PEACE and SECURITY

A Guide to Independent Groups and Funding Sources

PEACE and SECURITY

A Guide to Independent Groups and Funding Sources

Edited by Susan Forrester

Contributions from Professor Lawrence Freedman,
Dr David Hicks, Adrian Longley, Jonathan Steele
and Paul Sweeney

A Directory of Social Change publication

PEACE AND SECURITY:
A GUIDE TO INDEPENDENT GROUPS AND
FUNDING SOURCES

Edited by Susan Forrester

Cover design by The Graphic Partnership

Book designed by Michael Norton

The research for this book was undertaken with the financial support of the Barrow and Geraldine S Cadbury Trust and the Joseph Rowntree Charitable Trust

Published by the Directory of Social Change,
Radius Works, Back Lane, London NW3 1HL

© The Directory of Social Change 1988

No part of this book may be reproduced in any form whatsoever without prior permission in writing from the publisher. Permission will normally be given free of charge to non profit-making and charitable organisations. The Directory of Social Change is a registered educational charity.

Typeset by Scarborough Typesetting Services,
Scarborough, North Yorkshire.

Printed and bound in Britain by The Bath Press,
Lower Bristol Road, Bath, Avon.

British Library Cataloguing in Publication Data
Peace and security: a guide to independent groups and funding sources.
  1. Great Britain. Peace movements
327.1'72'0941

ISBN 0-907164-40-4

CONTENTS

Preface

Acknowledgements

PART ONE: ORGANISATIONS

The political context of independent groups,
by Professor Lawrence Freedman   2

Introduction   7

1. Policy-oriented research

Organisations   10
    University departments and centres   11
    Research groups, Working groups,
    Information centres   26
    International research establishments   39
    Research societies   44

2. Action research and campaigns

Campaigning groups: A personal viewpoint,
by Jonathan Steele   46

Organisations   47
    Individual membership groups   49
    Professional membership groups   58
    Non-membership groups   66
    Co-ordinatory bodies   72
    Church organisations and Religious groups   76
    Tracking/Direct action groups   84
    Peace camps   85
    Local peace councils and peace centres   86
    Service organisations   88

3. Nuclear Free Zones

Organisations   91

4. International relations (general)

Organisations   95

5. World studies, Education for peace, Development education

Education for peace, *by Dr David Hicks*   98
Organisations   101
    Local education authority initiatives   103
    Other initiatives   105
    Development education centres   120

6. Citizen Diplomacy

Organisations concerned with citizen diplomacy,
exchange visits, overseas service   122

7. Reconciliation work in Northern Ireland

Reconciling within Northern Ireland
by Paul Sweeney   133

Organisations   135

PART TWO: FINANCIAL SUPPORT

Charity law – Peace in our time,
by Adrian Longley   146

Check-list for organisations seeking
charitable status   154

1. UK Sources

Introductory note   155
    UK trusts listed alphabetically   155
    UK trusts by scale of grant making   157
    UK trusts with a particular interest in
    peace and defence   159
    UK trusts included for their interest in
    overseas aid and/or development education   159

Contents

UK trusts included for their support to work in Northern Ireland — 160
UK trusts listings — 160
UK awards and prizes listings — 218
UK governmental sources listings — 221

2. North American Sources

North American Foundations listings — 228

3. European Sources

European Foundations listings — 255

4. Japanese Sources

Japanese Foundations listings — 262

Bibliography — 265

Index of Organisations — 267

Index of Funding Sources — 270

Preface

This book has two distinct sections. The first half acts as a form of 'gazetteer' of organisations which are active in various aspects of peace, security and international relations, while the second half lists potential funding sources.

On the one hand we hope that organisations will themselves find the funding sources listings of practical benefit, and that new opportunities for obtaining funds will open to them. We also hope that the reference list of organisations will suggest new working links. On the other hand we hope that the guide, by displaying a panoply of varied initiatives, will encourage funding bodies to consider developing positive policies in this area of interest. Whilst this area of concern has not attracted a tradition of charitable support, the majority of organisations listed, even where they have not themselves contributed as charities, have the means of receiving charitable funding for appropriate work via related charities. It is an ironic fact that many grant making charities readily fund organisations working with the aftermath of conflict and distress, but either ignore or do not consider funding the preventative work which tries to reduce the prospect of war.

Acknowledgements

Particular thanks need to be made to all those individuals in the many and various organisations who have helped in providing the information for this guide and most particularly to its sponsors, the *Barrow and Geraldine S Cadbury Trust* and the *Joseph Rowntree Charitable Trust* who saw the need for this guide and who have been so helpful in seeing it through to fruition. In addition special thanks to *Ann McLaughlin* who has given her dependable and cheerful assistance with many laborious tasks and who has helped particularly with the search for relevant trusts.

PART ONE
ORGANISATIONS

The political context of independent groups

by Lawrence Freedman, Professor of War Studies, King's College, London.

During the first years of the 1980s a great debate was underway. This had been sparked by NATO's December 1979 decision to introduce Cruise and Pershing missiles into Europe, but soon came to involve a challenge to western strategic doctrine and the whole conduct of East-West relations. It created an enormous appetite for material which would allow activists to argue effectively with official spokesmen and encourage popular protest, and also which would allow concerned individuals simply to make sense of one of the major issues of the day.

But just as the decade began with East-West relations deteriorating and controversial new nuclear weapons programmes, it does not seem too optimistic to suppose that it will close with East-West relations much improved and less reason to worry about a nuclear arms race. Does this mean that sanity now rules and the protest movements should put away their banners, and that popular concern can shift towards a different set of issues?

Certainly as the national, and more widely European, debate has become less polarised, issues of peace and security have lost some of their intensity. In part, this is because more moderate policies are being pursued; in part, it is because any debate of this sort is eventually calmed by the intrusion of awkward considerations that make everything appear more complicated than it at first seemed. This may have reduced the scope and incentive for campaigning. It certainly has not made the subject less interesting.

There is an increasing sense that we are witnessing a period of historic change, brought about largely as a result of the declining influence (in quite different ways and to quite different extents) of the United States and the Soviet Union – the two powers that have dominated the international scene since 1945.

We do not yet know how this will work out. Great powers do not necessarily decline gracefully, and even when they do, the political vacuums created can create new forms of instability. Much current speculation revolves around Mr Gorbachev and his proclaimed policies of Perestroika and Glasnost in the Soviet Union. Opinions differ as to whether success in this venture will make the Soviet Union easier for others to live with or whether it would simply make it possible to pursue traditional expansionist goals with greater efficiency. Many doubt that Gorbachev can possibly succeed given that he is mounting such a fundamental challenge to the established system, or else fear that the process of reform once set in motion will be almost impossible to contain and is therefore as likely to end in violence as in a more liberal regime. This fear assumes that the Soviet system cannot operate except with strong centralised government, given the many distinct national groups it embraces. Of particular concern is the impact of the reform process in Eastern Europe where the Soviet-style regimes never really took root. Can these countries turn away from Soviet-style socio-economic system while still members of the Warsaw Pact? If not, might domestic reform lead to external vulnerabilities that could jeopardise the whole process?

While the pressures for domestic reform are less strong in the West there is a growing sense that the established Atlantic system, based on the United States cannot be sustained indefinitely. The United States no longer dominates the international economy, yet its reduced role in international economic affairs has yet to be matched by a reduced role in international security affairs. Recent economic problems have led to a questioning of the range of security commitments that it has acquired over the past few decades. This has been reflected in suggestions on both sides of the Atlantic for West Europeans to make a more substantial contribution to NATO. The Europeans themselves have become weary of dependence upon the United States and anxious to demonstrate their independence, while at the same time lacking confidence that they really can manage without American help, especially when it comes to nuclear deterrence. Perhaps the combination of improved relations between the superpowers and a loosening of the Soviet hold over Eastern Europe could create the conditions for a looser relationship within NATO.

If we are at the start of a process which could lead to the dissolution of the two alliances, what sort of security system will take its place? Will Germany be reunited – and what effect will that have on the security calculations of its neighbours, given that memories are long in Central Europe? Is there a danger that in the new security system new conficts will take over from the old, and that the discipline brought about by the fear of the dire consequences of superpower confrontation will give way to something more chaotic? Or are Europeans, still suffering the consequences of two great wars, now sufficiently wise and mature to create political structures that encourage prosperity and harmony and dampen down the fires of conflict that continue to smoulder around the continent?

Even if we can manage European security without major mishap,

The political context of independent groups

to what extent can we insulate ourselves from the stressful politics of the Middle East or the equally complicated situation in East Asia – both regions which have considerable relevance for the global economy? Even where the direct impact on the West may be marginal, political instability of various forms is often found to be behind those large-scale tragedies in the third world, usually manifested in the form of famines and refugee camps, that continue to move us.

This uncertain political future guarantees a continuing debate over military requirements. For many in the West, the world has not changed sufficiently to warrant any reduction of military effort; for others, the degree of western armament is part of the problem so that its reduction could stimulate a virtuous cycle in international relations, just as past increases have led to vicious cycles. Aside from debates over the level of armaments, there are intense controversies over the quality: what is the appropriate balance between conventional and nuclear forces? Is it the case that forces can be configured to avoid provocation and appear to be wholly defensive in orientation? Or is this, as many military specialists would insist, wholly fanciful? To deny offensive capabilities would not simply involve denying a capacity to invade another, but also to mount counter-attacks or interfere supply lines.

Nuclear deterrence has not survived the intense scrutiny to which it was subjected during the 1980s unscathed. Nobody has managed to explain how nuclear threats can be made credible when their implementation is likely to be suicidal. The various strategic debates of the past decade – including that over President Reagan's proposals for space-based defences against long-range missiles (popularly known as 'Star Wars') have addressed this problem but have failed to resolve it. On the other hand, nobody has explained how we can truly banish the weapons from our affairs. The best that we are left with is the thought that so long as there is a possibility that a major war would turn nuclear, no state will be inclined to start one. In terms of policy this argues for measures that reduce the antagonism between the superpowers; if antagonism persists, to reduce the risk of war starting by accident or miscalculation; if war nonetheless starts, to delay recourse to nuclear weapons by improving conventional forces. As the first two approaches are less expensive than improving conventional forces, we can expect them to be the focus of attention over the coming years.

Behind all these questions lies the thought that, if we get it wrong, then the consequences could be utterly disastrous. During the 1980s this thought stimulated many groups to campaign against established policies which, they feared, were more likely to lead to disaster than to prevent it. Part of the campaigning effort was to bring to the notice of the public the dangers that were being accepted on their behalf. In order to question official orthodoxy and to provide a basis for an alternative vision, it was considered necessary to ensure that there were alternative versions of current reality to those provided in government white papers, ministerial speeches and alliance communiqués.

Hence coincident with the growth of anti-nuclear protest in the late 1970s and early 1980s, there was a growth in organisations and journals devoted to informing the public, as well as activists, as to the state of the nuclear arms race, or the civil defence plans of government, or the latest disarmament proposals.

As the debate intensified this information effort became broadened in four ways. First, as governments were no longer able to take support for defence policies for granted, they were obliged to explain themselves in greater detail than before. They had to offer better information and more sophisticated interpretations.

Second, groups formed to counter the anti-nuclear movement and to put pressure on the government from a more hawkish position and this added to the diversity of views. Others became less concerned with influencing public opinion, and more concerned with developing new policies for government that demonstrated both sensitivity to its concerns and technical competence.

Third, it became apparent that to understand the nuclear problem it was necessary to look behind the weapons themselves to the whole history of their development, and then to the structure of international relations – which provided the rationales for this development and created the risks of their being used in anger. It was necessary to mount an intellectual critique of the doctrines of deterrence, and a political critique of the cold war.

Fourth, many individuals and groups interested in this debate, but less attached to a particular viewpoint, began to see their role in terms of doing what they could to keep the debate honest. To some, this simply meant providing reliable and comprehensive information. Others felt that this meant getting the adherents of the different views to engage and not talk past each other, perhaps in the hope that some new consensus might be forged. Yet more wanted to insure that neither side could duck awkward questions.

University departments and institutes, such as the International Institute for Strategic Studies and the Royal Institute of International Affairs, were reasonably well equipped to produce independent information and analysis, but they were less used to bringing this to a wider audience, and were properly inhibited from taking too high a political profile. Some academics threw themselves wholeheartedly into the debate, while others held back, believing polemics and campaigns to be inimical to scholarship.

Even within the academic world, there are many competing approaches to the issues of war and peace. There has been a long-established tradition of international relations in Britain, which tends to put questions of military force firmly in the context of the international political system. The strategic studies community (which in Britain is more historical and less technical than its

The political context of independent groups

American counterpart) accepts this political context, but then tends to narrow in its concerns. Although these more orthodox approaches support a great variety of views, they have been challenged by those who believe that alternative prescriptions require an alternative theoretical perspective. This is often expressed in approaches such as 'conflict research' and 'peace studies'. Within these approaches there are further controversies: for example, by peace do we mean the simple negative absence of war, or something more positive?

It should be noted that research in this area does not have to be policy-inspired to be useful. Indeed it may be that many of the critical changes in our thinking about international security result from impartial scholarship. Nor is policy utility the only test. The sources of international conflict and the means by which they are handled are of interest in themselves. Not all seem amenable to political action, but that is no reason not to attempt to understand them.

Thus, one of the legacies of the great nuclear debate, and a variety of other security issues from the arms trade to the Falklands War, has been the infrastructure to sustain serious discussion, even without the heat and political excitement of previous years. As we noted earlier, there is still plenty to talk about. For those anxious to enter into the debates, or simply to make themselves better informed, this book should provide invaluable assistance. One cannot but be struck by the range and diversity of the organisations allowing one to seek ideas and information without too great a risk of being confined to a particular partisan position or dependent upon a particular interpretation.

Introduction

The first section on organisations is intended to display the wide and various initiatives which can be included under the broad heading of 'peace', from group campaigns to academic work, from education in understanding in schools and colleges to cross-community initiatives for reconciliation in Northern Ireland. It has been organised into subsections, so that these differing types of activities can be more clearly identified and to assist comparisons and contrasts not only between sections but within the sections themselves.

Most reference books have some Procrustean features. Certain parameters are decided at the outset, then as work progresses these clear definitions become less clear as further overlaps and interconnections are discovered.

One initial parameter has been to include only those organisations whose central role is concerned with peace, security and international relations. As a result organisations such as Greenpeace and Friends of the Earth with well known anti-nuclear campaigns running along with other campaigns have not been included; similarly the Coalition for Peace through Security has been listed whilst the Freedom Association has not.

Another parameter has been to adopt a narrow use of the term 'peace' when deciding which groups to select. So whilst it is appreciated that the concept of peace is wider than the absence of war alone and is linked inextricably with issues of freedom and justice, the book has concentrated on the former and many organisations specifically concerned with human rights, civil liberties, anti-racism and anti-sexism have not been covered.

The organisations profiled are independent, based in the UK with a national scope and influence, or are international organisations based in the UK, for instance Pugwash Conferences and War Resisters International. A small number of international research organisations and associations have been included.

The local groups of national organisations are not covered, and on the whole local and regional projects are not profiled except in the sections covering peace camps and education for peace where they have a wider significance. It has however been thought helpful to include lists of addresses of local peace councils, peace centres and development education centres which are believed to be active.

The only departures from the general rule that all organisations be

Introduction

independent are the section on nuclear free zones and the listing of local education authority initiatives as an essential component of the section on education for peace.

The profiles have been compiled from information supplied directly from the organisations. Most have been particularly open and helpful in this respect; others have not wished to be included and their reasons for wishing to adopt a low-profile have not been explained. Where this has been the case the information published has been extracted from their own leaflets and has been supplemented, where the organisation is a registered charity, with information it has placed on file at the Charity Commission.

All organisations were sent a draft profile which they were invited to supplement, amend and update, and these comments have been incorporated. This method stimulated responses and also circumvented the time consuming and often fruitless mailing of questionnaires.

During the course of this research quite a few organisations ceased operating e.g. the Women's Peace Alliance, the Alternative Defence Commission, International Relations and Conflict Management at City University, Greater London Conversion Council to name a selection.

Information has been included to indicate the practical resources and administrative scale of the organisations. In this respect it should be noted that the 'Staffing' heading refers to paid employees only and the 'Sources of income' heading covers main supporting trusts and agencies in recent years not just the year for which an annual income figure has been quoted.

1. Policy-oriented research

Introductory note

The first part of this section covers university departments and centres where a significant body of research is conducted in the various aspects that can come under the heading of peace, security and international relations.

The compilation of data in this section began from the useful listing in '*Armament and Disarmament: An Introductory Guide to Sources, 1986*' published by the Armament and Disarmament Unit within the Science Policy Research Unit of the University of Sussex. It expanded with further reading and enquiry and as reports were received from the various departments, institutes, professional associations and from funding bodies in the UK and the USA. Whilst the following profiles cover an extensive range of academic study contributing to informed debate there are many individual research projects carried out in other establishments, particularly in many departments of politics, which inevitably could not be included.

All heads of department were asked to amend, update and expand on an initial draft prepared in advance from official reports and their assistance and cooperation in this respect has been appreciated. In only one case there was neither publicly available accounts of work, nor any direct response from the head of the department.

This review displays a vigorous body of interrelated research which illustrates the evolution of academic disciplines in order to meet the demands of a fast changing world. The departments of international politics and international relations developed when history, politics, international law and economics could not individually throw light on important world problems. After the First World War the study of international relations was launched at Aberystwyth, LSE, Chatham House and Oxford by a group of professors in sympathy with the League of Nations.

Today the area of peace studies is the youngest in a field of associated studies itself arising from the change after 1945 when the potential of nuclear weapons brought a whole new dimension and urgency to questions of survival. As Professor O'Connell of Bradford School of Peace Studies has said so cogently 'there are subjects such as peace that our civilisation cannot afford *not* to study'.

The rich mosaic of disciplines now includes: **War Studies**, the examination of how wars arise, are conducted, concluded and their impact on the social and economic fabric; **Strategic Studies**, which is concerned with many of the issues of war studies but with an emphasis on wider strategic issues; **Conflict Studies**, which examines not only international conflict, but industrial, social and racial conflict, and the various stages of negotiation and bargaining in peacemaking; and **International Relations**, which deals with the relationships between states, with diplomacy, international law and order, with international conflict and the processes of international peacekeeping.

University departments and centres along with other independent institutes play an important role, albeit a tenuous one, in fuelling or damping the policies of government, and also in furthering debate and in providing the necessary underpinning of intellectual resources and information for non-governmental organisations. There is, of course, a tension between the necessary detachment of academic enquiry and the demands for active involvement, but in their field of work the stereotype of academics as remote 'paper-pundits' seems remarkably out-of-date and irrelevant.

Policy-oriented research

List of contents

University departments and centres

Aberdeen University: Department of Politics and International Relations
Aberdeen University: Centre for Defence Studies
Birmingham University: Centre for Russian and East European Studies
Bradford University: School of Peace Studies
Bradford University: Commonweal Collection
Cambridge University: Centre of International Studies
Edinburgh University: Defence Studies
Glasgow University: Department of Sociology, Media Group
Keele University: Department of Politics and International Relations
Kent University: Board of Studies of Politics and International Relations
Kent University: Centre for the Analysis of Conflict
King's College, London: War Studies Department
Lancaster University: Centre for the Study of Arms Control and International Security
Lancaster University: Richardson Institute for Peace Studies
LSE: Department of International Relations
LSE: Centre for International Studies
Manchester University: Department of Science and Technology Policy
Southampton University: Department of Politics
Southampton University: Centre for International Policy Studies
Southampton University: International Nuclear Non-Proliferation Network
Sussex University: Institute of Development Studies
Sussex University: Science Policy Research Unit
Sussex University: Armament and Disarmament Information Unit
University of Ulster: Peace Studies Programme
University of Ulster: Centre for the Study of Conflict
University of Wales, Aberystwyth: Department of International Politics

Research institutes, Working groups, Information centres

British American Security Information Centre (BASIC)
Council for Arms Control
David Davies Memorial Institute of International Studies
European Proliferation Information Centre
Federal Trust for Education and Research
Foundation for Defence Studies
Foundation for International Security
Institute for European Defence and Strategic Studies
Institute for the Study of Conflict – Centre for Security and Conflict Studies
Institute for the Study of Terrorism
International Group of Researchers on the Anti-ballistic Missile Treaty (IGRAT)
International Nuclear Non-Proliferation Network (*see Southampton University*)
International Institute for Strategic Studies
Oxford Research Group
Pugwash Conferences on Science and World Affairs
Research Foundation for the Study of Terrorism
Royal Institute of International Affairs (Chatham House)
Royal United Services Institute for Defence Studies
Scientific Committee on Problems of the Environment (SCOPE ENUWAR), International Council of Scientific Unions
South Atlantic Council
Verification Technology Information Centre
Western European Defence Association
Working Party on Chemical and Biological Weapons

International research establishments

Atlantic Institute for International Affairs, Paris
International Peace Academy
Stockholm International Peace Research Institute
United Nations University
United Nations University for Peace
United Nations Institute for Disarmament Research

Research societies

Conflict Research Society
International Peace Research Association
International Society for Research into Aggression

POLICY-ORIENTED RESEARCH:
University departments and centres

ABERDEEN UNIVERSITY

Department of Politics and International Relations

Edward Wright Building, University of Aberdeen, Aberdeen AB9 2TY (0224-272713/7)

Contact: Professor Paul Wilkinson, Professor of International Relations and Head of Department.

Origins: Established as a full combined Department of Politics and International Relations of the University in the early 1960s.

Distinguished advisers: Captain John Moore (Honorary Professional Fellow since 1987) – adviser on research on maritime strategy and conflict; Philip Hodgson (former Security Director for BP International) – adviser on Industrial Security; Stuart Syrad – adviser on maritime security.

Personnel: 12 teaching/research staff; 35 postgraduates; 320 undergraduates.

Income: £75,000 (excluding salaries) for 1987/88.

Sources of income: Research foundations and industry.

Aims and objectives: To provide a comprehensive programme of teaching in political science and international relations at undergraduate and postgraduate levels, and to conduct a wide range of research and scholarly publication.

Research programme and examples of current projects: Terrorism and Low-level Conflict, Trends and Developments, Strategy and Western Defence Policy, Maritime Conflict and Strategy, Arms Control and Disarmament, Conflict in the Middle East, Public Administration and Policy Making, Politics and Social Change in North East Scotland, French Party Politics, Thomism and the History of Political Thought.

Teaching responsibilities: MA Hons (4 years); M.Litt (one year taught course in strategic studies); M.Litt by research (supervision provided); PhD by research (supervision provided); special in-service and professional training courses provided by arrangement with industry, the public sector and the professions.

Joint projects with other organisations: The Department contributes to work of the largest ESRC research project in the UK and also has a close relationship of co-operation and exchange of data with Rand Corporation, Santa Monica. It co-operates closely with the Aberdeen University Centre for Defence Studies, the RIIA, and other major institutes.

Specialist archive: The Department has special collections of materials on political violence and terrorism and on strategic and defence matters.

Publications: Members of the Department serve as Associate Editors and members of Editorial Boards of various professional journals. Books by members of the Department are numerous. Some examples are:

Wilkinson, Paul *'The New Fascists'* Pan Books, 1983;

Wilkinson, Paul, *'Terrorism and the Liberal State'* Macmillan, 1986;

Wilkinson, Paul and Stewart, Alasdair *'Contemporary Research on Terrorism'* Aberdeen University Press, 1987;

Sheehan, Michael *'The Arms Race'* Martin Robertson, 1981;

Sheehan, Michael and Wyllie, James *'Economist Pocketbook of Defence'* Economist Publications Ltd, 1987;

Criddle, Byron and Bell, P. *'The French Socialist Party'*, OUP, 1986;

Jordan, Grant and Richardson, Jeremy *'British Politics and the Policy Process'* Allen-Unwin, 1987.

ABERDEEN UNIVERSITY

Centre for Defence Studies

University of Aberdeen, Edward Wright Building, Dunbar Street, Old Aberdeen AB9 2TY (0224-272710)

Contact: David Greenwood, Director.

Policy-oriented research

Origins: Established in 1976.

Personnel: 3 Centre staff (established); 4 associates from the Department of Politics and International Relations; 5 Honorary Visiting Fellows; 2–5 Research Fellows/Assistants (short-term appointments).

Estimated budget: £90,000 for 1988.

Sources of income: University funds – 60%; Ministry of Defence funded lectureship, (since 1985) – 25%; small grants – 15%.

Aims and objectives: The Centre conducts research on national and international security affairs, including problems of arms control and disarmament, with particular emphasis on defence economics and security in northern Europe and northern waters. The Centre has contacts with parliamentary bodies and the media, and plays an important part in promoting informed debate on defence matters. Occasional colloquia are organised.

Research programme and examples of current projects: The aim is to produce analyses of British and European defence policy issues. Recent publications have included an assessment of the implications for the United Kingdom and Europe of the Americans' Strategic Defense Initiative (SDI), examinations of Nordic nuclear-free zone proposals and of Greenland's role in NATO, a three-part study of light forces in Western defence planning, and appraisals of 'area defence' and 'non-offensive defence' concepts. Work is in hand on an evaluation of proposals for strengthening conventional deterrence in Europe and an examination of measures leading to the more efficient use of resources in NATO (including role specialization). Exercises underway include:

British Defence Priorities - the United Kingdom's defence effort and issues likely to affect its evolution in the 1990s.

The Anglo Norwegian Defence Relationship – background, evolution, present position and prospects.

Teaching responsibilities: Contributions to the M.Litt in Strategic Studies – a course offered by the Department of Politics and International Relations in association with the Centre and to some undergraduate classes. Supervision of higher degrees.
Extra-mural activities include the organisation of short residential study periods, including some for the armed forces.

Working parties and joint projects with other organisations and institutions: The Centre supports the Northern Waters Study Group of the RIIA, Chatham House.

Publications: 'Aberdeen Studies in Defence Economics' (ASIDES) 27 have been published to date, including: Greenwood, David *'The SDI and Europe'*, 1986.

'Centrepieces', occasional papers on defence and disarmament including: Archer, Clive *'Greenland and the Atlantic Alliance'*; 1985; Gates, David *'Western Light Forces and Defence Planning 3: The US Light Divisions'*, 1986; Robertson, Myles *'Britain's Contribution to Norwegian Defence, 1940–1980'*, 1987.

BIRMINGHAM UNIVERSITY

Centre for Russian and East European Studies

University of Birmingham, P O Box 363, Birmingham B15 2TT (021-472 1301 x 3210 and 2124)

Contact: Professor R Amann, Director and Professor of Soviet Politics.

Origins: Established in 1962.

Personnel: A total of between 30–35; 4 Professors and Deputy Director; 7 Lecturers, 2 Honorary Senior Research Fellows; 3 Research Fellows; 10 Honorary Research Fellows; 6 Associate Members.

Annual budget: Information not disclosed.

Sources of income: These include (with reference to International and Security Studies) a Ministry of Defence Lectureship in Soviet Defence Studies and International Security; the Economic and Science Research Council and the Ford, Volkswagen, and MacArthur Foundations.

Aims and objectives: The Centre, as its name states, conducts professional academic study of the USSR and Eastern Europe.

Research programme and some examples of current projects: The Centre's research programme covers History, Economics, Econometrics and Statistics; Sociology and Labour Policy; Education; Geography and Environmental Studies; Russian Language and Literary Studies; Politics; Technology and Science Policy. Within its International and Security Studies programme recent projects have included the economic analysis of defence and arms control issues (Dr C. M. Davis) and research into Soviet perceptions of the prospects of peace, of the militarisation of space and of the nuclear winter (Dr S. D. Shenfield).

Teaching responsibilities: In 1985/86 the Centre staff provided courses, in full or in part, for some 750 undergraduates and 55 postgraduates in the faculties of Arts, Commerce and Social Science, Education, Engineering, Law and Science.
An Annual Research Conference is held for staff and students past or present. Cooperative conferences on projects are held with institutions in the UK and overseas including the School of Slavonic and East European Studies (SSES) at the University of London

and the National Association for Soviet and East European Studies (NASEES).

Library: The Alexander Bayker Library, located within the Centre, comprises some 85,000 volumes and microfilms, almost entirely in Russian and other Slavonic languages. It is one of the major libraries in Western Europe in the field of Soviet and East European studies.

Publications: A full list of books and articles by members and associates of the Centre is available. The journal *'Detente'*, receives the Centre's active support though it is not an official CREES publication.

BRADFORD UNIVERSITY

School of Peace Studies

University of Bradford, Bradford BD7 LDP
(0274-733 466 x 260)

Contact: Professor James O'Connell, Professor of Peace Studies and Head of School.

Origins: Established in 1973 with support from the religious Society of Friends (Quakers). A Quaker Peace Studies Trust was set up which matched University funds to establish the first Chair of the School.

Personnel: 10 permanent staff members; 3 full-time research fellows; 45 postgraduate students; 65 undergraduate students.

Estimated Annual Budget: £330,000 for 1985/86.

Sources of research income: (which totalled £120,000 in 1985/86) The Quaker Peace Studies Trust, the Joseph Rowntree Charitable Trust, the Joseph Rowntree Social Service Trust, the Barrow and Geraldine S. Cadbury Trust and the Economic and Science Research Council.

Aims and objectives: The school is the first university department in the UK to offer full degree courses in Peace Studies.
The school has identified five areas on which its teaching and research is centred:
 Peace theory;
 Nuclear and non-nuclear defence;
 Relations between economically developed and developing countries;
 Industrial societies, particularly race/ethnic relations in European countries, industrial/class divisions in Britain and the conversion of arms industries to other functions;
 Regions of conflict particularly Northern Ireland and the Middle East.

The school believes that one of its functions is to service and inform groups active in the discussion, study and promotion of peace.

Research programme and examples of current projects: A key interest is the documentation of the process of the arms race, the nature of and costs of various alternative forms of defence, and the proliferation of nuclear weapons.

Peace Studies at the school is not solely concerned with the nuclear issue. A major theme is the study of regions undergoing rapid change, such as Portugal and Nigeria, or in open conflict: most notably the Middle East and Northern Ireland. A central question that is relevant to all societies is how, under conditions of rapid change, can social progress and justice be achieved by non-violent means.

Teaching responsibilities: BA Honours; MA/Diploma; MPhil or PhD Supervision.

Library: *See separate entry for 'Commonweal Library'.*

Journals and recent publications:

'Peace Studies Papers (New Series)' present material in a popular style for a wide audience, e.g. Rogers, P. *'Guide to Nuclear Weapons'* Berg 1988.

'Peace Research Reports' published several times each year are aimed at specialists, e.g. Gregory, S. *'The Command and Control of Nuclear Weapons'*, 1986 Chalmers, M. *'Trends in UK Defence Spending'* 1986.

'Peace Studies Briefings' are not formally published but circulated to journalists and politicians e.g. No. 28 *'Third Generation Nuclear Weapons and the Prospects for a Nuclear Test Ban'*.

Other publications include:

Chalmers, M. *'Paying for Defence: Military Spending and British Economic Decline'*, London, Pluto Press, 1985;

Van den Dungen, P. (ed.) *'West European Pacifism and the Strategy for Peace'*, Macmillan, 1985;

McIntosh, M. *'Japan Re-armed: Japanese Defence Policy in the 1980s'*, Frances Pinter, 1986;

Gallagher, T. *'Glasgow: The Uneasy Peace'*, Manchester University Press, 1987;

Greene, Randle, Rogers and others, *'The Politics of Alternative Defence'*, Paladin, 1987;

Ramsbotham, O. *'Choices: Nuclear and Non-Nuclear Defence Options'*, Brasseys, 1987.

Policy-oriented research

BRADFORD UNIVERSITY

Commonweal Collection

c/o J. B. Priestley Library, University of Bradford, Bradford, West Yorkshire BD7 1DP (0274-733 466 x 8477).

Contact: Tim Wallis, Co-ordinator (part time).

Status: Charitable Trust.

Origins: The library, founded by David Hoggett, began in 1958 in Wales. In 1975 the library moved to the University.

Personnel: 1 part-time co-ordinator and about 10 volunteers.

Annual budget: Not disclosed.

Sources of income: Include the Lansbury House Trust Fund and the Philip Radley Charitable Trust.

Aims and objectives: The library is informally linked to the School of Peace Studies and the collection was designed for use by any individual or group concerned with social change and non-violence. It handles requests for bibliographical and research assistance and is developing its archival function.

The Commonweal Fellow, normally supported by the Trust, works as part-time co-ordinator of the collection and in part-time postgraduate studies at the School of Peace Studies.

Publication: Guide to the Commonweal Collection with key subject classification.

CAMBRIDGE UNIVERSITY

Centre of International Studies

University of Cambridge, History Faculty Building, West Road, Cambridge CB3 9EF (0223-335 333)

Contact: R. T. B. Langhorne, Director.

Adviser: Professor Sir Harry Hinsley, Chairman of the Committee of Management.

Staffing: Apart from 2 lecturers in Strategic Studies the Centre is serviced by between 15 to 40 other staff from various disciplines. There were 5 visiting fellows in 1987/88. The Centre has 40 to 50 graduate students.

Sources of income: These include 2 Ministry of Defence Lectureships in Strategic Studies, both until 1990 (Dr. P. A. Towle since 1980 and Dr I. Clark since 1982).

Aims and objectives: The Centre provides a one year course for a Master of Philosophy degree in International Relations which is administered by the Committee of Management of the Centre of International Studies and the Faculty of History through a Sub-Committee composed of members of the Faculties of Law, Economics and Politics, and History.

Students from many countries range from immediately post-graduate to quite senior serving officers from the British armed forces, occasionally American armed forces, bank officials, diplomats, civil servants, teachers, journalists, etc.

Journal: 'Cambridge Review of International Affairs' produced annually by the course students.

EDINBURGH UNIVERSITY

Defence Studies

University of Edinburgh, 31 Buccleuch Place, Edinburgh EH8 9JT (031-667 1011 x 6538)

Contact: Professor John Erickson, Director.

Aims and objectives: Defence Studies was established as a discipline at the University in 1967 and acquired departmental status in 1983 within the Faculty of Social Sciences.

'Though the smallest Department in the University, consisting of Professor John Erickson and a small group of Research Associates (it) carries out an extensive programme both of teaching, at undergraduate and postgraduate level, and of research (having produced well over 100 research papers, several monographs and a major two-volume history of the Soviet-German War 1941–45). Its special contribution lies in studies of the military organisation of the Soviet Union and the Warsaw Pact, with the emphasis on military-technical developments. Professor Erickson has played a pivotal role in the establishment from 1980 of the 'Edinburgh Conversations'. These have brought together under academic auspices for informal private discussions over the course of three days – usually once a year, alternatively in Moscow and Edinburgh – small groups of prominent national figures from Great Britain and the USSR. The Conversations have focused on international relations and strategic questions, latterly under the general heading of 'Survival in the Nuclear Age; towards common security'.

Specialist archive: A collection of Soviet military books, journals and newspapers, plus related microfilm/micro-fiche archives in Western Europe.

(Information supplied by the University's Information and Public Relations Section. Further basic data as supplied by other Departmental Heads were not available from Defence Studies directly despite several letters and telephone calls.)

Policy-oriented research

GLASGOW UNIVERSITY

Media Unit

Department of Sociology, Glasgow University, Adam Smith Building, Glasgow G12 8RT (041-339 8855).

Contacts: Professor J. E. T. Eldridge, Head of Department (extn. 4684); Greg Philo, Unit Research Director (extn. 5983).

Origins: Started in late 1974.

Personnel: 2 teaching/research staff; 3–4 postgraduate students; 1 technical assistant; 3 additional full time workers; 6 associate researchers; (plus contract workers for specific projects).

Estimated annual Budget: Not available.

Sources of income: During its first ten years the Media Unit's income received support from ESRC, UNESCO and the Joseph Rowntree Charitable Trust supplementing the basic office/administrative support in kind from the University. The BBC, Central Television and Channel 4 have also funded specific projects. Also the DHSS and the Central Office of Information for a study of the media coverage of AIDS.

Aims and objectives: Since 1981 the Unit has undertaken projects relating to aspects of peace/defence (e.g. analysis of TV coverage of the Falklands War).

Projects relating to aspects of peace, security and international relations have included:

War and Peace News, 1982–1984;

A Study of Defence News and Defence Correspondents;

The Ethiopian Famine and its Treatment as a News Story.

Teaching responsibilities: Honours course on Sociology of the Mass Media and input to basic introductory sociology course.

Joint Projects with other institutions: Approaches are being made to New York University and Moscow University to develop comparative studies in media treatment of peace and disarmament and their input to East/West relations.

Archive: All research projects are recorded on VHS video, and the Unit also has an entire video archive of TV news since the end of 1986 and a comprehensive press archive of 1983 and 1987 election coverage.

Publications and other materials: 'War and Peace News' Open University Press, 1985;

Philo, Greg 'Television and the Ethiopian Famine', Television Trust for the Environment/Central Television, 1986;

Videos on 'The Falklands War' and 'The 1984/85 Miners' Strike' (produced in Glasgow University) and a BBC Open Space Programme re the Media Unit, October 1985.

KEELE UNIVERSITY

Department of International Relations

University Of Keele, Keele, Staffs ST5 5BG (0782-3700/3690).

Contact: Professor Alan James, Professor of International Relations.

Sources of income: University Grants Committee. Funding for research projects on an individual basis has been received in recent years from ESRC, Nuffield Foundation, Leverhulme Trust, NATO Research Fellowship and assistance for travel costs from the British Academy.

Aims and objectives: The separate International Relations department and specialised International Relations degree dates from 1974. The 3 year degree course is unusual in that it is devoted to the study of the international scene.

Research programme and examples of current projects: The Department's research, though based on individual rather than team activity, has a measure of unity because of the converging interests of its members. It has a reputation for its work on international organisation and arms control, as a centre for the study of basic theoretical concepts whilst its Head is an authority on international peacekeeping. Current projects include work for books on 'International Peacekeeping', 'Domestic Analogy in Proposals for World Order', 'Britain and Compulsory Adjudication in the 1920s', 'Politics Among Strangers' and a NATO research project on 'The Implications for UK membership of NATO of the Labour Party's changed Perception of the Soviet Threat'.

Teaching responsibilities: BA Degree in International Relations; Taught MA in Diplomatic Studies (1 year full-time, 2 years part-time); Supervision of Masters or PhD in International Relations.

Joint projects: Regular joint seminars are held with the Department of International Relations and Politics of the North Staffordshire Polytechnic.

Recent publications:

These include the following:

James, Professor A. M. 'Sovereign Statehood: The Basis of International Society', Allen and Unwin, 1986; 'The UN on Golan: Peacekeeping Paradox?', Norwegian Institute of International Affairs, 1986; (with Sir Anthony Parsons) 'The United Nations and the Quest for Peace', Welsh Centre for International Affairs, 1986;

Policy-oriented research

Vincent, Dr R. J. *'Foreign Policy and Human Rights'* (edited) CUP 1986; *Human Rights and International Relations*, CUP 1986.

KENT UNIVERSITY

Board of Studies in Politics and International Relations

University of Kent, Canterbury, Kent CT2 7NX (0227-764 000).

Contact: Professor A. J. R. Groom, Professor of International Relations.

Personnel: 6 teaching/research staff; 15 PhD students; 30 one-year MA students; 15 two-year MA students; 50 undergraduate majors in a BA in Politics and International Relations and International Relations and French.

Source of income: University Grants Committee.

Aims and objectives: International Relations as taught at the University of Kent puts an emphasis on the conceptual and methodological aspects of the subject of with particular attention being paid to conflict research. International Relations is seen in the context of Social Science as a whole.

Research programme and examples of current projects: Staff and research students are working in a number of areas. Of particular interest to Peace Studies are: mediation and facilitation; peacekeeping; theory of conflict; international organisation of peace and security; strategic studies; ethnic conflict.

Joint projects with other organisations: The Department has particularly close ties through the Centre for the Analysis of Conflict with the home universities of Centre members which include several universities in south-east England and abroad. More specifically it has working ties with George Mason University, USA, University of Grenoble, France, and Eotvos Lorand University, Budapest.

Library: A specialist collection is kept on mediation.

Journals: The students have recently established a professional journal entitled *Paradigms*. For details please write to the Editor, *Paradigms*, Rutherford College, University of Kent, Canterbury, Kent, CT2 7NX.

KENT UNIVERSITY

Centre for the Analysis of Conflict

c/o Rutherford College, University of Kent, Canterbury, Kent LT2 7NX (0227–66822).

Contact: Professor A. J. R. Groom, Director.

Origins: Founded in 1965 at University College, London. In 1978 it moved its office to the University of Kent.

Annual budget: Not disclosed.

Sources of income: The centre has no direct financial support from the University funds. It raises income from donations, consultation fees and royalties from publications.

Research projects have been financed by trusts e.g. Joseph Rowntree Charitable Trust for Falklands Consultation in 1984, national research councils and clients in government.

Aims and objectives: The Centre consists of a small group of some dozen scholars in different universities who have a common interest in finding practical solutions to destructive conflicts. The academic disciplines represented include international relations, international law, political science, economics, sociology, anthropology, social psychology, conflict studies and systems analysis.

The function of the Centre is to promote research on conflict, on which it holds regular meetings and seminars, and prepares case studies and theoretical analysis for publication in books and learned journals. It serves as a channel for exchange between scholars of similar interests worldwide.

The Centre has concerned itself with conflict between groups at all social levels from industrial disputes through ethnic, political, religious and communal conflict to revolutionary violence and war.

The Centre has developed a problem solving technique which has the following advantages:

Total confidentiality both at the time and later;

The absence of any prior commitment by the parties to accept any outcomes, ideas or stances;

A research framework, non-judgemental and non-directive, which even if the dispute is not ended immediately is likely to afford new information and insights on processes and possible forms of resolution;

A low cost exercise where no party need be seen to negotiate.

Publications, teaching and training: Within the framework provided by the Centre, members collectively and individually undertake research and publish their findings. The Centre may also conduct teaching and training programmes in the field of conflict analysis upon commission on an *ad hoc* basis.

There are, naturally, strong links with the Conflict Research Society (*see separate entry*).

KING'S COLLEGE, LONDON

Department of War Studies

King's College (KQC), Strand, London WC2R 2LS (01-836 5454 x 2193).

Contact: Professor L. D. Freedman, Professor of War Studies.

Origins: Established during the 1950s.

Personnel: 6 full-time and 1 part-time teaching staff; 5 research staff; 40 post-graduate research students; about 30 MA/Diploma students (at least a third are from overseas and EEC).

Annual budget: Information not available.

Sources of income: University Grants Committee; Ministry of Defence Lectureship for five years from 1986; MacArthur Foundation, a three year grant for post-doctoral fellowships and students, support for the Liddell Hart Military Archive and some research; Ministry of Defence, Operations Analysis Establishment, for a research project on the pace of land battle, for three years from 1985; other MoD funded research projects have included one on the role of independent media commentators during the Falklands campaign, 1983/84; British Army, for support in developing military history component of new Higher Command Course; Rockefeller Foundation Research grant on the history of the Falklands War, from 1986/87; Joseph Rowntree Charitable Trust for the study of chemical warfare, from 1985; ESRC for Conference in 1987 on research on British defence and foreign policy, 1945 to 1956.

Aims and objectives: The Department is internationally renowned for postgraduate teaching and research in all aspects of War Studies. It is concerned with the historical, political, technical, economic and social problems which arise out of the preparation for and conduct of war, including questions of arms control and disarmament.

The courses offered are not only for academic specialists in defence questions and members of the Armed Forces, but also for those pursuing careers in public administration, politics, journalism and international affairs. The Department is physically close to the International Institute for Strategic Studies, the Royal United Services Institute, the Imperial War Museum, the Ministry of Defence and the Public Record Office, in all of which facilities are made available to students.

Core teaching programme: General Paper One: Military History from Napoleonic Times to 1945; General Paper Two: Contemporary Strategic Issues, including Ethics of War and Civil-Military Relations; Choice of ten special subjects. Research is undertaken in the Department on all aspects of war studies with a growing interest in post-1945 military history.

Teaching responsibilities: MA and Diploma in War Studies; MPhil and PhD supervision.

Joint projects with other organisations: A joint seminar series has been arranged with Pugwash (*see separate entry*) and a conference on Demographic Change and Security is to be organised with the University of Mississippi and other conferences in part organised with the Royal Navy and the RAF.

Archive: The Department is connected with the Liddell Hart Centre for Military Archives, a collection of over 200 sets of papers of higher commanders and senior civil servants reflecting on Britain's defence policy in the twentieth century.

Publications: All members of the Department publish widely, for example: '*King's College Studies in Military History*', (ed. M. L. Dockrill) a series published jointly with Macmillans.

Books based on conferences: Till, G (ed.) '*The Future of British Seapower and NATO's Northern Flank*', Macmillans; Sabin, P (ed.) '*The Future of British Airpower*' Brasseys.

LANCASTER UNIVERSITY

Centre for the Study of Arms Control and International Security

Department of Politics, University of Lancaster, Lancaster LA1 4YF (0524-65201 x 4890).

Contact: Professor Ian Bellany, Director.

Status: Charitable as a semi-autonomous section of the Politics Department.

Origins: Established in 1979.

Personnel: Research staff varies between 2–4.

Estimated annual budget: £50,000 for 1986/87.

Sources of income: The University contribution has so far not exceeded 20%. External grant funding covers the main part of the Centre's salary and office costs. Since 1979 the main contributors have been the Ford Foundation, NY, the ESRC and the Joseph Rowntree Charitable Trust. Staff have been awarded NATO (3) and Leverhulme Research Fellowships.

Aims and objectives: Members of the Centre concentrate on individual and joint research on

Policy-oriented research

international peace and security issues with special emphasis on Western Europe.

Research programme and some examples of current projects: Five main areas are studied:
  Nuclear non-proliferation;
  Theories and practice of arms control;
  British defence and disarmament policy;
  Technological problems for arms control;
  The procurement and control of conventional armaments.

ESRC research project: 'Procurement and operability of new conventional weapons'.

Leverhulme Trust research project: 'On-site verification of arms control agreements'.

Teaching responsibilities: CSACIS staff supervise PhD students (4 in 1987), mount post-graduate courses, including the MA degree in Science, Technology and International Affairs. The Director has also mounted under-graduate courses in Arms Control and Disarmament; the Politics of Security and 'Introducing International Relations'. Major conferences are organised e.g. 'Morality and Warfare', 1986 and 'New Directions in Arms Control', 1988.

Archive: An archive of some quarter of a million newspaper cuttings on international peace and security topics with a computerised data base is maintained.

Journals and recent publications:

Bellany, Ian and Huxley, Tim (eds) *'New Conventional Weapons and Western Defence'*, Cass, London, 1987.

Professor Bellany is founding editor of *'Arms Control'*, published by Frank Cass Ltd.

'Bailrigg Papers' – an occasional series:

No. 6 Bellany, Ian *'Why Men Enlist: The Royal Navy and the Royal Air Force, 1970–1980'*; No. 7 Dillon, G. M. *'Public Opinion and the Falklands Conflict'*; No. 8 Bellany, Ian *'British Defence Expenditure and Its Impact on Jobs and Energy Use: An Input-Output Analysis'*; No. 9 Bellany, Ian *'Inter-Service Rivalry and Military Innovation'*.

LANCASTER UNIVERSITY

Richardson Institute for Peace Studies

Department of Politics, University of Lancaster, Lancaster LA1 4YF (0524-65201 x 4568).

Contact: Dr Paul Smoker, Director.

Status: Charitable, as part of the university.

Origins: The Institute is named after a British Quaker who pioneered peace studies. It was originally founded in 1959 as the Lancaster Peace Research Centre and in 1965 Lancaster became the first university to appoint a Fellow in Peace Research. The Institute's Management Committee has strong representation from the Conflict Research Society.

Personnel: 1 Teaching staff; 8 postgraduate (MPhil, PhD) students; 5 MA students; 25 undergraduates.

Sources of income: University of Lancaster; Joseph Rowntree Charitable Trust; Quaker Peace Studies Trust; G. and H. Roberts Community Trust; The Institute solicits gifts and covenants via a Friends' Scheme.

Aims and objectives: The Centre's research and teaching roles have been extended over recent years to cover a broader community role with popular publications, conferences and public meetings.

Research and examples of recent projects: The Director, Dr Paul Smoker, has been working with Professor Ted Edwards, former Vice-Chancellor of Bradford University and co-founder of the School of Peace Studies, on a project to provide a strong defence of peace studies as a discipline.

Work has also proceeded on development of curriculum materials for teachers and students and some in-service training for teachers for the first A-level course in Britain on Peace and Conflict Studies scheduled to be introduced by the Joint Matriculation Board in September 1988.

Post-graduate students are researching:
  The Northern Ireland conflict;
  Politics of nuclear power;
  Non-violent action and contemporary peace movements;
  Images of the enemy;
  Children's perceptions of nuclear war;
  A cross-disciplinary survey of aggression;
  The possibilities of global action, a plea for internationalism of peace movements.

Teaching responsibilities: Undergraduate course in Peace and Conflict; MA in Peace Studies; MPhil; PhD programme supervision.

Joint project: A Conference on military and political options for alternative defence strategies in Europe was run in conjunction with Just Defence, in 1986.

Journals and recent publications:

Co-publisher and European distributor of *'International Accidental Nuclear War Newsletter'*.

Seventeen papers have been published on *'Accidental Nuclear War'*.

Policy-oriented research

'*Worldwise: Nuclear Weapons*', computer-based peace studies package.

Report of two Institute surveys in Barrow on attitudes towards the Trident submarine system, 1985–6.

A full list of publications is available.

LSE

Department of International Relations

London School of Economics and Political Science, Houghton Street, London WC2A 2AE (01-405 7686).

Contact: Professor Fred Halliday, Professor of International Relations and convenor of department.

Personnel: 17 full time, supported by about 6 part-time specialists and other distinguished visitors from overseas; 95 research students; 110 taught postgraduates; 154 undergraduates.

Sources of income: No information given.

Aims and objectives: The Department is a leading world centre in the teaching and development of international relations as a recognised subject with a separate department. It was founded 60 years ago as the first separate department in this field of academic study.

Research and examples of current projects: The full-time academic staff, their individual research interests and selected publications are given in the LSE booklet '*Graduate Studies in International Relations*'. These include:

Professor Fred Halliday: Research interests – Revolutions and International Relations; East-West relations; The Middle East; Theories on Imperialism and Underdevelopment.

Michael H. Banks: Research interests – General Theories of International Relations; Problems of Theory Construction and Methodology; Conflict Analysis and Conflict Resolution; Peace Research.

Dr Christopher Coker: Research interests – Third World Security; Southern African Politics; United States Defence and Foreign Policy; NATO Conventional Defence; (Current work in preparation: '*US Military Power in the 1990s*', scheduled for publication in 1987).

Nicholas A. Sims: Research interests – Diplomacy and Disarmament and Arms Limitation in the United Nations and Related Settings (with particular reference to multilateral treaty making, treaty reviews and negotiations: especially those pertaining to biological and chemical weapons); Disarmament Policy Processes and Institutions, in Britain and Elsewhere; International Verification Procedures and Compliance Diplomacy; Patterns of International Organisation in Commonwealth and UN systems.

Library: British Library of Political and Economic Science.

Journals and publications: Members of the Department publish widely.

'*Millennium: Journal of International Studies*' three times a year produced by postgraduate and undergraduate students. A yearly special issue brings together commissioned articles on a single theme (e.g. 1983 Special Issue on the Falkland Islands).

LSE

Centre of International Studies (CIS)

London School of Economics and Political Sciences, Houghton Street, London WC2A 2AE (01-405 7686).

Contact: Dr Michael Leifer, Chairman of Centre's Steering Committee and Editorial Board.

Origins: Established at the LSE in 1967 with a 5 year grant from the Ford Foundation.

Personnel: The Centre appoints 6 visiting fellows each year. It has a steering committee and editorial board with representation from five LSE departments including International Relations.

Sources of income: The LSE.

Aims and objectives: Soviet and Chinese studies have been, and still are, of central concern. New interests developed recently include European Studies (with East/West relations and external relations of European Community); international politics in Asia and the Pacific and international political economy.

Teaching responsibilities: The Centre sponsors an inter-disciplinary MSc in European Studies.

Publications:

'*L.S.E. Monographs in International Studies*' a series published by Cambridge University Press.

MANCHESTER UNIVERSITY

Department of Science and Technology Policy

University of Manchester, Mathematics Building, Oxford Road, Manchester M13 9PL (061-273 7121).

Contact: Dr Philip Gummett, Administrative Head of Department.

Origins: The Department was established in the mid 1960s.

Policy-oriented research

Personnel: 10 teaching/research staff; 25 research and visiting fellows; 10 PhD students; 15 MSc students; 60 undergraduates.

Estimated annual budget: £500,000 for 1987.

Sources of income: External funding for the department in 1985/86 amounted to more than £450,000. Organisations providing support included the Science and Engineering Research Council, Economic and Social Research Council, Department of Trade and Industry, Technical Change Centre, British Council, Commonwealth Science Council, Nuffield and Leverhulme Foundations, Royal Society, Wellcome Trust, Organisation for Economic Cooperation and Development, Commission of the European Communities, National Research Council of Italy, US National Science Foundation, Rand Corporation, and industrial and commercial firms.

SERC has accepted the PhD programme as suitable for tenure by their research studentships.

Aims and objectives: The Department was a pioneer in the study of science and technology as social phenomena. Their interrelationship with the economic, political and philosophical worlds is the subject matter of science and technology policy.

Research programme and examples of current projects: Five broad areas of research are carried out:
  Economics and technical change;
  Social and economic impact of science and technology;
  Government and industrial policy towards science and technology;
  Social history and science and technology;
  Evaluation of research and development.

The third includes specific projects on UK defence research and development policy carried out particularly by Dr Philip Gummett.

Teaching responsibilities: Three BSc degrees with the Analysis of Science and Technology running in conjunction with the Chemistry, Physics and Biological Sciences Departments. The third year includes courses in Risk Analysis and the Technology and Politics of Nuclear Weapons.

MSc course in Technical Change and Industrial Strategy in collaboration with six other departments or units also including Risk Assessment and Technology and Politics of Nuclear Weapons.

PhD research supervision: recent topics include 'Decision-making in National Nuclear Power Programmes', 'Problems of Nuclear Proliferation'.

Working parties and joint projects: Representation on the Working Group on Military Research and Development of the Council for Science and Society; the Innovation Working Group, Department of Trade and Industry; Resources from the Sea Committee, Department of Trade and Industry. Collaborative work on policy towards new materials with The University of Groningen, Netherlands; Four-country study on the impact of biotechnology within Europe for the European Commission; ESRC Working Group on Risk.

Publications: Books by departmental staff include:
Gummett, P. *'Scientists in Whitehall'* Manchester University Press, 1980.
Gibbons, M. and Gummett, P. (eds) *'Science, Technology and Society Today'*, Manchester University Press, 1984.
Council for Science and Society (Rapporteur: P. Gummett) *'UK Military R & D'*, OUP, 1986.
Gummett, P. and Reppy, J. (eds) *'The Relations between Defence and Civil Technologies'*, Dordrecht: Nijhoff, 1988.

SOUTHAMPTON UNIVERSITY

Department of Politics

The University of Southampton, Southampton SO9 5NH (0703-559122 x 2511/2512).

Contact: Professor Peter Calvert, Head of Department.

Personnel: 12 Teaching staff; 2 Research staff; 6 MPhil/PhD students; 11 MSc students; 45 undergraduates.

Estimated annual budget: £300,000 for 1988.

Sources of income: Include the Ford Foundation and the Rockefeller Brothers Fund.

Aims and objectives: The Department has a broad research and teaching programme. Its work ranges from one day special conferences to large scale externally funded research projects.

Research programme and examples of specific projects: Individual or collaborative research in areas of political studies includes:
  International relations, e.g. international economic relations, problems of nuclear proliferation;
  Defence policy studies – with special reference to weapons procurement systems;
  Comparative studies and police systems;
  The comparative study of political systems, e.g. the Latin American states, the USSR and the USA.
Specific projects include:
  Third World Security;
  International Nuclear Non-Proliferation Network (*see separate entry*).

Teaching responsibilities: BSc (Soc.Sci.) courses in politics and related studies e.g. International Studies; Certificate/Diploma/MSc (Soc.Sci.) courses include International Studies – useful for diplomats, military services, and those engaged in international trade; MPhil/PhD.

Journals and recent publications:
Staff have contributed to the Faraday Papers of the Council for Arms Control, and ADIU Reports etc.

Calvert, P. A. R. *'Guatemala, a Nation in Turmoil'*, Boulder, Colorado: Westview press, 1985.

Calvert, P. A. R., *'Britain's Place in the World'*, Inaugural Lecture, University of Southampton, Southampton, 1986.

Simpson, J., *'The Independent Nuclear State: The US, Britain and the Military Atom'*, 2nd revised edition, Macmillan, 1986.

SOUTHAMPTON UNIVERSITY

Centre of International Policy Studies

Department of Politics, The University, Southampton SO9 5NH (0703-559 122 × 2511).

Contact: Dr Dilys M. Hill, Director.

Origins: Established in 1983.

Personnel: Some 20 plus members drawn on a voluntary and co-operative basis from the University Departments.

The Centre confers the status of Visiting Fellow.

Sources of income: The Ford Foundation, for research into North/South Security Relations in the 1990s. The Nuffield and Ford Foundation and the Fulbright Commission have made grants for symposia and workshops. The Barrow and Geraldine S. Cadbury Trust for the International Nuclear Non-Proliferation Network.

Aims and objectives: The Centre brings together members of the Departments of Adult Education, History, Law and Politics to foster interdisciplinary and multi-disciplinary research into the domestic and external dimensions of policy. It also provides consultancy, training and conference services.

Research programme and examples of current projects: Centre members are involved in research on a wide range of policy issues. Recently published works have included books on the law of human rights, the Falklands War, the Carter Presidency, the European Community, intervention, the international nuclear non-proliferation regime and the military use of nuclear energy in the United Kingdom. Another major programme has investigated problems of North/South Security Relations in the 1990s for which the Centre was granted observer status at international diplomatic conferences.

Working parties and joint projects with other institutions: A Study Group 'Human Rights and Foreign Policy' and a Working Group on the European Community have been formed. Links have been established with the Centre d'Histoire Militaire of the University of Montpelier, and the Foundation Pour les Etudes de Défense Nationale, Paris. The Centre also participates in the work of the team on Political Culture in Eastern Europe at the Ecole des Hauts Etudes en Sciences Sociales, Paris. Members of the Centre have participated in the work of the European Science Foundation and the International Congress of Historical Sciences.

Publications:
The *'Southampton Series in International Policy'* published by Macmillan. Books by individual authors and the proceedings of conferences appear in this series.

SOUTHAMPTON UNIVERSITY

International Nuclear Non-Proliferation Network

Centre for International Policy Studies, Department of Politics, The University, Southampton SO9 5NH (0703-559122 x 2522).

Contact: Dr John Simpson, Rapporteur.

Status: Charitable as a project of a university centre.

Personnel: 3 part time staff.

Annual income: $120,000 for 1988.

Sources of income: Ford Foundation; Rockefeller Brothers Fund; Barrow and Geraldine S. Cadbury Trust; University of Southampton plus other assistance with overheads. Approaches are being made to the MacArthur Foundation (USA), the W. Alton Jones Foundation (USA) and Ploughshares Fund (USA).

Aims and objectives: The Network, administered as a project of the Centre of International Policy Studies, is a programme of information exchange, education, training and research to help strengthen the non-proliferation regime and support preparations for the next Review Conference of Non-Proliferation Treaty in 1990. The Network has two administrative bases in New York and Southampton.

Policy-oriented research

SUSSEX UNIVERSITY

Institute of Development Studies (IDS)

University of Sussex, Brighton B1N 9RE (0273-606261).

Contact: Professor John Toye, Director.

Status: Established in 1966.

Personnel: 45 academic staff; 55 MPhil and DPhil research students.

Budget: £2.4 million for 1987/88.

Sources of income: Overseas Development Administration fund half of the Institute's recurrent budget. Other income is from course fees and consultancies.

Research grants relating to its work in defence, disarmament and development are received from the United Nations University, Barrow and Geraldine S. Cadbury Trust and other funding agencies.

Aims and objectives: The IDS was established as a national centre concerned with Third World development and the relationships between rich and poor countries. The staff, which includes Fellows, visiting academics and research officers, work both at home and overseas.

The IDS is involved in research, teaching and operational assignments directed to a wide range of development problems, particularly those relating to poverty, employment and income distribution within Third World countries and to the unequal relationships between the Third World and the rest of the world economy.

There are 14 research 'clusters' at the IDS, one of which centres on 'Defence, Disarmament and Development'. A major project nearing completion in February 1988 is a comprehensive *Research Guide* to issues and sources relating to military technology, disarmament and development to act as a research tool for researchers based in the Third World where access to relevant literature and data is very limited.

Teaching responsibilities: MPhil and DPhil in Development Studies.

Joint projects: Collaborative projects and reports have been conducted with many organisations including – WIDER; SIPRI; International Broadcasting Trust; World Development Movement and Peace Research Centre, Canberra.

Library/archive: The IDS library is a national centre of documentation on Third World development and is an official depository for UN publications. The collection now exceeds 200,000 non-serial titles and can be used by scholars by arrangement.

Journals and recent publications:
'*IDS Bulletin*' quarterly, Vol. 16, No. 4, Special issue October 1985 – '*Disarmament and World Development: is there a way forward?*'.
Graham, M., Jolly, R. and Smith, C., '*Disarmament and World Development*', Oxford: Pergamon Press, 1986.

SUSSEX UNIVERSITY

Science Policy Research Unit

Mantell Building, University of Sussex, Falmer, Brighton, East Sussex BN1 9RE (0273-686758).

Contacts: Professor Geoffrey Oldham, Director or Julian Perry Robinson, Leader of Group on Military Technology and Arms Limitation.

Origins: Established in 1966.

Personnel: 50 teaching and research staff; 20 visiting fellows; 40 postgraduate students.

Annual turnover: £1.32 million for 1985/86.

Sources of income: The SPRU is a designated research centre of the ESRC. Funding was in the following proportions in 1985/86 – University 16%; the Research Councils 26%; overseas bodies (including international organisations) 21%; UK Charities 15%; central government agencies 10%; UK industry and commerce 5%; other sources 6%.

Aims and objectives: The primary aim of the Unit is to contribute through its research to the advancement of public knowledge of the relationships between scientific and technological developments on the one hand and economic, social and political processes on the other, and to assess their implications for the public policy.

The Unit's work divides into four broad areas – the fourth, *Global Studies of Science and Technology Policy* has two sections:

  Science and Technology Policy on Developing Countries.

  Military Technology and Arms Limitation, which comprises work on:

   The chemical industry and chemical warfare arms control;

   Aspects of chemical and biological armament;

   The SIPRI chemical warfare disarmament programme;

   The US cruise missile development programme;

   Military technology and the economy;

   The political economy of the East/West conflict in Europe;

   Alternative approaches to European Security;

Policy-oriented research

The Warsaw Treaty Organisation;
Armament and Disarmament Information Unit (*see separate entry*).

Teaching responsibilities: MSc course in Science, Technology and Industrialisation which includes options on aspects of Military Technology and Arms Limitations; MPhil and DPhil supervision.

Working parties and joint projects with other institutions and organisations: Collaborative projects have occurred with SIPRI, the United Nations University, the Transnational Institute, Amsterdam, the Pugwash Conferences on Chemical Warfare 1986–87, and Harvard University.

Publications:
Numerous contributions to journals; Graham, M. M. with Jolly, R. and Smith, C. M. '*Disarmament and World Development*', Oxford: Pergamon Press, 1986.

SUSSEX UNIVERSITY

Armament and Disarmament Information Unit (ADIU)

Science Policy Research Unit (SPRU), (*see separate entry*) Mantell Building, University of Sussex, Falmer, Brighton, East Sussex BN1 9RE (0273-686758).

Contact: Malcolm Spaven, Information Officer.

Status: Charitable as part of the University of Sussex.

Origins: Founded in 1978 as an independent information bank (with support from the Joseph Rowntree Charitable Trust) as part of the Military Technology and Arms Limitation research group with the Science Policy Research Unit.

ADIU's Advisory Committee: Includes Professor Sir Geoffrey Oldham the Director of SPRU as Chairman, the 13 members otherwise represent outside specialists and major sponsors.

Personnel: 3 full-time staff and 2 part-time staff.

Income: £72,000 for 1986.

Sources of income: Core support is given by Joseph Rowntree Charitable Trust, Barrow and Geraldine S. Cadbury Trust and the John D. and Catherine T. MacArthur Foundation.

Aims and objectives: The Unit has two principal aims: to facilitate more informed discussion and debate on matters of defence, disarmament and arms control through the provision of a documentation and information service, and to support research work in this field.

The Unit monitors over 200 specialist and non-specialist periodicals, the national and international press, government and intergovernmental documents, and academic papers, and maintains an information bank containing some 1,500 file headings. Specialist holdings are maintained on European defence affairs, military technology and strategy, arms control, and the British defence industry. Information is provided on request to journalists, parliamentarians, researchers and the general public. The Unit's resources are also available for personal consultation by appointment.

Journals and publications:

ADIU Report: A bi-monthly journal containing articles on topical issues, regular reporting of parliamentary proceedings on defence and disarmament, decisions in NATO, WEU, etc and progress on arms talks, together with comprehensive listings of recent literature.

ADIU Occasional Papers: This series was established in 1980 and includes: Robinson, J. Perry '*Chemical and Biological Warfare: Analysis of Recent Reports Concerning the Soviet Union and Vietnam*', 1980; Chirouf, L. '*From Giscard to Mitterand: French Disarmament Policy between the First and Second United Nations Special Sessions*', 1982; Clarke, M. '*The Alternative Defence Debate: Non-Nuclear Defence Policies for Europe*', 1985; Robinson, J. Perry '*NATO Chemical Weapons Policy and Posture*', 1986.

'*Armament and Disarmament: An Introductory Guide to Sources*', 1986. A subject-by-subject listing of literature, organisations and further sources of information.

'*Extremely Low Frequency Communications for Submarines: A Background Briefing on British plans*', 2nd Edition, 1986.

'*Statement on the Defence Estimates 1986, A Review*', 1986.

'*SDI Research: British Capabilities and Interests*', 1986.

ULSTER UNIVERSITY

Peace Studies Programme

Department of History, University of Ulster at Coleraine, Cromore Road, Coleraine, County Londonderry BT52 1SA (0265-4141 x 639).

Contact: Dr A. C. Hepburn, Course Director.

Personnel: 4 course staff (plus 15 drawn from 5 other departments); 12 Diploma/MA students; an undergraduate annual intake of 15.

Sources of income: Some funding for the course link with Limerick is from the EEC ERASMUS Programme which supports student exchange across national borders.

Policy-oriented research

Aims and objectives: The four year degree course which started in 1985 is concerned not just with overt violence but with the wider context in which violence occurs, and therefore with questions of social justice. It deals both with conflict between societies, and with conflict within societies, and it gives some consideration to the distribution of resources in the world and problems of development. In the first year, students are introduced to the disciplines on which the course is based. The main ones are History, Politics and Sociology with some subsidiary Psychology and Philosophy. The later years of the course include historical and theoretical perspectives, comparative study of the main themes in international relations and in ethnic conflict, and some case studies. The most important of the case studies is the conflict in Ireland and some of its broader themes are selected to place it in a wider perspective. Most of the third year is spent on placement in relevant employment.

The first intake for the postgraduate diploma/MA in Peace Studies started in 1987. The central aim of the course is to deepen students' understanding of the problems of conflict resolution and peace-building, with particular reference to divided societies. All students take:
  Concepts and Methods in Peace Studies;
  Conflict Management and Conflict Resolution;
  Divided Societies in the Modern World;
  The Northern Ireland Conflict.

Research programme: A case study of Cyprus with special reference to third party involvement in disputes; Irish politics with particular reference to syndicalism in Irish history; religion and society in Belfast and Derry; the history of community conflict in Belfast. Much of the research work is co-ordinated through the Centre for Conflict Studies.

Joint projects: A contribution on the Catholic minority in Belfast to a European Science Foundation funded research project on 'Government and Non-Dominant Ethnic Groups in Europe, 1850–1940'.

ULSTER UNIVERSITY

Centre for the Study of Conflict

University of Ulster at Coleraine, Cromore Road, Coleraine, County Londonderry BT52 1SA (0265-4141 x 649).

Contact: Professor John Darby, Director.

Origins: In 1977 as an informal cross-disciplinary group interested in Conflict. Now part of the University's research function.

Advisers: Include Dr Maurice Hayes, Parliamentary Commissioner for Complaints for Northern Ireland.

Personnel: 14 academic staff from 3 faculties are researchers with Centre projects. In addition 6 researchers with a primary affiliation to the Centre are funded by external grants.

Sources of income: External grants for 1986/87 were received from: British Council, Department of Education (NI) (Schools project), Department of Education (NI) (Churches project), European Science Foundation, European Community, Fondation Charles Veillon, Policy, Planning and Research Unit (Violence), Policy, Planning and Research Unit Review, Rank Foundation, Joseph Rowntree Charitable Trust, Ulster Quaker Peace Committee.

Aims and objectives: The central aim is to promote and encourage research on the community conflict in Ireland, to provide a forum for cross-disciplinary and comparative studies and to make an informed and impartial contribution to the public discussion of the conflict.

The Centre aims to do this by encouraging the growth of an academic community involved in conflict research, and supporting it through seminars, publications and liaison with other academic institutions. Conflict research is inter-disciplinary and comparative. The free-standing status of the Centre facilitates this approach, and much of the research based in the Centre is carried out by teams from more than one faculty.

There are close relations between the research activities of the Centre and the teaching activities of the Peace Studies courses based in the university's campus at Magee.

Research programme: The dominant interest in the Centre's research activities has been the internal dimensions – schools, churches and reconciliation groups – of the Irish conflict, and the light thrown on it by comparative study and the need to regard local problems within a broader context.

Eight externally funded projects were based at the Centre in 1987:
  The Task of Reconciliation Groups;
  Governments and non-dominant ethnic groups in Europe 1850–1940 (Group VIII: the city);
  Inter School Links;
  The Impact of Violence;
  The Role of the Churches;
  The Social Problems of Derry (joint project with the Universities of Paris and Liverpool);
  Consociationalism;
  Peace Education Project (at Magee College).

Joint projects: Most of the research projects at the Centre involve collaborative research as part of its policy. Formal conventions exist with the Centre for Irish Studies at Paris and the National Institute for

Higher Education, Limerick for the encouragement of co-operation in both research and teaching.

Journals and recent publications:
'*Research Communiques*', a quarterly series on developments at the Centre;

Cairns, E. '*Caught in the Crossfire: Children in Northern Ireland*' Appletree, Belfast and Syracuse University Press, NY, 1987;

Darby J. '*Northern Ireland: the Background to the Conflict*'. Appletree, Belfast and Syracuse University Press NY, 1987 (new edition);

Darby, Dodge and Hepburn (eds) '*Political Violence in Comparative Perspective*' Appletree, Belfast and Syracuse University Press, NY, 1988.

A list of recent articles contributed to journals and chapters to books is obtainable from the centre.

UNIVERSITY OF WALES

Department of International Politics

Llandinam Building, Penglais, University of Wales, Aberystwyth, Dyfed SY23 3DB (0970-3111 x 3234).

Contact: Professor John C. Garnett, Woodrow Wilson Professor of International Relations.

Origins: The Department was created as a result of a trust fund set up by Lord David Davies in 1919.

Personnel: 17 teaching and research staff; 15 postgraduate students; 100+ undergraduates.

Income: approx. £450,000 for 1986/87.

Sources of income: University Grants Committee and Ministry of Defence funding for a Defence Lectureship.

Aims and objectives: The Department claims to be the oldest department in the world on the subject of International Politics. It also pioneered the teaching of Strategic Studies in British universities in the early 1960s.

Research programme: Individual and collaborative research is pursued in many areas, including books on the following subjects:

Britain, NATO and Nuclear Weapons;

Research Guide to Strategic Studies;
Makers of Nuclear Strategy;
Soviet Foreign Policy;
Naval Strategy;
The Political Economy of the Arms Race;
The Political Economy of Soviet Defence Expenditure.

Teaching responsibilities: Undergraduate Studies – including single honours in International Policies and Strategic Studies and Joint Honours Degree Schemes; MSc Econ and Postgraduate Diploma in Strategic Studies. Postgraduate research in the following general areas:

Theories of International Politics;
Ethics and Foreign Policy;
History of International Thought;
Development of the International System;
International Organisation;
War and Strategy;
Disarmament and Arms Control;
Defence Policies of Major Powers;
International History since 1870;
American, Soviet, Chinese and British Foreign Policy, The Far East, Middle East and the Indian Sub-Continent.

Library: The Department's specialist library started in 1919 contains fine collections of foreign policy and International Organisations' documents going back to the League of Nations.

Publications:

Baylis, J. (ed.) '*Alternative Approaches to British Defence Policy*' Macmillan, 1983.

Garnett, J. '*Commonsense and the Theory of International Politics*', Macmillan, 1984.

Booth, K. and Baylis, J. '*Non-Nuclear Defence: For & Against*'; Macmillan, 1987.

Wright, M. (ed.) '*Rights & Objections in North-South Relations: Ethical Dimensions of Global Problems*', Macmillan, 1986.

POLICY-ORIENTED RESEARCH:
Research institutes, Working groups, Information centres

BRITISH AMERICAN SECURITY INFORMATION CENTRE (BASIC)

33 Southampton Street, London WC1E 7HQ (01-379 4924).

Contact: Dan Plesch, Director.

Status: Unincorporated association.

Origins: Set up in early 1987.

Staffing: 1 full time.

Income: £20,000 for 1987.

Sources of income: Joseph Rowntree Social Service Trust; Barrow Cadbury Fund Ltd; Network Foundation.

Aims and objectives: BASIC exists to promote contact between Britain and the US on international security issues. In particular BASIC seeks to improve mutual understanding of the possibilities for achieving security through decreased military power and greater democratic control.

BASIC provides an information service drawn from official US sources, organises seminars and speaking tours and produces research reports. Areas of special interest include NATO air/land and maritime strategies, nuclear weapons and the democratic control of decision making.

Recent publication:
NATO's New Nuclear Weapons, 1988 (Report).

COUNCIL FOR ARMS CONTROL

At King's College London, Manresa Road, Chelsea, London SW3 6LX (01-351 0654).

Contact: Dr Anthony Sivers, Research Officer.

Status: Registered charity.

Origins: Set up in 1981.

Officers: Professor Sir Ronald Mason, Chairman; General Sir Hugh Beach, Director.

Membership: 31 elected Council Members: about 50 Associate Members.

Staffing: 1 full time; 3 part time.

Estimated annual income: around £40,000 for 1986/87.

Sources of income: Trusts and some government support.

Aims and objectives: The Council is an independent research and educational organisation set up by a group of academics, church leaders, former diplomats and politicians from all the main parties in Britain, as a result of their common concern about the escalating arms race and the increasing polarisation between East and West. Its purpose is to promote research into the prospects for arms control and disarmament and to publish material designed to increase public understanding, especially among the young, of the realities of the political and military issues. Its members represent a wide range of views but generally support the active pursuit of international agreements for arms control to increase world stability.

Projects in 1987/88 included seminars on Conventional Arms Control and on Verification Techniques.

Journals and recent publications:
'*Bulletin*', the Council's bi-monthly journal free on request.

The '*Faraday Papers*' series analysis specific subjects, for example: No. 6, Bowker, Mike & Williams, Phil '*Misperceptions in Soviet-American Relations*' 1986;

No. 7, Sims, Nicolas A. '*Biological & Toxin Weapons: Issues in the 1986 Review*' 1986; No. 8, Martin, Laurence '*Minimum Deterrence*' 1987; No. 9, Freedman, Lawrence '*Why is Arms Control So Boring?*' 1987; No. 10, Croft, Stuart '*The United States and Ballistic Missile Defence: ABM and SDI*', 1987.

Annual Lectures are published, for example: 1985: Professor Michael Howard, '*Is Arms Control Really Necessary?*'; 1986: Professor Sir Ronald Mason, '*Innovation, Arms Control & Strategic Stabilities*'.

DAVID DAVIES MEMORIAL INSTITUTE OF INTERNATIONAL STUDIES

2 Chadwick Street, London SW1P 2EP (01-222 4063).

Contact: Sheila Harden, Director.

Status: Registered charity.

Origins: Formed in 1951 to commemorate and continue the work of Lord Davies (1880–1944) on ways to establish a viable world order.

Distinguished patrons: Lord Home of the Hirsel (President); Lord Hunt of Tanworth (Chairman); Professor Sir Keith Hancock, Miss M. M. Sibthorp, Professor Sir Francis Vallat, Professor Dr J. H. W. Verzijl, Lord Wilberforce (Vice-Presidents).

Membership: Not disclosed.

Staffing: Not disclosed.

Annual income: not disclosed.

Sources of income: Trusts and donations.

Aims and objectives: The Institute's main purpose is to advance and promote the development of the 'science' of international relations in all its aspects and to carry out or instigate research and study in this field. It initiates studies on current problems and on those where practical application or workable solutions may be proposed. It works chiefly through ad hoc groups, conferences and seminars drawing in expert participants in any given area and bringing together scholars, administrators, politicians and businessmen.

During 1956–64 the Institute's work centred on aspects of international law. Since then it has sponsored and published works on a wide range of subjects.

Its Annual Memorial Lectures held since 1954 contribute to the discussion of world problems. Copies of the lectures are available from the Institute, for example: Maurice Strong, 1985 '*Beyond the Famine: New Hope for Africa*'; Sir Oliver Wright, 1986 '*Anglo-American Relations: The Atlantic Grows Wider*'; Garet Fitzgerald, 1987 '*Thoughts on Two Cultures: Learning to Live Together*'.

Programme: Work in progress in mid 1987, 'The Frontiers of China', an annotated compilation of relevant treaties and other diplomatic exchanges, with maps. December, 1987, Study Group in 'Aspects of International Terrorism', chaired by Sir Anthony Parsons.

Journals and recent publications:

'*International Relations*', biannual journal, free to members.

'*Waters Round the British Isles: Their Conflicting Uses*' Report of a study group chaired by Professor R. B. Clark, OUP 1987.

'*United Nations and the Specialised Agencies: System Under Strain*' by Douglas Williams and a study group chaired by Mark Allen, Christopher Hurst, 1987.

'*Antarctica: The Next Decade*' Report of a study group chaired by Sir Anthony Parsons, Cambridge University Press, 1987.

'*South Africa: No Turning Back*' ed. Johnson, Shaun. Report of a study group chaired by Lord Bullock, Macmillans, 1988.

EUROPEAN PROLIFERATION INFORMATION CENTRE (EPIC)

258 Pentonville Road, London N1 9JY (01-278 2069).

Contact: Dr David Lowry, Director.

Status: Information consultancy.

Origins: EPIC was set up in May 1984 after a group of academics, researchers and journalists gave joint evidence on the history and implications of the links between civil and military nuclear technology to the Sizewell 'B' Public Inquiry.

Patrons and advisers: Hon President: Professor R. V. Hesketh; Advisory Board: Professor Frank Barnaby; Sir Kelvin Spencer; Professor Mike Pentz; Walter C. Paterson; Colin Hines.

Staffing: 1 part time.

Income: around £4,500 for 1986/87.

Sources of income: Initially from Joseph Rowntree Social Service Trust Ltd; Greenpeace International; Greenpeace (UK); Greater London Council.

Aims and objectives: EPIC is a research and consultancy organisation set up to serve journalists, environment, peace and development pressure groups and parliamentarians with information on a range of related issues comprising inter alia, civil and military nuclear links (reprocessing, waste management etc.); the increase and spread of nuclear weapons and their delivery vehicles; the increase and spread of biological and chemical weaponry; the implications of the

Policy-oriented research

Strategic Defence Initiative for arms control; the importance of the Nuclear Non-Proliferation Treaty (NPT) and its links with the Comprehensive Nuclear Test Ban Treaty (CTBT); the production of nuclear materials for military purposes; the application of nuclear safeguards against the diversion of civil nuclear materials and technologies to military use; the role of nuclear technology transfer to the industrially developing world.

In the course of its work EPIC drafts questions for British and European Parliamentarians, gives evidence to select committees, helps organise or make an input to international and national conferences. In particular EPIC has:

Provided regular information dossiers to the UK press and to the World Information Service on Energy (WISE);

Linked with SPACEWATCH, Congressional lobby group in Washington opposing SDI;

Assisted the UK National Nuclear Free Zone Steering Committee with presentation and information dossier on nuclear power/weapons links and dangers of spent nuclear fuel transport at AGM in 1986 (Dundee).

Affiliations and projects with other bodies: EPIC is a member of the (UK) National Peace Council and has worked with the Verification Technology Information Centre (VERTIC), Freeze, Greenpeace, Friends of the Earth, SERA, some trade unions and local authorities, Scientists Against Nuclear Arms, CND, World Disarmament Campaign and Third World First.

FEDERAL TRUST FOR EDUCATION AND RESEARCH

Europe House, 1a Whitehall Place, London SW1A 2HA (01-839 6625).

Contact: Roy Pryce, Director.

Status: Registered charity and company limited by guarantee.

Origins: Set up in 1945.

Patrons: Lord Thomson of Monifieth (President); Lord Briggs; Basil de Ferranti; Rt Hon Edmund Dell; Lord Ezra; Lord Forte; Lord Gladwyn; Rt Hon David Howell, MP; Professor Kenneth Kirkwood; Sir Arthur Knight; Kenneth Lindsay; Professor James Meade; Sir Michael Palliser; Lord Roll of Ipsden; Sir Brian Urquhart (Vice-Presidents); John Pinder (Chairman of Council).

Staffing: 2 full time (in academic year); 1 part time.

Income: £13,100 in 1986.

Sources of income: In recent years, the Trust has received grants for conferences, studies and educational activities from: the EC Commission, the European Cultural Foundation, the European Educational Research Trust, the Puckham Trust, the Federation Internationale des Maisons de l'Europe, Lloyds Bank, National Westminster Bank, Coutts & Co., Standard Chartered Bank, the John Lewis Partnership, Save and Prosper Group, Shell, British Aerospace, Ferranti, United Scientifc Holdings and Westland.

Aims and objectives: The Trust aims to contribute to the achievement of a more just, harmonious and peaceful world. The main thrust of its work in coming years is now focused on three major themes:

Building a stronger Europe;

Developing the Community's contribution to a better ordered world;

Encouraging a better understanding of the relevance and application of the Federalist principles at national, community and world levels.

The Trust co-ordinates study groups, conferences and lunchtime discussion groups.

Journals and recent publications:

Newsletter, twice yearly. '*The Federalist*' 3 times a year, The Trust promotes and distributes the English language edition for Movimento Federalista Europa.

A brochure on the first 40 years of Trust's work.

A bibliography on federalism.

Working papers and studies include:

Burrows, Sir Bernard & Tyrie, Andrew, '*European Defence Co-operation*' 1986.

Layton, Christopher, '*Europe and the Global Crisis*' 1986 (with IIED).

Affiliations: The Federal Trust is a founder member of the Trans-European Policy Studies Association (TEPSA) and affiliated to The European Movement and the Lothian Foundation.

FOUNDATION FOR DEFENCE STUDIES

c/o Beachcrofts, 100 Fetter Lane, London EC4A 1DN.

Contact: Air Commodore Alun Morgan, Director.

Status: Registered charity and company limited by guarantee.

Trustees: Toby Horton (Chairman); Viscount Lewisham; Rev Basil Watson; Ann Widdecombe MP; Lord Mulley; Lord Harris of Greenwich.

Policy-oriented research

Council for Defence Education: Rev Peter Mumford, Bishop of Truro; Field Marshal Lord Bramall; Professor Lawrence Martin; Lord Mulley; Lord Harris of Greenwich; Gerald Frost; Ray Whitney MP.

Staffing: 1 part time.

Income: £11,718 for 1985/86.

Sources of income: Not disclosed.

Aims and objectives: The Foundation was set up in 1985 'to advance the education of the public by promoting and advancing the study of, and increase the knowledge of, political and military science in all its branches, and promoting the exchange of information, knowledge and thought on international, political and defence issues arising from such study'.

It has carried out 2 major opinion studies on defence conducted by Gallup Poll. The Director's Report for 1985/86 with its accounts at the Charity Commission state 'the period's predominate activity was the organisation and production of a conference on 'Defence and Disarmament – facts and opinion'. This involved the commissioning of a wide ranging 'Gallup Poll' questionnaire which was subsequently analysed by a platform of international diplomats and academics. The opinion questionnaire results and the major contributions to the conference were published and distributed.

The remainder of the period was spent planning the establishment of a Council for Defence Education, the members of which we hope will join the board of directors in the next financial period and assist in the production of further conferences, seminars and publications.'

The Foundation has also subsidised trips to NATO and in 1987 launched a competition for university students.

FOUNDATION FOR INTERNATIONAL SECURITY

The Rookery, Adderbury, Oxon OX17 3NA (0295-810993).

Contact: Stan Windass, Director.

Status: Registered charity.

Origins: Set up in 1987.

Trustees: Field Marshal Lord Carver; Earl Castle Stewart; Professor Lawrence Freedman; Rt Rev Michael Hare Duke, Bishop of St. Andrews; Air Marshal Sir Reginald Harland.

Staffing: 5 full time; 5 part time.

Income: £100,000 for 1986/87.

Sources of income: Leverhulme Trust for study on future of European navies by Eric Grove. Funding is being sought from business and financial institutions in UK, Belgium, the Netherlands, Germany and the United States.

Aims and objectives: The Foundation for International Security is an independent, international body, set up to explore ways of lowering the level of East-West confrontation and encouraging international co-operation in resolving global problems.

It is based on the common sense assumption that in a global society states are increasingly interdependent for their security, and that all share a common interest in avoiding war.

It believes in two basic principles – that a robust defence is an essential condition of security and that co-operative security arrangements which reduce initial threat and military expenditure are equally essential. The Foundation developed from work carried out during 1985–7 focussing on European Security and known as the Common Security Programme. It intends to operate at a high level in three ways:

By means of a task force to help break up log jams in arms reduction negotiations;

By a series of specialised studies to be published in co-operation with Brassey's;

By seminars and other educational activities.

Journals and recent publications:

'*Common Security in Europe*', 2 volumes Brassey's, 1987.

'*Common Security Studies*', a series of specialised studies on long-term security-building was launched in 1987 in co-operation with Brassey's.

INSTITUTE FOR EUROPEAN DEFENCE AND STRATEGIC STUDIES

13–14 Golden Square, London W1R 3AG (01-439 8719).

Contact: Gerald Frost, Director.

Status: Registered charity (as the Centre for European Defence and Strategic Studies) and company limited by guarantee.

Origins: Founded in 1979.

Board of Management: Dr Edwin J. Feulner Jr. (Chairman); Professor Stephen Haseler (Secretary); Richard V. Allen; Rt Hon Sir Peter Blaker; Rt Hon Lord Chalfont; Dr Iain Elliot; Professor Antonio Martino.

Staffing: 4 full time.

Income: around £130,000 for 1986/87.

Policy-oriented research

Sources of income: Charitable trusts such as the Esmé Fairbairn Trust, the Smith Richardson Foundation, New York; donations from companies, individuals and the sale of publications. The Board Chairman is also President of the Heritage Foundation and substantial assistance is believed to be provided from that source.

Aims and objectives: The Institute studies political change in Europe and assesses its impact on strategic and defence issues. It is particularly concerned with developments which affect the future of the Western Alliance. It hopes that the findings of its authors and contributors will interest academics, politicians and others who influence the formulation of policy. Its activities are supervised by an international board of management (see above) and, where appropriate, it seeks the guidance of academics and public figures from Europe and the United States. Conferences and seminars are organised and regular inputs are made to journals and the press.

Journals and recent publications:

'*Survey*' a quarterly journal of East/West Studies, edited by Leopold Ladebz, is published in co-operation with the Institute.

Its *European Security Studies* series includes: '*Britain's Undefended Frontier: A Policy for Ulster*' A Report on an Independent Study Group; Mackenzie, Kenneth '*Turkey in Transition: The West's Neglected Ally*'.

Occasional Papers, of which there are 30, include: No. 4 Utley, T. E. & Norman, Edward '*Ethics & Nuclear Arms: British Churches and the Peace Movement*'; No. 7 Cox, Caroline & Scruton, Roger '*Peace Studies: A Critical Survey*'; No. 9 Kirkpatrick, Jeane '*Idealism, Realism and the Myth of Appeasement*'; No. 12. Chalfont, Alan '*SDI: The Case for the Defence*'.

INSTITUTE FOR THE STUDY OF CONFLICT

12a Golden Square, London W1R 3AF
(01-439 7381/7383).

Contact: Michael Goodwin, Director.

Status: Registered charity and non profit-making limited company.

Origins: Founded in 1970.

Council members: Frank Brenchley (Chairman); Lord Beloff; Professor Maurice Cranston; Lord Denman; Professor S. E. Finer; Air Chief Marshal Sir Christopher Foxley-Norris; D.C.B. Lieven; Vice Admiral Sir Louis Le Bailly; Professor L. W. Martin; Sir Edward Peck; Sir Robert Thompson; General Sir Harry Tuzo.

Staffing: 4 full time; variable number of part-time staff.

Estimated annual turnover: £74,000 for year ending June 1986.

Sources of income: Subscriptions and donations from trusts, foundations and corporations in the UK, USA and other countries. No government grants are received.

Aims and objectives: The Institute's main aims are:

To research into the causes, manifestations and trends of political instability and conflict throughout the world;

To study the subversive and terrorist activities of extremist organisations and their international links;

To publish balanced assessments of issues vital to international security based on the results of this research and analysis.

The Institute conducts conferences and seminars, usually in association with overseas associates and affiliates, and arranges briefings and round-table discussions for groups from universities, industrial and commercial organisations, the armed services and police, as well as for individuals.

Affiliations and projects with other bodies: The Institute is closely associated with the Center for Security Studies, Washington D.C.

Journals and recent publications: In 1986 the Institute established the Centre for Security and Conflict Studies, to be primarily responsible for its publishing activities. Publications include the quarterly '*Conflict Bulletin*' and the monthly '*Conflict Study*' dealing with a specific geographical area or aspect of political conflict. Occasional special reports arising from a conference or a series of study groups have been published on contemporary issues such as '*The Security of Middle East Oil*' and '*The Soviet Empire: Pressures and Strains*'.

INSTITUTE FOR THE STUDY OF TERRORISM (I.S.T. Research Associates)

65 Blandford Street, London W1H 3AJ (01-487 4858).

Contact: Jillian Becker, Director.

Status: Independent research institute.

Staffing: 6 full time (plus ad hoc specialists).

Income and recent sources of income: Not known.

Aims and objectives: The Institute describes its aims in its basic information leaflet as follows:

Collecting, classifying, and analysing information;

Supplying information and analysis on request;

Issuing information and analysis to the news media;

Publishing articles, papers, books;

Sponsoring public lectures, discussions and conferences;

Providing a centre for persons engaged in the study of terrorism, or in counter-terrorist activity, to contact or meet each other;

Building an archive for the Institute's own purposes, and as a facility for students, scholars and other researchers.

The Institute did not wish for an entry in this guide. It is understood that Lord Chalfont, Lord Orr-Ewing and Baroness Cox support its work as honorary officers/advisers, and that publications/reports may be available.

INTERNATIONAL GROUP OF RESEARCHERS ON THE ANTI-BALLISTIC MISSILE TREATY (IGRAT)

Alte-Bergsteige 47, D–6950 Mosbach, West Germany, (0049-6261-12912).

Contact: Dr Hans Günter Brauch, Research Co-ordinator.

Status: Unincorporated association.

Origins: Evolved in early 1986 to provide a focus for international researchers working on issues related to the 1972 ABM Treaty.

Staffing: 1 full time.

Income: £17,000 for 1987.

Sources of income: IGRAT is sponsored by the Lansbury House Trust Fund and has been funded by the Joseph Rowntree Charitable Trust, the Barrow ad Geraldine S. Cadbury Trust and the International Peace Education Fund, USA.

Aims and objectives: The ABM Treaty, threatened by developments from the United States and the Soviet Union, has provided the backdrop to all US/USSR nuclear arms control negotiations since its ratification. IGRAT monitors and reports on these developments. About 100 international researchers support the group. It also provides speakers' list for peace groups, academic and political organisations

Publications:

'*A Guide to the ABM Treaty*' (up to 10 free of charge).

Bulkeley, Rip and Brauch, Dr H. G. '*The ABM Treaty and World Security*' (available from the Armament and Disarmament Information Unit, University of Sussex, *see separate entry*).

INTERNATIONAL INSTITUTE FOR STRATEGIC STUDIES

23 Tavistock Street, London WC2E 7NQ, (01-379 7676).

Contact: Francois Heisbourg, Director.

Status: Registered charity and company limited by guarantee.

Origins: Founded in 1958 by a group of British analysts, academics, politicians, service officers and churchmen to study the growing complexity of security in the nuclear age. In 1964, the Institute became fully international with Council members respresenting some 16 countries in Europe, North America, the Middle East, East Asia and the Pacific.

Patrons and officers: Professor Sir Michael Howard (UK), (President); General Andrew Goodpaster (USA); Francois de Rose (France); Kiichi Saeki (Japan); Professor Carl Friedrich von Weizsacker (Germany); Chairman of Council, 1983–7, Sir Michael Palliser (UK); Chairman of Executive Committee, General Sir Harry Tuzo (UK) (Vice-Presidents).

Membership: 1,618 individual; 561 associate; 239 corporate; 247 student; (membership is drawn from 79 countries).

Personnel: 42 full time staff; 15 research associates.

Income: £1.432 million for year ended October 1986.

Sources of income: Until 1985 the Institute was dependent on a yearly general support grant from the Ford Foundation. An appeal for an endowment fund to support the Institute has raised £6 million from many sources including the Ford Foundation, the Rockefeller Foundation, and John D. and Catherine T. MacArthur Foundation, the Andrew W. Mellon Foundation and the William and Flora Hewlett Foundation. Support from research programmes and projects was received in 1986 from the W. Alton Jones Foundation; the Rockefeller Foundation; the Florence and John Schumann Foundation; the Stiftung Volkswagenwerk; the Kearney Foundation of Hong Kong; the Rockefeller Brothers Fund; the Arthur Vining Davis Foundation; the Agnelli Foundation; the Krupp Foundation; the Luce Foundation; the Leverhulme Trust; the Thyssen Foundation.

Aims and objectives: The Institute aims to analyse international security problems and to inject new thinking into the debate on these issues. Current priority areas of research are:

East-West relations;

Arms control;

Strategic defences;

Regional security (focusing in 1986–7 on South-East Asia).

Policy-oriented research

The Institute's role as an independent information source is served by its publications and library (see below). It acts as a major discussion forum with a prestigious annual conference and yearly Alastair Buchan Memorial Lecture complemented by seminars, study groups and twice-monthly meetings for members on current issues.

Library/Archive: The extensive library with independent collection is supported by a continuous press archive maintained since 1958.

Journals and recent publications:
'*Survival*', the Institute's bi-monthly journal.
'*The Military Balance*', Janes Publishing; an annual survey of military forces around the world.
'*Strategic Survey*'; an annual review of security-related events.
'*Adelphi Papers*' – monographs analysing current and future problems of international security concerns written by experts from many nations. Twelve to fifteen are published each year. By mid 1987, 220 had been published, for example: Nos. 216–218 – '*East Asia, the West and International Security: Prospects for Peace*' Papers from the IISS '28th Annual Conference, 1987; No. 219 – King, Ralph '*The Iran-Iraq War: The Political Implications*' 1987; No. 220 – Karsh, Ephraim '*The Iran-Iraq War: A Military Analysis*' 1987.

The Institute's book series available through booksellers are '*Studies in International Security*', '*Studies in Regional Security*' and '*The Adelphi Library*'.

INTERNATIONAL NUCLEAR NON-PROLIFERATION NETWORK

(*see University Departments and Centres, Southampton University*)

OXFORD RESEARCH GROUP

32 Warnborough Road, Oxford OX2 6JA (0865-242 819).

Contact: Scilla Elworthy McLean, Director.

Status: Unincorporated association; application for charitable status in train.

Origins: Established in 1982.

Board of Sponsors: Professor Frank Barnaby; Professor Elise Boulding; Professor Kenneth Boulding; Dr Malcolm Dando; Lady Franks; Nicholas Gillet; Rev Dr John Habgood; Mary Midgley; Sir Nevill Mott; Sheila Oakes; Professor James O'Connell; Dr Paul Rogers; Sir Kelvin Spencer; Rev Victor de Waal; Ben Whitaker.

Staffing: 3 full time; 6 part time.

Income: £54,074 for 1986/87.

Sources of income: B. and G. S. Cadbury Trust, J. A. Clark Trust, Puckham Trust, Joseph Rowntree Charitable Trust, Noel Buxton Trust.

Aims and objectives: The Oxford Research Group was established to carry out research on how nuclear weapons decisions are made, and by whom they are made, in all the nuclear nations. Its second aim is to communicate that information to the public. Its work is best described in their own words:

'We have examined all stages of production of nuclear weapons in the Soviet Union, the United States, Britain, France and China. We have studied the role of scientists in weapons laboratories, the role of intelligence analysts, military strategists, defence contractors and procurement officials, as well as examining interservice rivalry and foreign policy formulation.

'The work of the Group sprang from an early recognition that it is essential to understand the human side of the arms race – to understand how and by whom the decisions are made – if efforts to restrain the arms race are to be successful. Everything the Group undertakes is to increase this understanding, or to enable others to use it to focus their efforts for change.

'The Oxford Research Group is fiercely independent. The Group's function is to research and inform, not to campaign. We therefore have, as a Group, no policy on disarmament. Members of the Group vary in their personal convictions, but all would agree that the arms race must now be stopped. The Research Group comprises a core of some nine researchers who work in collaboration with specialist researchers on specific subjects'.

Joint projects with other organisations: The Group has carried out work for the United Nations University and is collaborating with the Harvard Medical School Centre for Psychological Studies in the Nuclear Age and with Bradford University School of Peace Studies.

From its inception the Group has made its research findings available to groups of citizens who want to engage in constructive dialogue with those involved in making key decisions about the design, manufacture, procurement and deployment of nuclear weapons.

Since 1983 some 70 UK groups have attempted to open and maintain a dialogue with a nuclear decision-maker in the UK and with another in China. The Group has supplied briefing sheets, and advice on how to manage constructive debate with a person who is likely to be unused to and wary of such a contact. Eleven groups have had meetings with a decision-maker. Most of the others have sustained a protracted and detailed correspondence. A similar project associated with the Oxford Research Group has started in the USA – the Nuclear Dialogue Project. The Group has also been supporting peace actions by women (e.g. a Women's Defence Dialogue with NATO in June 1987).

Journals and recent publications:
McLean, S. E. (ed.) 'How Nuclear Weapons Decisions Are Made' Macmillan, 1986.
Miall, H. 'Nuclear Weapons: Who's in Charge?' Macmillan, 1987.
McLean, S. E. 'Who Decides? Accountability & Nuclear Weapons Decision-Making in Britain', ORG, 1986.
McLean, Greene, Hamwee, Miall, Ponting, 'Do It Yourself Minister – Problems of Implementing a Non-Nuclear Defence Policy in a Nuclear World', ORG, 1987.
'Ask the Horse' 15 min. video describing those who shape nuclear weapons decisions worldwide.
'For Your Ears Only' Tape cassette describing powerlessness of Parliament made by Performing Artists for Active Enquiry.
Forthcoming in 1988: 'Nuclear Weapons Decision-making Yearbook' – a directory of main decision-making bodies in the 5 nuclear weapon nations and two alliances; 'Decide for Yourself' – a simulation game for students.

PUGWASH CONFERENCES ON SCIENCE AND WORLD AFFAIRS

Central Office: Flat A, 63A Great Russell Street, London WC1B 3RG (01-405 6661).

Contact: Dr Martin Kaplan, Secretary General.

Executive Office: 11A Avenue de la Paix, 1202 Geneva, Switzerland (022-33-11-80).

Origins: In 1957, a small group of scientists from East and West formed the Pugwash Movement, named after the village in Nova Scotia, Canada, where they first met to take up the challenge of the Russell-Einstein Manifesto of 1955 addressed to the world's scientific community to devise ways to avoid the danger of nuclear war.

Executive Committee: The ten member Executive Committee of the Pugwash Council includes Dr John Holdren (Chairman); Professor Bernard T. Feld; Professor Dorothy Hodgkin (President of the Pugwash Conferences); Dr Martin Kaplan; Professor Joseph Rotblat.

Membership: 2,300.

Staffing: 4 full time; 4 part time.

Annual income: Not disclosed.

Sources of income: The Pugwash Foundation, a fundraising charity registered in Switzerland was set up in 1986 to raise U.S. $3 million.

Aims and objectives: Since 1957 149 Pugwash Conferences, symposia and workshops have been held with an attendance of some 7,300 participants. The meetings are closed and without publicity. Major findings have been transmitted to governments, United Nations and leaders of the world scientific community. The private, unofficial and informal nature of Pugwash meetings mean that their influence on official government policy is not generally apparent. They claim influence on the negotiation of arms control agreements such as the Nuclear Test Ban Treaty 1963, the Nuclear Non-Proliferation Treaty, 1968, the Convention on the Prohibition of the Development, Production and Stockpiling of Bacteriological, (Biological) and Toxin Weapons and on their Destruction, 1972 and the Anti-Ballistic Missile Agreement 1972. Pugwash also helped in the groundwork for the Strategic Arms Limitations Talks (SALT), the Conference on Security Co-operation in Europe (CSCE), and the Mutual Balanced Force Reduction (MBFR) Talks. More recent examples are various governmental declarations for nuclear weapon-free zones, no-first-use of nuclear weapons and moratoriums on their testing and developments. International activities of Pugwash are organized by the Pugwash Council and its Executive Committee. National activities of Pugwash are the responsibility of 32 national groups working in co-operation with the Council. These groups organise and finance Pugwash meetings held in their own countries, and help in providing travel expenses when their scientists attend Pugwash meetings outside their own countries. They also contribute to the expenses of the Central and Executive Offices. Student/Young Pugwash groups have been established in 10 countries with chapters at many university campuses where the objectives of Pugwash are discussed.

Current Pugwash efforts include work towards deep reductions in nuclear forces, the prevention of accidental nuclear war, the achievement of a treaty for a total ban on chemical weapons, the prevention of the proliferation of weapons in space, the development of non-provocative defence postures, studies of conventional forces in Europe and elsewhere as a substitute for the military doctrine of relying on nuclear weapons for deterrence purposes, the definition of minimum deterrence and how to arrive at that state, and the establishment of crisis prevention and control networks in Europe, Africa, Latin America and Asia.

Affiliation: Pugwash has recognised status as a non-governmental organisation with the United Nations.

Policy-oriented research

Journals and recent publications:
Quarterly Pugwash newsletter; Proceedings of Annual Conferences; Annals of Pugwash; Monographs of Symposia.

British Pugwash Group: (address and telephone as for the Central Office of Pugwash); **Executive Committee:** Professor Joseph Rotblat (Chairman); Professor William F. Gutteridge (Membership Secretary); Maxwell Bruce (Organising Secretary). **Membership:** 190.

RESEARCH FOUNDATION FOR THE STUDY OF TERRORISM

40 Doughty Street, London WC1 2LF (01-405 5195).

or c/o University of Aberdeen, Department of Politics & International Relations, Edward Wright Building, Old Aberdeen AB9 2UB (0224-272713/7).

Contact: Professor Paul Wilkinson, Chairman.

Status: Educational charity.

Origins: Established in 1987.

Trustees: Professor Paul Wilkinson (Chairman of Trustees); Michael Ivens; Norris McWhirter; John Newton Scott; the Duke of Valderano (Chairman of Council).

Staffing: None paid.

Aims and objectives: The Research Foundation is designed to foster, sponsor and disseminate research into all aspects of terrorism. It produces briefing papers, reports and other information for industry, legislators, senior officials, professional people and the academic world. In December 1987 the Foundation ran a conference at Windsor on 'Terrorism, Business & Industry'.

ROYAL INSTITUTE OF INTERNATIONAL AFFAIRS

Chatham House, 10 St James's Square, London SW1Y 4LE (01-930 2233/3355).

Contacts: Admiral Sir James Eberle (Director); Brigadier W. Woodburn (Executive Director).

Status: Registered charity.

Origins: Set up in 1920 as a result of discussions between the British and American delegates at the Paris Peace Conference in 1919. In 1926 it received its Royal Charter.

Patron: The Queen. Presidents: Lord Callaghan; Lord Grimond of Firth; Lord Home of the Hirsel.

Membership: 2,973 members or associates, plus 322 corporate members.

Staffing: Approximately 70 full time.

Income: £1.002 million for 1986/87 (including research grants, etc.).

Sources of income: In 1986/87 some 46% of total revenue income (£461,000) was received in the form of research grants whilst some 27% was derived from subscriptions, individual and corporate. Grants during the two previous financial years were received from: American Academy of Arts and Sciences; Anglo-German Foundation; Arab-British Chamber of Commerce; Economic and Social Research Council; Ford Foundation; Foreign and Commonwealth Office; Fritz Thyssen Stiftung; ICI plc; Institute of Developing Economies; Japan Economic Foundation; Keizei Koho Centre; Le Poer Power Trust; Leverhulme Trust; MacArthur Foundation; Ministry of Defence; MITI; Nomura Research Institute; the Gatsby Charitable Institute; US Mission to NATO; Sir Daniel Stevenson Fund; Lothian Memorial Fund.

Aims and objectives: The Institute (often known has Chatham House) aims to promote the study and understanding of all aspects of international affairs through lectures, discussions, research and publications. Chatham House is primarily a working body and candidates for election to membership are usually in, or have a special knowledge of, international issues. The requirements of its Royal Charter mean that the Institute cannot express an opinion of its own so views expressed at meetings or in publications are those of the speakers and authors concerned.

The Institute has an active programme of meetings. General meetings, open to all members, are held usually once a week during lunch hour. Other discussions on specialised topics may be smaller and held privately by invitation only.

Conferences and briefings are fee-paying and analyse issues of special interest to business and industry. They are also open to non-members.

Research programme: The Institute's research programme is at the heart of its work. It covers the fields of International Security, International Economics, Western Europe, Soviet Foreign Policy, East Asia, the Middle East, Latin America and International Business and Technology. The Institute also collaborates with the Policy Studies Institute in a Joint Energy Programme. The research staff form the core of the research activities, commissioning work from outside collaborators as well as conducting research in-house. Visiting fellows from different countries and professional backgrounds also contribute to the Institute's research and publications. Some research takes the form of study groups which meet regularly over a period of one to two years. The

Policy-oriented research

products of this research are available in published form.

Working parties and joint projects: Joint projects with other institutions in 1986 included:

A comparison of French and British foreign policies with Centre d'Etudes et des Rècherches Internationales (CERI);

A collaborative study of Soviet and Western approaches to international economic security with the Institute for World Economy and International Relations, Moscow;

Selection as British participant in the 'Tokyo Forum', a network of institutions from the G5 countries sponsored by the Nomura Research Institute, Japan, to undertake co-ordinated research into the better management of the world economy along with the Brookings Institution (USA), IFRI, (France), IFO, (Germany) and Nomura.

Library and press library: The library is an outstanding specialist collection containing over 160,000 books and pamphlets with an emphasis on post Second World War but also covering the period since the Institute's inception. Some 650 periodicals are regularly received from all over the world. The library has depository status for United Nations publications and receives EEC documents. The press library has an extensive collection of cuttings from British and foreign newspapers and speeches by leading public figures with detailed classification and cross-referencing.

Journals and recent publications:

'*International Affairs*', quarterly journal;

'*The World Today*', monthly journal;

'*Chatham House Papers*' the RIIA's own paperback imprint started in 1979, since 1981 published by Routledge and Kegan Paul. There are some 36 titles including:

Freedman, Lawrence '*Arms Control: Management or Reform*', 1986;

Williams, Phil (ed.) '*The Nuclear Debate*' 1984;

Eberle, James and Wallace, Helen '*British Space Policy and International Collaboration*', 1987.

ROYAL UNITED SERVICES INSTITUTE FOR DEFENCE STUDIES (RUSI)

Whitehall, London SW1A 2ET (01-930 5854/2272).

Contact: Group Captain David Balcon, Director.

Status: Registered charity.

Origins: Formed in 1931; its first President, the Duke of Wellington.

Patrons: The Queen, The Duke of Kent, President.

Staffing: 20 full time (end Dec. 1987).

Membership: about 7,000.

Income: Not disclosed.

Sources of income: Ministry of Defence, donations from industry and membership subscriptions.

Aims and objectives: The Institute received its Royal Charter for 'the promotion and advancement of the military sciences and literature'. In seeking to set the military sciences in their current political, economic, social and technological context, in accordance with its Royal Charter, RUSI has three particular functions:

It is the professional association of the Armed Forces;

It brings together participants from a wide range of disciplines who have a legitimate interest in defence and international security;

It assists in developing a wider public undertaking of politico-military issues of the moment.

These functions underpin the studies of RUSI, its publications and its administration.

Its research is grouped into a series of Study Programmes which give a coherent structure to a range of meetings, lectures, research projects and publications. These programmes at the end of 1987 were:

The Soviet Union and Eastern European Programme.

European Security and the Atlantic Alliance Programme;

Technology and Defence Procurement Programme;

Middle East Programme;

Space and International Security Programme.

In addition RUSI each year adopts a main study theme for its lectures and presentations. The theme for 1986/87 was 'Conventional Defence: Into the 1990s' and for 1987/88 'NATO and the Warsaw Pact: the Next Fifteen Years'. There are regular visits from overseas defence colleges and official delegations. RUSI also runs 'Forum Lunches' for board members and investment managers from industry and the City.

Journals and recent publications:

'*Defence Studies and Military Power Book Series*'. The following titles have been published in 1987:

Williams, Air Commodore E. S. '*The Soviet Military: Political Education, Training and Morale*'; Sherr, James '*Soviet Power: The Continuing Challenge*'; Robertson, K. G. '*British and American Approaches to Intelligence*'; Hemsley, Brigadier John '*The Soviet Bio-Chemical Threat to NATO: The Neglected Issue*'; Cordesman, Professor A. H. '*The Iran/Iraq War and Western Security 1984–87*'.

The RUSI Defence Year Book, published with Brassey's

Policy-oriented research

Defence Publishers Limited. *Journal. Armed Forces*, published monthly with Ian Allan Ltd.

Whitehall Papers provide the essentials of a particular subject in a concise format, as well as offering the means of circulating conferences and seminar papers as soon as possible after the event. The following were produced in 1987: *'Conventional Defence: Issues and Prospects'*; *'British Forces Germany: Size Versus Prospects'*; *'Military Lessons of the Arab-Israeli Conflict'*; *'SDI: Will It Work? Can It Help?'*; *'War in the Gulf'*; *'Iran-Iraq War: Efforts at Mediation'*; *'Arms Transfers and the Iran-Iraq War'*.

RUSI Newsbrief provides background and analysis of topical defence and security issues. Coverage in 1987 included *'Soviet Industry and its Impact on Military Technology'*, *'US Bases in the Mediterranean'*, *'Yugoslavia: A Stable Future?'* *'The INF Agreement'*, an analysis of Southern Africa and also of Indonesia.

SCIENTIFIC COMMITTEE ON PROBLEMS OF THE ENVIRONMENT ENVIRONMENTAL CONSEQUENCES OF NUCLEAR WAR (SCOPE-ENUWAR)

SCOPE-ENUWAR Research Unit, Department of Chemistry, Essex University, Wivenhoe Park, Colchester CO4 3SQ (0206-873370).

Contact: Linda Appleby, Research Assistant.

Status: SCOPE-ENUWAR is part of the Scientific Committee on Problems of the Environment (SCOPE), created by the International Council of Scientific Unions (ICSU).

Origins: Initiated in 1983.

SCOPE Steering Committee: Sir Frederick Warner (UK) (Chairman); J. Bénard (France); S. K. D. Bergstrom (Sweden); P. Crutzen (Netherlands); T. F. Malone (ICSU); M. G. K. Menon (India); M. Nagau (Japan); G. K. Skryabin (USSR); G. F. White (USA).

Personnel: 7 (including 2 full time research assistants and 5 part-time including a professor, reader and lecturer).

Estimated annual budget: US $362,700 for 1988 (for both Essex University and USA-based work).

Sources of income: During the past 2 years support has been received from: W. Alton Jones Foundation; Rockefeller Brothers Fund; Royal Society of London; ICSU; University of Essex; SCOPE; Carnegie Foundation; The Joseph Rowntree Charitable Trust.

Aims and objectives: The Study of the Environmental Consequences of Nuclear War (ENUWAR) was established to examine critically the proposition that smoke injected into the atmosphere as a result of global nuclear war would have a major influence upon climate and consequently an adverse effect upon agricultural production. In 1985 the SCOPE published a two-volume technical report (SCOPE 28) summarising its investigations into the physical, atmospheric and biological effects of a nuclear exchange. The report brought together the conclusions of 300 scientists from 30 countries, following a series of major conferences and workshops held around the world. It concluded that the indirect effects of nuclear war (arising from environmental perturbations and consequent effects upon agricultural production and food distribution) resulting from a limited nuclear exchange could cause a greater loss of life (especially in non-combatant countries) than the direct effects of nuclear weapons.

The objectives of ENUWAR are: to continue to collate the latest scientific research on the environmental consequences of nuclear war and to disseminate this information; to continue to encourage and facilitate scientific work concerned with physical and biological consequences of nuclear war to resolve remaining uncertainties.

Programme: The current focus of the programme is upon refinement of predictions of indirect effects of nuclear war upon specific countries through case studies, and the communication of the results of the ENUWAR research to a wider audience. This entails:

Continued establishment of an international scientific consensus;

Communication to policy-makers, news media and educational establishments;

Facilitation of case-studies at national and regional level.

The SCOPE-ENUWAR unit organises international workshops to examine the physical, biological and radiological effects of nuclear war, and serves as an information/exchange. Detailed records of the research findings are maintained and updated. Some associated research is taking place in the Department of Chemistry on light absorption and scattering by smoke aerosols, evolution of smoke particle size with time due to coagulation processes, and morphology of smoke particles.

Publications:

'Environmental Consequences of Nuclear War' SCOPE 28 Vols. 1 & 2 John Wiley, UK, 1986.

'Planet Earth in Jeopardy' (Abridged version of above study) John Wiley, UK, 1986.

SOUTH ATLANTIC COUNCIL

c/o Department of Systems Science, City University, Northampton Square, London EC1V 0HB (01-253 4399 x 4617).

Contact: Dr Peter Willetts, Hon Secretary.

Executive Committee: Cyril Townsend MP (Chairman); Hugh Carless (Deputy Chairman); Dr Peter Willetts; George Foulkes MP.

Membership: 50 (limited by election).

Staffing: None paid.

Sources of income: For the three years to September 1987 the Barrow and Geraldine S. Cadbury Trust, the Joseph Rowntree Social Service Trust and the Joseph Rowntree Charitable Trust met the cost of the University salary and overheads of the appointment of the then Research Fellow/Director, Dr Alaine Lowe. Some funds also from subscriptions and other donations.

Aims and objectives: The Council is an all-party Parliamentary pressure group set up in December 1983 by members of the House of Commons Select Committee on Foreign Affairs. It now consists of a grouping of MPs, from all parties, members of the House of Lords, Churchmen, diplomats, academics and interested individuals. In 1984/85 the Council organised discussions at the University of Maryland between British and Argentinian politicians, ex-diplomats and academics. The Council has sponsored visits to the islands, and to Argentina, it publishes occasional papers and its members have contributed substantially to debate in the media. The former Research Director has researched attitudes to the dispute of both the Falkland Islanders (in 1985) and Argentinians (in 1986).

It has had close relations with the: British Council of Churches, Catholic Institute for International Relations, Baptist Church, United Nations Association, Anglo-Argentine Association, British/Argentine Women's Peace Initiative, Falkland Island Government Office.

Conferences have been held in November 1987 at the City University with members of the Fundacioun Universitaria del Rio de la Plata and a major Argentine/British Conference is planned for Spring 1989. It is hoped that this will initiate a biannual series of such conferences to be held alternately in Britain and Argentina.

VERIFICATION TECHNOLOGY INFORMATION CENTRE

33 Southampton Street, London WC2E 7HQ (01-379 7445).

Contact: Dr Patricia Lewis, Information Officer.

Status: Independent organisation.

Origins: Set up in 1986.

Staffing: 1 full time (plus 1 unpaid 'intern').

Estimated income: £20,000 for 1986/87.

Sources of income: The Lansbury House Trust Fund sponsors VERTIC. A start-up grant was given by the Joseph Rowntree Charitable Trust. The Barrow and Geraldine S. Cadbury Trust Fund has funded travel costs.

Aims and objectives: The Centre is a non-aligned, independent organisation which distributes technical information, especially briefings, on the verification of nuclear arms-control treaties, with the aim of promoting discussion and assisting informed debate. Material is sent on request to the media, Parliament, non-governmental organisations and individuals. Unsolicited briefings are distributed periodically, especially to MPs interested in disarmament and arms control. A library of press clippings and technical articles is maintained at the office and available for use by interested visitors.

VERTIC organises visits by overseas experts who give seminars and informal briefings. Its own associated scientist-specialists offer their services for public-speaking or technical advice.

Three working groups: Seismology (SWG), Remote Sensing (RSWG), and Verification Strategies (VSWG), are involved in the preparation of briefings. Eleven British scientists are involved in their spare time in the working groups, and each working group has one or more overseas advisers.

An independent Advisory Committee with members who represent the spectrum of arms-control activities supervises VERTIC's administrative and technical affairs.

Journals and recent publications: Scientific research papers:

Leggett, J. K. *'Clandestine nuclear testing: technologies and feasibility'* In: Cox, D. and Goldblat, J. (eds) *'A Comprehensive Test Ban: Problems and Prospects'*, SIPRI, 1987.

Leggett, J., Clark, R., and Westaway, R. *'The possible role of confidence-building measures in achieving a nuclear test ban'*, a paper presented at the Soviet Academy of Sciences 'Forum for Peace', Moscow, February 1987.

Clark, R. C. *'Verification of nuclear test bans'*. Lewis, P. and Greene, O. *'Verification of INF reductions'*. Both contributions to Barnaby F. (ed) *'A Verification Handbook for Arms Control and Disarmament'*, a publication of the London Centre for International Peacebuilding (*see separate entry*).

Policy-oriented research

Many other scientific review papers and commentary articles have been published.

WESTERN EUROPEAN DEFENCE ASSOCIATION

Blandford House, 65 Blandford Street, London W1H 3HA (01-402 9461).

Contact: Evelyn Le Chene, Director.

Status: Unincorporated association.

Aims and objectives: The Association, set up in 1985, is not a membership organisation. It acts as both a forum and research base and apparently is specifically concerned with chemical warfare, the Soviet application thereof and the imbalance in this area between East and West.

It is understood that Mrs Le Chene, the Director, is publishing a book on chemical warfare which should be publicly available in early 1988. Other research work is not made widely available.

Mrs Le Chene was not prepared to supply any further information about this organisation.

WORKING PARTY ON CHEMICAL AND BIOLOGICAL WEAPONS

Pencalenick, Polruan, Cornwall PL23 1NH (072-687782).

Contact: Elizabeth Sigmund, Co-ordinator.

Status: A project sponsored by the Lansbury House Trust Fund.

Origins: Members of the working party were associated with a 'grassroots' campaign against chemical and biological weapons in the 1960s which faded with the 1974 ban; in 1980 a scientist's petition led to the formation of the present group.

Staffing: 1 full time.

Income: £15,000 for 1987.

Sources of income: The Joseph Rowntree Charitable Trust and the Barrow Cadbury Fund Ltd.

Aims and objectives: The Working Group, chaired by Dr Alistair Hay, consists mainly of academics and aims to keep politicians, the media, churches and the general public aware of developments in the field of chemical and biological warfare by publishing information sheets and articles, holding briefing meetings and so on.

POLICY-ORIENTED RESEARCH:
International research establishments

ATLANTIC INSTITUTE FOR INTERNATIONAL AFFAIRS

9 avenue Hoche, 75008 Paris, France (42-25-58-17).

Contact: Dr Andrew Pierre, Director-General.

Status: Charitable.

Origins: Founded in 1961 as a result of a resolution from the 1958 Atlantic Parliamentarians Congress.

Officers: Dr Wilfried Guth (Chairman); Seiki Tozaki (Vice Chairman); Max Geldens (Finance Committee Chairman).

Membership: 130 Governors; 200 Corporate members; 200 individual members (drawn from 21 of the OECD countries).

Staffing: 6 full time.

Income: £450,000 for 1988.

Sources of income: Membership fees. In the past two years the Ford Foundation, the MacArthur Foundation, the Rockefeller Foundation, and the Thyssen Foundation.

Aims and objectives: The Institute operates internationally in the fields of economic affairs and international relations through self-conducted programmes of research, conferences, courses, publications and lectures. The studies programme is built around three main themes:

  Politics and military security problems affecting the Western community, and its relations with the Communist world;

  Economic and financial issues affecting the West;

  Developments in new technologies and their impact on policies and on economic and social structures and institutions.

Other activities include a Corporate Members Programme through which representatives of the business firms supporting the Institute meet twice a year to discuss common problems together with a select group of international experts. The Institute works closely with both international organisations and national institutes. Its location facilitates international gatherings and a close working relationship with the OECD. It also collaborates closely with NATO and the EEC. Various arrangements link the Institute with the activities of national institutes, the Trilateral Commission, the International Institute for Strategic Studies, the Brookings Institution, the Council on Foreign Relations and other similar organisations. The Institute also maintains a library covering a wide range of subjects relevant to its aims.

Current projects include 'Nato Institutions: the Management of Consensus'; 'Domestic Sources of Western Policy Towards the Soviet Union'.

Supporting and affiliated organisations: Atlantic Institute Foundation, USA; Keidanren, Japan; Atlantica, West Germany; The Atlantic Council of Canada.

Journals and recent publications: *The Atlantic Papers* (four monographs a year on topical international economic and security issues), for example: No. 62 Deschamps, Louis *'The SDI & European Security Interests'*; No. 63 Woods, Stanley *'Western Europe: Technology and the Future'*.

'Research Volumes' (books resulting from research projects), for example: Vine, Richard (ed.) *'Soviet-East European Relations as a Problem for the West'*.

INTERNATIONAL PEACE ACADEMY

777 United Nations Plaza, New York, NY 10017-3521 (212 949 8480).

Contact: Major General (Ret) Indar Jit Rikhye, Chairman of the Board and Chief Executive Officer.

Status: An independent non-profit organisation recognised as charitable in the USA, Canada and UK.

Policy-oriented research

Origins: Founded in 1970 by a 'multi-national' gathering of individuals led by Ruth Forbes Young (Mrs Arthur M. Young).

International Advisory Board: Its 22 members included in 1987 Cyrus R. Vance; Denis Healey. Its Honorary Chairpersons included Sir Shridath S. Rampal and the Archbishop of Canterbury, Dr Robert Runcie.

Staffing: Not disclosed.

Estimated annual budget: $1.3 million for 1987.

Sources of income: In order to maintain an impartial stance the IPA does not accept funds from the UN or the five major world powers. Project and basic support funding comes mainly from private sources – 70% from foundations, 25% from individuals and 5% from corporations all predominantly in the USA. Support has been given by the Ford, Rockefeller, Hewlett, McKnight, Pew Charitable Trusts, MacArthur Foundation and the Exxon and Honeywell Corporations.

Aims and objectives: The IPA is both a training and research institute devoted to methods of mediation and negotiation to resolve regional and international conflicts and a forum for dialogue about troubled areas of the world.

It has 'created' a network of some 4,000 professional people trained in techniques of conflict resolution. These include diplomats, military officers, policy-makers, academics and businessmen from 140 countries who are then available to assist in crisis-ridden areas e.g. Middle-East, Central America, South East Asia and Africa.

IPA describes itself as 'a moderator, messenger and mediator; a teacher and tactition of international security'. Its C.E.O. is the former head of the United Nations Peace Keeping Force to which the IPA provides aspects of support, stimulus and forward planning.

Journals and recent publications: The IPA publishes books, reports, simulation exercises, case studies, research and teaching materials. Its list of 12 books published up to 1987 includes:

'*The Peace Keeper's Handbook*' 3rd Edition, 1984; '*The Theory & Practice of Peacekeeping*' 1984; '*Conflict in Central America: Approaches to Peace & Security*', 1986.

There are some 23 reports based on workshops and research, for example:

'*Linkage for Peace through Economic Co-operation*' (1986); '*South African Peace and Security: Foundations for the Future*' (1985); '*Gulf Security: Quest for Regional Corporation*' (1985).

The President's Club Reports, the Newsletter and the Annual Reports are available to IPA supporters, or upon request.

STOCKHOLM INTERNATIONAL PEACE RESEARCH INSTITUTE

Pipers Vag 28, S-171 73 Solna, Sweden (468-559700).

Contact: Dr Walter Stützle, Director.

Status: International independent research institute.

Origins: Established in 1966 to commemorate Sweden's 150 years of unbroken peace and to examine questions of importance for peace and security. The staff, Governing Board and Scientific Council are international and researchers are drawn from countries with differing political and economic systems. SIPRI is neither Western or Eastern.

Governing Board: Ambassador Inga Thorsson, Chairman (Sweden); Egon Bahr (FRG); Professor Francesco Calogero (Italy); Dr Max Jacobson (Finland); Professor De Karlheinz Lohs (GDR); Professor Emma Rothschild (UK); Sir Brian Urquhart (UK), The Director.

Staffing: 60 full time.

Sources of income: Mainly financed by the Swedish Parliament (the Government grant for 1987/88 was Sw. Cr. 15.99 million). It also has the power to raise additional finance.

Aims and objectives: Over the past 20 years SIPRI has concentrated on questions of armament and disarmament pursuing a problem-orientated research approach.

It has a continuing interest in certain subjects, on which it has built up data banks. For example, it has a unique data bank on transfers of major weapons; it reports every year on the arms trade, and has produced a major study on arms sales to Third World countries. It also maintains a data bank on world military expenditure, and comments on trends annually. Researchers work either individually or in research teams on SIPRI projects: project proposals are considered by the Research Collegium and the Governing Board, and publications are refereed by independent experts outside the Institute. In addition to the researchers recruited for several years, guest researchers spend a short time at SIPRI, and the Institute also uses consultants who work in their own countries on SIPRI's behalf. SIPRI convenes symposia on various subjects, in order to bring in a wide range of expertise and views on some of the subjects which it studies. Contacts are maintained with other research institutes and individual researchers throughout the world. It is a basic rule of the Institute that SIPRI's research should be based on open sources.

Journals and recent publications:

'*World Armaments and Disarmament, SIPRI Yearbook*': The Institute's main publication each year has special studies of the current issues and provides

Policy-oriented research

an overview of the whole field of developments in armaments technology, in military expenditure, in the arms trade, and in the attempts to halt or to reverse the process. A popular version and/or a shorter brochure, based on the Yearbook, is published annually.

Over 70 books and some 20 research reports have been published over the past 20 years. The following publications were produced in 1987:

Jasani, B. '*Space Weapons and International Security*', OUP, 1987.

Jasani, B., Sakata, T. (eds) '*Satellites for Arms Control and Crisis Monitoring*', OUP, 1987.

Trapp, R. (ed.) '*Chemical Weapon Free Zones? (CBW 7)*', OUP, 1987.

Lodgaard, S. and Birnbaum, K. (eds) '*Overcoming Threats to Europe: a New Deal for Confidence and Security*', OUP, 1987.

Jacobsen, C. G. (ed.) '*The Uncertain Course: New Weapons, Strategies and Mind-sets*', OUP, 1987.

Ohlson, T. and Brzoska, M. '*Arms Transfers to the Third World, 1971–85*', OUP, 1987.

Sims, N. A. '*International Organization for Chemical Disarmament (CBW 8)*', OUP, 1987.

Stützle, W., Jasani, B. and Cowen, R. (eds) '*The ABM Treaty: To Defend or not to Defend?*', OUP, 1987.

Jacobsen, C. G. (ed.) '*The Soviet Defence Enigma: Estimating Costs and Burden*', OUP, 1987.

UNITED NATIONS UNIVERSITY

Information Services, Toho Seimei Building, 15-1, Shibuya 2-chome, Shibuya-ku, Tokyo 150, Japan (03-499-2811).

UNU Office in North America: United Nations, Room DC2-1457-70, New York, New York 10017, USA (212-963 6387).

UNU Office in Europe: Ship House, 20 Buckingham Gate, London SW1E 6LB, United Kingdom (01 630-9791/2/3).

Contacts: Professor Heitor Gurgulino de Souza, Rector of the University; John M. Fenton, Chief, Information Services, Tokyo.

Status: Functions as an autonomous academic institution rather than as an intergovernmental organisation. Its charter refers to it as an 'autonomous organ of the General Assembly'. Its financial administration is within the rules and regulations of the UN and audited by UN Board of Auditors. The University started operations in September 1975.

Income: US $44.80 million for 1986/87.

Sources of income: The main income source is an endowment fund to which the Japanese government pledged $100 million and also provided the Headquarters in Tokyo. A total of 43 member states has now made pledges and contributions totalling US $187.7 million.

Aims and objectives: According to its Charter, the United Nations University (UNU) is to be 'an international community of scholars, engaged in research, post-graduate training and dissemination of knowledge in furtherance of the purposes and principles of the Charter of the United Nations.' The University works on the pressing global problems of human survival, development and welfare through a network of research and post-graduate training centres in both the developed and developing countries, with planning and co-ordination provided by the central headquarters in Tokyo. As a worldwide system of research and training centres and programmes, the UNU has – in the words of its Charter – 'its location at the site of each centre or programme.' It is therefore strikingly different from the usual campus-based teaching university.

In practice, during the cycle (1982–87) the University's work has been organised into nine programme areas. These have been:

Peace and global transformation;
The global economy;
Energy systems and policy;
Resource policy and management;
The food-energy nexus;
Food, nutrition, biotechnology and poverty;
Human and social development;
Regional perspectives;
Science, technology and the information society.

Programme Area – Peace and global transformation: Research Items: Conflicts over natural resources; security, vulnerability and violence; human rights and cultural survival in a changing pluralistic world; regional peace and security; maintaining outer space for peaceful purposes.

Recent publication: Nandasiri Jasen-tuliyana (ed.) '*Towards a Liberating Peace, Maintaining Outer Space for Peaceful Uses*'.

UNITED NATIONS UNIVERSITY FOR PEACE

Apartado 199, Ciudad Colon, Costa Rica; PO Box 199-1250, Escazu, Costa Rica. (49-10-72/49-15-11).

Contacts: Dr Tapio Varis, Rector; Dr Francisco Barahona, Executive Secretary.

Policy-oriented research

Status: Independent organisation with academic freedom and with close ties with the United Nations General Assembly, UNESCO, UNIDIR, the United Nations University.

Origins: Set up in December 1980. By November 1985, 29 governments had signed the agreement for the establishment of the university; 16 from Central and South America, 2 African, 7 Asian, Spain, Italy, Cyprus and Yugoslavia in Europe.

Approximate annual income: US $3.6 million for the 7 months ending 31st July 1985.

Sources of income: $1 million from Japanese philanthropist, Mr Ryoichi Sasakawa, via the Japan Shipbuilding Industry Foundation, set up the university's endowment fund.

Aims and objectives: In 1984 the curriculum of the university was established culminating in the inauguration of the first Robert Schuman Master's Programme in Communications, Development and Peace. The university intends to operate at three integrated levels, basic (grassroots), intermediate and post-graduate.

The British Council for the University for Peace was launched in September 1985 at the Royal Albert Hall Festival to celebrate the International Day of Peace.

Journals:
'*In for Peace*' a regular fortnightly bulletin on arms, disarmament and development to inform world press and other media.

UNITED NATIONS INSTITUTE FOR DISARMAMENT RESEARCH (UNIDIR)

Palais de Nations, 1221, Geneva, Switzerland (34-60-11/31-02-11).

Contact: Jayantha Dhanapala, Director.

Status: Autonomous institution within the framework of the United Nations working closely with the Department of Disarmament Affairs.

Origins: Established in 1980, its statute was approved by the General Assembly in late 1984.

Board of Trustees: The UN Secretary General's Advisory Board on Disarmament Studies functions as UNIDIR's Board with representatives from 24 States including Sir Ronald Mason (School of Molecular Science, University of Sussex) for the UK.

Staffing: 10–14 (including permanent staff and consultant researchers).

Income: US $824,700 for 1988.

Sources of income: The UN contributes towards basic staff costs but UNIDIR's statute lays down that voluntary contributions from States and private organisations shall provide the major part of its finance. By 1988, seven States were contributing, the largest contributions being made by Japan, the USSR and France followed by Norway, Switzerland, Canada and Australia.

Aims and objectives: Its functions laid down in its statute are:

Providing the international community with more diversified and complete data on problems relating to international security, the armaments race and disarmament in all fields, particularly in the nuclear field, so as to facilitate progress, through negotiations, towards greater security for all States and towards the economic and social development of all peoples;

Promoting informed participation by all States in disarmament efforts;

Assisting ongoing negotiations on disarmament and continuing efforts to ensure greater international security at a progressively lower level of armaments, particularly nuclear armaments, by means of objective and factual studies and analysis;

Carrying out more in-depth, forward-looking and long-term research on disarmament, so as to provide a general insight to the problems involved, and stimulating new initiatives for new negotiations.

Current projects: Current projects and those near completion include:

A survey on the perception of priorities in the field of disarmament and arms control conducted among three groups – governments, the academic community and eminent representatives of public opinion such as Nobel Prize winners;

A pilot project for a computerized disarmament data base;

Disarmament: problems related to outer space;

Verification;

Disarmament and development.

Annual Conferences: These are held with a research institute which provides the logistical support. The conferences are small, for some 50 participants, and help 'shorten the distance between the academic and diplomatic community' e.g. 1987, at the Institute of World Economy and International Relations of the Academy of Sciences of the USSR (IMEMO) on 'Interrelationship of Bilateral and Multilateral negotiations on Disarmament'. For 1988 a conference on 'Conventional Disarmament in Europe' and a Symposium of Directors of Disarmament Research Institutes were scheduled.

Journals and recent publications: Totalled 23 by Spring 1987 and include:

Policy-oriented research

Cot, J-P., Guilhaudis, J-F. and Oudraat, C. de J. '*Repertory of Disarmament Research*', 1982 (to be updated shortly).

A quarterly UNIDIR Newsletter was planned for 1988, aimed at the academic community.

POLICY-ORIENTED RESEARCH:
Research societies

CONFLICT RESEARCH SOCIETY

c/o Rutherford College, The University of Kent, Canterbury, Kent CT2 7NX (0227-764000).

Contact: Keith Webb, Honorary Secretary.

Status: Registered charity.

Origins: Inaugurated in 1963.

Membership: 200.

Staffing: None paid.

Annual income: No information made available.

Aims and objectives: The Society's title is self explanatory and professional membership is drawn from many disciplines including biology, psychology, sociology, political science and economics. The Society does not align itself to any political persuasion and the membership contains a multiplicity of perspectives.

A specialist library is maintained at the Special Collections Section, Skinner's Library, the City University, London.

Annual Spring and Autumn Seminars disseminate current research work.

Society-sponsored working groups have included 'The Probability of Nuclear War' convened by Dr Paul Smoker and the 'Dispute Settlement Research Group' convened by Dr Christopher Mitchell.

In 1987 the Society ran an essay competition.

Journals: Newsletter, quarterly to members.

INTERNATIONAL PEACE RESEARCH ASSOCIATION

c/o Iuperj, Rua Paulino Fernandes 32, CEP 22270, Rio de Janeiro RJ, Brazil (021 246-1830-285-6197).

Contact: Clovis Brigagao, Secretary-General.

Origins: Founded in Europe in 1964.

Membership: 656 individuals, 74 corporate members, 4 national associations and some 350 other subscribers.

Staffing: 2 full time; 2 part time.

Income: Not known.

Sources of income: IPRA receives an annual subscription from UNESCO/ISSC to assist its running costs. Prior to its move to Brazil it received support from the Mershon Centre, Ohio State University its former office base. The General Services Foundation assisted its office relocation. Small grants have been received from the Flora R. and Isador M. Stettenheim Foundation USA, the Cambridge Institute for Societal Learning, USA and others.

Aims and objectives: IPRA is a worldwide community of peace researchers and educators. It aims to reflect the greatest possible diversity of perspectives on peace. Its headquarters have been rotated between five countries and moved in 1987 from the USA to Brazil. Its purpose is to advance interdisciplinary research into the conditions of peace and the causes of war and other forms of violence. It promotes, facilitates and serves as an information/exchange and contact point for co-operation and dissemination of the results of peace. It has established the Peace Education Commission (*see separate entry*) and has developed the following Study Groups:

Communication;
Food policy;
Human Rights;
Weapons Technology and Disarmament;
Non-violence;
Peace Movements;
Women, Militarisation and Disarmament.

Biennial conferences are arranged and have been held in 11 countries.

The Peace Movements Study Group: The Group was set up for the 11th General Conference in 1986 at Sussex University where 60 people attended sessions on six topics – Social Theory and Research on Peace Movements, Peace Movements as Transnational NGOs, Peace Movements as Social Movements, Community and Globalism, The International Peace Movement, Peace Movements and Non-Violent Action. The Study Group's co-ordination is by Katsuya Kodama, c/o Lupri, Dag Hammarskjolds vag 28, 223 64 Lund, Sweden.

The Non-Violence Study Group: This group was also set up following the 1986 Conference. The Convenor of the UK Section of the group is Graham Kemp, Richardson Institute for Conflict and Peace Research, University of Lancaster, Lancaster LA1 4YF (0524-65201 x 4568).

Affiliations: IPRA has Consultative Status with UNESCO and is a member of International Social Service Council (ISSC). Regional affiliates include the Asian Peace Research Association (APRA), the Latin America Council for Peace Research (CLAIP) and the Consortium on Peace Research Education and Development (COPRED).

Journals and recent publications:

'*International Peace Research Newsletter*' quarterly;

'*The Quest for Peace – Transcending Collective Violence and War among Societies, Cultures and State*' prepared by ISSC Issue Group on Peace for the International Year of Peace, 1986.

INTERNATIONAL SOCIETY FOR RESEARCH ON AGGRESSION

Dept of Psychology, University of Illinois at Chicago, Box 4348, Chicago, Illinois 60680, USA
(0101 312 996 4851).

Contact: Prof. L. R. Huesmann, Executive Secretary.

Status: Scientific association.

Origins: Organising sessions for the establishment of the society were held during the 20th International Congress of Psychology in Tokyo (August 1972).

Membership: Approx. 400.

Staffing: None paid.

Source of income: Membership dues.

Aims and objectives: The purposes of the society are exclusively scientific and educational – to promote and encourage the discovery and exchange of scientific information concerning the destructive and constructive aspects of aggression.

Affiliations: The Society has Consultative Status with United Nations/ECOSOC.

Journals:

'*Aggressive Behavior*': International journal Pub. AR Liss (N. York).

'*Bulletin of International Society for Research on Aggression*': membership newsletter published biannually, edited by Dr John Rodgers, University of Bradford.

2. Action research and Campaigns

Campaigning groups: A Personal Viewpoint

by Jonathan Steele, Chief Foreign Correspondent of the Guardian

The 1980s have seen a dramatic and unprecedented growth in the number and variety of independent, civic groups campaigning on the issue of peace and nuclear disarmament. The movement has not been confined to Britain, but has its counterparts in every Western European country, the United States, and even, at a more rudimentary and tentative level, in several Eastern European states and the Soviet Union.

It is as though people are saying that matters of national security and defence have for far too long been restricted to a narrow circle of politicians, defence specialists, and diplomats. In most Western European parliaments, debates on defence policy are rarely held. Political discussion tends to centre on the rival merits of different weapons systems, whether this one needs to be modernised, whether scarce resources should be spent on strengthening the navy compared to ground forces, and the like. The political scenarios which lie behind the country's defence posture are rarely mentioned. Under what circumstances is an attack likely? How can tensions be reduced? What would be the objectives of a potential enemy? Who indeed is the enemy? Is the Soviet 'threat' an unchanging part of the international environment, like the law of gravity in the natural world? Or are those who believe in it in danger of becoming political flat-earthers, overtaken by humanity's awareness that things are no longer what they once seemed?

The peace movement in its widest sense has had three currents. One was concerned mainly with the survival of the planet, given that nuclear weapons have the unique potential of ending all human life. The second was concerned with the whole industrial structure of which nuclear weapons are the extreme product, but which even in its beniger forms is causing unacceptable harm to our ecological environment. The third current worries over the human factor behind the arms race, the assumption and creation of enemy images which are used to justify military spending. The search is on for ways of overcoming these images by making contact and promoting exchanges with people from the 'other side'.

It is no accident that the treaty signed in Washington in December 1987 to destroy Cruise, Pershing-II, and SS-20 missiles in Europe and Asia was the first super-power arms control pact which actually *reduced* the number of weapons on both sides. Previous treaties merely curbed the future growth in numbers. The difference was that the original decision to deploy the missiles caused a massive public outcry. Public opinion was engaged in the issue as never before, and both superpowers were forced to negotiate for the first time in a blaze of publicity. They tried to outbid each other by arguing that each was more responsible, more reasonable, and more willing to make concessions than the other. Opinion polls in all the Western European countries which were due to host the new weapons consistently showed majorities against their deployment. In the period between 1979 when the NATO decision was taken and 1983 when deployment began, pro-Cruise politicians consistently argued that the public would accept them once they were installed. But this was not to be. In the end, NATO was obliged to recognise that the weapons were unpopular. As a result when the Soviet leader

Action research and campaigns

came to the conclusion that his own SS-20s were unpopular and offered to withdraw them all, with the shorter-range weapons in East Germany and Czechoslovakia thrown in for good measure, Western leaders matched him in what became known as the 'double zero'. It was a triumph for the peace movement, which had campaigned against both sides' deployments.

With that success under their belt, the three broad currents of the movement are focussing their energies on the deeper political questions. The prospect of a complete de-nuclearisation of Europe, coupled with cuts in conventional weapons, is now no longer fanciful. As NATO tries to work out its negotiating strategy for the post-INF period, the combined range of civic groups which have emerged over the last ten years is likely to want a voice in the debate.

They may well draw a lesson from the experience of the long process, known as the Helsinki process. In the run-up to the 1975 conclusion of the first Conference on Security and Co-operation in Europe, held in Helsinki, a new phrase entered the political vocabulary. It was known as 'Basket Three', short-hand for one of the three sets of questions exercising the diplomats of the thirty-five countries from East and West who took part in the conference.

'Basket Three' covered human rights. Western governments stressed this aspect of the accords, and encouraged civic groups to take part in the Helsinki debate, make proposals, and lobby the conference as a way of increasing the pressure on the Eastern European and Soviet side. The CSCE process is now a fixed part of the European scene and Western governments are setting a precondition for their acceptance of the Soviet Union's invitation to hold a conference on human rights in Moscow. They say that they will only attend if civic group and human rights lobbies are given visas to take part.

The time has come, in the view of many in the peace movement, for this initiative on Basket Three to be extended to Basket One, the set of questions which deals with security and defence matters. Why should civic groups not be encouraged to give evidence and make proposals to the CSCE conference on military issues too? Should Western European parliaments not open hearings on NATO's defence posture to as wide a circle of public interest groups as possible? Is it not time that the concept of an informed and independent input into the defence debate was not only tolerated by government, but welcomed?

It is clear from this book that a plethora of potential contributors already exists. Whether they are interested primarily in breaking the Cold War/enemy images by people-to-people detente through town-twinnings and exchanges, or in alerting the public to the dangers of nuclear weapons, they form the backbone of a powerful public constituency for change.

List of contents

Individual membership groups

British Atlantic Committee
Campaign for Demilitarisation of the Indian Ocean
Campaign for Nuclear Disarmament:
  Christian CND
  Green CND
  Labour CND
  Liberal CND
  Trade Union CND
  Youth CND
  Northern Ireland CND
  Scottish CND
  Welsh CND
Ecoropa
European Nuclear Disarmament (see Co-ordinatory bodies)
Families for Defence
Fellowship Party
Just Defence
Labour Action for Peace
Peace Pledge Union
Peace Tax Campaign
Pugwash Conferences on Science & World Affairs (see Section 1: 'Policy-oriented research')
Scottish Campaign to Resist the Atomic Menace
The European Atlantic Movement
United Nations Association, UK
Women's International League for Peace & Freedom
World Disarmament Campaign

Professional membership groups (and other social groups)

Architects for Peace
Book Action for Nuclear Disarmament
Clergy Against Nuclear Arms (see Church organisations and religious groups)
Electronics & Computing for Peace
Engineers for Nuclear Disarmament
Ex-Services CND
Farmers for a Nuclear Free Future
Generals for Peace and Disarmament
International Physicians for the Prevention of Nuclear War
Lawyers for Nuclear Disarmament

Action research and campaigns

Medical Association for the Prevention of War
Medical Campaign Against Nuclear Weapons
Members of Equity for Nuclear Disarmament
Musicians Against Nuclear Arms
Parents for Survival
Pensioners for Peace International
Psychologists for Peace
Scientists Against Nuclear Arms
Teachers for Peace (see Section 5: 'World studies, Education for Peace')

Non-membership organisations

Campaign Against Arms Trade
Campaign Against Military Research on Campus
Campaign for Defence & Multilateral Disarmament
Coalition for Peace through Security
Dunamis
Freeze (Nuclear Weapons Freeze)
International Institute for Peaceful Change
London Centre for International Peacebuilding
Peace through NATO
Peace through Parliament
Russell (Bertrand) Peace Foundation
Women Working for a Nuclear Free and Independent Pacific

Co-ordinatory bodies

British Peace Assembly
Campaign Against Arms Trade (see Non-membership organisations)
European Nuclear Disarmament
International Peace Bureau
London Nuclear Information Unit (see Nuclear Free Zones)
National Peace Council
National Steering Committee of Nuclear Free Zones (see Nuclear Free Zones)
National Trade Union Defence Conversion Committee
North Atlantic Network
Professions for World Disarmament and Development
War Resisters International

Church organisations and Religious groups

Anglican Pacifist Fellowship
Baptist Peace Fellowship
British Council of Churches International Division
British Council of Churches Peace Forum
Buddhist Peace Fellowship
Catholic Bishops' Conference of England and Wales, Department of International Affairs
Catholic Peace Action
Christian CND (see CND Section II, Membership organisations)
Clergy Against Nuclear Arms
Council on Christian Approaches to Defence and Disarmament
Diocesan Boards or Councils of Social Responsibility (local)
END Churches Lateral Committee
Fellowship of Reconciliation
London Mennonite Centre
Methodist Peace Fellowship
Northern Friends Peace Board
Pax Christi
Prayer for Peace
Quaker Peace and Service, Religious Society of Friends
Week of Prayer for World Peace

Tracking/Direct action groups

Cruisewatch
Cruise Resistance Network
Nukewatch (Polariswatch)
Snowball

Peace camps

Bull Point Peace Camp/Peace Bus
Faslane
Greenham Common
Menwith Hill
Molesworth
Upper Heyford

Local peace councils and peace centres

Service organisations

At Ease
Concord Film and Video Council
Exchange Services, EfP Ltd
GreenNet
Legal Support Group
Peace Advertising Campaign
Peacemakers' Relief Society
United Nations Information Centre

ACTION RESEARCH AND CAMPAIGNS:
Individual membership groups

BRITISH ATLANTIC COMMITTEE

5 St James's Place, London SW1A 1NP
(01-629 9289/90).

Contact: Major General Christopher Popham, Director.

Status: Educational charity.

Origins: BAC was formed in 1952 when similar organisations were set up in each of the NATO member countries.

Patrons: Sir John Killick (President); Vice-Presidents: Sir John Barnes; Earl of Bessborough; Lord Carrington; Sir Douglas Dodds-Parker; John Eppstein; Lord Gladwyn; General Sir John Hackett; Rt Hon Denis Healey; Rt Hon Edward Heath; Sir Nigel Henderson; Lord Home of the Hirsel; Sir Edmund Hulton; Lord Inchyra; Sir Fitzroy Maclean; Lord Mayhew; Gen Sir John Mogg; Rt Hon Lord Pym; Sir Peregrine Rhodes; Sir Frank Roberts; Rt Hon William Rodgers; Lord Shawcross; Sir Evelyn Skuckburgh; Lord Thomson of Monifieth. Ian Samuel (Chairman, Executive Committee).

Membership: 800.

Staffing: 3 full time.

Estimated annual income: £120,000 for 1987/88.

Sources of income: Foreign & Commonwealth Office, £57,500 in 1987/88; donations from various trusts and other bodies.

Aims and objectives: The Committee aims to contribute to informed public opinion in support of the Atlantic Alliance. A policy-making council of 60 from the political parties, churches, education, commerce, industry and retired members of the Armed Forces is presided over by the President and advised by a small Executive Committee. Specialist committees – for education, universities and youth also advise BAC. BAC provides speakers and information on NATO, arranges seminars and conferences on aspects of security, arms control and disarmament issues for educational institutions and voluntary groups. Visits to NATO political and military headquarters are arranged. In 1983 BAC formed '**Peace Through NATO**' (*see separate entry*) as an independent campaigning organisation without charitable status.

Journals and recent publications:
'*BAC Newsletter*', quarterly, for members and supporters.
'*A Peace Studies syllabus*', data sheets and posters are published for use in schools.
Briefing papers are also published by various authors at intervals.

CAMPAIGN FOR THE DEMILITARISATION OF THE INDIAN OCEAN

30 Stonedene Close, Forest Row, East Sussex RH18 5DB (034-282 4603).

Contact: Jaya Graves.

Status: Unincorporated association.

Origins: Started in 1982.

Membership: Around 100.

Income: From membership fees.

Aims and objectives: The Campaign works for the withdrawal of all foreign powers from the region and has focussed to date on the island of Diego Garcia (expropriated from Mauritius before its independence and loaned, as a British colony, to the USA for a base). It aims to provide information through networking, briefings, meetings and conferences. It works through interested MPs and pressure groups, including CND, and is making links with church and development groups. Efforts will concentrate on calling for the implementation of the Zone of Peace proposals in the months leading up to the United Nations Conference in 1989.

Action research and campaigns

Journals and recent publications:
Quarterly newletter; pamphlet by 'Raven' & Todd, Paul *'Disarming the Indian Ocean'.*

CAMPAIGN FOR NUCLEAR DISARMAMENT (CND)

22–24 Underwood Street, London N1 7JG
(01-250 4010).

Contact: Meg Beresford, General Secretary.

Status: Unincorporated association.

Origins: CND was launched in early 1958. Its origins were in the opposition to the development of the British hydrogen bomb in the late 1950s and grew from initiatives of the H-B National Council and the National Council for the Abolition of Nuclear Weapons Tests. Its first President was Bertrand Russell.

Officers: Bruce Kent (Chairperson); Linda Churnside (Treasurer).

Membership: 75,000 + individuals were members of the central national body at October 1987; the total number of supporters is estimated at around 200,000 individuals in membership of CND local groups (of which there are about 1,000).

Staffing: 26 employed at CND, HQ; 8 regional workers; 12 CND Publications Ltd workers.

Annual income: £927,110 for 1986/87 (not including CND Publications Ltd).

Sources of income: Membership and affilation subscriptions (47%), appeals (22%), donations (14%), other fund-raising events (16%). CND Publications Ltd, set up in 1983 as its trading arm, publishes magazines and books, organises the Glastonbury Festival and Annual Conference and is a partner in 'Books for a Change' the central London bookshop.

Aims and objectives: 'The aim of the campaign for nuclear disarmament is the unilateral abandonment by Britain of nuclear weapons, nuclear bases and nuclear alliances as a prerequisite for a British foreign policy which has the worldwide abolition of nuclear, chemical and biological weapons leading to general and complete disarmament as its prime objective.' (from the CND Constitution). These aims are pursued through a combination of public protest, including non-violent direct action, public education and lobbying Parliament and opinion-formers in the media, church and trade unions. Overall policy is made by CND Annual Conferences at which CND groups, regions, national bodies and affiliated organisations are represented along with individual members of the campaign. Some one thousand local CND groups are federated to British CND. They have their own membership schemes and decide their own campaigns and priorities within CND's overall policy. CND has a series of sections for specific membership interests: Christian CND, Youth CND, Trade Union CND, Labour CND, Liberal CND, and Green CND. These are described separately.

Affiliations: CND is affiliated to the following organisations: the International Peace Communication & Co-ordination Network (IPCC); the National Council for Civil Liberties (NCCL); the International Peace Bureau; the Campaign Against Arms Trade (CAAT); the National Peace Council (NPC); the United Nations Association (UNA); the END Convention 1987; the London Hazard Centre; and the Peace Tax Campaign.

Journals and recent publications:
'Sanity', monthly magazine; *'Campaign'*, monthly membership newspaper; *'CND News'*, national members' newsletter; *'Defence Briefings'* for MPs, journalists and opinion-formers; *'Beyond the Grapevine. A Campaigner's Guide to Using the Media'*; *'The Civil Defence Campaign Guide'*; *'Legal Advice Pack for Nuclear Disarmers'* (published in association with Lawyers for Nuclear Disarmament);

Reeve, Gillian and Smith, Joan *'Offence of the Realm, How Peace Campaigners Get Bugged'*;

Edwards, Rob *'The Deadly Connection, Nuclear Power & Nuclear Weapons'* 1985;

Dando, Malcolm and Rogers, Paul *'The Death of Deterrence, Consequences of the New Nuclear Arms Race'* 1984;

Rogers, Paul *'Guide to Britain's Nuclear Weapons'* 1985;

Holden, Gerald (ed.) *'The Second Superpower'*, *'The Arms Race & the Soviet Union'* 1985;

Chalmers, Malcolm *'Trident, Britain's Independent Arms Race'* 1984.

CHRISTIAN CND

(central office address & telephone number).

Contact: Barbara Eggleston, National Organiser.

Membership: A mailing list of approximately 6,000 with 150 local groups.

Origins: Founded as a specialist section in 1958 and re-established in 1976.

Staffing: 1 full time.

Aims and objectives: Christian CND seeks the support of all Christians who oppose the deployment and threatened use of nuclear weapons by any nation. Its membership is not distinct from CND itself but special conferences, events and vigils are organised and a special newsletter published (see below). There are

Action research and campaigns

regional co-ordinators to support local group work and develop grass roots activity.

A Christian Peace Co-ordinating Committee with representatives from all Christian Groups aims to develop co-operation and mutual reinforcement. Christian CND is represented on the British Council of Churches Peace Forum.

Journals and recent publications:

'*Ploughshare*', bi-monthly newsletter; '*Questions and answers about Christian and Nuclear Disarmament*' – leaflet; '*In God we Trust – Christian Reflections on the Nuclear Arms Race*' – booklet, 1986.

Further booklets, leaflets, posters, badges, audio-visual materials, speakers and advice are available for local Christian groups.

YOUTH CND/SCHOOLS AGAINST THE BOMB

(*central office address and telephone number*).

Contact: Clare McMaster, Co-ordinator.

Origins: Youth CND started in early days of CND. Schools Against the Bomb started in 1981 and originally worked autonomously though sharing office space and receiving funds from CND. Now the two groupings work in tandem with the same co-ordinator.

Membership: 10,000 members of Youth CND (who are 21 years or younger).

Staffing: 1 full time.

Aims and objectives: Youth CND organises a national campaigning conference, workshops, demonstrations, rallies and literature aimed to interest and involve the younger CND membership. Schools Against the Bomb as its name implies aims to raise awareness of nuclear issues specifically in schools. It organises debates for which it provides speakers and does this as often as possible in co-operation with Peace Through NATO (*see separate entry*). Both Youth CND and Schools Against the Bomb rely heavily on the enthusiasm and initiative of the local groups of supporters within the regions.

Journals and recent publications:

'*Protest*' Youth CND Groups bi-monthly bulletin; '*Sign of the Times*' Youth CND membership magazine 3 times a year; '*Schools Against the Bomb*, newsletter/poster, termly; '*Schools Against the Bomb, Information Handbook*', 1985; '*Organising Yourselves*' cyclostyled campaigning tips; '*Protest & Survive*' VHS Video 30 minutes (originally made for BBC 2's Open Door Programme and for hire from Concord Films, Ipswich).

A poster linking the high arms expenditure to starvation in the Third World has been jointly produced with UNA Youth.

TRADE UNION CND

(*central office address and telephone number*).

Contact: Jimmy Barnes, Secretary.

Origins: Formed in 1982.

Membership: About 1,000 Trade Union Branch Affiliates and 29 Trade Unions were in membership as at Autumn 1987: including ASLEF; ACTT; BF&AWU; BETA; CATU; COHSE; FBU; FTATU; GMBATU; IRSF; ISTC; MU; MSF; NALGO; NAPO; NCU; NGA; NIPSA; NUM; NUPE; NUR; NUS; NUTGW; SOGAT; STE; T&GWU; UCW; UCATT; USDAW.

Staffing: 1 full time.

Aims and objectives: The section promotes CND's aims in the Trade Union movement and assists any Union body/or CND group seeking to promote CND. Its regional structure parallels that of the regional TUCs and representatives of the regional TU-CND organisations sit on its Executive Committee along with 15 other people elected at the AGM.

In the past two years it has co-ordinated a series of issue campaigns:

On the link between unemployment and the level of spending on nuclear and related armaments;

(before 1987 General Election) on 'Welfare & Warfare – the Choice is Yours';

Against SDI,

On poverty and the arms race.

It has published a range of leaflets and posters for mass circulation to accompany each theme.

Journals and recent publications:

TU-CND News, bi-monthly; Chowcatt, John and Sawyer, Tom '*The Star Wars Threat*' pamphlet published jointly with the World Disarmament Campaign, 1987; Video on SDI, 1987, 10 minutes obtainable from CND offices.

Working links: Trade Union CND has observer status with the National Trade Union Defence Conversion Committee and the Barrow Alternative Employment Project.

GREEN CND

48 Grange Road, Hove, East Sussex (0273-738235).

Contact: Rob Jarrett.

Membership: Information not available.

Journal:

'*Green CND*' monthly newsletter.

Action research and campaigns

LABOUR CND

c/o Stodmarsh House, Cowley Estate, London SW9 6HH.

Contact: Carol Turner.

Membership: Information not available.

LIBERAL CND

c/o 6 Heeley Street, Wigan, NN1 2HN (0942-38941).

Contact: John McCarty, Secretary.

Membership: Information not available.

Journal:
'*Liberal CND Newsletter*' published bi-monthly.

The three national CND groups which follow each has financial and political autonomy:

NORTHERN IRELAND CND

c/o 15a Hopefield Avenue, Portrush, Co Antrim, BT56 8LT (0265-824456).

Contact: Elizabeth Breadon, Secretary.

Membership: 100 (+ 300 members of the Irish and British CND who are also serviced by NI, CND).

Staffing: None paid.

Income: £600 for 1986.

SCOTTISH CND

420 Sauchiehall Street, Glasgow G2 (041-331 2878).

Contact: Ian Davison, General Secretary.

Membership: 18,000 in the national body and in the local groups.

Staffing: 1 full time; 3 part time.

Annual income: some £55–60,000 in 1986/87.

Journal:
'*Nuclear Free Scotland*', quarterly free to members.

CND CYMRU – WALES

2 Plasturton Avenue, Pontcanna, Cardiff CD1 9HH (0766-831833).

Contact: Bob Cole.

Membership: Approximately 4,000 (+ 250 affiliated bodies).

Staffing: 1 full time.

Income: some £25,000 in 1986/87.

Journal:
'*Campaign Wales*' bi-monthly members' magazine.

ECOROPA LIMITED (European Group for Ecological Action)

Crickhowell, Powys, NP8 1TA (0873-810 758).

Contact: Fern Morgan-Grenville.

Status: Non-profit making limited company. Registered office in Switzerland.

Officers: Gerard Morgan-Grenville and Fern Morgan-Grenville, UK Directors.

Membership: Information not available.

Staffing: 3 part time.

Estimated annual income: Not disclosed.

Sources of income: The sale of leaflets, donations, membership subscriptions.

Aims and objectives: Ecoropa describes itself, 'a non-political, non-profit making, European organisation, primarily concerned with the safety of ecological or natural systems. Ecoropa is funded only by its supporters – Britons and Europeans – people who care about survival – our own and that of all natural systems on which our lives ultimately depend.'

Ecoropa's main activity is the sale of information leaflets which supporters distribute on their behalf. In 1987 membership of Ecoropa cost £10 p.a. As a result of this subscription members receive a 10% discount on the purchase of leaflets and books. This is a low cost method of raising awareness of their viewpoint.

Journals and recent publications: Ecoropa distributes posters, a small number of paperbacks and 16 leaflets. Leaflets include:
No. 5 '*Nuclear War – The Facts You Should Know*'; No. 6 '*Atomic Energy and Nuclear Weapons – The Intimate Connection*' by Dr. Frank Barnaby; No. 7 '*Nuclear Power – The Facts They Don't Want You To Know*'; No. 8 '*Defending Britain Without the Bomb*'; No. 9 '*Britain and The Arms Trade*'; No. 10 '*Chemical and Biological Warfare*'; No. 11 '*Falklands War – The Disturbing Truth*'; No. 15 '*Chernobyl Radiation & Nuclear Power*' (out of print); No. 16 '*Nuclear Power – More Facts You Should Know*'.

EUROPEAN NUCLEAR DISARMAMENT

(*see Co-ordinatory Bodies*)

Action research and campaigns

FAMILIES FOR DEFENCE

45 Bloomsbury Square, London WC1A 2RA (01-831 0180).

Contact: Lynne Dunn, Director.

Status: Unincorporated association.

Origins: Launched in 1983, (originally called 'Women and Families for Defence') by Lady Olga Maitland.

Patrons and officers: General Sir John Hackett (Vice President); Lady Olga Maitland (Chairperson).

Membership: Not disclosed.

Staffing: Not disclosed.

Annual income: Not disclosed.

Sources of income: Members' subscriptions and donations.

Aims and objectives: Families for Defence aims – in these words from its brochure – 'to support the NATO Alliance and NATO policies, to support Britain's independent nuclear deterrent; to draw attention to the Soviet arms build-up and the continuing massive military potential of the Soviet Union and to dispel the fallacy that the Soviet Union does not present a threat to Western Europe; to support all genuine efforts to achieve multilateral disarmament between the Soviet bloc and NATO and to explain the vital necessity of verifiable and balanced force reductions; to oppose Britain's one-sided abandonment of nuclear weapons; to show that the so-called 'peace movement' does not have the monopoly of concern in seeking peace; to oppose unilateralist and left-wing propaganda and indoctrination which is increasingly being disseminated through both the Church and through so-called 'Peace Studies' in our schools and colleges.'

The organisation has three campaigning committees on defence, education and the church. It provides speakers for groups. It runs a Patrons' Club founded in 1985, in which members attend dinners at the House of Commons and hear speakers of ministerial rank. It has a Youth Section for its membership.

Journals and recent publications: '*Deter*', quarterly newspaper. Booklets, briefings and pamphlets on defence, education and the churches include: '*A Layman's Guide to Defence*'; '*Peace Studies in our Schools – Propaganda for the Defencelessness*'; and '*Facts & Questions about Britain's and NATO's Defence Policy*'.

FELLOWSHIP PARTY

Woolacombe House, 141 Woolacombe Road, Blackheath, London SE3 (01-856 6249).

Contact: Ronald Mallone, General Secretary.

Status: Political party.

Origins: Formed in 1955.

Patrons: Donald Swann, Rowland Hilder (Presidents); Sidney Hinkes (Chair).

Membership: Not disclosed.

Staffing: None paid.

Annual income: Not disclosed.

Sources of income: Subscriptions and sales of literature.

Aims and objectives: The Party is in the words of its General Secretary – 'a pacifist political party, independent of all others, which believes in total world disarmament, the pooling of world resources for the use of all, the strengthening of international law, with all governments being obliged to take all disputes to the International Court at the Hague and to accept its decisions, and stronger support of the peaceful agencies of the United Nations, where it wants an end to the veto in the Security Council. It believes in the implementation of the Brandt Report, so as to give hungry nations the means to feed themselves by 1997 at the latest.' 'It also wants the UK to leave NATO and lead a Third Group of Commonwealth, neutral and uncommitted nations, to try to reconcile NATO and the Warsaw Pact.

Journals and recent publications:
'*Day by Day*', members' journal. Some 18 pamphlets on current topics are available as well as a Party tie, T-shirts, stickers and badges.

JUST DEFENCE

5 Pershore Hall, Pershore, Worcs. (0386-555779).

Contact: Cynthia Coulthard, Secretary.

Status: Voluntary organisation.

Origins: Formed in Oxford in 1983.

Distinguished Advisers: Professor Frank Barnaby (Chair); Advisory Council: Lord Beaumont; Sir Richard Doll; Dr. Bernard Dixon; Rev. Victor Guazzelli; Brigadier Michael Harbottle; Malcolm Harper; Professor Dorothy Hodgkin; Dr Anthony Kenny; Air Commodore Alastair Mackie; Rev Hugh Montefiore; Professor Robert Neild; Professor Joseph Rotblat.

Membership: 150.

Staffing: None paid.

Income: £2,000 for 1986.

Sources of income: Membership fees and private donations.

Action research and campaigns

Aims and objectives: Just Defence is a non-partisan organisation aiming to achieve a new consensus in Britain in support of defence policies based on the following principles:

'Defence must be seen to be effective, otherwise the policy will not command public support.

Defence must be non-provocative to others, so that the policy contributes to reducing international tension. Modern technology makes such a 'defence only' policy effective and powerful. Such a policy should be non-nuclear.

The defence system should contribute to 'crisis stability' and to reducing the risks of pre-emptive strike or war by miscalculation.

The policy should not provoke a new arms race by its choice of weapons.

Defence policy must be entirely consistent with international law and the UN Charter, and make a positive contribution to detente. Defence policy should lead to comprehensive disarmament and world security.'

Just Defence carries out educational activities, international liaison and lobbying work.

Affiliations and projects with other bodies: The United Nations Association circulated the Just Defence Charter to all its branches in 1987. A sister Just Defence group has been set up in New Zealand.

Journals and recent publications:
'*Just Defence*' Report, No. 2, May 1987; Discussion papers – No. 1 Barnaby, Frank '*Tomorrow's Weapons, Beyond Battleships, Bombers and Tanks*'.

LABOUR ACTION FOR PEACE

37 Hollingworth Road, Petts Wood, Orpington, Kent BR5 1AQ (01-467 5367).

Contact: Ron Huzzard, Hon Secretary.

Status: Voluntary group.

Origins: Formed in 1940.

Membership: 320 including 35 Labour MPs and 20 Labour MEPs plus 63 affiliations, including 12 national trade unions.

Income: £2,200 for 1987.

Sources of income: Subscriptions, sale of pamphlets.

Aims and objectives: Labour Action for Peace seeks to keep the issues of peace, disarmament and international socialism in the forefront of Labour's policies. Its membership is confined to Labour Party members. It provides speakers for party members, at grass-roots levels, and other interested bodies. It seeks to make contacts with socialist parties overseas and to ensure LAP representation at peace conferences e.g. at the Copenhagen 'International Year of Peace Conference' in 1986, the KEADEA Peace Conference, Athens and Peace Forum, Moscow in 1987.

Affiliations and projects with other organisations: Labour Action for Peace is affiliated to the National Peace Council, the United Nations Association, the World Disarmament Campaign (UK), the Campaign Against Arms Trade and the Labour Disarmament Liaison Commmittee.

Journals and recent publications:
'*Labour Peace Action*', newsletter produced 5 to 6 times a year; '*Labour, Arms and the Election*', pamphlet, 1986. '*What About the Russians?*' pamphlet, 1987.

PEACE PLEDGE UNION

6 Endsleigh Street, London WC1H 0DX (01-387 5501).

Contact: Jan Melichar, Campaigning/Publications Worker.

Status: Unincorporated association.

Origins: Founded in 1934 by Dick Sheppard.

Patron and sponsors: Sir Michael Tippett (President); Dr Alex Comfort; Professor Adam Curle; Cwynfor Evans; Ciaran McKeown; Very Rev The Lord MacLeod of Fuinary; Tony Smythe; Rev The Lord Soper; Donald Swann (Sponsors).

Membership: 1,500.

Staffing: 3 full time; 3 part time.

Income: £68,000 for 1986.

Sources of income: Subscriptions, donations and sales. Members and supporters are encouraged to covenant donations through the Lansbury House Trust Fund to the educational projects of the Union – 'Children and War', and 'Peace Education'.

Aims and objectives: The pledge for the Union is 'I renounce war and will never support or sanction another'. The Union works for non violent social change. By joining the Union, members also become members of the War Resisters International. The Union campaigns on a series of issues. Its main concerns are against militarism (particularly as exhibited at Remembrance time with the White Poppies), military recruiting, war toys, and war tax. It organises two projects specifically concerned with young people - 'The Children and War Project' aims to explore and draw attention to the influences on the young which make war acceptable. 'The Peace Education Project' aims to challenge the view, which the PPU sees as being reinforced by education, that violence, aggression and war are unavoidable. Both projects provide materials and support for those in education and for those concerned with the young who wish to further these views.

Affiliations: The PPU is affiliated to the Campaign Against Arms Trade, the National Peace Council, the War Resisters International, the National Council for Civil Liberties, the Peace Tax Campaign and the Central Board for Conscientious Objectors.

Journals and recent publications:
'*The Pacifist*' bi-monthly journal, free to members; the *Young Peace-Makers* magazine, ten times a year; '*PEP Talk*', a termly journal for supporters of the Peace Education Project; '*Studies in Non Violence*', theoretical journal, three times a year; '*The Pacifist Action Pack*' – an introduction to local campaigning. '*Remember and Disarm*' Action and information pack on militarism and the after effects of war. Learning packs for secondary schools on War and Society, Heroism, Human Rights, Violence and Non-Violence and The Life and Times of Martin Luther King.

A full resource list is available of all the books and other campaigning materials including leaflets, posters, postcards etc.

PEACE TAX CAMPAIGN

1A Hollybush Place, London E2 9QX (01-739 5088).

Contacts: David Ford, Jane Powell, National Co-ordinators.

Status: Un-incorporated association.

Origins: Started in 1977 by Stanley Keeble with the backing of the Peace Pledge Union; the Campaign was taken up by the Quaker Peace Committee in 1979; from 1981 the Campaign was run voluntarily by a retired couple and in 1986 a full time office with workers was set up.

Membership: 3,500 individuals plus some 30 national, regional and local groups which are affiliated.

Staffing: 2 full time.

Income: £30,000 for 1986.

Sources of income: All income comes from individual donations and from an annual appeal except for a grant of $5,000 in 1986 from the Speight Bequest, administered by the Society of Friends.

Aims and objectives: The Campaign aims to persuade Parliament to introduce legislation allowing people conscientiously opposed to war to have the military part of their taxes allocated to peace-building. The Campaign maintains a War Tax Resisters' Defence Fund to help support tax resisters who are facing financial hardship because of their actions.

Affiliations: The Campaign is a member of the National Peace Council.

Journals and recent publications:
Newsletter, bi-monthly. Booklets – '*Paying for Peace*', a guide to peace tax campaigns throughout the world; '*A Tax on Peace*', by Lawyers for Nuclear Disarmament. Leaflets (7), posters and badges are also produced.

PUGWASH CONFERENCES ON SCIENCE AND WORLD AFFAIRS

(*see Section 1: Policy-oriented research*)

SCOTTISH CAMPAIGN TO RESIST THE ATOMIC MENACE (SCRAM)

11 Forth Street, Edinburgh EH1 3LE (031-557 4283).

Contact: Steve Martin, Journal Editor.

Status: Unincorporated association.

Origins: Formed in 1975 at a gathering at the Torness site.

Membership: 1,000.

Staffing: 1 full time.

Income: £5,432 for 1985/86.

Sources of income: Subscriptions to journal and donations.

Aims and objectives: SCRAM is an anti-nuclear, safe energy organisation committed to achieving its aims through information dissemination and non-violent action. It maintains a reference library on nuclear and appropriate energy issues. It will take commissions to undertake background research into nuclear issues and is currently trying to establish a SCRAM News Service for media and groups.

Affiliation: SCRAM is affiliated to Scotland Against Nuclear Dumping (SAND), an umbrella organisation started in 1987.

Journals and publications:
'*SCRAM*', The Anti Nuclear and Safe Energy Journal, bi-monthly; pack of information leaflets.

THE EUROPEAN ATLANTIC MOVEMENT (TEAM)

Bailey House, Old Seacoal Lane, Ludgate Hill, London EC4M 7LR (01-236 4881).

Contact: J. E. Cullis, Vice-Chairman.

Action research and campaigns

Status: Registered charity.

Origins: Founded in 1958 by the late Mr John Sewell.

Patrons: Sir Frank Roberts (President); Patrons include Tom Arnold; Dr Harold C. Deutsch; Lord Gladwyn; Sir William Hayter; Lord Hill-Norton; Lord Jenkins of Hillhead; Dr Richard Mayne; Dr Roy Pryce; Professor Eugene V. Rostow; Lord Stewart of Fulham.

Membership: Approx. 100.

Staffing: None paid.

Income: £27,000 for 1985/86.

Sources of income: Donations and membership subscriptions.

Aims and objectives: TEAM aims to stimulate interest, understanding and participation in European and European-Atlantic affairs. The major areas of concern are armament, disarmament and arms control; the nature and intentions of ideologies opposed to democracy; the nature and purpose of the NATO Alliance; the effects of East-West tensions in the Third World. TEAM offers teachers, lecturers, educational planners, journalists and other 'multipliers' the opportunity to meet and discuss current issues with specialists, directly experienced in public affairs and policy implementation. TEAM promotes conferences, seminars and study tours enabling participants to have contact with people involved in European and Atlantic affairs on both sides of the ocean; diplomats, parliamentarians, businessmen, journalists, national and international civil servants. Its work aims to provide a complementary practical background to academic studies. Its annual Easter Study Tour takes participants to international institutions of Western co-operation. An annual International Seminar at Oxford, brings together participants from 10 to 15 countries to discuss economic, political, cultural and strategic issues of European-Atlantic affairs.

Publications: Occasional papers and reproductions of talks.

UNITED NATIONS ASSOCIATION, UK

3 Whitehall Court, London SW1A 2EL (01-930 2931/2).

Contact: Malcolm Harper, Director.

Status: Unincorporated association.

Origins: Established in 1945.

Patrons: Lord Caradon, Baroness Elliot of Harewood, (Presidents); Rt Hon Margaret Thatcher; MP, Rt Hon Neil Kinnock; MP, David Steel; MP, Robert McLennan; MP (Honorary Presidents).

Membership: 13,000.

Staffing: 11 full time; 7 part time.

Income: £220,000 for 1986/87.

Sources of income: The Foreign & Commonwealth Office grant-aid of £24,000 for 1986/87 has remained at this figure since 1980 and has therefore dropped substantially in real terms. The regional groupings and local branches which are financially autonomous contribute towards head office costs. Membership dues and contributions from local branches accounted for 43% of total revenue income in 1986/87. The UNA Trust, the charitable trust which funds UNA educational work, its volunteer programme and also supports the educational work of other organisations, contributed £30,000 (13.6%) to UNA, UK in 1986/87.

Aims and objectives: The United Nations Association of the United Kingdom is a voluntary organisation made up of individual members and groups. It is independent of the British government and of the United Nations. It works to:

Increase awareness in the United Kingdom of international issues, and particularly of the role of the United Nations and campaigns especially for disarmament, a fairer world economic order, and respect by governments for the human rights of their citizens;

Put pressure on the British government to fulfil Britain's national obligations to the international community through the United Nations;

Secure constructively critical support by the British people for the United Nations organisation.

Members work through branches in England, Wales, Scotland and Northern Ireland. Local church, trade union and other groups are encouraged to become corporate members of their nearest branch while their national bodies become national affilliates. Policy is decided by Annual General Council and by an elected Executive Committee. This committee is advised by four specialist committees – on disarmament, political matters, economic and social concerns and human rights. A Youth Council aims to involve young members. The International Service Department sends qualified volunteers to countries in Africa, Latin America and the Middle East (in 1986 40 people went to projects in 7 countries). UNAIS co-operates with other agencies of the British Volunteer Agencies Liaison Group. Through the World Federation of UNAs, based in Geneva, UNA-UK has close contact with UNAs in some 60 countries in all parts of the world. WFUNA has consultative status with the UN Economic and Social Council (ECOSOC). A major UNA-UK activity in 1986 was an appeal which raised almost a quarter of a million pounds for the programme of the UN High Commissioner for Refugees. The UNA has co-ordinated the meetings of the Disarmament and Development

Network, a grouping of some 15 organisations since 1982. In Autumn 1987 the Network agreed to meet in future on an irregular basis. The UNA continues to maintain a strong interest in this area of work.

Journals and recent publications:
'*New World*', bi-monthly members' newsletter; '*Briefings*', on specific topics available for a subscription; UNA publications include '*Common Security*', a summary of the Palme Report on Disarmament and Security Issues.

WOMEN'S INTERNATIONAL LEAGUE FOR PEACE & FREEDOM
(WILPF)

29 Great James Street, London WC1N 3ES (01-242 1521).

Contact: Elisabeth Goffe, President.

Status: Unincorporated voluntary organisation.

Origins: Founded in 1915 at The Hague.

Membership: 450.

Staffing: 1 part time.

Income: £12,500 for 1986.

Sources of income: Donations and legacies.

Aims and objectives: WILPF's objectives are peace and freedom with justice; removal of discrimination on grounds of sex, race or creed; total and universal disarmament. It is wholly opposed to war as a way of solving problems between nations, and works towards disarmament and international understanding. Other concerns are human rights and the status of women. It holds an annual council and a triennial international congress. Its sections unite in action on world problems. It co-operates with other international organisations with similar aims and has an international HQ in Geneva.

Affiliations and projects with other bodies: It has consultative status with the UN (ECOSOC and UNESCO) and specialised consultative status with FAO, ILO and WHO. It is a sponsor of the Campaign Against Arms Trade and a member of National Peace Council.

Journals and recent publications:
'*Peace & Freedom*', quarterly; '*Current Affairs*', bi-monthly; Annual Report and occassional publications.

Action research and campaigns

WORLD DISARMAMENT CAMPAIGN (UK)

45–47 Blythe Street, London E2 6LX (01-729 2523).

Contact: Duncan Rees, General-Secretary.

Status: Unincorporated association.

Origins: Formed in 1979.

Patrons and advisers: Lord Fenner Brockway (President); Lord David Ennals; Dame Judith Hart; Rev Kenneth Greet; Rev John Johansen-Berg; Ron Todd; Eric Messer (Vice-Presidents); Frank Barnaby; Tony Hart (Advisers).

Membership: 1,500 + 200 affiliated organisations.

Staffing: 1 full time.

Income: £25,440 for 1986.

Sources of income: Membership subscriptions, appeals and donations.

Aims and objectives: The World Disarmament Campaign (UK) was formed in 1979 to canvass support for the disarmament proposals of the United Nations 1st Special Session on Disarmament held the year before. These were endorsed by 148 member nations including Britain, the United States and the Soviet Union and called for:

The abolition of nuclear weapons and all weapons of mass destruction;

The abolition, by agreed stages, of conventional arms leading to general and complete disarmament;

Transference of military expenditure to end world poverty.

These remain the basic aims of the World Disarmament Campaign (UK). In its work of campaigning and liaison, WDC (UK) is served by three committees – international, churches and inter-faith work, trade union/labour liaison.

Women for World Disarmament has recently become a section of WDC (UK).

Affiliations and joint projects with other organisations: WDC (UK) is a member of the Special Non-governmental Organisations Committee on Disarmament in Geneva. As a co-ordinatory campaign its working associations are legion, some of the main ones being with UNA, the National Peace Council and Campaign Against Arms Trade.

Journals and recent publications:
'*World Disarm!*' bi-monthly members' newsletter.
Pamphlets, leaflets and stickers are produced and a full list is available on request.

ACTION RESEARCH AND CAMPAIGNS:
Professional membership groups (and other social groups)

ARCHITECTS FOR PEACE

41 St James Road, Sevenoaks, Kent, TN13 3NG (0732-452361).

Contact: Ian Abbott, Secretary.

Status: Voluntary association.

Origins: Set up in 1981.

Sponsors: Sir Hugh Casson; Lady Casson; Dame Sylvia Crowe; Edward Cullinan; Berthold Lubetkin; Professor Richard MacCormac; Malcolm MacEwen; Ann MacEwen; Peter Moro; Sir Philip Powell; Richard and Ruth Rogers; Sir Peter Shepherd.

Membership: 400.

Staffing: None paid.

Income: £1,765 for 1986/87.

Sources of income: Subscriptions.

Aims and objectives: Architects for Peace 'works for the abolition of nuclear arms and other weapons of mass destruction world-wide and to awaken the profession and the public to the unavoidably catastrophic effects of nuclear war'. Projects to date have included the free distribution of the organisation's publication '*Avenues for Peace*' to all local authorities.

Affiliations: Architects for Peace is affiliated to Profession for World Disarmament and Development and has links with architects' peace groups in USA, West Germany, Norway and New Zealand.

Journals and recent publications:
A quarterly newsletter; '*Avenues for Peace*', a handbook for design of parks and gardens.

BOOK ACTION FOR NUCLEAR DISARMAMENT (BAND)

15 Rokeby House, Lamb's Conduit Street, London WC1N 3LX (01-242 6104).

Contact: Michael Pountney, Co-ordinator.

Status: Unincorporated association.

Origins: Formed in early 1983 when the arrival of Cruise Missiles was imminent.

Membership: 250.

Staffing: None paid.

Income: £2,500 for 1986/87.

Sources of income: Membership subscriptions, events.

Aims and objectives: BAND includes people from all parts of the book world. It aims to act as a pressure group to oppose nuclear weapons and to argue for a total discontinuation of their use or possession. BAND organises regular open meetings with speakers to debate issues. In 1985 it organised National Peace Book Week in which more than 500 book shops and libraries took part, and in 1987 a variety show 'Bondemonium' for the book trade at the Commonwealth Institute.

Affiliations: BAND is affiliated to CND.

Journals and recent publications: Newsletter (occasional).

CLERGY AGAINST NUCLEAR ARMS

(*see Church Organisations*)

ELECTRONICS & COMPUTING FOR PEACE

28 Milsom Street, Bath, Avon BA1 1DP (*mail address*).

National contact: Paul Butler, (01-341 2509).

Status: Unincorporated association.

Origins: Started in 1982.

Membership: 300.

Staffing: None paid.

Income: £5,000 for 1986.

Sources of income: Half the society's income comes from membership subscriptions. Support has been given by the Barrow & Geraldine S. Cadbury Trust, the Noel Buxton Trust and by Allied Dunbar.

Aims and objectives: The Society's aims are stated as:

To promote social responsibility within industry, commerce and government;

To develop positive, socially appropriate technology;

To publicise misuse of technology;

To reduce the involvement of electronics and computing in military research, development and manufacture;

To link and support those concerned about the military implications of their work;

To encourage technologists to determine the use of their technology;

To provide accurate technical information and informed opinion.

Its principle activity is the provision of technical information to the general public as well as to members. Speakers are available for groups. A major conference is planned for Easter 1988 on military expenditure and economic growth. The Society has provided finance towards a 25 minute video 'Star Wars: Artificial Intelligence in Space' produced by TV Choice, a production company specialising in information technology.

Affiliations: It is affiliated to the National Peace Council.

Journals and recent publications:
Bi-monthly newsletter, free to members.
'The Ground Launched Cruise Missile, a Technical Assessment'; *'Careers in the Defence Industry'*; *'SDI'*; *'The Nuclear Electro-Magnetic Probe'*; *'The Reliability of Military Systems'*.

ENGINEERS FOR NUCLEAR DISARMAMENT

1 Oatlands Park, Linlithgow, West Lothian EH49 6AS (0506-842451).

Contact: David Shirres, Treasurer and Membership Secretary.

Status: Unincorporated association.

Origins: Set up as 'Civil Engineers for Nuclear Disarmament' in 1982 and took its current name in 1984.

Patrons: P. Newton (President); J. Ashcroft; J. Davis, W. Cranston; Prof. M. Thring; P. Thompson; Prof. R. Butterfield; D. Evans; R. Macintosh; B. Bennell.

Membership: 200+.

Staffing: None paid.

Income: £1,000 for 1985/86.

Sources of income: Membership subscriptions and donations.

Aims and objectives: The association's aims are:

To work for the abolition of nuclear weapons;

To awaken the profession and the public to the catastrophic effects of nuclear war;

To publicise the diversion of resources from much needed public works to expenditure on nuclear weapons.

The primary function of the group is to provide a forum for engineers to discuss, debate, question and research the issues of nuclear weapons and the implications for engineers. EngND considers that engineers have a fundamental responsibility to provide technical information to policy makers and the public and a responsibility to examine these issues because of the direct involvement of the engineering profession in the design, development and production of nuclear weapons.

Affiliations: It has contacts with Professions for World Disarmament and Development, Architects for Peace and other professional groups.

Journals and recent publications:
'Nuclear Attack and the Man-Made Environment', a report of a working party on the effect of nuclear attack on water supplies, structures, transportation and energy, 1987.

Action research and campaigns

EX-SERVICES CAMPAIGN FOR NUCLEAR DISARMAMENT

Contacts: Stanley Dent, Chair, 61 Lanchester Road, London N6 4SX, (01-883 5367); Bob Lawrence, International Secretary, 49 Grand Avenue, London N10 3BS (01-883 6654).

Status: Unincorporated association.

Origins: Started at a meeting of Bristol war veterans in 1983.

Patrons: John Stanleigh, President (founding Chairman); The Very Reverend H. A. Dammers, Dean of Bristol; Professor Robert A. Hinde; Bruce Kent; Air Commodore Alastair Mackie; Deaconess Olive Price; Harry Ree; Professor Hugh Tinker; Vice-Presidents.

Membership: 1,200.

Staffing: None paid.

Income: Approximately £6,000 for 1986/87.

Sources of income: Members' subscriptions, donations and fundraising events.

Aims and objectives: The campaign aims for the removal of all nuclear weapons from Britain irrespective of the actions of other countries. It presents arguments based on the members' military experience and knowledge; provides speakers for public and private meetings; distributes reprints of the Earl of Mountbatten's 1979 Strasbourg speech against nuclear weapons; promotes Mountbatten Day Commemorations at local war memorials in May each year.

It plans to develop international action with ex-services associations in other countries.

It is affiliated to CND.

Journal:
Ex-Services CND Newsletter, quarterly.

FARMERS FOR A NUCLEAR FREE FUTURE

Georgeteign Barton, Ashton, Near Exeter, Devon (0647-52461).

Contact: J. Horsman, Chairman.

Status: Independent group.

Sources of income: The Group has no regular income; it is largely self supporting and funded from publication sales. 'Nuclear Harvest', its educational video, received a grant from the Lansbury House Trust Fund.

Aims and objectives: The group of some 15–20 farmers arose from the concern over the lack of government information on the effects of radiation on farming. Since Chernobyl the group has concentrated its activities on nuclear energy. They aim to provide a professional information service and have no particular political viewpoint.

Publications:
'*Guide to the Effects of a Nuclear Disaster on Agriculture*', 1984; '*Chernobyl, Becquerels and British Agriculture*', 1986; '*Nuclear Harvest*', video (30 minutes) available from Chairman.

GENERALS FOR PEACE AND DISARMAMENT

(*London Office*), c/o London Centre for International Peacebuilding, Wickham House, 10 Cleveland Way, London E1 4TR (01-790 2424).

Contact: Brigadier Michael Harbottle.

Status: Independent organisation.

Origins: Formed in 1981.

Membership: 15.

Staffing: None paid.

Estimated annual income: £10,000.

Sources of income: Donations and sale of literature.

Aims and objectives: This small group of retired senior officers from NATO countries questions the wisdom of current NATO defence strategies in their dependence upon the nuclear deterrent. It meets periodically to analyse current political and military decisions affecting arms control and disarmament.

In May 1984, a meeting was initiated with a comparable group of retired Generals from all the Warsaw Pact countries to create a working relationship based on common professional experience and understanding of the military issues affecting East-West security. Meetings have since been held annually.

Publications:
'*10 Questions Answered*' (re sighting of Cruise and Pershing missiles); '*The Arms Race to Armageddon: Generals Challenge US/NATO Strategy*'. Berg. German language books: '*Generale fur den Frieden*' 1981; '*Generale gegen Nachrustung*'; '*Generale fur Frieden und Abrustung*'. Bulletins, Memoranda, Posters and postcards are also produced.

Action research and campaigns

INTERNATIONAL PHYSICIANS FOR THE PREVENTION OF NUCLEAR WAR

126 Roger Street, Cambridge, MA 02142, USA (617-868 5050).

Contact: William W. Monning, Executive Director.

IPPNW, European Office: South Bank House, Black Prince Road, Lambeth, London SE1 7SJ (01-587 1110).

Contacts: Marlene Laubli, Co-ordinator (Part time), Mark Lister, Project Co-ordinator.

Status: A non-profit making educational organisation.

Origins: From Physicians for Social Responsibility, founded in Boston in 1961, grew a series of Soviet/American medical dialogues on nuclear war which culminated in the incorporation of the International Federation in 1980. The two prime movers and later Co-Presidents were Dr Lown, Professor of Cardiology at the Harvard School of Public Health and Dr Eugueni Chazov, then Director of the USSR Cardiological Institute (who resigned in 1987 when created Soviet Minister of Health of the USSR).

Co-Presidents: Dr Bernard Lown and Acad. Mikhail Kuzin.

Membership: National Affiliates are the only true members of the Federation but some 170,000 physicians in 58 countries are involved in this organisation. The largest affiliates are Physicians for Social Responsibility, USA (28,000) and the Soviet Committee of Physicians for the Prevention of Nuclear War (60,000).

Staffing: 12 full time.

Income scale: Not given.

Sources of income: Foundation grants 6%; affiliate dues 6%; individual donations 82%; miscellaneous 6%.

Aims and objectives: IPPNW is a federation of national affiliates. Its International Council consists of one delegate from every member nation. This elects an executive committee headed by Co-Presidents from the US and USSR. Its primary objective is to alert the people in the governments of the world to the medical dimensions of the nuclear arms race. IPPNW has agreed; 'that it would restrict its focus to nuclear war and the nuclear arms race; that physicians would work to prevent nuclear war as a consequence of their professional commitments to protect life and preserve health; that it would involve physicians from around the world; that the same information about nuclear war would be circulated widely to the public and leaders of all nations; that though it might advocate certain steps to prevent nuclear war, it would maintain a neutral, non-partisan character.'

IPPNW has encouraged its affiliates to develop policies and programmes which are exclusively national in focus. As a global Federation it has taken broad positions with world-wide applications e.g. a verifiable freeze on the development and deployment of all nuclear weapons systems; an explicit declaration of no-first-use by the nuclear powers; a recognition by governments of the 'illusory nature' of civil defence plans for nuclear war.

In 1985 the International Council voted unanimously to endorse the IPPNW Medical Prescription. The call for a moratorium on all nuclear explosions became the Federation's prime recommendation to governments. A nuclear test ban remains the single arms-control measure that all IPPNW affiliates have agreed to emphasise accompanied by a world-wide campaign to educate the public on its merits. In 1985 the IPPNW was awarded the Nobel Peace Prize. Seven world conferences have been held since 1981; in Moscow in 1987 and in Montreal in 1988.

The IPPNW European Office is setting up a computerised index of international speakers to be made available to all European affiliates.

Journals and recent publications:
'*Report*' a newsletter published 3 times a year; Freeman, W. H. '*Last Aid: The Medical Dimensions of Nuclear War*', New York, 1982.

LAWYERS FOR NUCLEAR DISARMAMENT

2 Garden Court, Temple, London EC4.

Contact: Owen Davies, Secretary.

Status: Unincorporated association.

Staffing: None paid.

Aims and objectives: The Society's aims are stated as:

To research and publicise the legal implications and consequences of the production, possession, deployment and use of nuclear and other weapons of mass destruction;

To support, advise and assist individuals, groups and authorities who object to the existence of such weapons and to the production of materials for their manufacture and use;

To propose, publicise and foster relevant national and international legislation and to pursue its implementation.

A Nuclear Warfare Tribunal was held in 1986 and a videotape is available of a BBC 'Open Space' programme covering this.

Action research and campaigns

A booklet is being prepared with the International Peace Bureau and the International Progress Organisation on legal resistance to nuclear weapons.

Journals and recent publications:
Newsletter, quarterly. Pamphlets include: *'The Illegality of Nuclear War'*; *'Trade Unionism and Nuclear Disarmament'*; *'A Tax on Peace'*; *'The Legal Status of Nuclear Weapons'* – inaugural lecture to the Society by Professor Ian Brownlie; *'Nuclear Free Zones'*, a series of 6 Working Papers; *'A Legal Advice Pack for Nuclear Disarmers'*.

MEDICAL ASSOCIATION FOR PREVENTION OF WAR (MAPW)

Sudbury, 16b Prince Arthur Road, London NW3 6AY (01-794 1430).

Contact: Martha Pinnons, Administrator.

Status: Unincorporated association. The Lionel Penrose Trust which is a registered charity, receives support for its educational activities.

Origins: Founded in 1951, with the objective to study causes and effects of war, and the ethical position of the medical profession.

Patrons and officers: Prof. Sir Richard Doll (President); Dr Martin Bax (Chairman); Dr John Hutchins (Hon Secretary); Mr Nick Lewer (Hon Treasurer).

Membership: 530.

Staffing: 1 part time.

Estimated income: £6,500 for 1986/87.

Sources of income: Subscriptions.

Aims and objectives: The Association aims are 'to formulate ethical responsibilities of health workers in relation to war; to study causes and results of war; to examine psychological mechanisms which condition acceptance of war as a necessity; to oppose use of medical science for any purpose other than prevention and relief of suffering; to urge that energies and money spent in preparation for war be diverted to development and health care.'

Conferences run by MAPW in recent years, have centred on the nuclear threat, on the relationship between arms expenditure and health care and development. The 1987 conference was on terrorism.

Future plans include the amendment of the Hippocratic Oath to include consideration of weapons of mass destruction and medical responsibility.

Affiliations and projects with other bodies: MAPW is affiliated to the International Physicians for Prevention of Nuclear War (IPPNW) and the National Peace Council. It participates in the work of Professions for World Disarmament and Development and the International Peace Bureau.

Journals and recent publications:
'Medicine and War', quarterly journal in association with Medical Campaign Against Nuclear Weapons and MAPW, Australia. It is free to members. (Available from MAPW or from the publishers, John Wiley.)
Quarterly Newsletter.

MEDICAL CAMPAIGN AGAINST NUCLEAR WEAPONS (MCANW)

Trees House, 3 Stamford Street, London SE1 9NT (01-261 1266).

Contact: Jane Oberman, National Co-ordinator.

Status: Unincorporated association.

Origins: Founded in 1980.

Membership: 4,000.

Staffing: 2 full time; 2 part time.

Income: Around £80,000 for 1987.

Sources of income: The Campaign relies for funds on membership subscriptions, (60%), an annual Hiroshima Day Appeal (30%) and donations (10%). Support was provided in 1985 and 1986 by the Greater London Council. Donations for educational work can be made to the Medical Educational Trust, a registered charity.

Aims and objectives: The association is open to all health-care workers and has 49 branches throughout the country. The Campaign states that it:

Supports nuclear disarmament as the only way to prevent nuclear war;

Calls for a reallocation of resources from nuclear arms to health care;

Opposes the deployment of Cruise missiles and Trident;

Endorses the findings of the two British Medical Association reports and the Royal College of Nursing report and condemns medical civil defence planning for nuclear war which ignores their conclusions;

Supports a world-wide freeze on the testing, production, delivery and deployment of nuclear weapons;

Recognises links between nuclear power and the production of nuclear weapons.

Policy is decided at its Annual Conference and at the National Council meetings held three times a year. Special interests within the Campaign are served by a number of different Working Groups, such as the Nurses Group, the Civil Defence Working Group, and the Scottish Working Party on Psycho-Social Issues and War.

MCANW produces a range of materials including leaflets, posters, books and briefings; provides expert speakers for groups and for the media; lobbies Parliament and professional organisations on nuclear weapons issues; runs an information and briefing service for the media and organises national campaigns.

In 1983 MCANW members set up the UK-USSR Medical Exchange Programme (*see separate entry*).

Affiliations: The Campaign is a UK affiliate of International Physicians for the Prevention of Nuclear War (IPPNW) and a sister organisation of the Medical Association for the Prevention of War (MAPW).

Journals and recent publications:
Newsletter, 3 times a year;
Farrow and Chown (eds) '*The Human Cost of Nuclear War*', 1983;
Humphrey, Prof John, Hartog, Dr M. and Middleton, Dr Hugh '*The Medical Consequences of Nuclear Weapons*', 1983;
Holdstock, Dr Douglas '*World at the Crossroads*', 1986.
A full list of other leaflets and campaign materials is available.

MEMBERS OF EQUITY FOR NUCLEAR DISARMAMENT

94a Uplands Road, London N8 (01-341 7116).

Contact: Lynne Brackley.

Membership: around 100.

Income: Largely from membership fees.

Aims and objectives: MEND aims to use the skills of the entertainment profession to further the cause of nuclear disarmament. Those who are not members of Equity are welcome to join.

Workshops were taking place in Autumn 1987 on a proposed television serial on the 'World Without Nuclear Weapons'. Other activities have included street theatre, non-violent direct action and peace videos.

MUSICIANS AGAINST NUCLEAR ARMS

The Premises, 201 Hackney Road, London E2 8JL (01-729 0885).

Contacts: Colin Dudman, Treasurer; Matilda Hamilton, Secretary.

Status: Unincorporated association.

Patrons: John Williams (President); Simon Rattle; Charles Groves; Michael Tippett; Jessye Norman.

Membership: 500.

Staffing: 1 part time.

Income: £3,500 for 1986/87.

Sources of income: Membership subscriptions and concerts.

Aims and objectives: MANA works to promote peace by putting on concerts in London and the regions. It also provides musicians for the fundraising work of other peace groups.

Journals: Quarterly members' newsletter.

PARENTS FOR SURVIVAL

Sandybrae Cottage, 10 Sandybrae Road, Skelmorlie, Ayrshire PA17 5AT (0475-521410).

Contact: Mary McGlashan.

Status: Unincorporated association.

Origins: Founded in 1981 in Edinburgh and Glasgow, it now operates in all Scottish cities, and has members from Mull to Middlesex.

Membership: 1,000.

Staffing: None paid.

Income: £5,000 for 1986/87.

Sources of income: Membership subscriptions and fund-raising events.

Aims and objectives: Their primary purpose is to bring about a halt to the nuclear arms race. They have no party political affiliations and do not adopt a specifically unilateralist position (although members are free to take that view). They aim to give support to other parents worried about nuclear war and undertake basic education on nuclear issues. They also aim to translate parents' anger and fears into a positive vehicle for change and have been responsible for several major campaigns and events, including an Anti-Trident postcard campaign, the start of the Freeze campaign in Scotland, and, in Autumn 1986, the Arms Around Scotland demonstration. This event was undertaken in support of the UN International Year of Peace and involved over 40,000 people who linked arms across the central belt of Scotland.

An exhibition is to be housed with the Peace Garden Project at the Glasgow Garden Festival in 1988.

Action research and campaigns

PENSIONERS FOR PEACE INTERNATIONAL

c/o 43 Dickerage Road, Kingston-Upon-Thames, Surrey KT1 3SR (01-942 0204).

Contact: Margaret Smith, Secretary.

Status: Unincorporated association.

Sponsors: Lord Fenner Brockway; Lord Hugh Jenkins of Putney; Sir Hugh and Lady Margaret Casson; Spike Milligan; Dame Judith Hart; MP, Dervla Murphy; Frank Allaun; Jack Jones.

Membership: 2,000.

Staffing: None paid.

Annual income: Not disclosed.

Sources of income: Voluntary subscriptions and occasional donations.

Aims and objectives: PPI was founded in 1981 by Jack Sheppard who also ran it as international organiser until his death in 1987. It aims 'to rally the older generation to work for Peace with Justice and for World Disarmament, and for the abandonment of nuclear, biological and chemical warfare'. It supports CND and other organisations, holds occasional meetings to discuss current issues and can supply speakers to pensioners' groups and other gatherings.

Affiliation: Pensioners for Peace International is affiliated to CND.

Journal: Quarterly newsletter.

PSYCHOLOGISTS FOR PEACE

Dept of Psychology, University of Surrey, Guildford, Surrey GU2 5XH (0483-571 281 x 728).

Contact: Professor David Canter.

Status: Unincorporated association.

Origins: In 1982, from the impetus of 3 separate groups of psychologists.

Membership: 525 (Dec. 1985).

Staffing: None paid.

Income: Not disclosed.

Sources of income: Subscriptions only.

Aims and objectives: As psychologists three broad areas of concern are examined:
  The systems of nuclear confrontation – from civil defence to negotiation;
  The unconscious processes that motivate our reactions – anxiety, denial and helplessness – and dealing with these;
  The consequences of unrelenting threat on developing minds.

Local meetings and events are arranged by eight regional groups in Scotland, Wales, Avon, South West, Birmingham, Manchester, Sheffield and the South East. Speakers are provided for meetings and national and international conferences are organised.

Affiliations and projects with other bodies: The Association co-operated with Scientists Against Nuclear Arms in the Summer Conference, 1986, at Hungarian Academy of Sciences, Budapest on 'Social & Psychological Aspects of the Arms Peace', and is co-operating with the Medical Campaign Against Nuclear Weapons in a survey of doctors' views on the arms race, (1985 onwards). It is a member of Professions for World Disarmament and Development.

Journal: Newsletter, quarterly, free to members.

SCIENTISTS AGAINST NUCLEAR ARMS (SANA)

9 Poland Street, London W1V 3DG (01-734 5281/2).

Contact: Rebecca Miles, Co-ordinator.

Status: Independent organisation.

Origins: Formed in 1981.

Distinguished supporters: In 1987 SANA had some 60 distinguished sponsors including Nobel prize winners, Fellows of the Royal Society, politicians and media figures.

Membership: 900+ scientist members; non-scientist associates 100+ (a new category).

Staffing: 1 full time; 2 part time.

Estimated income: £42,000 for 1987.

Recent sources of income: Donation for research and educational activities from the Joseph Rowntree Charitable Trust; support also from the Barrow Cadbury Fund Ltd and the Joseph Rowntree Social Service Trust which provides free office accommodation. Funding also from subscriptions and the sale of publications.

Aims and objectives: SANA promotes and co-ordinates the activities of scientists working to halt and reverse the nuclear arms race. It does so through the provision of information and speakers, publications, input to the mass media and scientific journals.

SANA has a national co-ordinating committee and national office but its organisation is largely based in its regional groups and research and study groups, i.e. civil defence, nuclear winter, non-provocative defence, accidental nuclear war, arms control/disarmament negotiation, disarmament education, Trident/ASW etc, nuclear power, nuclear weapons proliferation, SDI, verification, biological effects, political – social context of science and the arms race and others:

SANA has, for example:

Co-ordinated a Star Wars' Research boycott by over 500 scientists;

Briefed MPs and Parliamentary candidates;

Provided evidence to Government enquiries and the British Medical Association;

Provided local authorities with technical information and advice on the effects of nuclear weapons the effectiveness of civil defence, etc;

Carried out a campaign on the long-term consequences of a nuclear war (the Nuclear Winter) and, with Nuclear Free Zone authorities, organised a speaking tour of scientists from USA and USSR;

Convened two major International Symposia of scientists on Problems and Prospects of Nuclear Disarmament, in 1982 and 1986.

Journals and recent publications:

Newsletter, quarterly;

'*Defence and Disarmament: Issues and Counter issues*', 1987; A pack of 20 leaflets;

'*Star Wars: the Terminology and Politics of Space Weapons*' August 1986, pamphlet;

SANA video '*A Change in the Weather*', VHS 30 mins;

Arms Race Slideshow;

Greene, Percival and Ridge '*Nuclear Winter: The Evidence and the Risk*' Polity Press, 1985.

TEACHERS FOR PEACE

(*see World Studies, Peace Education*)

ACTION RESEARCH AND CAMPAIGNS:
Non-membership organisations

CAMPAIGN AGAINST ARMS TRADE

11 Goodwin Street, Finsbury Park, London N4 3HQ (01-281 0297).

Contacts: Stephen Chappell and Ann Feltham, Joint Co-ordinators.

Status: Independent organisation.

Origins: Set up in 1974 by organisations concerned about the growth of the arms trade following the Middle East war.

Sponsors: The Anglican Pacifist Fellowship, CND, Fellowship of Reconciliation, Friends of the Earth, Green Party, Housmans Bookshop, Labour Action for Peace, London Greenpeace, Methodist Division of Social Responsibility, National League of Young Liberals, National Peace Council, Pax Christi, Peace Pledge Union, Plaid Cymru, Quaker Peace and Service, Socialist Environment and Resources Association, TAPOL (Indonesia Human Rights Group), Third World First, United Nations Association, Women's International League for Peace and Freedom.

Staffing: 3 full time.

Income: £50,000 for 1987.

Sources of income: Support comes largely from individuals and sponsoring organisations and some 30% from the sale of campaign materials. Grants amounting to less than 10% of total income have been made recently by the Barrow Cadbury Fund Ltd and the Joseph Rowntree Social Service Trust.

Aims and objectives: The campaign is a coalition of groups and individuals committed to ending the international arms trade, and Britain's significant role in this. It is also committed to the conversion of military industry to socially useful production. The campaign has no formal membership structure. It has some 120 affiliated groups and a supporters' mailing list of 2,000 people. Local branches of peace organisations, trade unions, churches etc. support the campaign. Local contacts cover much of the country and focus work against the arms trade in their area by trying to encourage other groups and individuals to include questions about the arms trade in their concerns.

These local contacts and representatives of the sponsoring organisations come together twice yearly as the Campaign Development Group. This group reviews the campaign's work and exchanges ideas about future operations. A monthly steering committee guides everyday work which also includes working groups on the following topics – human rights, development education, and the churches.

Affiliations and projects with other bodies: The fourth 'Bread Not Bombs Week', 1987 was promoted jointly with CAFOD, Christian Aid, Fellowship of Reconciliation, Oxfam, Pax Christi, Quaker Peace and Service, United Nations Association, Voluntary Service Overseas, War on Want, World Disarmament Campaign, and Women's International League for Peace and Freedom.

The major campaign in 1988 is against the biennial British Army Equipment Exhibition, in conjunction with several human rights organisations.

Journals and recent publications:
Newsletter, bi-monthly.

A major publication of the campaign is *The Arms Traders*, a listing of Britain's arms exporters giving their addresses and product range. It is organised in two parts, a register of the major arms traders and in the second part a listing of the exporters by geographic area.

'Arms Unlimited', A slide/tape show also available on VHS video (30 minutes). Exhibitions are available, e.g. *'Trade in Misery'* a set of 8 colour posters, *'Alternatives to the Arms Trade'*, a 27 panel exhibition (free), *'Punch Up in Arms'*, 125 cartoons mainly from Punch magazine (free).

Leaflets, pamphlets, briefings, aids to local action, postcards, posters, badges, stickers, are produced.

Action research and campaigns

CAMPAIGN AGAINST MILITARY RESEARCH ON CAMPUS (CAMROC)

190b Burdett Road, Bow, London E3 4AA (01-980 2455).

Contact: Rob Evans, Co-ordinator.

Status: Independent group.

Origins: Started in 1986.

Staffing: None paid.

Income: £800 for 1987/88.

Source of income: Donations.

Aims and objectives: The campaign aims to inform students and the general public about the extent and nature of military-funded research in British universities and colleges and to press for a reduction in the amount of military research both nationally and in universities. It is seeking a complete ban on research contracts from Porton Down and Aldermaston and on secret research in universities. The campaign is based in college/local groups which work autonomously. There is a national co-ordinating group.

Affiliations and joint projects with other organisations: CAMROC is affiliated to the British Society for Social Responsibility in Science and the Working Party on Chemical Weapons.

Conferences have been organised in association with the National Union of Students.

Journals: A termly newsletter is produced.

CAMPAIGN FOR DEFENCE AND MULTILATERAL DISARMAMENT

Conservative Central Office, 32 Smith Square, London SW1P 3HH (01-222 9511/9000).

Contacts: Harvey Thomas, CDMD Secretary; Keith Simpson, Defence Research Department.

Aims and objectives: The Campaign, chaired by Gerry Neale MP, has a 16 member Council and Campaign Committee. The Campaign, funded by the Conservative Party, provides speakers and information along with some co-ordinatory work with a grouping of defence organisations committed to multilateral disarmament.

It produces a '*Briefing Pack*', updated about three times each year, to assist MPs and other campaigners. It contains:

Lists of the Campaign's Council & Committee members, Defence & Foreign Office ministerial teams and relevant Conservative office personnel; journalists & lobby correspondents; 'multilateral' defence organisations; briefing documents, speeches, booklets;

Party-political comparisons; documents and leaflets from the Conservative, Liberal/SDP & Labour Parties, the MoD the Conservative Research Department and the Coalition for Peace through Security.

COALITION FOR PEACE THROUGH SECURITY

2nd Floor, 35 Westminster Bridge Road, London SE1 (01-261 0134/01-928 9524).

Contacts: Dr Julian Lewis, Ms Catherine Marshall.

The Coalition did not wish to supply information for this book. The Campaign for Defence and Multilateral Disarmament (CDMD), includes its leaflets in its briefing pack. These display its stance as a leading anti-CND organisation pledged to 'campaign' against the drift towards neutralism in Britain, in favour of multilateral and balanced arms reductions, Britain's continued membership of NATO, and the maintenance of Britain's nuclear deterrent.

It has close links with the Freedom Association with which it jointly produces the leaflets below.

Journals and recent publications: Leaflets include:

'*30 Questions & Honest Answers about CND*'; '*CND – The Things They Say – 40 quotes about Peace*'.

It distributes the book, Mercer, Paul '*Peace of the Dead – the Truth behind the Nuclear Disarmers*'.

DUNAMIS

St. James's Rectory, 197 Piccadilly, London W1V 9LF (01-437 6851).

Contact: Ronald Higgins, Director.

Status: Charitable as an educational project of St. James's Church.

Origins: Founded in 1980. The organising committee is chaired by Jenifer Wates, a co-founder with Neil Wates.

Distinguished advisers: Advisory Council members include: General Sir Hugh Beach; Julian Critchley MP; Professor William Gutteridge; Lord Henniker; Frank Judd; Professor Joseph Rotblat and Elizabeth Sidney.

Staffing: 2 part time.

Estimated annual income: £22–25,000 for 1986/87.

Source of income: Commonwork Trust.

Aims and objectives: Dunamis believes 'the national defence debate is absurdly polarised with too little

Action research and campaigns

room left for real listening or the exploration of real alternatives. Parliament and politics generally are performing poorly in a critical area. Dunamis seeks to provide a model for genuine dialogue by providing a truly open public forum and a safe private space in which rival positions can be sensitively explored'.

It works by the following methods:

Lecture series on all aspects of international security and from all points of view;

Suppers and evening seminars;

Weekend seminars for decision makers and opinion formers, mostly on North/South issues (usually at Commonwork, Kent).

Written material, two books on peacemaking theory and practice, and sponsorship of booklets, articles, etc.

Tapes of lectures are on sale.

Dunamis worked with BBC and Open University on a linked series of TV and radio programmes for the course *'Nuclear Weapons, Enquiry, Analysis and Debate'* (*see separate entry*).

FREEZE RESOURCES LTD (NUCLEAR WEAPONS FREEZE)

National Office, 82 Colston Street, Bristol BS1 5BB (0272-276 435).

Contact: Dr Will Howard, National Co-ordinator.

Status: Non-profit making limited company.

Origins: Started in 1985.

Distinguished patrons and officers: FREEZE has over 350 eminent patrons from the fields of religion, medicine, science, education, media, the arts, sport and politics. These include: Countess Mountbatten; Lord Brabourne; Lord Ennals; Jonathan Miller; Lord Len Murray; The Rt Rev Lord Coggan; The Bishop of Liverpool; Professor Dorothy Hodgkin; Ben Kingsley; Dame Peggy Ashcroft; John le Carré; Laurie Lee; and Catherine Cookson. The Directors, of which there are 17, include: Sir Geoffrey Wilson; Sir Rudolf Peierls; Professor Andrew Haines; Dr Frank Heller; Dr Frank Barnaby; and Mary Midgley. FREEZE is not a membership organisation but has some 5,000 paying supporters.

Staffing: 5 full time; 4 part time.

Estimated annual income: £130,000 for 1986/87.

Sources of income: Individual donations; Barrow Cadbury Fund Ltd; Joseph Rowntree Social Service Trust.

Aims and objectives: FREEZE was launched as a new non-partisan initiative to help halt the momentum of the nuclear arms race.

Specific campaigning objectives are:

Comprehensive Test Ban, to halt introduction of new types of weapons;

Plutonium freeze, to end the production and reprocessing of nuclear materials used for making nuclear bombs; and further measures to stop the spread of nuclear weapons to currently non-nuclear countries;

Preservation of the treaties which prevent the placing of nuclear weapons in space.

The FREEZE movement developed in the late 1970s in the USA through a series of local referenda. In Britain, a number of local groups formed the national FREEZE campaign in 1984. FREEZE carries out parliamentary lobbying; scientific and arms control research; receptions and meetings countrywide; presswork; conferences. Supporters throughout the country carry out local lobbying and persuasion particularly through: the FREEZEVOTE, a rolling national referendum on the FREEZE proposal; and the FREEZE Bandwagon, a huge poster, which travels around the country collecting signatures. A Marplan poll has been commissioned annually to date – the response in 1987 was 79% in favour of a freeze (78% of Conservative, 86% of Alliance, 82% of Labour voters).

FREEZE conducts a specific research project in conjunction with the United Nations Association Trust. This commissions and publishes its findings.

Journals and recent publications:

Supporters receive FREEZE *'Update'*, a quarterly newsheet. Other publications include:

Barnaby, Frank *'Mad Nuts, First Strike & a Nuclear Freeze'* 1986; Thompson, Gordon and Haines, Andrew, *'The Nuclear Freeze Revisited'*, 1987; a compilation of Mary Midgley's Guardian articles *'FREEZE Matters'*, 1987.

INTERNATIONAL INSTITUTE FOR PEACEFUL CHANGE

Lochiel House, 2 Ormonde Road, Hythe, Kent CT21 6DN (0303-69416).

Contact: James Saunders.

Status: Registered charity.

Hon. Officers: Lord Ennals, Professor Walter Isard, Jonathon Porritt (Vice-Presidents); Dr Jack Grobstein, Patricia Holt, Sean Kennedy, Kenneth Lee, Alan Mayne, Louis Alfred Pinna (Trustees).

Staffing: 1 part time.

Annual income: Not disclosed.

Action research and campaigns

Sources of income: The Institute's PEACEAID Campaign encourages individual donors to give £3.65 with the slogan – 'A penny a day to give peace a chance' and seeks sponsors for its publishing and campaigning enterprises. The Peace Science Publishing Trust Co Ltd is its publishing arm and underwrites its other activities.

Aims and objectives: The Institute is inspired by Clause 106 of the UN Special Session on Disarmament which calls for all governments and non-governmental organisations to develop programmes for disarmament and peace studies. Its current aim is to try to give the 1986 UN Year of Peace a lasting impact via its publications. These introduce 'new, multi-disciplinary holistic scientific skills concentrating on peace and sex education and having poetic and musical elements'. The Institute started a new PEACEAID campaign in mid 1987.

Publications:

'*In a Child's Eyes Wondering. Journeying towards the New Peace Sciences*'; '*Aids: Why Ignorance Can Kill*'; '*Poetry for a Changing World and Changing Moods*'; a street-play record with PEACEAID: theme songs '*Now's the Hour, We've the Power, Make Love not War*'.

LONDON CENTRE FOR INTERNATIONAL PEACE BUILDING

Wickham House, 10 Cleveland Way (Mile End Road), London E1 4TR (01-790 2424).

Contacts: Brigadier Michael Harbottle, William Hawthorne, Directors.

Status: Independent organisation.

Origins: Founded in 1983 with the maxim 'Peace is everybody's business'.

Staffing: 5 full time.

Income: Not disclosed.

Sources of income: The Centre relies solely on donations and receives no grants from governments or official bodies. The Caroline Gourlay Trust receives charitable donations for the Centre's educational project work.

Aims and objectives: The Centre has been established to bridge the gap between academic peace research and the activist movement. It enjoys the support of a number of eminent people who act as consultants and help implement its projects to help advance international understanding and peaceful co-existence.

Projects include:

Disarmament: the preparation of a Handbook of Verification Procedures to assist in the negotiation and monitoring of arms control agreements, due for publication in 1988;

Confidence Building: the development of an East-West 'peoples' detente through inter-action by professional, artistic, media, business and other common interest groups;

Collective Security: research into collective security systems which will enable countries of the Third World to live and develop peacefully, using as a basis the recommendations of the Palme Commission's Report on Common Security;

Environmental Education (The Gaia Initiative) to promote an awareness of the World Conservation Strategy and to assist in its implementation in schools and community groups.

Affiliations: The Centre is registered with the United Nations as a non-governmental organisation and has an Agreement of Co-operation with the University of Peace, Costa Rica (*see separate entry*).

Publications:

Leggett and Waterlow '*War Games that Superpowers Play*' 1983, revised 1985;

Jasani and Barnaby '*Verification Technologies: The Case for Surveillance by Consent*' Berg, 1984;

Harrison, Levi, von Hippel and Barnaby, '*Verifying a Nuclear Freeze*' Berg, 1985.

PEACE THROUGH NATO

46–47 Chancery Lane, London WC2 1JB (01-831 2220).

Contact: Ken Aldred, Secretary General.

Status: Unincorporated association.

Origins: Founded as a campaigning organisation in 1983 – under the auspices of the British Atlantic Committee (*see separate entry*).

Distinguished patrons: Lord Home of the Hirsel (President); Lord Hooson, Lord Mulley (Vice Presidents).

Staffing: 3 full time; 1 part time.

Income: £120,000 for 1987/88.

Sources of income: Foreign Office grant aid. Donations from companies and individuals.

Aims and objectives: As its name indicates the organisation campaigns in favour of NATO and its policies of deterrence and negotiated arms control. An all-party organisation with a nationwide network of supporters and groups, all of whom are ready and

Action research and campaigns

willing to spread the NATO message and to counter the arguments of those who promote unilateralism. It seeks to promote these arguments to the widest possible audience. PTN is not a membership organisation but by 1987 had some 4–5,000 supporters with a network of over 100 groups throughout England, Scotland and Wales. (About 36 of these groups are in schools, polytechnics and universities as part of the 'Youth for Peace throughout NATO' aspect of PTN's campaign work.) It offers speakers, exhibitions, publicity material, leaflets about NATO and defence, films and videos.

Joint project: For the 1986 International Year of Peace, Peace through NATO started working jointly with 'Schools Against the Bomb' (*see separate entry with Youth CND*) and continues to do so.

Journals and recent publications:
'*Peace through NATO News*', biannual newsletter; Regan, David '*It Costs a Bomb: the Local Government Anti-Nuclear Campaign*', 1985.
A full publication/resource list is available.

PEACE THROUGH PARLIAMENT

9 Beversbrook Road, London N19 4QG (01-263 4027).

Contact: Jeremy Polmear.

Status: Unincorporated association.

Annual income: Not disclosed but very small apparently.

Sources of income: Supporters' donations.

Aims and objectives: Peace through Parliament started in 1983 and encourages the lobbying of MPs on nuclear issues for which it provides practical advice and discussion sheets. Whilst the group has no formal membership its mailing list covered some 300 interested people in 1987.

In 1986, inspired by the Oxford Research Group's work (*see separate entry*) on lack of accountability in decision-making about nuclear weapons in Britain, Peace through Parliament lobbied MPs specifically on this issue. It runs role-playing workshops on lobbying for campaigning groups e.g. the Peace Tax Campaign (*see separate entry*).

BERTRAND RUSSELL PEACE FOUNDATION

Bertrand Russell House, 45 Gamble Street, Nottingham NG7 4ET (0602-784 504).

Contact: Ken Fleet, Secretary.

Status: Company limited by guarantee.

Origins: Set up in 1963.

Board of Directors: Michael Barrett Brown; Stephen Bodington; Ken Fleet; Tony Topham.

Staffing: 2 full time; 1 part time.

Estimated annual income: £85,000 for 1986/87 (*including publishing*); £25,000 for 1986/87 (*excluding publishing*).

Sources of income: Individual donations; royalties from some of Bertrand Russell's books; occasional grants for specific projects.

Aims and objectives: The Foundation aims to pursue issues of disarmament and social justice through conferences, campaigns and publications. (It is not a grant-making body.) The Foundation was instrumental in the establishment of the European Nuclear Disarmament movement and provides secretarial services for the International Liaison Committee which organises the annual END conventions (1987 in Coventry, 1988 in Lund, Sweden).

Its facilities include a library, art gallery and printing press. The publishing company with the 'Spokesman' imprint publishes books and the journal '*END papers*' (originally '*Spokesman*'). A full publications list is available.

WOMEN WORKING FOR A NUCLEAR FREE AND INDEPENDENT PACIFIC

c/o 82 Colston Street, Bristol 1 (0272-743 224/550 905).

Contact: Sigrid Shayer.

Status: Unincorporated association.

Origins: The founders met at Greenham Common Women's Peace Camp in 1984.

Staffing: None paid.

Income: Not disclosed.

Sources of income: WWNFIP runs 2 funds – the Pacific Fund, a general campaigning account and the Rongelap Resettlement Fund. Local groups raise their own money for local work.

Aims and objectives: The Group is a feminist network with no formal membership. It is non hierarchical and decentralised and works in support of the grass roots movement in the Pacific. Much of the work is in disseminating information through speaking tours, meetings, conferences, videos and publications. They run two funds (see above) to raise money to support their campaign and local groups in the Pacific.

Action research and campaigns

Local and national actions range from demonstrations, leafletting and picketting to letter-writing campaigns and petitions. A national 'telephone tree' alerts activists about French nuclear tests at Moruroa atoll.

Joint projects with other organisations: Work is often done in co-operation with other campaigns, such as Friends of the Earth, the Medical Campaign Against Nuclear Weapons, CND and the Green Party.

Journals and recent publications:
NFIP *Bulletin*, bimonthly; *'Pacific Women Speak – Why Haven't You known?'* ed. WWNFIP, published by Greenline magazine; *'Pacific Paradise – Nuclear Nightmare'* ed. WWNFIP, CND Publications; *'Nightmare in Paradise'* 20 min. slide/tape or video.

ACTION RESEARCH AND CAMPAIGNS:
Co-ordinatory bodies

BRITISH PEACE ASSEMBLY

3rd Floor, 5–11 Lavington Street, London SE1 0NZ (01-928 9028).

Contact: Rosemary Bechler, Secretary.

Yorkshire, Humberside and Derbyshire Region: c/o 5 St Martin's Terrace, Leeds LS7 4JB (0532-624 185). **Contact:** Dave Levy.

Scottish Region: 43 Marwick Street, Dennistun, Glasgow (041-423 4719). **Contact:** Frieda Park.

Status: Independent organisation.

Origins: Founded in 1980.

Officers: James Lamond MP (President); Alf Lomas MEP; Gordon Schaffer; Beryl Huffinley (Vice-Presidents).

Membership: Some 200 affiliated organisations and 100 individual associates.

Staffing: None paid.

Annual income: Information not made available.

Sources of income: Affiliation fees and sales of literature.

Aims and objectives: The Assembly is a broad-based peace organisation which seeks to play its part in the wider peace movement by emphasising its international links. Among its affiliates are peace groups, trade unions, political parties and solidarity organisations.

The BPA is linked to the World Peace Council, based in Helsinki, and affiliated to the United Nations Association of Great Britain. The Yorkshire Region organised *Peace March '87*, between Chesterfield and Leeds in September, with local union support and under the slogans: 'No Space Weapons', 'Nuclear Disarmament in Europe' and 'Ban Nuclear Tests'. As part of the campaign against the US 'Star Wars' space weapons programme, it brought together scientists, trade unionists and peace activists to organise a major conference 'Star-Wars: The Threat' scheduled for early 1988.

Journals and recent publications: *'Facts the Media Ignore'*, bi-monthly newsletter; A new series of 'Background Briefing' documents was launched in 1987 with *'INF Briefing'* and followed in 1988 with briefings on the Gulf, Star Wars and the Western European Union; World Peace Council literature and other campaigning materials are circulated upon request.

CAMPAIGN AGAINST ARMS TRADE

(*see Non-membership Organisations*)

EUROPEAN NUCLEAR DISARMAMENT (END)

11 Goodwin Street, London N4 3HQ (01-272 9092).

Contact: Andy Roberts, Organising Secretary.

Status: Independent organisation.

Origins: Founded in 1980, after the launch of the 'END Appeal' which called for a nuclear-free Europe and 'people to people' detente between East and West. The Appeal was signed by thousands of people throughout the world. In Britain its signatories formed the END organisation.

Honorary Officers: Kate Soper (Chair); Keith McClelland (Treasurer); Mary Kaldor (Editor END Journal).

Membership: Started in 1986.

Staffing: 1 full time; 3 part time.

Estimated annual income: £65,000 for 1987/88.

Sources of income: During 1986, END relied mainly on donations – 61% (42% from USA, the remainder from UK and elsewhere); subscriptions and publications – 32%. No grants have been received from UK foundations since 1985.

Action research and campaigns

Aims and objectives: The END idea is neither a 'policy' nor an imposed 'line' for each peace organisation to follow but a common goal, for each individual and/or group to achieve in their own way. The END Appeal calls for peoples to act together to 'free the entire territory of Europe, from Poland to Portugal from nuclear weapons, air and submarine bases and from all institutions engaged in research into or manufacture of nuclear weapons. It asks the two superpowers to withdraw all nuclear weapons from European territory'.

Since 1980, END has grown significantly and there are active END groups within the churches, universities, trade unions, women's groups and in towns and regions. The London office helps to co-ordinate this activity.

END campaigns for a Europe free of nuclear weapons, East and West, works for a non-aligned Europe free from the domination of both superpowers, defends the right of all citizens, East and West, to work for peace and the free exchange of ideas, stresses that people-to-people detente is as important as confidence-building between governments, builds contacts throughout the world, promotes an internationalist perspective in Britain, supports unilateral and multilateral trust-building and disarmament measures, and calls for the creation of nuclear free zones throughout Europe.

END is both a campaigning organisation and information resource centre. It takes part in international demonstrations and events; organises conferences, dayschools and speakers tours; facilitates twinning of local peace groups and initiates letter writing campaigns. It co-ordinates many specialist working groups in particular, its five East European working groups on the Soviet Union, Czechoslovakia, Poland, Hungary and GDR.

Annual END Conventions are organised by an International Liaison Committee with a local preparatory committee in the host country. The 1987 Coventry Convention preparatory committee included END, CND, the Bertrand Russell Foundation, the Nuclear Free Zones Authorities and the Labour, Liberal, Green and Communist parties.

Affiliations: A major part of END's work is co-ordinatory and its working links are numerous. It is affiliated to CND, the National Peace Council, the International Peace Communication & Co-ordination Centre IPCC, Holland and various networks, such as the North Atlantic Network.

Journals and recent publications: *END-Journal*, bi-monthly; END Special Reports (14) (e.g. No. 14 '*Documents on the Peace Movement in Hungary*'); END Briefing Sheets (14); Books and Pamphlets (19) (e.g. No. 19 '*Mad Dogs: the US Raid on Libya*' Thompson, Kalder *et al.*).

INTERNATIONAL PEACE BUREAU

Rue de Zurich 41, CH-1201 Geneva, Switzerland (022-316 429).

Contact: Rainer Santi, Secretary General.

Status: Unincorporated association.

Origins: Founded in Rome in 1892; received the Nobel Peace Prize 1910.

Patrons: Bruce Kent (President); Sean MacBride (President Emeritus).

Membership: 38 organisations as full-members.

Staffing: 1 full time; 1 part time.

Income: Swiss francs 110,000 for 1986/87.

Sources of income: The Swedish Lottery Fund, via the Swedish Peace Council; membership fees and extra donations by member bodies.

Aims and objectives: The Bureau is a network of independent, non-aligned peace organisations, international, national and local. Full members are active peace organisations which decide its policy, action and elect its executive bodies. Associate members are those organisations which work for peace as one of their aims – labour unions, research institutions, churches, etc. The action programme for 1986/87 included monitoring of the official Arms Control Negotiations, a Telex information service on nuclear tests and port calls of nuclear-capable ships, international arms trade, legal resistance to nuclear weapons, co-ordination of actions against foreign military presence and bases, support for the right of conscientious objection, prevention of nuclear war and elimination of nuclear weapons, and a series of seminars on issues relevant to the peace movement.

An appeal to lawyers, throughout the world, to condemn nuclear weapons as illegal was launched by the Bureau in 1987. Eminent lawyers, including Sean McBride (Nobel Peace Prize), Alexandre Soukarev (President, Association of Soviet Lawyers) and Ramsey Clark (former Attorney General, USA) have signed the petition.

Affiliations: Consultative status with UN/ECOSOC.

Journals and recent publications:
'*Geneva Monitor – Disarmament*' bulletin; '*Geneva News*' monthly; '*The Right to Refuse to Kill*'; '*Children & War*'; '*Campaigns against Peace Movements*'.

NATIONAL PEACE COUNCIL

29 Great James Street, London WC1N 3ES (01-242 3228).

Contact: Al McLeod, Co-ordinator.

Action research and campaigns

Status: Unincorporated association.

Origins: Founded in 1908.

Main patrons: Rev Bishop Trevor Huddleston (President); Elnora Ferguson (Chairperson); Lucy Beck (Vice-Chairperson).

Membership: Some 180 national and local organisations and 80 individuals.

Staffing: 2 full time; 1 part time.

Income: £14,300 for 1985/86.

Sources of income: Over half the income is from affiliation fees and individual subscriptions, about a fifth comes from donations. (The Council's educational charity, the United World Education & Research Trust funds its information work). In 1987, the Council raised £22,000 from the Barrow Cadbury Fund Ltd to employ a second full-time worker for 3 years.

Aims and objectives: The National Peace Council is not a campaign. It encourages and facilitates the work of its member organisations by providing them with a range of information, a regular forum for discussion of issues of common concern, and links with organisations concerned with other issues (such as world development or human rights) and other constituencies (such as trade unions or churches). It is not directly aligned with any group political, social or religious but does support peace groups in Britain and abroad whose aims and policies coincide with its own.

Affiliations and joint projects: The Council is a member of the International Peace Bureau and the Non-governmental Organisations Special Committee on Disarmament based in Geneva. It sponsors the Campaign Against Arms Trade which has subsequently become a member of the Council, and also liaises particularly with Anti-Apartheid Movement, Human Rights Network, Freedom of Information Campaign, Disarmament & Development Network.

Journals and recent publications:
'Newsletter', 10 times a year; 'Peace Information Resources', 1987; Occasional papers (published by the United World Trust)
e.g. Merryfinch, Lesley 'What They Say, What They Do: The British Government & Military Exports'; Rogers, Paul & Crossley, Gordon 'Unilateral Action for Multilateral Disarmament'; Oakes, Sheila 'The Nuclear Freeze'.

NATIONAL TRADE UNION DEFENCE CONVERSION COMMITTEE

c/o 22–24 Underwood Street, London N1 7JG.

Contact: Jimmy Barnes, Secretary.

Aims and objectives: The Committee was formed in September 1984 to develop the debate around the future of the defence industry and the need to plan for defence conversion. It consists of representatives from a number of national trade unions including T&GWU, TASS, IPCS, UCATT, SPCS, GMBATU and ASTMS. Permanent observers at the Committee are the Centre for Alternative Industrial & Technological Systems, TUCND and the Greater London Conversion Council. Ron Todd was the founding chair of this Committee. The Committee organised the first national arms conversion conference, Manchester, March 1987.

Journals and recent publications:
'The Defence Converter' newsletter; 'Defence Jobs & Arms Conversion' Report of 1987 Manchester Conference.

NORTH ATLANTIC NETWORK WORKING GROUP

c/o Scottish CND, 420 Sauchiehall Street, Glasgow G2 3JD (041-331 2878).

Contacts: Vivien Kendon or Martin Meteyard.

Origins: Established in 1983.

Aims and objectives: The Network is a group of activists, from countries bordering the North Atlantic, who focus their campaigning on the arms race and increasing militarisation at sea. Representatives come from Britain, Ireland, Canada, the United States of America, Iceland, the Faroe Islands, Greenland, mainland Scandinavia and other relevant countries. Networking, amongst some 130 peace groups, is its main activity; an annual conference and other actions are also organised. The 1988 conference was held in Glasgow.

Affiliations: The Network links with Scottish CND and local groups in the rest of the UK, Indian, Pacific Ocean and Caribbean peace groups and peace groups in the member countries e.g. Mobilisation for Survival in the United States.

Journals and recent publications:
'Newsletter', published occasionally; 'Portswatch', bulletin published quarterly from Tromso, Norway.

PROFESSIONS FOR WORLD DISARMAMENT AND DEVELOPMENT

1 North End, London NW3 7HH (01-458 5316).

Contact: Hugh Gordon, Honorary Secretary.

Status: Independent group.

Action research and campaigns

Participating Organisations: Architects for Peace, Artists for Peace, British Association of Social Workers, Engineers for Nuclear Disarmament, Clergy Against Nuclear Arms, Electronics and Computing for Peace, Farmers for a Nuclear Free Future, Journalists Against Nuclear Extermination, Lawyers for Nuclear Disarmament, Medical Association for Prevention of War, Medical Campaign Against Nuclear Weapons, Members of Equity for Nuclear Disarmament, Musicians Against Nuclear Arms, Psychologists for Peace, Scientists Against Nuclear Arms, Teachers for Peace, Veterinary Nuclear Weapons – Information Group.

Staffing: None paid.

Income: £300 for 1986.

Sources of income: Supporting organisations.

Origins, aims and objectives: PWDD started in 1982 following a suggestion from Lord Fenner Brockway about the special role for professional people. Subsequently, the grouping has arranged conferences e.g. in December 1987 on 'Disarmament & Development'. Its aims are:

To further the cause of Disarmament and Development with emphasis on their relationship, by means of research, publications, conferences and in other appropriate ways.

To act as a reference, information and support group for participating organisations and to further co-operation between them.

WAR RESISTERS INTERNATIONAL

55 Dawes Street, London SE17 1EL (01-703 7189).

Status: Voluntary association.

Origins: Founded at an international conference in the Netherlands in 1921. Members make the declaration – 'War is a crime against humanity, I therefore am determined not to support any kind of war and to strive for the removal of all causes of war.'

Membership: 26 Sections in 19 countries; British sections are the Peace Pledge Union and Fellowship of Reconciliation (*see separate entries*).

Staffing: 3 full time.

Income: £50,000 for 1985/86.

Sources of income: Sale of badges, publications, etc; affiliation fees; individual donations. Supporting trusts include New York Friends Group, A. J. Muste Memorial Institute, Lansbury House Trust Fund, Asia Partnership for Human Development, Barrow Cadbury Fund, Joseph Rowntree Social Service Trust, Puckham Trust, Radley Trust, Noel Buxton Trust, Italian Peace Tax Campaign, Quaker Peace and Service.

Aims and objectives: WRI aims to support war resisters all over the world and to promote non-violent alternatives and non-violent action. It carries out networking, organising seminars, conferences, non-violent action, non-violence training, preparing briefings for co-ordinated international actions. It co-ordinates international working groups on the Middle East, South/Central America, Non-Violence Training and Non-violent Social Defence. It arranges European speaking tours and is the international communications point for war tax resisters.

Some examples of recent and future initiatives are:

An international women's gathering on 'Feminism and Non-violence' held in Ireland in 1987;

A peace treaty delegation with Wolnosc i Pokoj (Freedom and Peace in Poland) at Wroclaw in November 1987;

The WRI Triennial Conference on 'People's Power: to Change the World without Weapons' in Finland, 1988;

An international seminar on 'How to develop non-violent social defence from below' planned for Belgium, 1989;

The appointment of a South/Central American field-worker in 1989.

Affiliations: WRI has recognised status as a non-governmental organisation with UN (ECOSOC and UNESCO), is affiliated to the International Peace Bureau, a member of the END Convention Liaison Committee and a participant in GreenNet.

Journals and recent publications:
'*WRI Newsletter*', bi-monthly in English; '*The Broken Rifle*', bi-annual newsheet in English, French and German; '*WRI Women*' bi-annual in English; '*Prisoners for Peace Honour Roll*' every December in English, French and German; '*War Resister*', an annual review is planned for 1989.

ACTION RESEARCH AND CAMPAIGNS:
Church organisations and Religious groups

ANGLICAN PACIFIST FELLOWSHIP

St Mary's Vicarage, Bayswater Road, Headington, Oxford OX3 9EY (0865-61886).

Contact: Rev Sidney Hinkes, Hon Secretary.

Status: Recognised as a charity.

Origins: Founded in 1937.

Membership: 1,400.

Staffing: None paid.

Income: £16,000 for 1986/87.

Sources of income: Subscriptions and covenants.

Aims and objectives: All members of the Fellowship sign the following statement – 'We, communicant members of the Church of England, or of a church in full communion with it, believing that our membership of the Christian Church involves the complete repudiation of modern war, pledge ourselves to renounce war and all preparation to wage war, and to work for the construction of Christian peace in the world.' An annual Summer Conference and an annual retreat are organised. The Fellowship is represented on the END Churches Lateral Committee (*see separate entry*).

Journals and recent publications:
'*Challenge*', free membership journal, bi-monthly. Fifteen short pamphlets are also published (e.g. '*Let's Love Russia*', '*Pacifism and Politics*', '*Christianity is a Pacifist Faith*'). Also, Barrett, Rev Clive '*Peace Together, a Vision of Christian Pacifism*', James Clarke/Lutterworth, 1987 (published to celebrate the Fellowship's Jubilee year).

BAPTIST PEACE FELLOWSHIP

c/o 19 Kathdene Gardens, Ashley Down, Bristol BS7 9BN (0272-43416).

Contact: Mrs T. Parsons, Hon Secretary.

Status: Independent group.

Patrons: Tom Harrison, President.

Membership: 841 (300 of which belong also to FOR).

Staffing: None paid.

Income: £280 for 1986.

Sources of income: £100 from the Fellowship of Reconciliation and subscriptions.

Aims and objectives: New members sign the Fellowship of Reconciliation 'Basis' (*see separate entry*) and thus become members jointly of FOR and the Baptist Peace Fellowship. An annual conference is organised. Talks and discussions are held. Members share in local and national pacifist witness. Representatives sit on the general Committee of FOR, co-operate with the Standing Joint Conference of Pacifist Organisations, and take part in the International Affairs Group of the Department of Social Responsibility of the Baptist Union.

BRITISH COUNCIL OF CHURCHES

Division of International Affairs

Interchurch House, 35-41 Lower Marsh, London SE1 7RL (01-620 4444).

Contact: Michael Smart, Divisional Secretary.

Staffing: 6 full time (including its Forums).

Income: £72,150 for 1986.

Sources of income: BCC budget plus grants from churches and charitable trusts for work on Africa, peace and human rights.

Aims and objectives: The purpose of the Division is to help the British and Irish churches to bring a

Christian judgement to bear on international affairs. It seeks to achieve this aim by:
  Bringing together groups of Christians and people in sympathy with the churches who have knowledge or experience relevant to particular international problems;
  Preparing suitable information or study material for use by churches;
  Lobbying Government and Parliament on matters which the churches wish to bring to their attention.

The Board of the DIA, working closely with the Boards of Christian Aid and of the Conference for World Mission, is backed by advisers including Roman Catholics working in international relations in the Justice and Peace Commission and the Catholic Institute for International Relations. Expert committees advise the Board on:
  East/West Relations;
  Southern Africa;
  The Middle East.

Asian questions are largely handled through the Conference for World Mission and a member of its staff, and Latin America questions with the aid of CIIR and a member of its staff.

The Division also services and works closely with the Peace Forum (*see separate entry*) and the Human Rights Advisory Committee appointed by the BCC.

BRITISH COUNCIL OF CHURCHES 'PEACE FORUM'

Interchurch House, 35–41 Lower Marsh, London SE1 7RL (01-620 4444).

Contact: Suzanne Long, Executive Secretary.

Status: Charitable, as a project of the British Council of Churches.

Membership: 25.

Staffing: 2 part time.

Annual income: Not known.

Sources of income: The Churches especially Free Church Federal Council, Church of Scotland, United Reformed Church, Quaker & Peace Service, Methodist Division of Social Responsibility. Trusts which have contributed in recent years are the Rowan Charitable Trust, the Westcroft Trust, the Barrow & Geraldine Cadbury Trust and the Joseph Rowntree Charitable Trust.

Aims and objectives: The Forum was set up, in 1984, following a resolution of the British Council of Churches Assembly, as a place of dialogue and mutual education in which all the viewpoints of those

Action research and campaigns

committed to peacemaking could be represented within a Christian framework. It consists of representatives of member churches and associated bodies of the BCC and representatives of Christian groups concerned with peace and disarmament. Specific topics such as SDI and the nuclear winter have been discussed in depth with the help of technical experts, and reports issued. In future, the forum intends to give more emphasis to educational work within the Churches on the issue of peace.

Journals and recent publications:
Leaflets include: *'The Nuclear Freeze'*, a study pack for churches; *'On Making Peace in a Nuclear World'* – BCC Assembly resolution; *'The SDI and the Churches'*; BCC Peace Forum reading list on peace and defence issues.

BUDDHIST PEACE FELLOWSHIP

16 Upper Park Road, London NW3 2UP (01-586 7641).

Contact: Aleda Erskine, Secretary.

Status: Unincorporated association.

Origins: Started in 1983.

Membership: 250.

Staffing: None paid.

Income: £800 for 1986.

Sources of income: The Fellowship is funded entirely by membership subscriptions.

Aims and objectives: The Fellowship is a network 'to reduce all suffering caused by all violence, including our own, and to bring a Buddhist perspective to peacemaking'. Quarterly retreats are arranged and a regional and national network of local groups and contacts are being fostered. It is represented on the Religious Advisory Committee of the United Nations Association.

Journals and recent publications:
Quarterly membership newsletter; fourteen Peace Fellowship books are available (e.g. Jones, Ken *'Buddhism and the Bomb'*, Macy, Joanna *'Dharma and Development'*).

CATHOLIC BISHOPS' CONFERENCE OF ENGLAND AND WALES

Department of International Affairs (Committee for International Justice and Peace, Committee on Nuclear Issues)

39 Eccleston Square, London SW1V 1PD (01-834 5138).

Action research and campaigns

A new structure was created at the 1984 Bishops' Conference with a Department for International Affairs incorporating the following separate committees for International Justice and Peace, Nuclear Issues, Migrants & European workers. The Department is financed by the National Catholic Fund.

Committee for International Justice and Peace.

Contact: Rev Robert Beresford, Secretary.

Aims and objectives: The Committee has an episcopal Chairman (Bishop James O'Brien) and about 12 members. It appoints working parties on particular topics, arranges conferences and seminars; prepares reports for the Bishops' Conference which in appropriate cases are recommended for publication. It has close links with diocesan justice and peace groups, and with Commissions formed by national hierarchies in Europe and elsewhere, as well as with the Pontifical Commission. It co-operates with Catholic bodies whose fields of interest overlap with its own, and with ecumenical and other bodies. The Office is responsible for the organisation of Peace Sunday in January or February each year and deals with individual enquiries and requests for literature.

The Committee on Nuclear Issues with some 15 members is also chaired by Bishop James O'Brien and serviced by Rev Robert Beresford.

CATHOLIC PEACE ACTION

c/o 7 Putney Bridge Road, London SW18 1HX.

Contact: Dan Martin.

Status: Voluntary group.

Origins: Started in 1982.

Sources of income: Donations.

Aims and objectives: Catholic Peace Action is an affinity group (not a membership organisation) which witnesses against the nuclear threat by engaging in periodic acts of non-violent civil disobedience outside the Ministry of Defence. Since 1983 the group has also been conducting a dialogue with workers at the Ministry through the distribution of leaflets twice monthly. The group has some 150 supporters who assist with their funds, prayers and with other forms of support.

Journals and recent publications:

Occasional newsletter; videos, *'Blessed are the Peace Makers?'* 26 minutes and *'Repentance and Resistance'* 36 minutes.

CLERGY AGAINST NUCLEAR ARMS

38 Main Road, Norton, Evesham, Worcestershire WR11 4TL (0386-870 918).

Contact: Reverend John MacDonald Smith, Hon Secretary.

Status: Unincorporated association.

Origins: Set up in 1982.

Sponsors: The Reverends John Austin Baker; Donald Black; Ronald Bowlby; Dr Kenneth Greet; Victor Guazzelli; John Johansen-Berg; Andrew Morton; The Lord Soper.

Membership: 550 clergy and ministers of all denominations.

Staffing: None paid.

Income: £3,000 for 1986.

Sources of income: Support received from the Joseph Rowntree Charitable Trust in 1987 and from the Barrow and Geraldine S. Cadbury Trust for an Annual Lecture.

Aims and objectives: CANA, an ecumenical organisation, aims to give support to all clergy seeking practical ways of making peace. It has produced a statement for signing by members of the ministry, it also solicits subscriptions by means of the statement which 'urges Her Majesty's Government to conform its nuclear weapons policy to the principles of true deterrence, as an interim measure, leading to the adoption of a non-nuclear defence policy'. It arranges about 3 or 4 national events each year, such as public lectures and conferences. Its 30 or so area contacts set up local meetings.

Affiliations and projects with other bodies: CANA has links with the Ash Wednesday Protest with Catholic Peace Action, the Fellowship of Reconciliation, Pax Christi and Christian CND.

Journals and recent publications:

'Koinonca' newsletter produced 3 or 4 times a year; CANA Occasional Papers No. 1; Williams, Professor Rowan *'Star Wars, Safeguard or Threat?'*

COUNCIL ON CHRISTIAN APPROACHES TO DEFENCE AND DISARMAMENT (British Group)

33 Southampton Street, London WC2E 7HQ (01-836 3809).

Contact: Anne-Marie Sutcliffe, Administrative Secretary.

Status: Registered charity and company limited by guarantee.

Action research and campaigns

Origins: Established in 1963 by the Rt Rev Robert Stopford, then Bishop of London, to study problems relating to defence and disarmament within a Christian context.

Distinguished patrons: The Archbishop of York (President); Professor Sir Michael Howard; Rev Arthur MacArthur; Sydney Bailey; John Jukes (Vice-Presidents).

Membership: 101 (by invitation).

Staffing: 1 part time.

Income: £10,000 for 1986/87.

Sources of income: Around 15% of income is from the churches themselves. Joseph Rowntree Charitable Trust; Wates Foundation; Ford Foundation (for specific project).

Aims and objectives: The British group is made up of Christians from different traditions. Since 1963, autonomous groups have been set up also in the USA, Federal Republic of Germany, France, the Netherlands, Norway, Belgium, Finland and Sweden. The main activities of the group are discussion meetings, one major open meeting each autumn, a publications programme and an international conference hosted in turn by the different national groups.

The Division of International Affairs of the British Council of Churches has asked the British Group to advise it on matters relating to defence and disarmament.

Recent publications:
Paskins, B. (ed.) *'Ethics & European Security'* Croom Helm, 1986; Hockaday, Arthur *'The Strategic Defence Initiative, New Hope or New Peril?'* CCADD pamphlet, 1987.

DIOCESAN BOARDS OR COUNCILS OF SOCIAL RESPONSIBILITY

In the last ten years almost all the 43 dioceses of the Church of England have established Boards or Councils for Social Responsibility. Almost all have appointed workers whose task it is to help people in local churches become more aware of what is happening in Britain and the world, and to think out the social implications of being a Christian today. The Directory *'Social Responsibility: A Directory of Resources in the Church of England'* is a quick reference guide to some of the work in this field including details of social work, community work and residential work, as well as information on the main issues which dioceses have chosen to make a priority. The range is wide; the directory covers work organised or managed by boards for social responsibility. There are many other schemes and projects run by church groups or with strong church involvement. The information is organised by dioceses.

Diocesan Social Responsibility Officers have indicated the following interests as priorities in their areas (inevitably this information is not up-to-date and some changes will have occurred).

Arms trade – Portsmouth.

Conciliation – Chichester, Exeter.

Development (World Development) – Bradford, Canterbury and Rochester, Chester, Gloucester, Guildford, London, Portsmouth, Salisbury, Wakefield, Winchester, General Synod BSR.

International Affairs – Chelmsford, General Synod BSR.

Nuclear Issues – Carlisle, Chelmsford, Exeter, Liverpool, General Synod BSR.

Peace Convoy – Winchester.

Peace Issues – Bradford, Exeter, Lincoln, Portsmouth, Salisbury, Sheffield, Winchester, Worcester, York, General Synod BSR.

Contact: *'Social Responsibility: A Directory of Resources in the Church of England'* can be obtained from: Alison Webster, Board of Social Responsibility, Church House, Great Smith Street, London SW1P 3NZ (01-222 9011).

END CHURCHES LATERAL COMMITTEE

4 The Square, Clun, Shropshire, SY7 8JA (05884-398).

Contact: Stephen Tunnicliffe, Co-ordinator.

Status: Independent group.

Staffing: None paid.

Income: £3,000 for 1986/87.

Sources of income: *'Register'* subscriptions and sales; appeals.

Aims and objectives: The Committee set up in 1981, has some 15 members including representatives from the following organisations: Anglican Pacifist Fellowship, Christian CND, Christian Peace Conference, Clergy Against Nuclear Arms, Coventry Cathedral, Fellowship of Reconciliation, International Fellowship of Reconciliation, Pax Christi, Unitarians with representatives also from Action Reconciliation, West Berlin and the British Council of Churches, Division of International Affairs. It aims to bring together church members and other Christians in Europe, the USA and beyond, who share a common concern about nuclear weapons and the arms race and who wish to promote nuclear disarmament as a first

Action research and campaigns

step to a more peaceful and more Christian world. The Committee has no defined corporate policy beyond this. In late 1987, the Committee organised a second international seminar in Budapest on the theme 'Towards a Theology of Peace'.

Journals and recent publications:
The '*Register*' started in 1982 and published quarterly, is currently in abeyance for lack of funds.

FELLOWSHIP OF RECONCILIATION

40–46 Harleyford Road, Vauxhall, London SE11 5AY (01-582 9054).

Contacts: Doreen Hudson-Tobin, National Co-ordinator; Ginnie Dengel, Administrator.

Status: Registered charity.

Origins: The Fellowship is an ecumenical Christian pacifist network which started in 1914 on the initiative of a German Lutheran and a British Quaker, Friedrich Siegmund-Schultze and Henry Hodgkin, who parted with the words 'We are one in Christ and can never be at war'.

Patron: Lord Soper, President.

Membership: 3,000+.

Staffing: 5 full time; 2 part time.

Approximate annual income: £51,000 for 1986.

Sources of income: The Fellowship is financed entirely by its members. There is no fixed subscription.

Aims and objectives: Members of the Fellowship agree with a five-point statement, the Basis, formulated at a conference in Cambridge in late 1914.

FOR is committed to non-violence as a way of life and social change – active peacemaking rather than a passive response to violence. Its Basis enables it to campaign on a range of issues. Because of its philosophy its witness concentrates on the themes of reconciliation, non-violent communication, Christian pacifism, social justice, disarmament and international peace. It suffers from an ageing membership and various projects aim to redress this imbalance such as a joint youth education project with Pax Christi, a FOR/Methodist Association of Youth Clubs travelling peace workshop and summer play schemes run in Lurgan since 1973 and the Tiger Bay/New Lodge areas of Belfast since 1986. Independent national Fellowships exist in Scotland, Wales and Ireland (see addresses below). All four national bodies are co-ordinated through a general committee serviced by the London Central Office staff. An embryonic regional structure exists in England – London, Southern, South West, East Anglia, Yorkshire and Humberside, Leicestershire/Nottinghamshire/Derbyshire. FOR members meet in local groups – some 'pure' FOR, others jointly with Peace Pledge Union, or via a local Peace Council. At a national level, FOR co-operates with other peace movements in general through the Standing Joint Pacifist Committee and the National Peace Council, and in particular with the Anglican Pacifist Fellowship, Pax Christi and others. The Methodist Peace Fellowship maintains a separate identity for work within the Methodist Church but is incorporated into FOR by means of a common membership. The Baptist Peace Fellowship and the Unitarian Peace Fellowship are affiliated to FOR.

FOR is one of the sponsoring organisations of the Campaign Against Arms Trade.

Journals and recent publications:
'*Reconciliation Quarterly*'; '*Peace Links*', bi-monthly membership magazine started mid-1987; '*Dialogue and Resistance*', three times a year, a journal of non-violence for religious peace activists; '*Fellowship Briefings*', (14 by mid-1987) summaries of current thinking on various issues (e.g. No. 14. Barritt, Denis '*Northern Ireland: the Background to the Anglo-Irish Agreement*') available as a Briefing Pack.

The Fellowship publishes some 24 other short booklets and pamphlets, including '*We'd Rather Freeze Now Than Later*' on the nuclear freeze proposals, co-sponsored by FOR with other peace and development groups, and '*Agenda for the UK*', an international programme for Parliament dealing with disarmament, development, the UN's security role, confidence building and human rights.

A list of youth peace resources has been compiled.

A full publications list is available, including details of videos, audio tapes, badges etc.

Fellowship of Reconciliation (Ireland)
24 Pinehill Road, Ballycairn, County Antrim (0231-26 341). **Contact:** Denis Barritt, Chairperson.

Fellowship of Reconciliation (Scotland)
10 Thomson Road, Currie, Midlothian EH4 5HP (031-449 3659). **Contact:** Alan Wilkie, Hon Secretary.

Fellowship of Reconciliation (Wales)
2 Oak Mews, Heol-y-Dderwan, Llangollen, Clwyd LL20 8RP (0978-860 835). **Contact:** Nia Rhosier, General Secretary.

LONDON MENNONITE CENTRE

14 Shepherd's Hill, London N6 5AQ (01-340 8775).

Contact: Alan Kreider, Director.

Status: Registered charity.

Staffing: 4 full time; 1 part time.

Income: £21,000 year 1986.

Aims and objectives: The Mennonites, descendants of the Anabaptist Movement, are one of the historic pacifist churches, known for their mission and development work. The London Centre opened, in 1951, as an international hostel and student ministry but since 1981 has operated with a different emphasis as a library, resource and meeting place. The library stocks some 3,500 books, plus tape cassettes and periodicals.

A Church, the London Mennonite Fellowship, exists alongside the Centre. The Centre runs 'Metanoia', (named from the Greek for 'repentance'), a book service of some 400 titles mainly stocked from Herald Press, the North American Mennonite publisher. The centre is the sole distributor in the UK. Some 50 titles are on peace-making, and war and peace studies.

METHODIST PEACE FELLOWSHIP

c/o Fellowship of Reconciliation, 40–46 Harleyford Road, London SE11 5AY (01-582 9180).

Contact: Rev Rex Hallam, Hon Secretary, 16 Paddocks Close, Wellington, Telford, Shropshire TF1 3ND (0952-42133).

Status: Registered charity.

Patrons: Lord Soper (President); Kenneth Greet (Chairperson).

Membership: 800.

Staffing: None paid.

Income: £11,000 for 1987/88.

Sources of income: Subscriptions and a grant from Fellowship of Reconciliation.

Aims and objectives: The Fellowship is comprised of Methodists who accept the Basis of the Fellowship of Reconciliation (*see separate entry*) and its pacifist witness.

Publications: Chairperson's Biannual Newsletter.

NORTHERN FRIENDS PEACE BOARD

1 The Grange, Hall Lane, Horsforth, Leeds LS18 5EH (0532-585 631).

Contact: Marion McNaughton, Co-ordinator.

Status: Charitable, as part of the Religious Society of Friends.

Origins: Founded in 1913.

Action research and campaigns

Staffing: 1 full time.

Sources of income: Financed by Northern Quaker Monthly Meetings and private donations. Income scale not disclosed.

Aims and objectives: The Board was established to work among Friends (Quakers) in the northern half of Great Britain on issues of justice and peace. In the past it has also played a prominent part in work for the right of conscientious objection to war service, understanding issues in Northern Ireland, and the promotion of peaceful East-West relations. Its current work is based among Friends, and aims to raise awareness and understanding of all aspects of peace, and to strengthen the traditional Quaker opposition to war and militarism. It provides seminars, workshops, speakers and occasional publications.

The Board works closely with Quaker Peace and Science.

Recent publication: Leavitt, M. L., '*Star Wars – The Spiritual Challenge*' (booklet).

PAX CHRISTI (British Section)

St Francis of Assisi Centre, Pottery Lane, London W11 4NQ (01-727 4609).

Contact: Michael Winter, Office Administrator.

Status: A part of the Roman Catholic Church; the National President is appointed by the English bishop.

Origins: Pax Christi International began in 1946; The British Section started in 1970 and in 1971 merged with Pax.

Honorary Officers: Cardinal Franz Koenig (International President); Bishop Victor Guazzelli (National President); Valerie Flessati; Fr Gerry Hughes; Owen Hardwicke; Bruce Kent; Fr Oliver McTernan (Vice-Presidents).

Membership: 2,200 plus some 20 local groups.

Staffing: 2 full time; 2 part time.

Income: £75,175 for 1986.

Sources of income: Subscriptions; sales of literature; Peace Sunday and Chairman's appeals; income from London hostels; National Catholic Fund.

Aims and objectives: Pax Christi is an international Catholic peace movement with its main secretariat in Antwerp. It helps Christians to understand that faithfulness to either of the twin traditions of non-violence and a 'just war' also demands that they work for an end to nuclear deterrence policies. Its London based East-West Group arranges visits and assists British-Soviet understanding; the Human Rights Co-ordinating Group runs a Prisoner of Conscience scheme

Action research and campaigns

and supports the work of other human rights organisations particularly Amnesty International and Action of Christians Against Torture; the Disarmament Consultative Group in 1986 prepared and promoted 'Disarmament: A Window of Opportunity' a broad statement to attract support from Bishops and leading Catholic figures; the British Irish Group publishes leaflets, organises study days and visits. In 1986, 60 volunteers were trained to run five 3-week playschemes in Northern Ireland attracting several hundreds of 5–15 year olds. Peace Education in schools is a continuous part of Pax Christi's work. Contact has been made with some 300 Catholic schools in London and a teachers' in-service course was organised at the London University Institute of Education in 1987.

Affiliations: Pax Christi has recognised non-governmental organisation status with the United Nations and is a founder/sponsor of Campaign Against Arms Trade.

Journals and recent publications:
'*Justpeace*', membership newsletter, 8 times a year; '*Peace notes*', a termly magazine for young people. Pax Christi also publishes church statements and a range of publications and leaflets covering disarmament, arms race and non-violence; Northern Ireland; South Africa; human rights. It also produces posters, cards and badges. A full publications list is available.

PRAYER FOR PEACE

70 Weymouth Road, Frome, Somerset BA11 1HJ (0373-71317).

Contact: John Careswell, Secretary.

Status: Unincorporated association.

Origins: To support the build up of public interest in and awareness of the United Nations Special Session on Disarmament, July 1982, with a particular emphasis on spiritual support.

Patrons: Bishop George Appleton; Satish Kumar.

Staffing: 2 part time.

Sources of income: Voluntary contributions; sales of cards, posters, stickers etc. Entirely self supporting with no income from trusts or agencies.

Aims and objectives: The Prayer for Peace is international, interfaith and non-sectarian. It is not a membership organisation. People everywhere are invited to offer a simple prayer (the 4-verse Prayer for Peace) at noon local time everyday – thus forming an hour-by-hour chain of prayer around the world and emphasising the personal and spiritual basis of peace.

The Prayer is publicised by the distribution and sale of cards, posters, stickers, etc., and a twice-yearly newsletter.

QUAKER PEACE AND SERVICE

Friends House, Euston Road, London NW1 2BJ (01-387 3601).

Contact: Andrew C. Clark, General Secretary.

Status: Registered charity.

Staffing: Some 80 in all; 36 in London, of which 33 are full time and 3 are part time.

Income: £1,229,000 in 1986.

Sources of income: In 1986, grants for project work overseas were made by the following aid agencies: ODA; Irish Foreign Ministry; Swedish Foreign Ministry; Christian Aid; Oxfam; World Council of Churches; Trocaire; Kinderspotzegels; ICCO; Federal German Republic; EZE; Netherlands; Dutch Inter-Church Aid.

30% of income comes from non-Quaker sources.

Aims and objectives: Quaker Peace and Service is the department of the Religious Society of Friends in Britain and Ireland concerned with international understanding, world development, human rights, peace work and witness. This derives from religious conviction first publicly expressed in a declaration presented to Charles II in 1660 – the Peace Testimony written by George Fox. This denies 'all outward wars and strife, and fightings with outward weapons, for any end, or under any pretence whatever'. Its activity spreads in a network of some 40 diverse projects in a score of countries as well as Britain and Northern Ireland. All the projects support local self-development. In London, the work of QPS is organised into sections each with an advisory committee. These sections usefully indicate its fields of operation. They are Africa; Asia; Middle-East; Latin-America; Europe; East-West; Peace; United Nations; Sharing world Resources (which disburses grants from the 1% Fund (*see separate entry*); Study-Travel Bursary (*see separate entry*). entry).

It is worth quoting from the 1986 Quaker Peace and Service Report, and specifically from its section on peace work in Britain, since it illustrates the nature of this work, although by 1988 new emphases are bound to have developed.

'Giving help in local activities and spreading the skills involved in peacemaking were a major focus in 1986. Five Networkers appointed in October have begun to find Friends in their areas whose skills in mediation,

Action research and campaigns

counselling, facilitation and nonviolence training can be made available to Quakers and those who turn to Friends for help.

'Support for peaceworkers in Hertfordshire, Scotland and Newbury, Berkshire, continued. In Newbury a resident Friend at the Meeting House works to overcome the divisions between the Greenham peace campers and the townsfolk. A grant was also given to the Reading Mediation Centre, a concern of Friends, for a coordinator.

'Peace Section staff were involved in a 'Women and Peace' course, and in running workshops on such subjects as strategic thinking for peacemakers, nonviolence in action, taking sides in peace and justice, overcoming barriers in local peace campaigning and the Quaker Peace Testimony. They have assisted the development of the national network of Quaker facilitators, and established a group to consider issues of security and defence and how to go beyond protest to positive policy recommendations.'

An Education Advisory Programme offers advice on resources and methodology, one day and half day in-service courses and visits to schools across the broad range of interconnecting issues covered by Quaker Peace and Service.

Affiliations: Quaker Peace and Service is affiliated to or works jointly with a range of organisations including the United Nations Association, the Campaign Against Arms Trade (CAAT), Amnesty International, Action by Christians Against Torture (ACAT), Campaign for Nuclear Disarmament, World Disarmament Campaign and the National Peace Council.

Journals and recent publications:

'QPS Reporter', quarterly with supplementary Action Resource Sheets inserted.

A wide range of some 40 booklets includes: Merritt, Sandy 'Speaking our Peace: Exploring Non-violence and Conflict Resolution', 1987; Tod, Ruth and Saunders, Pat 'Poverty & Peace: Reviewing the Development Debate'.

QPS has a variety of resources available to Friends and others to help them in their local peace and service work. They may be borrowed from Home Organisation Section, or the Section concerned, at Friends House, Euston Road, London NW1 2BJ. Normally no charge is made for the loan of these materials, but borrowers are expected to meet postal or delivery charges, and may feel able to make a donation to QPS funds.

These resources include exhibitions, a range of slide-tape shows on disarmament and development, videos, a peace education library, a 16 mm cine projector. A wide range of items are available for sale: badges, balloons, stickers, carrier bags, ties, dusters, tea towels, T-shirts, postcards. In addition some 40 different posters are published.

Order forms are available for all items.

WEEK OF PRAYER FOR WORLD PEACE

Wickham House, 10 Cleveland Way, Mile End Road, London E1 4TR (01-790 2424).

Contact: Canon Gordon Wilson, Secretary.

Status: Independent group.

Origins: Started in 1974.

Officers: Rev Dr Edward Carpenter, former Dean of Westminster (Chairman); Ronald Gandy (Treasurer).

Staffing: 2 part time.

Income: £12,826 for 1986.

Sources of income: The main income is from the sale of leaflets although $6,000 was given by Rissho Kosei Kai, the Japanese lay Buddhist group in 1986. Some support has been received in the past from certain Quaker trusts.

Aims and objectives: The Week of Prayer for World Peace is an independent interdenominational and interfaith initiative. It runs from Sunday to Sunday in the week in which United Nations Day (October 24th) falls (i.e. 23rd–30th October in 1988).

Prayer leaflets are distributed throughout the country. The week has no individual membership as such. Its mailing list comprises some 3,000 local groups, churches and individuals. Whilst the week has some overseas contacts they are now being helped to develop worldwide to every religion with support from Rissho Kosei-Kai. The British Council of Churches will undertake administrative support with the UK mailings starting from the 1988 week.

ACTION RESEARCH AND CAMPAIGNS:
Tracking/Direct action groups

CRUISEWATCH

PO Box 28, Newbury, Berks.

Cruisewatch is an informal network of peace activists in the South of England which has tracked, monitored, and publicised each of the deployment exercises from Greenham Common since March 1984. They assert they have given the lie to Heseltine's boast 'that Cruise would melt into the countryside'. Through non-violent direct action, Cruisewatchers have stopped the convoys on several occasions. It has received funds from CND but is otherwise autonomous.

CRUISE RESISTANCE NETWORK

c/o CND Office, 13 Paton Street, Manchester M1 2BA.

Cruise Resistance is an informal network of CND members, Greenham Common women, Cruisewatchers and other peace campaigners throughout the UK with many contacts in Europe and the USA. It meets quarterly always in different towns and each host group takes responsibility for producing the next *Cruise Resistance Bulletin* (address for the bulletin and contributions above).

The Network relies entirely on donations and subscriptions.

NUKEWATCH

c/o CND, 22–24 Underwood Street, London N1 7JG (01-250 4010).

Contact: Janet Convery.

CND set up Nukewatch as a national tracking network in November 1985. It has some 26 national co-ordinators, and has grown from the activities started around 1982 such as those by Faslane and Burghfield Peace Campers who continue with Nukewatch to track warhead convoys between Coulport, near Glasgow and Burghfield, near Reading. Polariswatch maintains its name and separate existence in Scotland, but is otherwise absorbed into the larger Nukewatch network.

Publication: *A briefing sheet.*

SNOWBALL

48 Bethel Street, Norwich, Norfolk NR2 1NR (0603-631 007).

Contacts: Tigger and Annie Zelter.

Aims and objectives: Snowball started in October 1984 at Sculthorpe base and has since spread to over 30 bases involving over 2,200 people. It aims by non-violent means to persuade the government to undertake at least one disarmament measure:

1. That Britain starts voting in the United Nations in favour of multilateral disarmament and supports the Comprehensive Test Ban Treaty or,

2. That Britain publicly encourages Nuclear Freeze proposals or

3. That Britain takes some unilateral step towards on Freeze or reduction, by abandoning Trident or returning Cruise, or publicly rejecting the forthcoming USA chemical weapons storage proposal.

The methods used to achieve this are a 'snowball' of letters, and a 'snowball' of people prepared to cut the perimeter fence at a 'snowball base', that is a site with any military link including nuclear power stations. The actions are synchronized to take place on the same day throughout the country with each snowballer writing a statement and insisting, where possible, on arrest thus gaining publicity. Over 200 people have been imprisoned.

Publications: Briefing document; '*Snowball, Statements and History of the Campaign*'; '*Holloway for Beginners*', 1987 (pamphlet).

ACTION RESEARCH AND CAMPAIGNS:
Peace camps

BULL POINT PEACE BUS/PEACE CAMP

c/o 41 Ingra Walk, Belliver, Plymouth, Devon PL6 7DS (0752-783 513).

Contact: Shirley.

Aims and objectives: The Peace Bus evolved from the Peace Camp which was set up outside the Royal Naval Armament Depot, Bull Point in January 1987. The camp only survived for nine days due to frequent evictions but the campers decided to take to the road, hence the Peace Bus.

The Peace Bus acts as a mobile information centre on nuclear issues working with peace groups around Plymouth and the West Country. In August 1987 a four day peace camp set up outside RNAD Ernesettel, Plymouth to commemorate Hiroshima and Nagasaki. Other peace camps have been held over long weekends in October and November 1987 and January 1988.

FASLANE PEACE CAMP

Below St Andrew's School, Shandon, Near Helensburgh, Dunbartonshire (0436-820 901).

The camp was set up in June 1982. There is a constant presence at the camp with larger demonstrations, festivals etc. As the camp land is owned by Strathclyde Regional Council, the campers have not faced endless evictions. A phone tree and legal support group have been established.

GREENHAM COMMON WOMEN'S PEACE CAMP

Outside USAF Greenham Common, Newbury, Berks.

The camp was set up in September 1981. December 1982 saw the massive 'Embrace the Base/Close the Base' demonstration which attracted 35,000 women. This event is repeated annually in December. Other special events celebrated are Dora Russell's birthday, 3rd April, Hiroshima and Nagasaki days, 6th and 9th August and 'Time off for Women', 24th-25th October. Local support groups exist throughout the country.

MENWITH HILL PEACE CAMP

Outside US Spy Base, Menwith-With-Darley, Near Harrogate, North Yorks.

The peace camp was set up to protest against the US National Security Agency's communications spy base.

MOLESWORTH PEACE CAMP

Peace Corner, Outside USAF Molesworth, Brington, Huntingdon, Cambs PE17 5SE.

The peace camp was set up in December 1981. The campers were evicted in February 1985. The base continues to be a focal point for demonstrations and tracking of missiles.

Contact: Molesworth Cruisewatch, PO Box 35, Cambridge CB1 2NX.

UPPER HEYFORD PEACE CAMP

Portway, Camp Road, Upper Heyford, Oxon OX5 3LP.

Contact: Steve Chasey (0869-40321).

The camp was established over the Easter weekend in 1982. Planes from the base were involved in the US raid on Libya in April 1986 and a vigil was held in April 1987 to mark the first anniversary. Numbers at the base have fluctuated dramatically, at the moment Quakers predominate but this is a recent development and all are welcome.

ACTION RESEARCH AND CAMPAIGNS:
Local peace councils and peace centres

The range of activities of these groups varies. Most have a co-ordinating function for local peace campaigns. This list cannot claim to be comprehensive but covers those groups believed to be active in early 1988.

Aberdeen Association of Peace Groups
Aberdeen Peace Centre, 334 George Street, Aberdeen AB1 1HJ, (0224-64883).

Brighton Peace Centre
28 Trafalgar Street, Brighton BN1 4ED, (0273-692 880).

Contacts: Duncan Blinkhorn, Mabel Platt.

Affiliated to National Peace Council. Shop, library and meeting room, a 'campaign' office is also planned.

Cleveland Peace Campaign
72 The Avenue, Linthorpe, Middlesborough, (0642-824 194).

Contact: Pat McEndoo.

Affiliated to the National Peace Council.

Cumbrians for Peace
13 Solway View, Sunny Hill, Whitehaven, Cumbria CA28 7HL.

Contact: Cath Smith.

A newsletter is published.

Derbyshire Federation of Peace Groups
c/o County Offices, Matlock, Derbyshire (0773-835 433).

Contact: Sue Groom.

Affiliated to National Peace Council. Sponsored by Derbyshire County Council.

Publishes: '*World Friendship Day*', A Celebration of Events in 1986 (booklet/20 min. video).

Dorset Peace Council
The Square, Broadwindsor, Beaminster, Dorset DT8 3QD (0308-68966).

Contact: Charles Radcliffe.

Affiliated to the National Peace Council. One full-time paid worker. Newsletter; *Peace 1986* (magazine).

Durham Peace Action
2 Diamond Terrace, Sidegate, Durham (0385-62595).

Affiliated to the National Peace Council. Peace Action Durham News, 8 yearly.

Edinburgh Peace and Justice Resource Centre
St John's Church, Princes Street, Edinburgh EH2 4BJ (031-229 0993).

A newsletter is published.

Finchley Centre for Peace and Non Violence
Quaker Meeting House, 58 Alexandra Grove, London N12 8HG (01-445 6212).

Glasgow 'Centrepeace' Peace Centre
143 Stockwell Street, Glasgow G1, (041-552 8357).

Newsletter and shop.

Halifax Nuclear Disarmament Group
17 Bankhouse Lane, Salter Hebble, Halifax, West Yorks (0422-50006).

Action research and campaigns

All Kent Alliance for Peace
33 Lansdown Road, Sittingbourne, Kent ME10 3AY.
A newsletter is published.

Manchester Peace Council
199 Dane Road, Sale, Cheshire M33 2NA (061-973 2606).
Contact: Mary Mander.
Affiliated to the National Peace Council.

Milton Keynes Peace and Justice Centre
4 Church Street, Wolverton, Milton Keynes MK12 5JN (0988-3128430).

Norwich and District Peace Council
89 Rosary Road, Norwich.
Contact: Heather Edwards.
Affiliated to National Peace Council. Monthly Calendar.

Nottingham Rainbow Centre
180 Mansfield Road, Nottingham (0602-585 666).
Newsletter. Rainbow Databases.

Scottish Justice and Peace Commission
28 Rose Street, Glasgow G3 6RE (041-333 0238).

Selly Oak Peace Council
35 Tillyard Croft, Birmingham B29 5AH (021-472 4540).
Contact: Michael Jones.

South East Hants Peace Council
37 Wilson Road, Stamshaw, Portsmouth PO2 8LE (0705-699 006).
Contact: Chris Lowndes.
Affiliated to the National Peace Council. Newsletter.

South East Peace Newsletter
12 The Pasture, Kennington, Ashford, Kent TN24 9NG (0233-629 975).

South Glamorgan Peace Forum
c/o Peace Shop, 56 Mackintosh Place, Roath, Cardiff CF2 4RQ (0222-489 9260).
Contact: Robert Jones.

Stafford Peace Action
Friends Meeting House, Foregate Street, Stafford ST16 2PX (0785-40282).
Contact: Janet Woodworth.

Surrey Peace Action Network
Maybury Lodge, 83 Reigate Road, Surrey RH2 0RE (0737-71007).

Sussex Alliance for Nuclear Disarmament
187 Eastern Road, Brighton BN2 5BB.
Contact: Eileen Daffern.

Tadcaster Peace Centre
Inholmes, Tadcaster, North Yorkshire LS24 9LP (0937-833 752).

West London Peace Council
4 Coombe Road, London W4 (01-994 6388).
Contact: Peggy Heath.

West Yorkshire Peace Centre
9 Market Buildings, Vicar Lane, Leeds LS2 7JF (0532-451421).

West Yorkshire Peace Newsletter
2 Lascelles Road, Leeds LS8.
Affiliated to the National Peace Council. Newsletter is published bi-monthly.

York Peace Centre
15a Clifford Street, York YO1 1RG (0904-642 493).
Affiliated to National Peace Council. Newsletter/Diary.

ACTION RESEARCH AND CAMPAIGNS:
Service organisations

AT EASE

c/o 1 Secker Street, London SE1 8UF (*Address for mail*).

Contact: Liz Urben.

Membership: 32.

Staffing: None paid.

Income: £200 for 1986.

Sources of income: Support has been made available in previous years from the Barrow Cadbury Fund Ltd and the Cheney Peace Settlement.

Aims and objectives: At Ease is an advisory and counselling service for members of the armed forces. It was started by a small group of people connected with the Central Board for Conscientious Objectors and the Peace Pledge Union who were aware of the difficulties of soldiers who are not naturally conscientious objectors and who therefore do not get help from pacifist organisations. Sessions are held every week at St John's Church, Waterloo Road, London on Sundays from 5.00–7.00 pm.

Affiliations: At Ease is affiliated to The Central Board for Conscientious Objectors.

CONCORD VIDEO AND FILM COUNCIL

201 Felixstowe Road, Ipswich, Suffolk IP3 9BJ (0473-715 754).

Contact: Lydia Vulliamy, General Secretary.

Status: Registered charity and company limited by guarantee.

Staffing: 10 full time; some 15 part time.

Income: £244,270 for 1985/86.

Sources of income: Film rentals and sales.

Aims and objectives: The Council distributes educational films on health, development, environmental and social issues and the general maintenance and improvement of life on earth. It handles over 3,000 titles and out of these it publishes a specific catalogue of 'peace' films for educational use.

Publications:

'Videos & Films for Peace – A Selection of Videos and Films for use in Peace Education', April 1987.
Full catalogue of Concord's films is obtainable from the Council.

EXCHANGE RESOURCES, EfP Ltd

28 Milsom Street, Bath, Avon BA1 1DP (0225-69671/2).

Contact: Tony Wilson, Managing Director.

Status: Limited company.

Origins: Started in 1986.

Staffing: 4 full time; a variable number of part-time staff.

Income: £50,000 for 1986/87.

Sources of income: Barrow and Geraldine S. Cadbury Trust assisted with a start-up grant.

Aims and objectives: An employment agency and business consultancy, set up in July 1986, for engineers and computer professionals who are seeking ethically acceptable work or who are concerned about the implications of their work. Exchange Resources' main function is recruitment. It also holds workshops, speaks at universities and polytechnics, takes stands at career fairs and encourages socially useful technological ventures. There is an initiative to involve local groups of campaigning organisations to identify likely business.

GREENNET

26–28 Underwood Street, London N1 7JQ (01-490 1510).

Action research and campaigns

Contact: Mitra, Founder/Co-ordinator.
Status: Non-profit making limited company.
Origins: Started in 1985.
Staffing: 3 full time.
Income: Information not made available.
Sources of income: GreenNet has been largely funded by its founder with support from charitable funds for discrete parts of its work.
Aims and objectives: GreenNet is part of a global federation of computer networks designed specifically to serve environment and peace groups. By mid 1987, it had some 200 subscribers using its electronic mail service. It links with PEACENET in the USA bringing access to over 1,600 peace groups worldwide.

LEGAL SUPPORT GROUP

c/o Quaker International Centre, 1 Byng Place, London WC1E 7JJ.

Contact: David Polden.
Status: Independent group.
Origins: The Group started in 1983.
Membership: 8.
Staffing: 1 part time.
Approximate annual income: £2,000 for 1987/88.
Sources of income: CND.
Aims and objectives: The Group exists to provide legal advice for the peace movement and though financed by CND is an independent group and prepared to work with anyone involved in non-violent activities.

It runs a weekly 'Legal Support Unit' to answer legal queries over the phone. It will also consider further legal support activities, but its resources are limited and it needs plenty of advance notice. (Times of the legal support unit: Wednesday 10.00 am to 6.00 pm, excluding 1.00 pm to 2.00 pm. on 01-388 9689).

PEACE ADVERTISING CAMPAIGN

PO Box 24, Oxford OX1 3JZ (0865-723 011).

Contact: Dr Mark Levene, Administrator.
Status: Non-profit making limited company.
Origins: Set up in 1980 by a group of Quakers involved in media work.
Staffing: 1 full time; 1 part time.
Income: around £40,000 for 1986.
Sources of income: Most income derives from its sales and services. Some income comes from individual donations and appeals but no support is received from trusts.
Aims and objectives: The Campaign provides resources and services to the peace movement and other sympathetic organisations such as nuclear free authorities, in the area of advertising and media. Much of its work has been to provide billboard posters on peace themes to local peace groups, providing at the same time a comprehensive service of billboard space buying through the national contractors, plus back-up to the local groups through PR and press work. Its new sister organisation, Peace Advertising Services, has a wider remit and will tailor resources to specific direct requirements.
Publications: The Campaign's 1987 Spring Catalogue lists: Billboard posters (14); A3 Posters (20); Stickers (6); Postcards (4); Films/video for cinemas (3).

PEACEMAKERS RELIEF SOCIETY

c/o CND, 22 Underwood Street, London N1 7JG (01-250 4010).

Contact: Meg Beresford.
Status: Independent society.
Origins: In 1983 a group of individuals in the peace movement felt a need for a fund to relieve hardship for those who are faced with financial loss because of their non-violent direct action.
Founder members: Lord Caradon; James Cameron; Lady Piper; Malcolm Harper; Andrew Clark; Oliver Postgate; Rev Dr Kenneth Greet; Lord Fenner Brockway; Jane Blom-Cooper; Adam Curle; Sheila Oakes; Terry Marsden; Dr Paul Rodgers; Joan Ruddock.
Staffing: None paid.
Income: About £3,000 in 1986/87.
Sources of income: Donations from members of the peace movement.
Aims and objectives: Women and men who suffer financial hardship through making a non-violent witness for peace for a variety of reasons including court appearances, can apply for help from the Peacemakers Relief Society but fines are not paid. Help can also be provided for families and dependents. The Society is a last resort after other sources of assistance have been exhausted. It is a revolving fund and it is hoped that people helped will make every effort to repay any grant received, as soon as possible, so that the money can be made available to other peacemakers.

Action research and campaigns

The original management committee members all had to relinquish their involvement. In 1986 CND was asked if they would manage the fund. The terms remain the same and by advertising in appropriate journals and newsletters it is hoped that donors and potential recipients will again become aware of its existence.

UNITED NATIONS INFORMATION CENTRE

20 Buckingham Gate, London SW1E 67B (01-630 1981).

Contact: Dr Erik Jensen, Director.

The Centre supplies information about the work of the United Nations and its agencies. Its library is open on Mondays, Wednesdays and Thursdays between 10.00 am to 1.00 pm and 2.00 pm to 5.00 pm.

3. Nuclear Free Zones

Introductory note
by the London Nuclear Information Unit

Nuclear Free Zone local authorities feel that activities involved in the nuclear cycle pose an unacceptable risk to the health and wellbeing of their communities. Many people are concerned about the threat of nuclear war and following the disaster at Chernobyl concerns are growing about the possibility of nuclear accidents.

Currently the Nuclear Free Zones are in the process of seeking to protect their communities from the threat of nuclear accidents by setting up radiation monitoring networks and by making emergency plans and preparations. War however remains the major threat and there are many important targets in Britain. The Nuclear Free Zones believe that civil defence measures proposed by central government would be ineffective against nuclear attack and that the civil defence demands made on local government amount to an activity primarily of military use, rather than about protecting the population from nuclear attack.

Clearly the nuclear threats cannot be abolished by simply making a declaration but the Nuclear Free Zones are working in difficult circumstances to protect their communities while bringing their attention to the nature of the risks.

List of contents

London Nuclear Information Unit
National Steering Committee of Nuclear Free Zones
NFZ Forums:
  County Councils
  Metropolitan Districts
  Non-Metropolitan Districts
  Scotland
  South East Region
  Wales
Listing of NFZ local authorities

LONDON NUCLEAR INFORMATION UNIT

Room 326a Camden Town Hall, Euston Road, London NW1 2RU (01-860 5747/8).

Contact: Christine Kings.

Status: Joint body of local government.

Origins: Formerly the GLC Nuclear Policy Unit. After abolition in April 1986, Camden Council, the lead borough, joined with other NFZ London boroughs to continue the unit with 3 staff transferred from the GLC NPU.

Membership: London Boroughs Nuclear Policy Committee and 12 London Boroughs – London Boroughs of Camden, Ealing, Greenwich, Hackney, Hammersmith and Fulham, Haringey, Hounslow, Islington, Lambeth, Lewisham, Southwark and Waltham Forest.

Staffing: 4 full time.

Estimated income: £120,000 for 1988/89.

Aims and objectives: The Unit promotes NFZ issues in London. Main issues at present include civil defence, the transportation of 'spent' nuclear fuel through the capital, peace education and emergency planning for nuclear accidents. It:

  Provides information and advice to officers, councillors and members of the public through briefings, reports, seminars and public meetings;

  Conducts research, both within the unit and commissioned by the unit on behalf of London Boroughs;

  Provides an organising and publicity service;

  Produces materials and resources including leaflets, posters, booklets, audio visual materials, exhibitions, etc.

Affiliation: The Unit is affiliated to the National Steering Committee for Nuclear Free Zones.

Publications:

Booklet: 'Nuclear London, a Guide to the Nuclear Maze', 1st edition June 1987, 2nd edition January 1988.

Nuclear Free Zones

Report by Large Associates, Consultant Engineers *'The Transportation of Irradiated fuels'*, 1988. A free 16-page summary is available.

'The Nuclear Trains, an Investigation'.

Assorted leaflets include: *'Why London needs Nuclear Free Zones'*; *'Nuclear Waste Transport through London'*.

Exhibitions: *'London as a Nuclear Free Zone'*; *'Blackout to Whitewash Civil Defence exhibition'*; *'Greenham Winter'*; *Hiroshima exhibition*.

NATIONAL STEERING COMMITTEE OF NUCLEAR FREE ZONE AUTHORITIES

PO Box No 532, Town Hall, Manchester M60 2LA (061-234 3244).

Contact for correspondence: Vernon E. Cressey, Honorary Secretary and City Administrator of Manchester City Council.

Administrative Contact: The National Secretariat at Nuclear Policy and Information Unit, Manchester.

Status: Joint initiative of supporting local authorities.

Origins: Set up in 1983 following a national conference called by Manchester City Council, Britain's first local authority to make a Nuclear Free Zone (NFZ) declaration.

Membership: 184 local authorities.

Staffing: 1 full time; 3 part time.

Estimated expenditure: £65,320 for 1987/88.

Sources of income: Payments for services from supporting authorities and conference receipts.

Aims and objectives: The National Steering Committee (NSC) aims to encourage individual NFZ authorities to:

Develop policies in respect of those responsibilities of the local authority which are affected by the nuclear state, in particular an authority's responsibilities for its citizens' safety, general education and future livelihood and well being;

Inform the democratic process by providing information to local people about how living in a country with nuclear weapons and power affects the services provided by the Council, their health and safety, and livelihood;

Promote international understanding through friendship and peace agreements with towns from different parts of the world.

In Spring 1987 the NSC decided the following priority areas of work:

Assistance and guidance to supporting authorities on civil defence matters, particularly those relating to the 1983 Civil Defence Regulations, the carrying out of Planning Assumptions Studies and the Home Office 'civil protection' public relations campaign;

Guidance and information on initiatives relating to the road movement of nuclear warheads and components;

Advice and guidance relating to environmental health and emergency planning initiatives in response to nuclear accidents (eg the promotion of local authority radiation monitoring and research into the risks, the effects and emergency planning implications of major accidents);

Exchanging information regarding peace education initiatives and developments;

Guidance and information relating to the local authority role in conversion of the nuclear and defence industries;

Assistance and guidance on how to produce a range of public information materials on nuclear related issues.

In addition to considering and recommending action to supporting authorities on the above issues, the national secretariat facilitates the work of the International Secretariat Committee.

The NSC also wishes to include a further range of issues and initiatives in its work programme, including: the promotion of alternatives to nuclear power, initiatives relating to the transportation of nuclear materials and the disposal of nuclear waste, and the promotion of international initiatives such as 'peace links' and friendship agreements. The NSC has invited supporting authorities to take a 'lead' role on such issues on behalf of and in conjunction with the NSC.

The NSC meets approximately once every two months. The membership of the NSC is made up of representatives from each of the NFZ Forums. The composition is as follows:

	No. of Places
Chair	1
Vice Chair	1
Scottish Forum	4
Welsh Forum	4
Counties Forum	3
Metropolitan Districts Forum	3
Non-Metropolitan Districts Forum	3
South-East Region	4
(NSC Secretary)	1

Affiliations and projects with other bodies: The administration of the NFZ International Secretariat Committee (ISC) is assisted by the NSC. It was formed following the Third International NFZ Conference in Perugia in 1986. Its first President is Councillor Roger Barton, Sheffield Metropolitan Borough Council and Chair of the UK National Steering Committee. An International Bulletin and NFZ Register is organised by Perugia.

The NSC employs a Planning Assumptions Study Co-ordinator based at the Bradford School of Peace Studies.

Earth Resources Research Ltd is undertaking work commissioned by the NSC concerning local authority emergency planning for peace-time emergencies and civil defence planning assumptions studies.

The NSC has worked in conjunction with employees at the Centre for Local Economic Strategies (CLES), SANA, END, CND and London Nuclear Information Unit.

Journals and recent publications:

'NSC National Bulletin', bi-monthly to supporting local authority Chief Executives and member contacts.
Briefing Documents include: 'Planning Assumptions Studies: The Basic Guide'; 'The Road Transport of Nuclear Warheads'; 'The Nuclear Fuel and Weapons Cycle in Great Britain'; 'Local Authority Monitoring of Radiation'; 'A Critical Review of Emergency Planning for Reactor Accidents'; 'The Hazards of Promoting Civil Defence: A Critical Examination of the Home Office's new 'Civil Protection Policy''; and a briefing on the Home Office Civil Defence circular on the 'Planned Programme of Implementation'.

NUCLEAR FREE ZONES: Local Authority Forums

County Councils' Forum

c/o Chief Executive's Department, Nottingham County Council, County Hall, West Bridgford, Nottingham NG2 7QP (0602-823 823).

Contact: P. A. Rivett.

Metropolitan District Councils' Forum

c/o Leeds City Council, Peace and Emergency Planning Unit, Selectapost 8, Dudley House, 133 Albion Street, Leeds LS2 8PP (0532-463 3988).

Contact: George Grossley.

Non-Metropolitan District Councils' Forum

c/o Chief Executive's Department, Cambridge City Council, The Guildhall, Cambridge CB2 3QJ (0223-358 977).

Contact: George Brewster.

Scottish Forum

c/o City of Glasgow, Town Clerk's Office, City Chambers, Glasgow G2 1DU (041-227 4164).

Contact: Mrs R. Slaven.

South-East Forum

c/o Chief Executive's Department, London Borough of Greenwich, Town Hall, Wellington Street, London SE18 6PW (01-854 8888 x 2054).

Contact: Nigel Karney.

Welsh Forum

c/o Chief Executive's Department, South Glamorgan County Council, County Headquarters, Newport Road, Cardiff CF2 1XA (0222-499 022 x 3476).

Contact: Peter Davies.

NUCLEAR FREE ZONES: A list of supporting Local Authorities as at January 1988

ENGLAND

Metropolitan Districts (30)

Barnsley	Oldham
Bolton	Rochdale
Bradford	Rotherham
Bury	St. Helens
Calderdale	Salford
Coventry	Sandwell
Doncaster	Sheffield
Gateshead	South Tyneside
Kirklees	Sunderland
Knowsley	Tameside
Leeds	Trafford
Liverpool	Wakefield
Manchester	Walsall
Newcastle-upon-Tyne	Wigan
North Tyneside	Wolverhampton

Nuclear Free Zones

Non-Metropolitan Counties (11)

Bedfordshire
Cleveland
Cumbria
Derbyshire
Durham
Humberside
Lancashire
Northumberland
Nottinghamshire
Shropshire
Staffordshire

Non-Metropolitan Districts (59)

Allderdale
Barrow-in-Furness
Basildon
Blackburn
Blyth Valley
Bolsover
Brighton
Bristol
Burnley
Cambridge
Cannock Chase
Carlisle
Chesterfield
Chester-le-Street
Cleethorpes
Corby
Crawley
Darlington
Derby
Derwentside
Durham
Exeter
Halton
Harlow
Hastings
Hyndeburn
Kingston upon Hull
Langbaurgh
Leicester
Lincoln
Malvern Hills
Middlesborough
Milton Keynes
Newcastle under Lyme
N E Derbyshire
N W Leicestershire
Norwich
Nuneaton/Bedworth
Oxford
Pendle
Peterborough
Preston
Redditch
Rossendale
Scunthorpe
Sedgefield
Slough
South Somerset
Stevenage
Stoke-on-Trent
Thamesdown
Thurrock
Wansbeck
Watford
Wear Valley
Welwyn Hatfield
Worcester
Wrekin
York

WALES

Welsh Counties (8)

Clwyd
Dyfed
Gwent
Gwynned
Mid Glamorgan
Powys
South Glamorgan
West Glamorgan

Welsh Districts (22)

Afan (Now Port Talbot)
Arfon
Blaenau Gwent
Brecknock
Ceredigion
Cynon Valley
Dinefwr
Dwyfor
Glyndwr
Isle of Anglesey
Islwyn
Llanelli
Meirrionnyd
Merthyr Tydfil
Newport
Ogwr
Rhonnda
Rhymney Valley
South Pembrokeshire
Taff-Ely
Torfaen
Wrexham Maelor

SCOTLAND

Regions (7)

Central
Fife
Grampian
Lothian
Shetland Isles
Strathclyde
Tayside

Districts (27)

Aberdeen
Clackmannan
Clydebank
Clydesdale
Cumbernauld/Kilsyth
Cumnock/Doon Valley
Cunninghame
Dumbarton
Dundee
Dunfermline
East Kilbride
East Lothian
Edinburgh
Falkirk
Glasgow
Inverclyde
Kirkcaldy
Kilmarnock/Loudoun
Midlothian
Monklands
Motherwell
Renfrew
Stirling
Strathkelvin
West Lothian
Western Isles
Wigtown

London Boroughs (17)

Barking/Dagenham
Brent
Camden
Ealing
Greenwich
Hackney
Hammersmith/Fulham
Haringey
Hounslow
Islington
Kingston upon Thames
Lambeth
Lewisham
Newham
Southwark
Tower Hamlets
Waltham Forest

4. International relations (general)

Introductory note

This small section covers those organisations which do not fall happily under the other section headings in this guide but which are included since they demonstrate significant aspects of European, transatlantic and international cooperation. The section makes no claim to be a comprehensive review of organisations in the field of international relations, but to highlight other strands in the network of organisations concerned with peace and security.

List of contents

Ditchley Foundation
European-Atlantic Group
European Movement
Inter-Parliamentary Union

DITCHLEY FOUNDATION

Ditchley Park, Enstone, Oxon OX7 4ER (060872-346).

Contact: Sir John Graham, Director.

Status: Registered charity.

Origins: Incorporated in 1958 with general charitable objects and in particular 'any branches or aspects of education, likely to be for the common benefit of British subjects on the one hand and of the United States on the other'.

The first Anglo-American conferences were held at Ditchley in 1962 and in 1964 the American Ditchley Foundation was established.

Patrons and office bearers: Sir David Wills (President); Lord Hunt of Tanworth (Chairman of Council of Management); Lord Windlesham (Vice-Chairman).

Income: £462,256 for 1986/87.

Sources of income: Two thirds from dividends, interest and rents, and one third from donations. The American Ditchley Foundation assists with travel costs of participants from the USA.

The Ditchley Park Conference Centre Ltd, a wholly owned subsidiary company, runs guest conferences at Ditchley. The number of such conferences is limited.

Aims and objectives: The Ditchley Foundation firmly states in its annual report that it 'has no political objective. The people who support them represent a wide range of interests and opinions and they believe that on both sides of the Atlantic there is need for greater study of the problems which affect the other side and the world in general. They have therefore sought to provide opportunities for people concerned with the formation of opinion in the United States of America and Britain, and also in other countries of the European Community and in Japan, Canada, Australia and elsewhere, to meet in quiet surroundings to

International relations (general)

discuss, study and learn about the great issues and difficulties facing their countries.'

The British Ditchley Foundation is administered by a Council of Management composed of British and American members resident in the United Kingdom and drawn from the list of Governors of the Foundation. The Governors (some 122) represent a wide variety of interests in the United Kingdom and include a number of Americans and prominent citizens from other major countries.

All Ditchley Foundation conferences take place over weekends at Ditchley Park. Attendance is by invitation. There are 12 to 14 of them a year with an annual aggregate of about 500 participants, of whom 150 or so are from the United States and about 100 from other countries.

EUROPEAN-ATLANTIC GROUP

6 Gertrude Street, London SW10 0JN (01-352 1226).

Contact: Mrs Elmar Dangerfield, Honorary Director.

Status: Registered charity.

Origins: The Group was founded in 1954 by the late Lord Layton (then Vice-President of the Council of Europe) together with other Members of both Houses of Parliament, industrialists, bankers, economists and journalists.

Officers: The Lord Layton (President); Lord Rippon of Hexham (Chairman); Sir Antony Buck MP, Lord Stewart of Fulham, Sir Wynn Hugh Jones (Vice-Chairmen).

Membership: Individuals 700; Corporate 160.

Staffing: 3 part time.

Income: £17,230 for 1986.

Sources of income: Corporate subscriptions; individual subscriptions; functions.

Aims and objectives: The main object of the Group is to promote closer relations between the European and Atlantic countries by providing a forum in Britain for discussion of their problems and possibilities for better economic and political co-operation with each other and with the rest of the world. The main activities are the monthly meetings in the House of Commons and dinner-discussions. In 1987 these have included a joint meeting and seminar with the ESU and others on the Marshall Plan addressed by Casper Weinberger and Norman Tebbit MP; Lord Chalfont speaking on 'British Defence Policy and European Atlantic Co-operation'; Admiral Lee Baggett speaking on 'Western (NATO) Naval Strategy'.

Journal: *'The European Atlantic Journal'* published annually since 1984.

THE EUROPEAN MOVEMENT

Europe House, 1 Whitehall Place, London SW1A 2DA (01-839 6622).

Contact: Peter Luff, General Secretary.

Status: Company limited by guarantee.

Patrons: The Rt Hon David Owen MP; The Rt Hon David Steel MP; The Rt Hon Margaret Thatcher MP.

Membership: 2,100 individuals; 140 corporate members.

Staffing: 4 full time; 3 part time.

Income: £105,000 for 1987.

Sources of income: Individual membership subscriptions; corporate membership subscriptions; HM Government grants; European Commission grants. No grants from Trusts.

Aims and objectives: The European Movement was set up after the Second World War to work for an end to rivalries between European nations. Its principal task is to persuade the government, parliament and the public at large, to back proposals for European Union and thus to ensure that its objective of a fully united Europe is finally achieved. In Britain, the Movement worked to persuade successive British governments to seek membership of the European Community. Its current campaign is to inform the British people and business about opportunities that will be created by the completion of the single internal market in 1992.

The Movement is supported by members of all political parties and by people belonging to no party. Membership enables individuals to join local branches as well as a political party group, and other associated organisations, if eligible. Branch activities include meetings, seminars and educational programmes, often run in co-operation with other organisations locally. A number of branches have direct links with similar groups in other European countries. The national Movement is governed by an elected Council. This elects the officers and the Management Board responsible for daily management of the Movement's activities.

Journals: *'Facts'* quarterly by European Movement; *'European Trade Unionists'* quarterly by Trade Union Group, *'Europe Left'* quarterly by Labour Movement Group.

INTER-PARLIAMENTARY UNION

Headquarters: Place du Petit-Saconnex, B.P. 438, 1211 Geneva 19, Switzerland (010-4122- 34 41 50).
Contact: Pierre Cornillon, Secretary General.

International relations (general)

Inter-Parliamentary Union, British Group: Palace of Westminster, London SW1A 0AA (01-219 3013/3011). *Contact*: Captain P. J. Shaw, General Secretary.

Status: The IPU's juridical capacity and international status are recognised by a Headquarters Agreement concluded with Switzerland's Federal Council.

Origins: In 1889, a first Inter-Parliamentary Conference for international arbitration attended by delegates from nine countries met in Paris.

Membership: 108 member parliaments.

Staff: 24 full time.

Approximate annual income: Swiss fr. 5.4 million for financial year 1988.

Sources of income: National groups contribute according to a scale established by the Inter-Parliamentary Council.

Aims and objectives: The IPU is the only world-wide organisation for the linking of parliaments and its work is carried out in two fields: action for peace and the strengthening of parliamentary institutions. Delegations meet twice yearly at major conferences. In addition to topical issues of a political nature often concerning local or regional conflicts, recent conferences have adopted resolutions on disarmament, ways of strengthening the United Nations, development of parliamentary institutions, equality of rights between men and women, hunger in the world, support for measures adopted at UNCTAD VI, population problems, refugees, environment, youth employment, decolonization and protection of the rights of minorities.

The work of the Union is guided by its Council, Executive Committee and four committees, (the first of which is concerned with 'Political Questions, International Security and Disarmament') supported by a secretariat. Its International Centre for Parliamentary Documentation (CIPD) contributes to the study and promotion of representative institutions.

Affiliations: IPU has consultative status, category 1 with Economic and Social Council of the United Nations and close relations with ILO, UNESCO, WHO, UNICEF and other specialised UN agencies. It also has regular relations with organizations such as the Council of Europe, the Organization of American States, the Commonwealth Parliamentary Association, the Union of African Parliaments, the Arab Inter-Parliamentarians' Union and the ASEAN Inter-Parliamentary Organization.

Publications include: *'Inter-Parliamentary Bulletin'* official quarterly; *'Summary Records of the Inter-Parliamentary Conferences'* and *'Verbatim Records'* of the symposia.

5. World studies, Education for peace, Development education

Education for Peace

by Dr David Hicks, Director, Centre for Peace Studies

The term education for peace has been in use now for over a decade by teachers and others in this country, and a lot longer by many educators in other countries. In the United Kingdom, this concern is part of our long-standing tradition of education for international understanding. It should also be seen in conjunction with a range of other educational initiatives, all of which seek in different ways to offer a curriculum more relevant to the needs of both children and society today. Such fields include personal and social education, world studies, development education, multicultural education, equal opportunities, human rights education and political education. Whilst each field may have its distinct origins and concerns they often overlap in practice. Taken together they have much to offer in the creation of a socially relevant education for the 1990s.

The interest amongst teachers in education for peace began for a variety of reasons. Specifically, during the last decade, teachers in many different countries have looked variously at the state of the planet, of their country, of education, or of their pupils, and were disturbed by what they saw. In particular, they were concerned about increasing levels of direct violence between people, as in the case of assault, riot or war, and the equally damaging structural violence which may be built into oppressive social, political or economic systems. Noting the crucial importance of both peace and conflict in this latter part of the twentieth century, they asked themselves what the implications might be for teaching and learning in school. 'Education for peace', both in this country and elsewhere, thus began as a grassroots concern amongst teachers in response to what they, and many others, saw as an increasingly violent world, a violence epitomised initially by the arms race and the threat of nuclear war.

It is worth noting, in passing, that the *World Directory of Peace Research Institutions*, published by Unesco, lists some 300 bodies involved in some way with peace and conflict research. Peace research as a distinct field of enquiry emerged in the early 1960s, and, although teachers with an interest in education for peace generally have little to do with peace researchers in universities, it is useful to recall this parallel academic backdrop of concern.

Three broad assumptions generally underlie most definitions of education for peace, and these are as follows:

1. War and violent conflict are not conducive to human well-being;
2. Neither are war and conflict necessarily the result of inevitable aspects of human nature;
3. Peace, that is alternative ways of being, organising and behaving, can be learnt.

World studies, Education for peace, Development education

One of the central concerns of education for peace has, therefore, been to widen the debate about the nature of human aggression. Thus, whilst it is currently popular to consider human aggression as an innate characteristic, much research has also been carried out which refutes such ideas and focusses instead on the learnt nature of both aggression and non-aggression.

The overall aim of education for peace is to develop the skills, attitudes and knowledge which are needed to resolve conflict peacefully in order to work towards a more just and less violent world. More specifically, education for peace aims to:

1. Explore **concepts of peace** both as a state of being and as an active process;
2. Enquire into the **obstacles to peace** and the causes of peacelessness, both in and between, individuals, groups, institutions and societies;
3. **Resolve conflicts** in ways that will contribute to a more just and less violent world;
4. Study ways of constructing a range of **alternative futures**, in particular ways of achieving a more just and sustainable world society.

Specific objectives for education for peace must, of course, be consonant with the above aims. For example, under **knowledge** objectives, one might expect to look at issues to do with conflict, peace, war, nuclear matters, justice, power, gender, race, ecology and futures. Such issues are, of course, seldom found together in one place on the timetable. They may be part of topic or project work or part of, say, Humanities, Geography, History, English or Religious Education. Education for peace, it should be made quite clear, is seldom seen as a separate subject but more often as a dimension across the whole curriculum.

Appropriate objectives must also include **skills** such as critical thinking, co-operation, empathy, assertiveness, conflict resolution and political literacy, together with **attitudes** such as self-respect, respect for others, ecological concern, open-mindedness, vision and a commitment to justice. These attitudes and skills do not belong, quite properly, to one particular part of the curriculum. Education for peace is thus seen as an approach to teaching and learning as well as having its substantive content. In particular, attention is paid to the need for congruence between medium and message, so there is considerable stress on participatory and experiential styles of learning.

Whilst such concerns necessarily involve the exploration, on a variety of scales, of a range of issues to do with violence, conflict and peace – some of which will inevitably be deemed controversial – it is also important to recall the legitimation for such concerns. The educational rationale for education for peace thus has a three-fold basis, relating to: a) the aims of education; b) the nature of childhood socialisation; and c) educational ideologies.

Amongst the broad aims of education set out in *The Curriculum From 5–16*, from Her Majesty's Inspectorate in 1985, are the following: to help pupils to develop lively, enquiring minds, the ability to question and argue rationally and to apply themselves to tasks . . .; to instil respect for religious and moral values, and tolerance of other races, religions and ways of life; to help pupils understand the world in which they live, and the interdependence of individuals, groups and nations. Education for peace quite specifically attempts to respond to, and elaborate on, broad aims such as these.

Childhood socialisation plays an important role in young people's perception of the world in which they live. Thus, not only are racist and sexist beliefs acquired at quite an early age, so are attitudes to violence, to war and to peace. Children appear to have fairly well defined ideas about war and peace by the age of seven or eight. Whilst younger children can often see no justification for war whatsoever, the majority of fifteen-year olds believe war is morally valid to punish an aggressor. Their concepts of peace, it seems are much less clear than those of war. Recent research from many countries, including Britain, also indicates that many primary-aged children are worried about the threat of nuclear war, and that such fears increase in adolescence. Education for peace specifically attempts to respond in a positive way to issues such as these.

Finally it should be noted that education for peace has its roots in, and tries to combine, two broad educational traditions: the person-centred tradition and the reconstructionist tradition. In the first, there is a particular focus on personal worth and personal growth; in the second, an emphasis on the need for educators to engage in social, political and economic debate and for classrooms to be seen as potential arenas for change.

Interest in education for peace grew rapidly in the early and mid-1980s amongst teachers, educators and parents. Support came from teachers' groups, teacher unions and a variety of voluntary agencies, as well as from members of HMI. Several LEAs, such as Nottinghamshire, Avon, Manchester, Sheffield and Birmingham, have produced their own guidelines on education for peace, and some have also appointed advisory teachers. As already mentioned, education for peace initiatives often overlap, or run parallel with, developments in the allied fields.

It is important to note that most of the critical comment that has arisen in relation to education for peace has been ill-informed and bears little relationship to what most teachers are actually doing in schools. Six points will be briefly mentioned here:

1. It has been argued that peace studies is not a proper subject, and should therefore not be included on the timetable. However, few teachers are proposing a completely new subject called 'peace studies', but rather are asking what teaching and learning could go on *within* existing subjects to help children understand issues to do with peace and conflict.

2. It is argued that peace studies is really a cloak for teaching about unilateral nuclear disarmament. This is only *one* of the issues, however, that teachers may explore and, quite clearly, if disarmament is discussed it should include a variety of perspectives. It has been suggested by some researchers that most teachers seem to be *avoiding* the nuclear issue rather than confronting it in the classroom.

3. It has been argued that peace studies is really just training in good manners, something that has always been part of good education. But education for peace is about much *more* than this. In particular it stresses the need for all students to develop a positive self-concept, to learn about ways of resolving conflicts less violently, and to develop skills of co-operation and empathy, critical judgement and political literacy.

4. It has been suggested that peace studies is a tool for the deliberate indoctrination of pupils, not least through the use of biased resources. Since one of the aims of education for peace is to develop children's critical judgement, so that propaganda in *any* form may be more readily identified, this seems an unwarranted criticism. It is, of course, based on a view of education which wishes to exclude the study of any contemporary issues from the classroom.

5. It is argued that peace studies pays a lot of attention to conflicts in the capitalist world, but no attention to the evils of communism, which are much more substantial. Clearly, as children get older, they need to be aware of the world's major political systems, their origins, assumptions and achievements. They need to study, as objectively as possible, life in both capitalist and communist countries, and weigh up some of the advantages and disadvantages of each to the inhabitants themselves.

6. It has been suggested that it is dangerous to study issues of peace and conflict with younger children, due to their inability to grasp complex ideas. However, schools merely intervene in an on-going educational process, wherein parents, peer group and media, constantly teach children about such issues, whether on a local or a global scale. Reports from teachers involved with the *World Studies 8–13 Project* also indicate that children are very interested in, and in their own terms can be quite knowledgeable about, events in the wider world.

Most comment has thus been based not on classroom experience but on hearsay. Education for peace, as a vital and flourishing approach to education, is here to stay. Indeed its concerns remind us that without creative resolution of conflict – whether local or global – and without our own visions of peace and justice to hold before us, our dreams of a better world may yet stay unrealised.

Introductory note

This section covers educational initiatives, courses and projects which introduce a global and peace dimension into the classroom and community education. Because the scope of the subject area is so broad it naturally displays differing emphases as shown in the titles – World Studies, International Studies, Global Education, Education in World Citizenship, Peace Studies, Education for Peace, Development Education. The issues covered range from the macro to the micro, and underline the theme of interdependence and interconnectedness running through these studies – from Third World/First World issues to an understanding of interpersonal conflict, from issues about defence and disarmament to an appreciation of different cultural perspectives.

In the context of formal education, a short list has been compiled of those local education authorities with a policy and/or staff specifically employed to help generate a wider acceptance of education for peace as a cross-curricula subject. This list shows the authorities where the subject is likely to be more advanced. Initiatives have of course been taken by many schools elsewhere. Indeed the subject has been developed also by pilot projects in independent schools and colleges (see Atlantic College) and given particular impetus by Quaker colleges and schools.

World studies, Education for peace, Development education

This work in schools and colleges is now helped by the support networks for teachers (e.g. Peace Education Network, and internationally by the Peace Education Commission).

Parallel with these projects a range of independent centres helps to underpin the growth of education for peace by conducting pilot projects and research for curriculum development, by providing in-service teacher training courses and by acting as resource centres (e.g. Centre for Peace Studies, Centre for Global Studies, Centre for International Studies, etc.). Where such curriculum development is part of a wider programme, for instance the work on an A' level course in Peace Studies developed at the Richardson Institute for Peace Studies, Lancaster University, a cross-reference is made. Also cross-referenced in this section, but included in full in 'Section 1: Policy-oriented research Universities', are the courses in Peace Studies at Bradford and Ulster Universities and at the United Nations University for Peace. This pioneering work was given particular momentum in the UK by the Quakers. Other churches are active in the field of education for peace (e.g. Pax Christi), and many have come to it as an extension of their overseas relief work (e.g. Christian Aid, CAFOD). The major relief agencies form the backbone of support for development education work within the UK, and are important also in their support to local development education centres.

Other educational projects aimed at adults as well as young people are organised by groups aiming to raise awareness on a particular issue; again these are cross-referenced to 'Section 2: Campaigning Groups'. They include Youth CND, Peace through NATO, Peace Pledge Union, Campaign Against Arms Trade and United Nations Association.

List of contents

Local Education Authority initiatives

Barnsley
Birmingham
Bradford
Derbyshire
Kirklees
Leeds
Manchester
Nottinghamshire
Sheffield

Other initiatives

Bradford University, School of Peace Studies (*see Section 1: Policy oriented research, Universities*)
Campaign Against Arms Trade, development education project (*see Section 2: Action research and campaigns, Non-membership organisations*)
CAFOD: the Catholic Fund for Overseas Development
Catholic Institute for International Relations
Centre for Global Education
Centre for International Studies
Centre for Peace Studies
Centre for World Development Education
Christian Aid
Council for Education and World Citizenship
Fircroft College
Gandhi Foundation
National Association of Development Education Centres
National Peace Action Foundation
One World Trust
One World Week
Open University
Oxfam
Oxford Project for Peace Studies
Pax Christi (*see Section 2: Action research and campaigns, Church organisations*)
Peace Education Commission
Peace Education Network
Peace Education Project (West Midlands)
Peace Education Resource Centre, Belfast (*see Section 6: Northern Ireland*)
Peace Pledge Union (*see Section 2: Action research and campaigns, Membership organisations*)
Peace Through NATO (*see Section 2: Action research and campaigns, Non-membership organisations*)
Play for Life
Quaker Peace and Service (*see Section 2: Action research and campaigns, Religious groups*)
Richardson Institute for Peace Studies, Lancaster University (*see Section 1: Policy-oriented research, Universities*)
Schools Against the Bomb (*see CND/Youth CND, Section 2: Action research and campaigns, Membership organisations*)
Sheffield Post 16, Peace and Conflict Studies Working Party
Student Peace Project
Teachers for Peace
Third World First
Trade Union International Research & Education Group
Ulster University, Peace Studies Programme (*see Section 1: Policy-oriented research, Universities*)
United Nations Association (*see Section 2: Action research and campaigns, Membership organisations*)
United Nations University for Peace (*see Section 1: Policy-oriented research, International*)

World studies, Education for peace, Development education

United World College of the Atlantic
War on Want
Welsh Centre for International Affairs
Woodbrooke Quaker Study Centre
World Development Movement

Youth CND (*see CND in Section 2: Action research and campaigns, Membership organisations*)

Development education centres

A listing of centres with paid staff

WORLD STUDIES, EDUCATION FOR PEACE, DEVELOPMENT EDUCATION:
Local Education Authority Initiatives

Listed below are those authorities which have made and are making some advisory provision to develop cross-curricular interest in education for peace. Of course, many schools, at all levels, have undertaken their own individual programmes, not only in these local authorities, but in many other parts of the country. The Peace Education Network (*see separate entry*) is a source of information about where these initiatives are currently taking place.

Barnsley Metropolitan Borough Council

The LEA has adopted a Policy Statement – 'Education for a Less Violent World'.

A Handbook of *'Resources & Suggestions'* has been compiled.

Contact: Dr Mary Jefferson (*until summer '88*); T. Higginbottom, Chief Adviser (*thereafter*). Contact address: Adviser in Humanities, Barnsley Education Department, Berneslai Close, Barnsley, South Yorks (0226-287 621).

Birmingham City Council

In September 1985, the Education Committee approved a *'Policy Statement on Education for Peace'* which was then circulated to all governing bodies, colleges and schools for implementation. The Education Committee emphasised that the statement aims to promote discussion of ideas rather than to be prescriptive since the work crosses all phases of the curriculum and levels of education. It is the first local authority to have agreed a policy statement specifically entitled 'Education for Peace'.

Contact: Mary le Breuilly, Co-ordinator of Peace Education, The Bordesley Centre, Camp Hill, Stratford Road, Birmingham B11 1AR (021-772 5912).

Bradford Metropolitan District Council

The Council has declared its area a nuclear free zone. A working party was set up to review the issue of peace education and a teacher has been seconded for the 1987/88 academic year and to study the issue of introducing peace education in the curriculum and to service the working party.

Contacts: Mrs B. Thomson, Senior Adviser, Directorate of Educational Services, Provincial House, Bradford BD1 1NP (0274-752 111); or David Fitch, Advisory Teacher, c/o Willowfield First School, Legrams Lane, Bradford, W. Yorks. (0274-578 898).

Derbyshire County Council

The Council has declared its area a nuclear free zone. In 1983, the Education Committee in its document *'A Derbyshire Approach to Personal and Social Education in the Secondary School'* outlined its policy on Peace Education.

An annotated catalogue *'Resources for Peace Education'* was published for schools in 1987 listing materials available in the County's P.S.E. resources centre. An advisory teacher for Peace Education was seconded for the academic year 1987–88.

Contact: David Cooper, Advisory Teacher for Peace Education, Education Offices, County Offices, Matlock, Derbyshire DE4 3AG (0629-580 000 x 6584).

Kirklees Metropolitan District Council

Guidelines on peace education were produced in 1985 and an Inspector appointed with responsibility for this field of work. In-service teacher training courses are run at the Teachers' Centre and in schools and a pool of resources has been gathered for wide use.

World studies, Education for peace, Development education

Contact: Mark Pattison, Inspector, Humanities, Peace Education, Oldgate House, 2 Oldgate, Huddersfield, West Yorkshire HD1 6OW (0484-22133 x 3244).

Leeds City Council

A shared peace education development post was set up in 1987 for a two year period. It first started within the Peace and Emergency Planning Unit as part of its work as a nuclear free zone and transferred to the Education Department in December 1987. A rationale and programme for the implementation of peace education appropriate to the whole range of educational provision in Leeds is being developed with the help of a Working Group. A *Peace Education Resources* list has been published.

Contacts: Juliet and Martin Pierce, Peace Education Development Officers, Leeds City Council, Department of Education, Selectapost 17, Merrion House, 110 Merrion Centre, Leeds LS2 8DT (0532-462 875).

Manchester County Council

Manchester Education Committee appointed an advisory teacher, on a two-year secondment to work two days a week on education for peace, to:

Service a working party preparing policy guidelines;

Research and acquire necessary resources;

Develop an in-service training programme;

Work in schools with teachers.

Two booklets were published in late 1987 – *Policy Guidelines* and *Case Studies of Education for Peace in Manchester* (covering some 20 examples).

Contact: Dave Cooke, Manchester County Council, Education Development Service, South District, Royal Oak Road, Wythenshawe, Manchester M23 8ED (061-998 5256).

Nottinghamshire County Council

This is the first authority to have produced guidelines for peace education within its Personal and Social Education Programme. These guidelines have apparently become recognised internationally as a useful model.

The two major documents, both produced under the heading 'Personal and Social Education, A Process for Life' are essential reading for any newcomer to this field of work: *'Report to the Education Committee of the Working Party on the Development of a Curriculum for Peace Education'*; and *'Some Curriculum Implications for Peace Education'*.

At the time of going to press the post of adviser in this area was not filled but was expected to be by Paul Mein.

Contact: Advisory & Inspection Service, The Mandela Centre, Green Street, The Meadows, Nottingham NG2 2LA (0602-860 232).

Sheffield City Council

The Council has created a permanent post of Advisory Teacher with specific responsibility for peace education.

Contact: Fiona Cooper, Westbourne Teachers' Centre, 17 Westbourne Road, Sheffield S10 2QQ (0742-685 976).

WORLD STUDIES, EDUCATION FOR PEACE, DEVELOPMENT EDUCATION:
Other initiatives

BRADFORD UNIVERSITY, SCHOOL OF PEACE STUDIES

(see Section 1: Policy-oriented research – Universities)

CAMPAIGN AGAINST ARMS TRADE

(see Section 2. Action research and campaigns – Non-membership organisations)

CAFOD – the Catholic Fund for Overseas Development

2 Garden Close, Stockwell Road, London SW9 9TY (01-733 7900).

Contact: Julian Filochowski, Director.

Status: Registered charity.

Origins: Founded in 1962.

Trustees: Rev Anthony Hitchin; Rev Derek J. H. Worlock; the Duke of Norfolk.

Staffing: 44 full time (in London), plus 6 regional officers.

Income: £5,375,000 for year ending September 1986.

Sources of income: Government and other grant-aid i.e. ODA, EEC, Jersey, other official sources. Special appeals, donations, legacies, Family Fast Days, etc.

Aims and objectives: CAFOD is the official development agency of the Catholic Church in England and Wales. Its management committee (including representatives of the leading lay Catholic organisations) makes major policy decisions with the final approval of the Bishop's Conference.

Over half CAFOD's income is spent in supporting over 500 development projects in some 25 countries; over a third is spent on emergency aid. A small proportion of total revenue (5%) is spent on development education within Britain. CAFOD encourages the formation of groups in parishes, schools and religious communities to support its work on a regular basis. These groups can relate through a partnership scheme to a specific development project or to a particular issue.

A Development Education Committee advises on its work in Britain. The Development Education Campaign for 1986/87 was 'Proclaim Jubilee' covering issues of land, debt and slavery.

Projects supported by CAFOD in Britain include a mobile resource library run by the Birmingham Catholic Teachers' Federation to help integrate issues of development, justice and peace into teaching. *'Education Dialogue'* is a newsletter for teacher contacts.

Affiliations and joint projects with other organisations: CAFOD co-operates with the Department for Internal Affairs of the Bishops' Conference, the National Missionary Council, and the Catholic Institute for International Relations (CIIR). It also works with other agencies, such as Christian Aid, on joint programmes and projects.

Internationally, CAFOD is a member of two Catholic networks; CIDSE (International Co-operation for Solidarity and Development), which is a partnership for Catholic development and Caritas, the Catholic network for emergency and disaster relief – on which it forms the English and Welsh representation together with the Bishops' Social Welfare Committee.

Joint promotion of 'Bread not Bombs' week, 1984–1987 with the Campaign Against Arms Trade and its other sponsors.

Journals and recent publications: The Resource Centre at CAFOD stocks an extensive range of books, pamphlets and leaflets, posters, films and videos, simulation games etc. as part of its Development Education Campaign. Much of this is directly published by CAFOD: *'Link'* free newsletter of the Development Education Department, produced quarterly; *'Campaign*

World studies, Education for peace, Development education

News', free bi-monthly newsletter for Campaign groups; '*The CAFOD Bulletin*', free monthly newsheet on new projects and emergency funding.

The numerous books, pamphlets and leaflets include: '*Action for Justice and Peace, A Handbook for Groups*' 1986; '*The New Name for Peace is Development*', a free leaflet for colleges and universities.

CATHOLIC INSTITUTE FOR INTERNATIONAL RELATIONS

22 Coleman Fields, London N1 7AF (01-354 0883).

Contact: Ian Linden, General Secretary.

Status: Registered charity and company limited by guarantee.

Origins: The Institute started life in 1940 as 'The Sword of the Spirit' and took its current name in the late 1950s.

Patrons: Cardinal Basil Hume, Archbishop of Westminster (President); Rev David Konstant, Bishop of Leeds (Episcopal Adviser).

Membership: 3,150.

Staffing in London office: 24 full time; 4 part time.

Income: £1.3 million for 1986/87.

Sources of income: The Institute's volunteer programme is financed almost entirely (90%) by the ODA. Other financial sources are the EEC, Oxfam and SIDA, the Swedish government development agency. Membership subscriptions comprise 1.5% of total revenue income.

Aims and objectives: The Institute exists 'to promote a better understanding of justice, peace and development issues in the poor countries of the world'. Its work falls into two main areas – its overseas volunteer programme and its publishing work. Its volunteer programme is entirely secular. In Spring 1986, 67 professionally and technically qualified people worked on local development projects in North Yemen, Somalia, Zimbabwe, Central and South America.

The Institute also conducts research and publishes books and pamphlets on international social, economic and political issues. Its Desk on Development liaises with the EEC and monitors its development policy.

Affiliations and joint projects with other organisations: The Institute produces its series, 'Church in the World' and 'Third World Theology' with the Inter-Agency Group comprising CIIR, CAFOD, Pax Christi and the Scottish Catholic International Aid fund (SCIAF). CIIR co-operates with the British Volunteer Committee.

Journals and recent publications:
'*CIIR News*' is produced quarterly and circulated free to members. Briefing papers entitled '*Comment*' are also circulated free to members and include issues on: '*Guatemala*', 1987; '*Sanctions against South Africa*', 1986; '*Common Agricultural Policy*', 1986.

Book publications include: Hanlon, Joseph '*Beggar Your Neighbours*'; '*Apartheid Power in Southern Africa*' CIIR/James Currey, 1986.

CENTRE FOR GLOBAL EDUCATION

University of York, Heslington, York YO1 5DD (0904-413 267/415 157).

Contact: Dr David Selby, Director.

Status: Charitable as part of a university department.

Origins: Set up in 1982 under the aegis of the University of York Education Department, and originally called the World Studies Teacher Training Centre.

Personnel: 5 Academic staff; 3 support staff; 1 Centre Fellow; 30 part-time Diploma Course students.

Income: £140,000 for 1987/88.

Sources of income in recent years: World Wildlife Fund; EEC Development Fund; School Curriculum Development Committee; Joseph Rowntree Charitable Trust; Christian Aid; Oxfam and Calouste Gulbenkian Foundation.

Aims and objectives: The Centre aims to promote in primary and secondary schools a more 'global' perspective through curriculum and materials development and through pre- and in-service teacher training programmes in world studies and selected fields, i.e. education for peace as well as development issues, environmental concerns, human rights and multi-cultural, anti-racist, anti-sexist approaches. A hallmark of the Centre's work is the development of curriculum materials and teaching/learning styles which encourage participation, interaction and co-operation in the classroom during the first years on 'World Studies' Teacher Training Project.

Projects: 'Perspective Consciousness' a four year project begun in 1985 to enable students to see through the eyes, minds and hearts of those of other cultures. Student packs for primary and secondary schools are being produced around the themes: environment, development, human rights, childhood, futures and conflict resolution. Individuals from a number of countries and cultures will 'speak' for themselves through these packs.

'Global Impact' three-year project started 1986 and funded by the World Wildlife Fund, seeks to promote the inclusion of the related issues of development and environment in schools in the UK.

Teaching: Part-time Diploma Course in Global and Multi-cultural Education. In-service consultancies with LEAs and international schools.

Journals and recent publications:
'*Global Education News*', quarterly; '*World Studies Journal*', occasional. Short documents include: Selby, David '*World Studies, the Participatory Classroom, the Open School*'; Duczek, Stephanie '*Peace Studies, the Atlantic College Experience*'; '*CGE 1982–1986*', a report of the Centre's activities in its first four years.

Teaching and learning materials/resources are stocked e.g. '*Global Statistics*' – a complete software package for the mathematics and world studies classroom; Pike, Graham and Selby, David '*Global Teacher, Global Lecturer*' CGE/Hodder & Stoughton, 1987; Greg, Sue, Pike, Graham and Selby, David '*Earthrights, Education as if the Planet Really Mattered*' Kogan Page/WWF, 1987.

A full catalogue is available.

CENTRE FOR INTERNATIONAL STUDIES

Box 18, Exmouth, Devon EX8 (0395-264 902).

Contact: Roger W. R. Morgan, Director.

Status: Independent organisation.

Origins: Set up in 1976 to promote international understanding through education. The Centre has a Board of distinguished international educators.

Membership: 800+.

Staffing: 3 full time; 5 part time.

Estimated annual income: £100,000 for 1986/87.

Sources of income: European Commission, UNESCO, LEAs, Oxfam, Christian Aid, World Wildlife Fund.

Aims and objectives: The Centre aims to:
Facilitate and stimulate communication about international issues in both the formal and non-formal education sectors;
Promote the exchange of information between educational and non-educational institutions and individuals working in this area;
Encourage projects which facilitate the use of expertise in this area to fulfil such objectives.

It does this by organising the following activities – conferences and workshops; translation of teaching materials; promotion of exchanges by professionals working in this area; co-operation with curriculum development bodies, ministries, non-governmental organisations and project leaders; the preparation of audio-visual packs.

Affiliations and projects with other bodies: The Centre provides the secretariat for the Standing Conference on Education for International Understanding (SCEIU), European Development Education Curriculum Development (EDECN), the Transatlantic Network on Global Education (TNGE). It is a member of executive of UK Centres for European Education (UKCEE) and a member of the National Association of Development Education Centres (NADEC).

Journals and recent publications:
'*Conceptual Clarification, Europe and International Understanding*' (Sponsored by SCEIU and UKCEE), 1986; '*Global Environmental Programme – Earthwatch Now*', 1986; '*Eurogame*', 1987.

CENTRE FOR PEACE STUDIES

St Martins College of Higher Education, Lancaster LA1 3JD (0524-37698).

Contact: Dr David Hicks, Director.

Status: Responsible to a Consultative Committee and to the Academic Board of this voluntary Church College.

Origins: The Centre was established in 1980.

Patron: Adam Curle, Emeritus Professor of Peace Studies, Bradford University.

Staffing: 1 full time; 1 part time.

Estimated annual income: £25,000 for 1987/88.

Sources of income: European Commission, Oxfam, Christian Aid and other donations.

Aims and objectives: The Centre aims to:
Assess national needs in relation to education for peace and world studies;
Promote awareness of issues relating to peace and conflict within education;
Interpret and clarify the existing educational responses to such issues: education for peace, world studies, multi-cultural education and development education;
Identify priorities for curriculum development and innovation in these fields, at primary and secondary level;
Provide educational resources and support for the development of peaceful strategies and skills to cope with global and local change in 1990s and beyond;

World studies, Education for peace, Development education

Reinforce, and build on, existing regional, national and international networks concerned with education about, and for, peace.

In particular the centre provides an advice and enquiry service for teachers, schools and LEAs; a series of occasional papers and other publications; responsibility for the national curriculum project World Studies 8–13 operating in over 40 LEAs; specialised in-service training for schools and LEAs; lectures and workshops; international links and contacts.

Journals and recent publications:
Fisher, Simon and Hicks, David 'World Studies 8–13: A Teacher's Handbook', Oliver and Boyd, 1985.

CENTRE FOR WORLD DEVELOPMENT EDUCATION

Regent's College, Inner Circle, Regent's Park, London NW1 4NS (01-487 7410).

Contact: Derek Walker, Director.

Status: Registered charity and company limited by guarantee.

Origins: In 1966 was first set up as the Voluntary Committee on Overseas Aid and Development which became the Centre in 1977.

Patrons and Trustees: HM The Queen (Patron); Sir Kenneth Durham (President); Nicholas Hinton; Frank Judd; Lady Nourse; Christopher Reeves (Vice-Presidents); David Kingsley (Hon Treasurer), T. W. F. Allan; Donald Chesworth; Sir Leslie Kirkley; John Machin; Dame Margaret Miles; Gordon Scotney (Trustees); Colin Craig (Chairman, Council of Management).

Staffing: 7 full time; 2 part time.

Income: £250,000 for 1986/87.

Sources of income: Overseas Development Administration; project support from Marks & Spencer plc and the Calouste Gulbenkian Foundation; donations from some 20 companies and the World Bank.

Aims and objectives: CWDE promotes 'education in Britain about world development issues and Britain's interdependence with developing countries'.

It organises workshops, conferences, in-service education, exhibitions and displays of teaching resources. It runs a series of Study-action Groups in which teachers and lecturers produce resources and help organise training events. It co-ordinates a Development Journalists Group with a membership of over 140 journalists. It also provides programmes of seminars on development issues for the business community. Its resource centre is an extensive display of books, pamphlets, audio visual materials and other teaching aids for sale produced by both the Centre and many other organisations.

Journals and recent publications: An extensive catalogue lists all educational materials from the centre (which includes many titles published by other organisations covered in this book).

CHRISTIAN AID

PO Box 100, London SE1 7RT.

Interchurch House, 35 Lower Marsh, London SE1 7RL (01-620 4444).

Contact: Rev Michael Taylor, Director.

Status: Charitable as a division of the British Council of Churches.

Origins: Started in 1950; received its present name in 1964.

Board of Directors: Sir Brian Young (Chairman); Mrs Anne Booth-Clibborn (Deputy Chairman).

Staffing in UK: 200 full time; 40 part time.

Income: £16,757,000 for 1986/87.

Sources of income: Government grants from the ODA, EEC, the Government of Jersey, Republic of Ireland. Special appeals, the annual Christian Aid Week and donations, covenants and legacies.

Aims and objectives: 'Christian Aid helps those victimised by poverty and the abuse of power to change their circumstances and prospects. It is at work both within the Christian fellowship and beyond it, among people of all races and all faiths helping the poor and the oppressed without political or other discrimination'.

In 1986/87 Christian Aid allocated the following funds:

Development	£7,400,000
Refugees	£1,100,000
Emergencies	£2,000,000
Development education in UK	£1,800,000*
Overseas students	£430,000
World Council of Churches	£165,000
Community and Race Relations	£60,000
Inter-Church aid	£133,000

(* includes £600,000 in grants to other educational groups)

Every year Christian Aid runs its appeal week – its theme in 1986 was 'Change Things for Good', and in 1987 'Power to the Poor'. Christian Aid sees the affluence of the West as one of the causes of world poverty 'that we ourselves are part of the problem and therefore hold the key to part of the solution'.

World studies, Education for peace, Development education

Journals and recent publications:

'*Christian Aid News*', quarterly; '*The Collector*', annual magazine for collectors of money for the charity; Policy statement of Christian Aid and World Development.

An extensive range of publications and support materials is produced and a full catalogue is available including the following with specific relevance to this book's interests: '*The Arms Trade*', free fact sheet; '*It's Not Fair*', an A4 handbook on world development for youth readers; '*Seeking Peace*', a study guide for small groups; '*The Big If*', 9 minute animated film on the arms trade, 1982.

COUNCIL FOR EDUCATION IN WORLD CITIZENSHIP (CEWC)

Seymour Mews House, Seymour Mews, London W1H 9PE (01-935 1752).

Contact: Margaret Quass, Director.

Status: Registered charity.

Origins: Founded in 1939.

Distinguished patrons: HRH Duke of Gloucester (Patron); Professor William Taylor (President).

Membership: Some 2,000 member schools and colleges.

Staffing: 6 full time; 2 part time.

Estimated annual income: £90,000 for 1985/86.

Main sources of income: Department of Education and Science; Scottish Education Department; Overseas Development Administration; Ministry of Education, Northern Ireland; LEA grants and school subscriptions; UNESCO; Lloyds Bank sponsorship.

Aims and objectives: The Council was founded to 'promote throughout the educational system such studies and teachings as may best contribute to mutual understanding, peace, co-operation and good-will between all peoples'. An autonomous body representing local education authorities, teachers' associations, youth organisations and other specified educational bodies, its main area of activity is among its member school colleges. Each of these receives regular newsletters, current affairs broadsheets, information about CEWC activities, publications and materials, UN and UNESCO literature, conferences and any information or practical help relating to the teaching of international affairs in its widest context. Hundreds of speakers are sent each year to individual and inter-schools meetings covering all subjects from democracy to disarmament; from China to the E.E.C.

CEWC has at its London headquarters an extensive resource centre available to teachers and pupils.

Annotated lists of new material are circulated twice a term.

The Annual Conference 1986 was held, for the first time, outside Britain at the UNESCO headquarters, Paris, on the theme 'The Defences of Peace'.

Journals and recent publications:

'*Citizens of the World*' by Curriculum Development Working Party on Criteria for Education in International Understanding; '*A World Studies Resource Guide*' listing over 100 governmental and non-governmental organisations in the field of international affairs.

Broadsheets for Seniors (and adapted for Juniors) include:

Baines, John '*Learning to Live on Planet Earth*' 1985; Sims, Nicholas A. '*Disarmament and Arms Control*' 1985; Pankhurst, Richard '*Famine in Ethiopa*' 1985; Funnell, Victor '*Vietnam and Kampuchea*' 1985; Blackburn, Kari '*Uganda since Amin*' 1985; Sinclair, Stephen '*The Refugee Nation*' 1986; Adam, Gordon '*Pakistan – A New Beginning?*' 1986; Walker, Rt Hon Peter and Wynn, Brian '*Nuclear Energy*' 1987; Brooke, Penny '*China*' 1987; Preston, Ros and Adams, Michael '*Middle East*' 1987; Joffe, George '*The Gulf War*' 1987; Lampert, Nicholas '*USSR under Gorbachev*' 1987.

FIRCROFT COLLEGE

1018 Bristol Road, Selly Oak, Birmingham B29 6LH (021-472 0116).

Contact: Brian Wicker, Principal.

Status: Part of the federation of nine Selly Oak Colleges.

Staffing: 5 full time; 3 part time.

Income: about £350,000 for 1986/87.

Sources of income: The College is funded almost entirely by the Department of Education and Science by direct grants and student bursaries.

Aims and objectives: Fircroft is a residential college offering a full-time one year course to about 50 students. Anyone over 20, regardless of formal qualifications, may apply. All students commit themselves to studying three of the six main subjects on offer. The courses are mostly introductions to their subjects and include: Economics, Literature, Philosophy, Politics, Sociology, Peace Studies, Mathematics (History, Better English and Study Skills are also available).

Peace Studies is an introduction to the possibilities and the problems of peace in the modern world. It includes studies of the contemporary international scene and of the various military and political options open to states and groups within them, discussion of alternatives to current military strategies, the various competing philosophies of peace which underlie conventional defence, non-violent resistance, pacifism and other approaches to the problem. Visiting experts take part. The course presupposes no particular answers. Students from other Selly Oak colleges may take part.

GANDHI FOUNDATION

Kingsley Hall, Powis Road, London E3 3HJ (01-981 5017).

Contact: Surur Hoda, General Secretary.

Status: Registered charity and Friendly Society.

Origins: Established in 1983 with help from the Joseph Rowntree Charitable Trust.

Patrons: Sir Richard Attenborough (President); Lord Ennals (Chairman).

Staff: 1 part time.

Income: £5–6,000 for 1986.

Sources of income: The Joseph Rowntree Charitable Trust, the Jubilee Trust and the Gandhi Trust, a registered charity set up to raise money for the Foundation's educational work.

Aims and objectives: The Foundation aims 'to relate the teachings of Mahatma Gandhi to the problems of our time by non-violent actions, public education, training and by promoting a better understanding among all peoples of the principles of truth (Satya) and non-violence (Ahimsa).

The programme to date has included the following – a series of summer schools, the third in 1987 on the subject 'Gandhi, Education and Training in Non-Violence'; an annual lecture; a Working party on inner cities problems; a 'Torch For Freedom' carried during 1986 on the first Sunday of each month to Downing Street to draw attention to the problems of the peoples in South Africa.

Journal: Newsletter, quarterly.

NATIONAL ASSOCIATION OF DEVELOPMENT EDUCATION CENTRES

6 Endsleigh Street, London WC1H 0DX (01-388 2670).

Contact: Tony Williams, National Worker.

Status: Registered charity and company limited by guarantee.

Origins: NADEC was formed in 1979; its office base was set up in 1981.

Membership: 50 development education centres and 100 affiliated organisations.

Staffing: 1 full time; 1 part time.

Income: £43,720 for 1986/87.

Sources of income: Initially funding was made available by Oxfam, Christian Aid and War on Want for the first workers in the early 1980s. Almost half the funding in 1987 came from Oxfam and Christian Aid with support also from War on Want, Methodist Church, United Reformed Church, Quaker Peace and Service, CAFOD and project funding from World Wildlife Fund.

Aims and objectives: NADEC exists to support and co-ordinate the work of Development Education Centres in the UK. In 1986/87 it organised 8 one-day training workshops, its annual conference and a series of working groups on relations with the formal sector and on the issues of women, youth and anti-heterosexism. NADEC provides a specialised service to assist centres in submitting their applications for funds to the EEC. In 1988 it will publish a directory of development education centres.

Journals and recent publications:
'Newsdec', quarterly magazine, each issue dealing with a specific theme. Also available are: 'Responding to Media Coverage of Development Issues' 1987; report from a NADEC Working Group set up by Birmingham DEC; reports of the 1986 and 1985 conferences and a publishing workshop are available.

NATIONAL PEACE ACTION FOUNDATION

435a Kingswood Road, Nuneaton, Warwickshire (0203-387 159).

Contact: Pat Bidmead.

Status: Independent group.

Origins: Started in 1983.

Patrons: Dr Sir Nelson Brunton; Canon Peter Berry; Stan Banks; Peter Cadogan; Dennis Gould; Len Gibson; Rev Graham Hardwick; Rev Sidney Hinkes; C. L. R. James; Bruce Kent; Dorothy Kuya; Sam Lee; Harry Mister; Angela Needham; Professor Mike Pentz; Susannah York; Father George Sebalka.

Staffing: None paid.

Income: about £3,000 for 1986.

Sources of income: Donations and publication sales.

Aims and objectives: The Foundation is a small multi-cultural collective which aims to educate and inform in aspects of peace and racial harmony. It arranges for speakers to visit groups and makes no charge except for travelling expenses.

Publications:
Some dozen information packs are produced.

ONE WORLD TRUST

Room 325, St Stephens House, Victoria Embankment, London SW1A 2LA (01-930 0034).

Contact: Katrina Holgate, Secretary.

Trustees: Brendon Sewill (Chairman); Peter Archer MP; Mrs Islay Doncaster; Mrs Celia Goodhart; Christopher Layton; Mrs Wendy Reves; Richard Tames; Sir John Tilney; Henry Usborne.

Status: Registered charity.

Origins: The Trust was set up in 1951 by the Parliamentary Group for World Government.

Staffing: 1 part time.

Aims and objectives: The Trust aims to raise funds for the promotion of education and research and to investigate ways in which to encourage a greater sense of 'world community'.

In the early 1980s the Trust helped to initiate the 'World Studies 8–13 Project'. In recent years the Trust has not been so active but is now in the process of developing new programmes which include plans for:

A new teachers' handbook;

Conferences for sixth formers;

Seminars for foreign representatives;

A campaign to promote better understanding of the EEC in collaboration with the Federal Trust;

A newsletter.

ONE WORLD WEEK

PO Box 1, London SW9 8BU (01-733 5500).

Contact: Pat Gerrard, Tany Alexander, Programme Workers.

Status: A project of the Action for World Development Fund, a registered charity, related to the World Development Movement.

Origins: In 1976, the World Development Movement's Churches Committee launched a 'development week' inspired by programmes in Canada, Sweden and the Netherlands. The Committee has representatives from the following churches; Baptist Union, Church of England, Methodist Church, Roman Catholic Church, Society of Friends, Unitarian Churches, United Reformed Church, CAFOD, Christian Aid, Church Missionary Society, United Society for the Propogation of the Gospel, World Development Movement, Y-Care International, YWCA, Scottish Churches through Scottish Churches Action for World Development.

Staffing: 2 full time.

Income: £35,700 for 1986.

Sources of income: The organsations listed above provide some 90% of total income. Christian Aid provides office space and a large financial contribution.

Aims and objectives: One World sees itself as an opportunity for people to share concerns about justice, peace and development. It takes place particularly in churches, community groups and in schools and involves networks such as the development education centres. There are national co-ordinatory offices in London, Edinburgh, Cardiff and Belfast. The week has a different theme each year: in 1988, 'Making Peace with the Planet'; in 1987, 'Who Gets the Credit?'. Themes in earlier years have been: 'Listen for a Change'; 'Recipes for Justice'; 'Women and Children First'; 'Breaking Barriers'.

Projects with other organisations: In 1986 a radio tape was produced with the International Broadcasting Trust.

The 1987 theme provided for co-operation with other development education networks concerned about the debt issue: these included WDM, War On Want, CAFOD, UNICEF and Friends of the Earth. Each yearly theme aims to involve new groups.

Recent publications:
'*One World on Your Doorstep*'; a Handbook giving advice to local planners based on the experience of planners so far. '*1987 Supplement*'; ideas for local planners on the theme, activities and resources. A supplement is prepared each year along with other resource materials.

OPEN UNIVERSITY

2nd Level Course 'Nuclear Weapons, Inquiry, Analysis & Debate'

Walton Hall, Milton Keynes, MK7 6AA (0908-74066).

Contact: Mike Lewsey, Course Manager.

Personnel: Professor Lawrence Freedman of the Department of War Studies at Kings College is the main course assessor with eight other assessors for the different units within the course.

World studies, Education for peace, Development education

Sources of income: Government funding via the DES and student fees. In addition support from the Barrow and Geraldine S. Cadbury Trust and Dunamis to enhance the broadcasts and a.v. programmes.

Aims and objectives: This nine-month course starting annually in February has an eight year presentation life between 1986 and 1993.

Programme: 'The starting point of the course is people's concern about security in the nuclear age. Some see the existence of nuclear weapons as a stabilising influence on the international system and hold that their possession is essential to national security, while others believe that the possession of nuclear weapons is a source rather of insecurity. The situation is a dangerous one, in which the actual use of nuclear weapons is a possibility.'

The course aims to help students to apply intelligent thought and to help them reach their own reasoned judgements in the light of available information. The course is interdisciplinary, providing information and skills from history, international relations, philosophy, physics and technology.

Unit 1 Introduction to the Course – The Atomic Bombs, 1938–1945.
Unit 2 The Nature of the Debate.
Unit 3 Nuclear Physics and Nuclear Weapons.
Unit 4 The Effects of Nuclear Weapons and Nuclear Wars.
Unit 5 Nuclear Weapons Technology.
Unit 6 The European Cold War and the Origins of the Problem of 'Extended Deterrence'.
Unit 7 Nuclear Strategy.
Unit 8 European Independent Nuclear Capabilities in Historical Perspective.
Unit 9 Nuclear Weapons and the Causes of War.
Unit 10 Nuclear Arms Control and Disarmament.
Unit 11 Nuclear Proliferation and Global Security.
Unit 12 Ethical Aspects of the Nuclear Debate.
Unit 13 Prescriptions I.
Unit 14/15 Prescriptions II.

Fee: £210 Half credit Second level, 8 TV programmes, 8 radio programmes, 2 audio cassettes. Transferable towards a BA degree.

OXFAM

Youth and Education Department, 274 Banbury Road, Oxford OX2 7DZ (0865-56777) (*for grants see separate entry*).

Contact: Barbara Bond, Head of Department.

Status: Registered charity and company limited by guarantee.

Origins: Oxfam's work for development education in Britain started over 20 years ago.

Oxfam Officers: Christopher B. Barber (Chairman); W. Mary Cherry (Chairman of Executive Committee); Joel G. Joffe (Vice Chairman); Frank Judd (Director).

Staffing of Youth and Education Department: 31 full time posts, 7 of which are at Oxfam's Oxford HQ (the majority are qualified teachers).

Income: Separate figures are hard to estimate but believed for the department to be over £½ million in 1986/87. Oxfam's Public Education and Campaigning work cost £2.23 million in 1986/87. This includes work with schools, the costs of the Information and Visual Aid Department and the Public Affairs Unit programme of research. Oxfam's total income in 1986/87 was £44.24 million of which £32.16 million was spent on overseas aid.

Aims and objectives: Oxfam's work for development education within Britain 'is concerned with recognising our involvement in world affairs, raising our awareness of our own potential for influencing them, and developing the skills necessary for effective participation. It examines the relationship between industrialised and 'Third World' countries; it promotes respect for all cultures and lifestyles, and it confronts the fact that we, while consuming far more than our share of the earth's resources, look down on the very countries and people whom we are depriving.

Through its work with teachers, youth workers and young people, Oxfam's Youth and Education Department aims to contribute to the effectiveness of development education work in the UK through:

The production and marketing of a wide variety of learning resources;

Offering professional advice and support to teachers and youth workers who want their work with young people to have an international perspective;

Initiating experimental development education projects;

Funding development education programmes in the UK.' (*See separate entry in Part Two – Funding Sources*).

Oxfam's development education work is based on 40 years' direct work with poor people in some 80 countries throughout the world. Each year it is involved in relief operations in situations of conflict in the Third World and sees how scarce resources are diverted from health, education and development to pay for imports of military equipment.

Affiliations: Oxfam has been one of the many joint sponsors of the Bread Not Bombs Week of the

World studies, Education for peace, Development education

Campaign Against Arms Trade which was held annually up to 1987.

Oxfam is one of the 20 sponsors of the Annual Central America Week in March. The 1988 theme of this national event was 'Peace for People, People for Peace'.

Journals and publications: A free catalogue of all Oxfam's schools and youth materials is available. This includes work by local development education centres as well as from other related organisations. Each year a booklet of new resources is also produced. Oxfam's Audio Visual Resource Unit has a wide range of materials available for sale or loan. Oxfam's Information Department produces a range of free information sheets.

OXFORD PROJECT FOR PEACE STUDIES

30 Sunderland Avenue, Oxford OX2 8DX (0865-58684).

Contact: Dr George Johnson, Hon Secretary.

Status: Registered charity.

Origins: A group of people with a concern for peace came together in 1980 at the invitation of George Johnson.

Trustees: Mrs Mary Allsebrook; Sir Richard Doll; Dr Frank Ellis; Professor John Ferguson; Professor Kenneth Kirkwood.

Staffing: None paid.

Estimated income: £6,000 for 1986.

Sources of income: Grants from trusts, covenanted subscriptions from its Friends Scheme and other donations.

Aims and objectives: The Project aims to promote teaching and research in the field of peace studies in Oxford. Links have been developed with academic institutions in Oxford and elsewhere. Activities to date include an essay competition in 1984 for students in higher education on the theme 'The Search for Peace', and an annual series of lectures from 1984 at St Antony's College exploring 'Peace Studies' from different academic perspectives. The project aims to establish a new academic centre for peace studies at Oxford.

Publications: *'Peace Studies: The Hard Questions'*, Rex Collings, 1987. Pamphlets of lectures.

PAX CHRISTI

(see Section 2. Action research and campaigns – Church Organisations)

PEACE EDUCATION COMMISSION

International Peace Research Association, Centre for Comparative and International Studies in Education, School of Education, La Trobe University, Bundoora, Victoria 3083, Australia (0347-92639).

Contact: Robin Burns, Executive Secretary.

Origins: Founded by IPRA in 1972.

Membership: 220.

Staffing: None paid.

Income: US $1,100 for 1987.

Sources of income: International Social Science Council (UNESCO).

Aims and objectives: The Commission is developing links between individuals and groups by focusing on a series of project areas: children and violence; textbook analysis; sexism and sex role socialisation; peace education in the Third World; non formal and adult education for peace; tertiary and teacher-training peace education programmes; implementation of peace education; evaluation of peace education; and effective aspects of peace education.

Projects include:

'Controversies Surrounding the Relationship between Education and Development' edited by R. Aspeslagh (Netherlands) and M. Haavelsend (Norway) to be published in collaboration with the Gandhi Peace Foundation;

Preparation by Betty Reardon and other PEC members of a kit on women and peace for the UN;

A book on images of war in school textbooks.

International conferences;

A newsletter is produced.

PEACE EDUCATION NETWORK

c/o 11 Alexandra Road South, Whalley Range, Manchester M16 8GE (061-226 6328).

Contact: Gil Fell, Development Worker.

Status: Independent non-profitmaking organisation.

Origins: Formed in 1981 during a meeting at Atlantic College on 'Education for Peace'.

Membership: 150.

Staffing: 1 full time.

Sources of income: Barrow Cadbury Fund Ltd support for full-time worker for 3 years (starting mid 1986); subscriptions.

Aims and objectives: The Network aims to:

Provide communication between and practical

World studies, Education for peace, Development education

support for teachers and local groups wishing to make education a force for peace;

Promote peace education amongst the public at large;

Promote links with those similarly involved in other countries, and with those with related concerns;

Promote research and development in the field of peace education.

An annual conference, termly residential weekend and occasional day schools are organised. In-service training is provided for LEAs on request.

Journal: *'PEN newsletter'*, termly.

PEACE EDUCATION PROJECT (West Midlands)

Woodbrooke, 1046 Bristol Road, Birmingham B29 6LJ (021-472 7242).

Contact: Andrew Chandler, Organiser.

Status: Charitable as a project of the Warwickshire Monthly Meeting of Quakers.

Staffing: 1 full time; 1 part time.

Income: Not disclosed.

Sources of income: Warwickshire and Staffordshire Monthly Meetings; Quaker Peace and Service; Barrow and Geraldine S. Cadbury; other Quaker Trusts.

Aims and objectives: This three year project has been set up and is jointly administered by the Staffordshire and Warwickshire Monthly Meetings. Staff started work in May 1987. The aim is to provide a resource for teachers in the nine local authority areas of the West Midlands and to be of specific relevance to the school children of the area.

PEACE EDUCATION RESOURCE CENTRE, Belfast

(see Section 7: Northern Ireland)

PEACE PLEDGE UNION

(see Section 2: Action research and campaigns – Membership organisations)

PEACE THROUGH NATO

(see Section 2: Action research and campaigns – Non-membership organisations)

PLAY FOR LIFE

31b Ipswich Road, Norwich NR2 2LN (0603-505 947/616 098).

Contact: Elizabeth Stutz, Joint Director.

Status: Registered charity and company limited by guarantee.

Origins: Play for Life was started, in 1984, by a small group of people concerned about the effects of war toys and other undesirable toys and the need for worthwhile alternatives.

Founding sponsors: Green Party, Peace Pledge Union, Quaker Peace and Service and Traidcraft Educational Foundation.

Staffing: 1 part time (plus an arrangement with Concord Film and Video Council for distribution of materials).

Membership: 120.

Trading turnover: £5,700 for 1986.

Sources of income: Sale of toys and activity books through mailorder, party plan agents and stalls at events; grants from the Invicta Trust and the Barrow and Geraldine S. Cadbury Trust; membership subscriptions.

Aims and objectives: Play for Life aims to develop co-operation between parents, educators and the toy industry in promoting 'life-affirming' playthings. Their main tool for this is their *'Guide to Playthings for Life'* which describes some 200 'life-affirming' toys, games activities and materials. The toys are submitted by the manufacturers for inspection and Play for Life believe a constructive relationship is developing with the toy industry – well over 5,000 copies of the Guide have been sold.

Play for Life also runs an annual conference, workshops, provides speakers and workshop leaders. They have been represented at many conferences including the World Peace Congress, Copenhagen, 1986, the 'International Competition for Toys and Games preparing for Life in Peace' by the Polish Peace Committee, 1987, in Warsaw.

Play for Life plan to produce their own playthings, kits and games to supplement those listed in the guide.

Affiliations: Play for Life is affiliated to the International Association for the Child's Right to Play and the National Peace Council.

Journals and publications:
Members' quarterly newsletter;
'A Guide to Playthings for Life', 3rd edition, 1987;
Butterworth, Lesley, *'Do-it-Yourself Toys'*, pamphlet;
Stutz, Elizabeth, *'Growing up to love nature'*, pamphlet.

QUAKER PEACE AND SERVICE

(see Section 2: Action research and campaigns – Church organisations)

RICHARDSON INSTITUTE FOR PEACE STUDIES, Lancaster University

(see Section 1: Policy-oriented research)

SCHOOLS AGAINST THE BOMB

(see CND entry in Section 2: Action research and campaigns – Membership organisations)

SHEFFIELD POST 16 Peace and Conflict Studies Working Party

Richmond College of Further Education, Spinkhill Drive, Sheffield S13 8FD (0742-342 497).

Contacts: Chris Hyde; Eric Deamer; Brian Hamilton-Tweedale (Research assistant).

Aims and objectives: The working party, which began at a Sheffield conference in 1984, has received funding from the Joseph Rowntree Charitable Trust and aims to:
  Develop an 'A' level syllabus in Peace and Conflict Studies to be available nationally (the project is an official development of the Joint Matriculation Board in Manchester);
  Develop a resource centre in Sheffield for such studies.

STUDENT PEACE PROJECT

77 Hungerdown Lane, Lawford, Manningtree, Essex CO11 2LX (0206-230 434).

Contact: Ted Dunn, Co-ordinator.

Status: The Project works in association with the Lansbury House Trust Fund, an educational charity.

Sponsors: Lord Caradon; Professor Adam Curle; Robin Richardson; Professor John Ferguson; Professor James O'Connell; Conflict Research Society.

Income: £2,000 for 1986.

Sources of income: Donations have been made by the Joseph Rowntree Charitable Trust, the Puckham Trust and the C. C. Morland Charitable Trust.

Aims and objectives: The Project aims to highlight the need to study the interdisciplinary nature of peace. Awards are made to students relating their work to peaceful relationships. Awards to sixth-form, graduate and postgraduate students range between £10 and £100.

The peace research considered need not be limited specifically in the area of peace studies, anthropology, law, architecture, agriculture and philosophy are all subjects which can be related to the understanding of the nature of peaceful relationships.

Students can submit their research projects/studies at any time accompanied by a short abstract to enable a wider dissemination of the work in the project's published 'Collection of Abstracts'.

Journals and recent publications:
Collection of Abstracts.

TEACHERS FOR PEACE

c/o 22–24 Underwood Street, London N1 7JG (01-250 4010).

Contact: Pat Allen, Chair.

Status: Unincorporated association.

Origins: Founded in the late 1950s and re-formed in 1981 at a CND conference.

Membership: Information not supplied.

Staffing: None paid.

Income: Not known.

Sources of income: Subscriptions and donations.

Aims and objectives: Teachers for Peace is a membership organisation of teachers, lecturers, youth workers, parents and others with an interest in education which aims to answer young people's questions about nuclear war. It believes that information about the dangers of nuclear war and the possible alternatives to such a war should be widely available in schools and colleges in forms designed for each age group. The group believes that teachers have a duty to discuss the means by which disarmament could be achieved, whether unilateral or multilateral, although it is opposed to the use of the classroom as a recruiting ground for any organisation.

It encourages education authorities to adopt peace education and serves as an educational contact network distributing peace education materials of its own as well as from other sources.

Affiliations: Teachers for Peace is recognised as a non-governmental organisation by UNESCO, is a member of Professions for World Disarmament &

World studies, Education for peace, Development education

Development and is affiliated to CND and the National Peace Council.

Recent publications:

'*Lesson Notes on Nuclear Weapons*', pilot pack by Iain Farrell and Julian Cohen, 1985; '*Peace Studies Resource Guide*', 1986.

THIRD WORLD FIRST

Central Office, 232 Cowley Oxford OX4 1UH (0865-245 678).

Offices also in Newcastle (091-261 1649) **and London** (01-434 4220).

Contact: Mary Wright, Fundraiser/promotions (based in London).

Status: Unincorporated association. The Third World First Educational Trust and the Anti-Poverty Trust carry out its charitable activities.

Origins: 3WI was founded in 1969 and was originally a part of Oxfam. It became independent in 1976.

Membership: 60 groups with over 5,000 members.

Staffing: 6 full time; 1 part time.

Income: £120,000 for 1986/87.

Sources of income: Oxfam, Christian Aid and CAFOD with half coming from members' subscriptions.

Aims and objectives: Third World First is a national student-based campaign against world poverty. It exists to:

'Publicise the facts of international poverty;

Support the growing actions of the poor and oppressed as they organise to build their own futures;

Expose and oppose the interests of the rich and powerful that stand in their way.'

It organises educational programmes, campaigns and conferences. Membership is open to all who support its aims, and is not limited to students. Their 1% Self-Tax Scheme encourages people to commit 1% of their income to 3WI. Half the contribution goes to self-reliant development in the Third World or Britain, of the member's choice; the other half pays for membership of 3WI.

Projects with other organisations: A research project on charity and media representation of black and Third World people is funded by the CRE and the Joseph Rowntree Charitable Trust.

Journals and recent publications:

'*Links*', quarterly publication to members, distributed more widely by Third World publications. Thirty issues by December 1987, including: No. 18 '*Disarmament & Development*', No. 26 '*Critical Mess, the Real Cost of Global Nuclearisation*'.

Published by Pluto Press in association with 3WI: Hayter, Teresa '*Creation of World Poverty*'; Hill, Jeremy and Scannell, Hilary '*Due South*'.

A full publications list, including resource packs, is available.

TRADE UNION INTERNATIONAL RESEARCH AND EDUCATION GROUP (TUIREG)

Ruskin College, Walton Street, Oxford OX1 2HE (0865-54599/56564).

Contact: Carol Cotmore, Co-ordinator.

Status: Registered charity status as a project within Ruskin College.

Origins: Founded 1976, by staff and students at Ruskin after a TUC Conference.

Staffing: 4 full time; 1 part time.

Income: £150,000 for 1987.

Sources of income: EEC; Oxfam; Christian Aid; Action Aid; CAFOD; Save the Children Fund; TUIREG courses and schools commissions; a sponsorship scheme.

Aims and objectives: TUIREG is a group working for development through educational activities across the world and in the UK.

It aims to promote education and research on international issues at all levels of the labour movement, where they affect workers as producers or consumers; to increase understanding of and support for international initiatives conducted in the interests of workers by institutions including trade unions, governments and international agencies; to provoke discussion and action, leading to a growth of international understanding and solidarity amongst workers.

TUIREG offers a combination of resources for use in development education including: audiovisuals, publications, teaching, and courses. It also undertakes research and audio-visual commissions.

Journals and recent publications:

Newsletter, quarterly and free to sponsors of TUIREG.

Video programmes with background notes are available for hire or sale on a range of topics e.g. the Brandt Report.

A catalogue is available upon request.

World studies, Education for peace, Development education

ULSTER UNIVERSITY, Peace Studies Programme

(see Section 1: Policy-oriented research – Universities)

UNITED NATIONS ASSOCIATION

(see Section 2: Action research and campaigns – Membership organisations)

UNITED NATIONS UNIVERSITY OF PEACE

(see Section 1: Policy-oriented research)

UNITED WORLD COLLEGE OF THE ATLANTIC

(Atlantic College), St Donat's Castle, Llantuit Major, South Glamorgan CF6 9WG (04465-2530).

Contact: Ian Wilson, Head of History Department.

Status: Registered charity.

Origins: The College was founded by Kurt Hahn and Lawrence Darvall in 1962. The pilot scheme for their peace studies course started in 1978.

Patron: HRH The Prince of Wales, President.

Personnel: (involved in the Peace Studies Project) 1 teacher with responsibility for Peace Studies; 20 students a year.

Sources of income: (for the Peace Studies Project) Between 1975 and 1981 support was provided by the Leverhulme Trust for development on the course.

Aims and objectives: The college curriculum provides an International Baccalaurate, administered in Geneva, which fulfils university requirements in most countries.

The United World Colleges are particularly concerned to promote international understanding through education.

The Peace Studies course is multidisciplinary, linking with the materials and methods of related disciplines, i.e. History, Economics, Psychology and Politics. It covers the study of major world problems (e.g. East-West and North-South conflict) and examines concepts of peace and conflict within and between individuals (e.g. aggression) and nations (e.g. racism). The course deals not only with examples of open violence but also with the wider contexts in which violence and injustice occur.

WAR ON WANT

Central Office, 37-39 Great Guildford Street, London SE1 0ES (01-620 1111).
Offices also in Manchester, Glasgow and Cardiff.

Contact: Francis Khoo, General Secretary.

Status: Registered charity and company limited by guarantee.

Origins: In 1952 Victor Gollancz wrote a letter to the Manchester Guardian on the link between poverty and the arms race. This elicited over 5,000 affirmative responses, and led to the setting up of War on Want.

Honorary officers: Simon Fanshawe (Chairperson).

Membership: Individuals 4,000; Local groups 65–70.

Staffing: 38 full time in London; 9 Regional (3 of which are part time).

Income: £6,532,000 million for 1985/86.

Sources of income: ODA; Jersey government; EEC; CAFOD; Christian Aid; CIIR; Local groups.

War On Want Campaigns Ltd the non-charitable campaigning associate, was formed in 1980. This particularly concerns itself with aspects of the debt crisis.

Aims and objectives: War on Want works through its local groups raising local awareness on Third World issues, organising campaigns and fundraising.

Since 1983, War on Want has been the lead agency for the Eritrea Inter Agency Consortium and the Tigray Transport & Agriculture Consortium and has been raising funds for these projects on behalf of the Consortia from many different agencies.

War on Want funds projects in Southern Africa, North Africa and the Middle East, Central America and the Caribbean, South Asia. It also makes a particular feature of the position of women, and speaks out on development for women.

In 1985/86 it funded the following projects based in Britain:
  Education/Information Programme (Carila);
  Central America Human Rights Co-ordination;
  Central America Information Service;
  Film on El Salvador;
  Latin American Debt Campaign;
  Nicaragua Solidarity Campaign;
  Development Under Fire (Film on Nicaragua).

Affiliations and joint projects with other organisations: Co-operation with 'Bread not Bombs' campaign; Hiroshima Day Long March, 1985, by Bruce Kent raised funds for both CND and War on Want's work in Eritrea and Nicaragua. One of its best known

World studies, Education for peace, Development education

slogans is 'Arms sales to the Third World amounts to more than the value of relief aid'.

Publications: Information broadsheets (which also serve as fundraising leaflets) are published on specific campaign areas (e.g. Mozambique, Nicaragua, Bangladesh).

WELSH CENTRE FOR INTERNATIONAL AFFAIRS

Temple of Peace, Cathays Park, Cardiff CF1 3AP (0222-28549/395 664).

Contact: W. R. Davies, Director.

Status: Unincorporated association; the UNA (Welsh Centre) Trust is its charitable arm.

Origins: The Centre was established in 1973; (the Temple of Peace was built in 1938 by Lord Davies of Llandinam).

Patrons: Sir Alun Talfan Davies (President); Hon Jonathan Davies (Chairman of Co-ordinating Committee); Hon Edward Davies; Viscount Tonypandy (Past Presidents).

Staffing: 6 full time; 1 part time (plus 1 full-time secondment from Metal Box).

Income: £58,756 for 1986.

Sources of income: Interest from an endowment fund and donations.

Aims and objectives: The Centre has no individual membership but comprises representatives of organisations, public and private, from all over Wales. The Centre works in four main areas:

Schools and Colleges – to initiate a range of conferences to cover all levels of education activity, primary to university, and to encourage practical support for international understanding.

A Conference Structure – to develop an all Wales conference structure so that issues of international importance which affect people's day to day life can be discussed.

Humanitarian assistance – to strengthen links with humanitarian aid agencies represented in Wales, more especially UNICEF in an effort to reduce the level of poverty, disease and deaths in the developing world.

International service – to develop an all Wales network of international service work camps where young people from many countries can work side by side on social service projects with the youth of Wales and to provide similar opportunities overseas.

The Centre is both a forum, a co-ordinating body, an instigator and a servicing agency. It services the following constituent organisations in Wales:
Welsh National Council, United Nations Association;
Freedom From Hunger Campaign (Wales);
Council for Education in World Citizenship – Cymru;
UNA (Welsh Centre) Trust;
David Davies Memorial Institute for International Studies;
United Nations Association (Wales) International Youth Service;

The United Kingdom Freedom from Hunger Campaign Committee is administered from the Centre. The Centre has committees on Development Education and Information, and on Legal Affairs.

The Centre acts also as an information/resource centre and also compiled a Register of Speakers in Wales on various aspects of development education.

Journals and recent publications:
Half yearly newsletter. An annual topic paper is published: Paper No. 11, in 1986, was *The United Nations and the Quest for Peace* by Professor Alan James and Sir Anthony Parsons.

WOODBROOKE QUAKER STUDY CENTRE

1046 Bristol Road, Birmingham B29 6LJ (021-472 5171).

Contacts: June and Roland Ellis, Wardens.

Status: Autonomous educational institution, part of the federation of nine Selly Oak Colleges.

Origins: Founded in 1903 when George Cadbury gave his former family home as a base.

Income: £360,838 for year ended September 1986.

Sources of income: Well over half the revenue comes from visitors' and course fees and the remainder from donations, particularly from Quaker Trusts, and investment income.

Aims and objectives: Woodbrooke is an international Quaker adult study centre. It exists to provide a learning community in which individuals and groups can study, discuss, explore new ideas and experiences, and seek to grow spiritually. It is open to any who want to share in its programme. It offers term-time residential courses; short periods of study or reflection during term-time; residence for those studying elsewhere in Birmingham; short courses at Woodbrooke in term-time and vacations; short courses 'On-the-Road' at Friends' Meetings in Britain and abroad. In 1986, some 1,200 people studied at Woodbrooke. (Limited funds are available for bursaries.) Courses are offered in Quaker Studies,

Biblical Studies, Contemporary Religious Thought and in particular in:

Peace Studies, including individual and corporate conflict, violence and injustice, the theory of practice of non-violence and the relevance of the Quaker Peace Testimony.

International Affairs, including development and environmental issues and the approaches to a more just and peaceful world.

Social Responsibility, various topics such as racism, women's issues, the problems of industrial societies and a consideration of alternative futures.

Every summer a Peace Week is organised. In 1987 its theme was 'Living Our Visions' and in 1988 'Networking for Change'. Courses in Autumn/Winter 1987/88 included 'Defence and Security in the Nuclear Age', 'Women and Peace' and 'Justice, Peace and the Integrity of Creation'.

Journals and recent publications:
The Woodbrooke Association publishes a biannual newsletter. Study packs and recordings are produced to be used widely in any part of the world.

WORLD DEVELOPMENT MOVEMENT

Bedford Chambers, Covent Garden, London WC2E 8HA (01-836 3672).

Contact: John Mitchell, Director.

Status: Company limited by guarantee.

Origins: Started in 1969.

Council officers 1987/88: Charlotte Mbali (Chairperson); John Tanner (Vice-Chairperson); Co-opted Council members: Paul Boateng MP; Eric Deakins MP; Bowen Wells MP.

Membership: 4,850.

Staffing: 10 full time; 2 part time.

Income: £220,000 for 1986 (WDM/AWDF joint income) £140,000 for 1986 (WDM only).

Sources of income: The first figure above represents the combined accounts of the Movement and of the Action for World Development Fund (AWDF), an educational charity which co-operates with the Movement in funding a large part of its educational, as opposed to its political work. AWDF's support to One World Week (*see separate entry*) and Third World Publications is not included in the above total income figure.

Nearly half the income is in grants mainly from the Churches and the major aid agencies.

Aims and objectives: The Movement aims to encourage Britain to play a leading role in helping to create a just world and help change the structures which perpetuate poverty. Some 200 locally based groups and individual members assist the campaign for changes in Britain's policies which will benefit the poorest groups in the Third world. In 1986 WDM jointly campaigned for Sport-Aid and co-ordinated a successful EEC-wide campaign that EEC food aid should be provided for disaster relief and for feeding the very poor and not as a way of dumping EEC food surpluses. During the General Election period in 1987, WDM members and supporters managed to raise development issues with the main party candidates in virtually every constituency in Great Britain. Other major campaigns during 1987 included work on the sugar trade and international debt crisis.

Affiliations and joint projects with other organisations: Much of the WDM's work is in close association with other organisations.

Journals and recent publications:
'*Spur*', monthly newspaper. A resource list of campaigning booklets, leaflets, posters, balloons and badges is available.

YOUTH CND

(*see entry for CND in Section 2: Action research and campaigns – Membership organisations*)

WORLD STUDIES, EDUCATION FOR PEACE, DEVELOPMENT EDUCATION:
Development Education Centres

This section includes only those centres with paid staff or involved in publishing (as at January 1988).

Bangor: World Development Education Centre School of Education, St Mary's College, Lon Pobty, Bangor, Gwynedd LL57 1DZ (0248-351 151 x 2947).

Bath: Bath Development Education Group, 7 Barton Buildings, Bath, Avon BA1 2JR (0225-313 274).

Belfast: One World Centre (NI), 4 Lower Crescent, Belfast BT7 1NR (0232-41879).

Berkshire: WEB Bus Project, Haymill, 112 Burnham Lane, Slough, Berks SL1 6IZ (06286-67401).

Berkshire: Reading International Support Centre, 103 London Road, Reading RG1 4QA (0734-586 692).

Birmingham: Development Education Centre, Gillett Centre, Selly Oak Colleges, Birmingham B29 6LE (021-472 3255).

Brighton: Brighton Development Education Group, Brighthelm Church and Community Centre, North Road, Brighton (0273-698 064).

Bristol: BREAD, 84 Colston Street, Bristol BS1 5BB (0272-230 458).

Carmarthen: Centre for Development Education, Maenllwyd, Llangynog, Carmarthen, Dyfed SA33 5JA (0267-82278).

Cleveland: Development Education Centre, 41 Tedworth Close, Hunters Hill, Guisborough, Cleveland TS14 7PR (0287-39316).

Coventry: Development Education Centre, 300 Walsgrave Road, Coventry CV2 4BL (0203-44502).

Derry: Development Education Centre, 12 London Street, Derry BT48 6QR (0504-269 183).

Dorset: Development Education in East Dorset (DEED), South-East Dorset Teachers' Centre, Lowther Road, Bournemouth, Dorset BH8 8NR (0202-295 184).

Dundee: The World Centre, Blackness Project Office, 1 Westport, Dundee (0382-201 424).

Edinburgh: Multi-Agency Centre (MAC), Old Playhouse Close, Moray House College of Education, Holyrood Road, Edinburgh EH8 8AQ (031-557 3810).

Edinburgh: SEAD, (Scottish Education and Action for Development), 29 Nicholson Square, Edinburgh EH1 3LT (031-667 0120).

Exmouth: Centre for International Studies, Box 18, Exmouth, Devon (0395-264 902).

Hull: Development Education Centre, 161 High Street, Hull HU1 1NQ (0482-210 168).

Leamington: Warwickshire World Studies Centre, 32a Bath Street, Leamington Spa, Warwickshire (0926-881 980).

Leeds: Development Education Centre, 151-153 Cardigan Road, Leeds LS6 1LJ (0532-784 030).

Leicester: Leicester World Development Centre, 10a Bishop Street, Leicester (0533-540 957).

Liverpool: World Development Studies Centre, Liverpool Institute of Higher Education, St Katharine's College, Stand Park Road, Liverpool L16 9JD (051-722 2361 x 267).

London (North): Women's International Resource Centre, 173 Archway Road, London N6 (01-341 4403).

London (North-West): Development Education Centre, 26 Cressy Road, London NW3 2LY.

London – Africa Centre: 38 King Street, Covent Garden, London WC2 8JT (01-836 1973).

London (East): Tower Hamlets International Solidarity, Oxford House, Derbyshire Street, London E2 (01-739 9001).

Manchester: Development Education Project, c/o Manchester Polytechnic, 801 Wilmslow Road, Didsbury, Manchester M20 8RG (061-445 2495).

World studies, Education for peace, Development education

Milton Keynes: World Development Education Centre, Block A, Bridgewater Hall, Stantonbury Campus, Milton Keynes MK14 6BN (0908-310 951).

North Staffordshire: Development Education Centre, Newcastle under Lyme College, Liverpool Road, Newcastle, Staffs ST5 2DF (0782-711 455).

Nottingham: MUNDI, c/o YMCA, 4 Shakespeare Street, Nottingham, Notts. NG1 4FG (0602-480 080).

Norwich: Norfolk Education and Action for Development, 38–40 Exchange Street, Norfolk NR2 1AX (0603-610 993).

Oxford: Oxford Development Education Centre, 33a Canal Street, Jericho, Oxford OX2 6BQ (0865-511 095).

Preston: Lancashire Development Education Centre, Room 1, Avenham Building, Avenham Lane, Preston PR1 3SS (0772-52299).

Pendle: Centre for Development and Peace, Unit 20, Colne Commercial Centre, Exchange Street, Colne, Lancs, BB8 0SQ (0282-862 505).

Sheffield: South Yorkshire World Development Education Centre, Burngreave Middle School, Earldom Road, Sheffield S4 YEJ (0742-739 216).

Southampton: Tools For Self Reliance, Netley Marsh Workshops, Southampton SO4 2GY (0703-869 697).

Winchester: Hampshire Development Education Centre, Mid-Hants Teachers' Centre, Elm Road, Winchester, Hampshire (0962-56106).

6. Citizen diplomacy: Citizen diplomacy, Exchange Visits, Overseas Service

Introductory note

Citizen's diplomacy is an evocative phrase coined by Claire Ryle and Jim Garrison (who themselves set up East-West Reach – see entry) to describe those many and varied independent contacts with other countries, particularly between countries with which official diplomatic relationships are strained and uneasy.

This small section merely acts as an 'indicator' of the myriads of ways in which creative communication occurs between individuals and groups making links with their counterparts in other countries; links which help to forge mutual understanding and to bring about a change in attitudes and alter misconceptions.

First there are the many exchange programmes – in this area, the work of the Central Bureau for Educational Visits and Exchanges is focal and their guides to the hundreds of opportunities and individual organisations are invaluable information sources (see list with entry).

The legacy of the Commonwealth still acts as a vast tree of interconnections between many different cultures and in the UK the Royal Commonwealth Society, the Victoria League for Commonwealth Friendship and the Commonwealth Youth Exchange Council are a few of the organisations fostering these relationships.

Societies and associations which facilitate links with a specific country are legion. In this section the English Speaking Union, the Great Britain–China Centre and the Great Britain–USSR Association are representative of organisations which support a wide variety of contacts, professional trade and cultural. The UK–USSR Medical Exchange Programme is an example of an exchange programme for a specific profession.

Within other sections of this guide there are other organisations, centres, institutes or departments where scientific and academic collaboration flourishes as a central part of their raison d'être – Chatham House, the Centre for Russian and East European Studies, the Pugwash Conferences and the International Physicians for the Prevention of Nuclear War to name but a few.

Town twinning, which started between European towns after the First World War, is now widening its geographical scope and extending to towns in Eastern Europe, Russia and The Third World. Within their programmes many towns aim to forge links which provide some form of developmental value. These are working links which echo the example of the voluntary work camps and programmes of voluntary work overseas.

List of contents

Agencies

Central Bureau for Educational Visits and Exchanges
Christian Fellowship Trust
Christian Movement for Peace
Commonwealth Youth Exchange Council
East West Reach
English Speaking Union
Experiment in International Living
Great Britain – China Centre
Great Britain – USSR Association
Joint Twinning Committee of the Local Authorities Association of Great Britain and Northern Ireland

Mothers for Peace
Royal Commonwealth Society
Schools' Partnership Worldwide
Servas
UK One World Linking Association
UK – USSR Medical Exchange Programme
United Towns Organsation
Victoria League for Commonwealth Friendship

Volunteer programmes

Catholic Institute for International Relations (CIIR) (*see Section 5: Education*)
International Voluntary Service (IVS)
United Nations Association International Service (UNAIS) (*see Section 2: Action research and Campaigns, Membership organisations*)
Voluntary Service Overseas (VSO)

CENTRAL BUREAU FOR EDUCATIONAL VISITS AND EXCHANGES

Seymour Mews House, Seymour Mews, London W1H 9PE (01-486 5101).

Contact: A. H. Male, Director.

Edinburgh office: 3 Bruntsfield Crescent, Edinburgh EH10 4HD (031-447 8024).

Belfast office: 16 Malone Road, Belfast BT9 5BN (0232-664 418/9).

Status: Registered charity.

Origins: Established in 1948 by the British Government.

Trustees: The Central Bureau is governed by a Board of Trustees appointed and charged by the Secretaries of State responsible for Education and the Youth Services in the four countries of the United Kingdom. The UK Education Departments appoint assessors; the Foreign and Commonwealth Office and the British Council have observer status.

The Chairman is J. A. Carter, County Education Officer, East Sussex.

Staffing: 74 full time; 1 part time (as at end 1987).

Income: £2,226,000 for 1985/86.

Sources of income: Department of Education and Science; Scottish Education Department; Department of Education, Northern Ireland.

Aims and objectives: The Central Bureau is the national office responsible for the provision of information and advice on all forms of educational visits and exchanges; the development and administration of a wide range of curriculum related pre-service and in-service exchange programmes; the linking of educational establishments and local education authorities with counterparts abroad; and the organisation of meetings and conferences related to professional international experience.

Journals and recent publications:
'*Working Holidays*', An annual guide to short-term paid and voluntary vacation jobs in Britain and overseas,
'*Volunteer Work*', A guide to medium and long-term voluntary work and service, with information on over 100 organisations recruiting volunteers for projects in the UK and in 153 countries worldwide; published in co-operation with the National Council for Voluntary Organisations;
'*Home from Home*', A guide to homestays and exchange visits with detailed information on organisations arranging exchanges and family homestays;
'*Young Visitors to Britain*', A guide to study, work and leisure opportunities in Britain for young people from

Citizen Diplomacy

overseas. (Published in English, French, German, Italian and Spanish).

'*Pupil Exchange News (PEN)*', a termly newsletter for schools (free on receipt of SAE); '*How to Make the Best of Teacher Exchange*' A guide for schools, colleges and LEAs.

CHRISTIAN FELLOWSHIP TRUST

c/o 19 Denbigh Road, Ealing, London W13 8QA (01-997 1095).

Contact: Alison Harvey, Secretary.

Status: Registered charity.

Origins: Founded in 1964 in South Africa.

Management: Dr Anthony Barker (Chairman) and Committee of 15.

Staffing: 1 part time.

Annual income: £10,000 in 1986 – excludes ODA contribution.

Sources of income: ODA/EEC; Joseph Rowntree Charitable Trust, British Churches (United Reformed Church and Methodist).

Aims and objectives: The Trust aims 'to further the interests of the christian churches in Southern Africa by arranging for personal exchanges of leaders and lay people of the Church between Southern Africa and Europe. It arranges study tours to and from Southern Africa and Namibia and the UK for concerned Christians working for change. Such visits provide a vital opportunity to 're-charge batteries' and to broaden perspectives away from the pressure of Southern Africa. People in the UK keen to learn about the Southern Africa crisis also gain much from the grantees. The Trust is plannig to set up a 'Friends of the Trust' to strengthen the links of solidarity established by people involved in the projects.

Publications: All grantees produce written reports – which are circulated to interested institutions or bodies. The Trust does not have the resources to publish these.

CHRISTIAN MOVEMENT FOR PEACE

Bethnal Green United Reformed Church, Pott Street, London E2 0EF (01-729 7985).

Contact: Mark Roberts, Co-ordinator.

Status: Unincorporated association.

Origins: The Movement was started in Alsace after the First World War by French and German Christians committed to working for reconciliation and friendship between people. The British branch was formed in 1961.

Patron: Paul Ostreicher.

Membership: 60 (300 volunteers).

Staffing: 1 full time.

Approximate annual income: £10,000 for 1986.

Sources of income: Some support from EEC Youth Exchange funds but largely self-financing.

Aims and objectives: CMP is an ecumenical and international movement with branches in Belgium, Canada, France, Portugal, Germany, Holland, Malta, Italy and Switzerland. The main activity of the British branch is organising summer voluntary work in Britain and Ireland as well as sending volunteers to projects abroad. Internationally CMP organises over a hundred projects a year in Europe and Canada and exchanges volunteers with non CMP organisations in Eastern Europe and North America. (Volunteers have to be able to cover their own travel costs).

International seminars are organised by the European Secretariat in co-operation with local branches, recent themes have included 'Nicaragua' and 'Star Wars'.

Affiliations and projects with other bodies: CMP is a member of the umbrella group 'Praxis' which also includes Church Action on Namibia, Emergency, Salvador Allende Cultural Centre and a theology and worship group.

Journals and recent publications:
An annual guide to summer voluntary projects is published each year.

COMMONWEALTH YOUTH EXCHANGE COUNCIL

18 Fleet Street, London EC4Y 1AA (01-353 3901).

Contact: Roderick Gray, Executive Secretary.

Status: Registered charity

Origins: Established in 1970.

Distinguished patrons: The Duke of Westminster (President); Sir Mervyn Brown; Michael H. Caine; Pete Murray; Ian Taylor (Vice Presidents).

Membership: 172 (79 national voluntary bodies; 93 statutory bodies).

Staffing: 3 full time; 1 part time.

Estimated annual income: £205,000 for 1985/86.

Sources of income: HM Government through the British Council and the Youth Exchange Centre;

Queen's Silver Jubilee Trust; member local education authorities and voluntary youth organisations; commercial organisations.

Aims and objectives: The Council aims to promote among young people and youth leaders a wider understanding of the Commonwealth and a greater sense of tolerance and purpose in our multi-racial society. It does this by assisting two-way exchanges between groups of young people in Britain and the Commonwealth particularly for young people in need. It advises with planning and preparation of visits, establishes pilot exchange projects, assists project organisers, runs information services and training courses. Some £148,000 was available in 1986/87 for grants to youth exchange projects (*see separate funding entry*).

Affiliations and projects with other bodies: The Council collaborates with many agencies, in particular the Youth Exchange Centre, Oxfam Education and the Joint Agency Group, placing Commonwealth youth exchange within the wider context of the Youth Service and school curriculum.

Journals and recent publications:
'*A Handbook for Commonwealth Youth Exchange*'; Course reports.

EAST-WEST REACH

6 Catherine Court, Lake Road, Wimbledon SW19 7EW (01-947 1980).

Contact: Barbara Laird.

Status: Unincorporated association.

Origins: Founded in 1983 by Jim Garrison, Pyare Shivpuri and Claire Ryle; recently restarted by Barbara Laird and Pyare Shivpuri.

Consultant: Brigadier Michael Harbottle.

Membership: 83.

Staffing: None paid.

Income: £700 for 1987.

Sources of income: East-West Reach aims to give groups and individuals the opportunity to help in building bridges between the UK and the USSR. It expects to take at least two groups each year to the USSR; to organise talks and discussions on the arts, culture and history of the USSR; to create a network of pen friends.

It works with advice from and in close co-operation with Quaker Peace and Service, and Goodwill Holidays, a Quaker tour operator.

Journals and recent publications:
Bi-annual newsletter; Ryle, Claire and Garrison, Jim '*Citizens' Diplomacy; A Handbook on Anglo-Soviet Initiatives*', Merlin Press, 1986.

ENGLISH SPEAKING UNION OF THE COMMONWEALTH

Dartmouth House, 37 Charles Street, London W1X 8AD (01-493 3328).

Contacts: Rear Admiral Richard Heaslip, Director-General; David Griffiths, Director, Current Affairs.

Status: Registered charity.

Patrons and trustees: HM The Queen (Patron); the Duke of Edinburgh (President); Sir Patrick Dean (Deputy President); Lord Pym (Chairman of the Board of Governors).

Membership: Corporate members 100; Individual members 3,500.

Staffing: 15 full time; 5 part time.

Annual income: £533,000 for 1986/87.

Sources of income: Income from premises, subscriptions, donations and legacies.

Aims and objectives: The ESU is a leading worldwide voluntary society promoting international understanding and friendship between peoples. It describes itself as 'especially concerned with the promotion of understanding and friendship between peoples of the Commonwealth and the USA and, on a non-discriminating basis, with peoples everywhere who share our common values and find English a useful international medium'.

The ESU pursues its cause through educational means. It organises:

Educational interchanges of young people and adults to study in each other's countries;

Current affairs meetings, courses and conferences for people to learn about each other's countries;

Hospitality for its scholars and sponsored visitors so that they can participate in the life of the country they visited;

English language study to facilitate international communication and understanding;

Book exchanges;

Youth and travel programmes.

The ESU believes from experience that as countries and peoples become steadily more interdependent in the modern world there is ever more need of international friendship, and that this cannot be left to governments alone.

The Current Affairs committee, chaired by Sir Philip Adams, takes European–American relations as its major theme. It hosts an annual international summer conference in Oxford. Forum meetings on topical issues, and many other seminars e.g. 'Western Europe and Peacekeeping Worldwide' co-sponsored by the International Peace Academy (*see separate entry*).

Journal: '*Concord*', members' newspaper is published twice a year.

EXPERIMENT IN INTERNATIONAL LIVING (EIL)

'Otesaga', Upper Wyche, Malvern, Worcestershire WR14 4EN (06845-62577).

Contact: Andrew L. McLeod, National Director.

Status: A non-profit making, educational travel association with Training and Induction Ltd is a limited liability company, administering most of its affairs in the UK along with the Trust for Education in International Living, a registered charity.

Origins: Founded in the States in 1932 by Dr Donald Watt who believed 'Men Learn to Live Together by Living Together'. The British Section started in 1936.

Membership: 2,000+.

Staffing: 6 full time; 5 part time.

Income: An annual turnover of £½ million and an operating surplus of £14,000 in 1986.

Sources of income: (*over the past 2 years*) Subscriptions; EIL is contracted by the British Council to run training and induction programmes for study fellows, particularly from Africa; sponsors include the Ernest Cook Trust, Thwaites Brewery, and the Girl Guides Association.

Aims and objectives: EIL aims to promote understanding, respect and friendship between people from different cultural backgrounds.

EIL is part of a federation of autonomous national organisations in 47 countries in all 6 continents, and organises:
  Group programmes during vacation periods;
  Individual homestay placements, world-wide, year-round;
  Intensive language training programmes;
  Special programmes for common-interest groups;
  Academic programmes at secondary, university and post-graduate levels;
  Social service programmes in third-world nations.

EIL believes that understanding comes about through sharing family life rather than as a tourist or guest and this is reflected in its programmes.

Affiliations and joint projects: EIL has consultative status Category B with UNESCO and recognition as Category II non-governmental organisation by UN Economic and Social Council. Nationally and internationally, EIL co-operates with groups such as the International Association for the Exchange of Students for Technical Experience (IAESTE), the Association International des Etudiants de Sciences et Commerce (AISEC), AFS International Scholarships, the Council on International Youth Affairs and Educational Exchange (CIEE), the Peace Corps, Ministries of Youth Affairs and Education, and many similar groups.

Journals and recent publications: '*The Experimenter*', quarterly newsletter for members.

GREAT BRITAIN-CHINA CENTRE

15 Belgrave Square, London SW1X 8PG (01-235 6696/9216).

Contact: Nicola Macbean, Director.

Status: Company limited by guarantee.

Origins: The Centre was opened in 1974. Its predecessor, the Great Britain-China Committee, co-operated with 'Times Newspapers' in organising the exhibition of Chinese archaeological finds at the Royal Academy in 1973. The profits from the exhibition were used to set up the Centre and the China Educational Trust (administered also by the Centre).

Patrons: Lord MacLehose of Beoch (President); Lord Callaghan; Edward Heath; Sir Denis Hamilton (Vice-Presidents); Graham C. Greene (Chairman); Sir Alan Traill; Lady Youde; John Swire (Vice-Chairmen).

Membership: 130 corporate; 500 individual.

Staffing: 3 full time; 1 part time.

Income: £130,000 for 1987/88.

Sources of income: Foreign and Commonwealth Office.

Aims and objectives: The Centre exists to promote closer cultural, economic, scientific, social and other contacts between Britain and China and to encourage mutual knowledge and understanding. It organises direct exchange activities with China of delegations, individuals and exhibitions; work placements in Britain for Chinese professionals and special seminars and briefings on China. Members can attend monthly lectures. To aid its advice and information work, the Centre is setting up a computerised database on general, political and cultural contacts.

Journals and recent publications:
'*Britain-China*' – Newsletter, published three times a year, free to members; '*The Directory of British Organisations with a China Interest*'.

GREAT BRITAIN-USSR ASSOCIATION

14 Grosvenor Place, London SW1X 7HW (01-235 2116).

Contact: John C. Q. Roberts, Director.

Status: Independent, membership association.

Patrons: Sir Fitzroy Maclean, The Rt Hon Lord Wilson (Past Presidents); The Archbishop of Canterbury, Sir John Lawrence, Sir Frank Roberts, Lord Shackleton (Vice Presidents); Sir Curtis Keeble (Chairman).

Membership: 1,300.

Staffing: 4 full time servicing countrywide activities (*see below*).

Income: £153,000 for 1987.

Sources of income: Foreign and Commonwealth Office.

Aims and objectives: The Association fosters on a politically impartial basis professional, cultural and human contacts of all kinds between the United Kingdom and the Soviet Union. A British organisation, it works in consultation with the Foreign and Commonwealth Office, and the British Council. It enjoys the active support of the British Government and of the Opposition, and is also in touch with official bodies in the USSR and with the Soviet Embassy in London. Its Council includes representatives of British organisations, professional, educational and artistic bodies, businesses and trade unions. Its services for its members include introductions to opposite numbers in the Soviet Union, receptions in London and in branches throughout the country for members to meet visitors from the USSR, the use of an extensive library, lectures and film shows, the provision of information and advice to researchers and to those wishing to visit the USSR. There are branches in Scotland, Wales and Northern Ireland as well as representatives who help arrange local events in major cities throughout the country.

Journals and recent publications:
'*Britain–USSR*', members' periodical, 3 times a year and occasional joint publications with the School of Slavonic Studies.

JOINT TWINNING COMMITTEE of the Local Authority Associations of Great Britain and Northern Ireland

10 Spring Gardens, London SW1A 2BN (01-930 8466).

Contact: David R. Herbert, Secretary.

Origins: Started in 1962 by the Association of Municipal Corporations.

Members: Association of County Councils, Association of District Councils, Association of Local Authorities of Northern Ireland, Association of Metropolitan Authorities, Convention of Scottish Local Authorities, National Association of Local Councils.

Associate members: The British Council, Central Bureau for Educational Visits and Exchanges, Council of European Municipalities and Regions (British Section), International Union of Local Authorities (British Section), Department of Education and Science, Department of the Environment, Foreign and Commonwealth Office, Society of Local Authority Chief Executives, Youth Exchange Centre, United Kingdom One World Linking Association.

Staffing: 3 full time.

Annual income: £57,000 in 1987/88.

Sources of income: British Council.

Aims and objectives: The Joint Twinning Committee (JTC) was set up to co-ordinate the development of twinning and avoid overlapping. In 1972, when the UK was poised to enter the EEC, the British Council was given funds to develop closer contacts with other European countries and since that time the Council has also provided the JTC secretariat.

The Committee of nominated representatives of the six associations meets three times a year. Its Secretariat:

Keeps records of all registered British twinning links and requests for new links from Britain and overseas;

Keeps closely in touch with the national sections of the Council of European Municipalities and other international organisations concerned with links, in order to put tentative partners in contact with one another;

Provides advice and encouragement at the initial stages of twinning to local authorities in Britain;

Holds two regional twinning seminars each year in different parts of Britain.

In 1986 there were some 1,300 twinnings in Britain and Northern Ireland, 75% with France and Germany. The following is the current breakdown by area:

Australia (12), Austria (4), Belgium (23), Botswana (1), Bulgaria (2), Canada (11), Caribbean (2), China (8), Cyprus (1), Czechoslovakia (7), Denmark (13), Eire (2), Falkland Islands (1), Finland (3), France

Citizen Diplomacy

(589), Gambia (4), Germany (382), East Germany (4), Gibraltar (1), Hungary (3), Iceland (1), India (1), Israel (5), Italy (18), Jamaica (2), Japan (2), Korea (1), Luxembourg (2), Mongolia (1), Netherlands (40), New Zealand (10), Nicaragua (3), Nigeria (1), Norway (10), Poland (4), Romania (1), Sierra Leone (2), Somalia (2), South Africa (1), Spain (2), Sri Lanka (1), Switzerland (2), Sweden (7), Tanzania (1), Tonga (1), Uganda (2), USA (68), USSR (15), Yugoslavia (12), Zambia (2), Zimbabwe (3).

The JTC, through the British Council, has funds available to assist in the establishment of new links. Grants may be given for the exchange of up to three key people concerned with the promotion of a link. For western European countries this covers fares for an outward visit and a small hospitality grant for an inward visit. For other countries the JTC has set a ceiling for grants for outward visits. The small hospitality grant is also available.

Journals and publications: *'Twinning News'*, a biannual newsletter; *'A Twinning Handbook'*, 1985; *'List of Twinnings'*, 1986.

MOTHERS FOR PEACE

70 Station Road, Burley-in-Wharfedale, Ilkley, West Yorkshire LS29 7NG (0943-864 577).

Contact: Beryl Milner, National Co-ordinator.

Status: Voluntary association.

Origins: In 1980, two elderly Quakers, Lucy Behenna and Marion Mansergh, inspired by the words of the poster 'World peace will come through the will of ordinary people like yourself' put the bulk of their life savings into a fund to send mothers to the USA and the USSR with a message of peace, in the belief that the common bond of motherhood, and wish for a peaceful future for children would unite them and break down barriers of fear and mistrust which stand in the way of peace.

Membership: About 320.

Staffing: 1 part time.

Income: £11,000 for 1985/86.

Sources of income: Donations have been made by the Joseph Rowntree Charitable Trust.

Aims and objectives: Mothers for Peace aims to create personal informal links of friendship between women of East and West. 'We believe that fear and mistrust between people of different cultures and ideologies can be reduced by meeting and learning about each other. We arrange reciprocal visits between women from Britain, USA, USSR and other European countries. Together we try to find ways to create the right conditions for disarmament in the belief that women everywhere want a peaceful future for their children. We provide speakers and information about our experiences. 'Mothers for Peace' plans to continue by the means we already use to nurture the contacts we have made, particularly in the Eastern Bloc countries, and explore new possibilities as they arise.'

Journals and recent publications: A quarterly newsletter; *'Tears and Rainbows – Mothers for Peace, Birmingham discussion week*, 1983; *'Mothers for Peace – Spring and Autumn visits to USA and USSR*, 1984.

ROYAL COMMONWEALTH SOCIETY

18 Northumberland Avenue, London WC2N 5BJ (01-930 6733).

Contact: Sir Michael Scott, Secretary-General.

Status: Educational charity.

Origins: The Society received its Royal Charter in 1882, having started life in 1868 as the Colonial Institute.

Patrons: HM the Queen; HM The Queen Mother (Grand President); HRH The Duchess of York (President).

Membership: 21,000 worldwide including 125 corporate members.

Staffing: 19 full time.

Income: £348,560 for 1986.

Sources of income: Membership subscriptions.

Aims and objectives: The first article of the Society's Royal Charter states its objectives 'to promote within our United Kingdom and overseas the increase and spread of knowledge respecting the peoples and countries of the Commonwealth'. It is both a learned society and a club. It provides meeting places and accommodation for members, a meetings' programme e.g. joint seminars on development with the Crown Agent and a seminar of lectures on South Africa in 1986–7, an annual international Commonwealth Essay Competition and periodical Commonwealth Inter-Change Study Group Operations (CISGO) which are intensive study foci for young executives. The library is extensive and open to all bona fide students of the Commonwealth.

Affiliations: Close relations are maintained with other Commonwealth-oriented organisations including the Royal Over-Seas League, Victoria League, English Speaking Union, Commonwealth Institute and the Commonwealth Secretariat, the Commonwealth Foundation and Foreign and Commonwealth Office.

Journals and publications:
Chairman's Review and Annual Report and Accounts; Newsletters, three times a year for members; *'Library Notes'*; *'Expatriate Briefings'* published by Monitor Press (56 in the series).

SCHOOLS' PARTNERSHIP WORLDWIDE

17 Dean's Yard, London SW1P 3PB (01-222 5738).

Contact: J. A. Cogan, Director.

Status: Registered charity.

Origins: Founded in 1985.

Patrons and trustees: Lord Ennals (Patron); Michael Brearley; James Cogan; Rev Dr Charles Elliott; Christopher Martin; Howard Green; Professor Sir Kenneth Stuart; Derek Dutton; Jean Burroughs.

Staffing: 4 part time.

Income: £25,000 for 1987/88.

Sources of income: The organisation started with the help of grants from the Linbury Trust, the Headley Trust, the Weston Family Trust and the Queen's Silver Jubilee Trust. The scheme is largely self-financing.

Aims and objectives: The Partnership enables young people from schools and colleges to take part in the scheme to work for up to six months in a third-world school, orphanage, community project or other organisation. The Partnership's aims include persuading UK schools and colleges to sustain regular financial commitments to counterpart agencies in the developing world. When joining the scheme a school or college pledges a continuing commitment to the overseas organisation which it wishes to support. In return that organisation offers up to six months' work experience to young people from the school or organisation that raised the money (one visit for every £500/£700).

Once these contacts have been formally established, member schools and colleges are encouraged to develop and extend any twinning arrangements that they wish to pursue.

The Partnership is a new initiative. In the initial phase twenty schools, from both maintained and independent schools, have taken part. More than eighty school leavers had already worked overseas by the end of 1987. The scheme may be particularly attractive to schools to whom the traditional 'volunteering' approach seems inappropriate and who would welcome a more structured means of both giving practical help to Third World institutions and of channelling the urge felt by many young people to give their time and energy as well as their money to such a cause.

SERVAS

British Contact, 77 Elm Park Mansions, Park Walk, London SW10 0AP (01-352 0203).

Contact: Graham Thomas, Hon Secretary.

Origins: This international movement started in 1949 with the name 'Peace Builders' through an American conscientious objector, Bob Luitweiler, who sought a positive expression of his pacifist beliefs.

Staffing: None paid.

Income: £6,840 for 1986.

Aims and objectives: Servas is a network based on enabling work, study and travel between groups of people working for peace and social justice all over the world. In 1952 the movement acquired the name 'Servas' from Esperanto 'ni servas' – 'we serve'. Approved travellers receive lists of hosts in different countries. In some 100 countries and six continents there are over 9,000 host addresses, with individuals, families, neighbourhood centres, ashrams and communities. In 1972 'Servas International' was incorporated in Switzerland as an international, non-profit making association. It is a cultural, non-governmental, non-partisan, interracial and inter-faith organisation with links with many other international peace, human rights, environmental and world development groups.

There are regional co-ordinators for Africa, Europe and Near East, Southern Asia, East Asia, South Pacific, Central America, Caribbean and Mexico, South America, United States and Canada.

Affiliation: Servas has consultative status as a recognised non-governmental organisation with the UN Economic and Social Council.

Journal: *'Servas International News'* bi-annually, free to members.

UK ONE WORLD LINKING ASSOCIATION (UKOWLA)

Chestnut Lodge, Oare, Marlborough, Wilts SN8 4JA (0672-62749).

Contact: Pat Lovelace, Treasurer.

Status: Voluntary organisation.

Origins: Set up in 1985 particularly in response to the growing interest in 'North-South' and 'Third World' community linking.

Membership: 50 One World Link Groups in the UK.

Staffing: None paid.

Citizen Diplomacy

Income: £600–1,000 for 1987 (excluding specific projects).

Sources of income: Subscriptions. Sponsorship has been received for specific projects from e.g. the Commonwealth Foundation, the British Council and the Joint Twinning Committee.

Aims and objectives: The Association provides support, information and advice as well as representation on national and international bodies. Linking comes in many forms and is organised by local authorities, voluntary groups and institutions such as schools, hospitals or dioceses. The prime aim may be cultural exchange, friendship, development co-operation, solidarity, or joint problem solving. Often a mixture of aims is involved and always the process is educational.

Journals and recent publications: 'Community Link' Association Journal, quarterly; 'Handbook on Linking'; 'Community Links' (the first study in linking); 'Towns & Development' (a survey of European–Third World Links).

UK–USSR MEDICAL EXCHANGE PROGRAMME

480 Banbury Road, Oxford OX2 8EN

Contact: Dr Stewart Britten, Hon Secretary.

Status: Independent organisation.

Origins: Founded in 1984 by the Medical Campaign Against Nuclear Weapons and the Medical Association for the Prevention of War, now independent.

Sponsors: Prof J. W. Boag; Prof Z. A. Butenko; Sir Raymond Hoffenberg; Prof J. H. Humphrey; Academician Y. M. Lopukhin; Prof V. S. Moiseyev; Dr Ian Munro; Lord Rea; Prof J. Rotblat; Dr Anthony Storr; Prof F. E. Vartanian.

Membership: 50.

Staffing: None paid.

Income: £1,000 for 1986.

Sources of income: Funds come from subscriptions and donations of members.

Aims and objectives: The Programme aims are – to achieve the exchange of medical knowledge between Soviet and British doctors and other professionals working in health to our mutual benefit – to broaden understanding between Britain and the Soviet Union by promoting exchanges among health workers – to encourage co-operation among the developed countries of East and West in the fair distribution of medical resources throughout the world.

The Programme provides three kinds of medical tours in the Soviet Union, general medical, student and specialist tours, each lasting two weeks and visiting Moscow, Leningrad and one other city. Every opportunity is taken to welcome Soviet medical visitors and to support co-operative research particularly in areas lying outside those formally selected by the British and USSR governmental agreement on co-operation in the field of medicine and public health.

UNITED TOWNS ORGANISATION
(UTO)

(Federation Mondiale Des Villes Jumelées – Cities Unies), 2 rue de Logelbach, 75017 Paris, France (010-331-47.66.75.10).

Contact: Michèle Gayral, Service Presse.

Status: Non-profit making organisation.

Patrons: M. Pierre Mauroy, President (past Prime Minister of France and Mayor of Lille).

Membership: 3,000 towns worldwide (15 in the UK).

Staffing: 29 full time.

Sources of income: Members' subscription fees (based on population size of the member town) government subsidies, particularly the French government. Specific projects funded by UNESCO, the Council of Europe and the EEC.

Aims and objectives: UTO was established in 1957 and helps towns set up twinning links involving the whole population. UTO's basic principles are non-discrimination, non-interference and free circulation of people and information. There are various kinds of twinning:

Twinning set up between two or more towns at a similar stage of economic development; these are the most frequent types of twinnings and they usually take place between towns in countries which are not too far apart;

When one of the partners is a Third-World town, twinnings lead to real development projects. The promotion of such 'co-operaton-twinnings' has become one of UTO's priorities, as local authorities and the people they represent are thus directly involved in the struggle against underdevelopment. Such links also have the advantage of increasing the number of small-scale projects, which are adapted to the real needs of people in the Third World.

UTO recommends that each partner town create its own twinning committee or association, backed by the municipality, to inform as many people as possible about the twinning and involve them in exchange activity.

United Towns' Day is the last Sunday of April every year.

Affiliations: Consultative Status 1 with UNESCO, the UN Economic and Social Council, UNICEF and the Council of Europe.

Journals: *'Cités Unies'*, quarterly magazine in French, English and Spanish. Monthly or bi-monthly newsletters.

VICTORIA LEAGUE FOR COMMONWEALTH FRIENDSHIP

18 Northumberland Avenue, London WC2N 5AP (01-930 1671).

Contact: Sylvia Barnett, General Secretary.

Status: Registered charity and company limited by guarantee.

Origins: Founded in 1901.

Patrons: The Queen; the Queen Mother (Patrons); Princess Margaret (President); the Duchess of Devonshire; the Earl of Selkirk; Lord MacLehose of Beoch; Dame Anne Bryans; Sir John Prideaux, Sir John Peel; Lady Binney (Deputy Presidents).

Membership: 4,000 in the UK and 50 elsewhere.

Staffing: 6 full time.

Income: £70,000 for 1988.

Source of income: Investments.

Aims and objectives: The League aims to promote friendship and understanding between peoples of the Commonwealth. It welcomes and helps members and visitors from the Commonwealth – in particular, to give such visitors to the United Kingdom chances of meeting British people and to offer them a wide variety of invitations and opportunities during their stay, whether its purpose is study, business or pleasure. It also provides student accommodation in London.

Besides Headquarters in England and Scotland there are Leagues in all the Australian States, in many cities in New Zealand, in Zimbabwe, South Africa, the West Indies, Nigeria and Papua New Guinea, and an affiliated organisation in Canada. In most other Commonwealth countries there are League representatives.

Affiliations: The Victoria League is a member of the Joint Commonwealth Societies Council and a corporate member of the Royal Commonwealth Society and Royal Overseas League.

INTERNATIONAL VOLUNTARY SERVICE

162 Upper New Walk, Leicester, LE1 7QA (0533-549 430).

Contact: Malcolm Goldsmith, General Secretary.

Status: Registered charity and company limited by guarantee.

Patrons: The Right Rev Trevor Huddleston (President); Stanley Burton; Barbara Castle MEP; Douglas Childs; Lord Elwyn Jones; Greville Janner MP; Sir Leslie Kirkley; The Earl of Lanesborough; Michael Meadowcroft; Mary Peters; Rt Hon Peter Walker MP; Tim Yeo MP (Vice-Presidents).

Membership: c 1,200.

Staffing: 24 full time (in Britain).

Income: £680,210 for 1986.

Sources of income: Overseas Development Administration (85% of total income); over 70 company and trust donations (9% of total income); membership subscriptions (6% of total income).

Aims and objectives: Service Civil International, of which International Voluntary Service is the British branch, was founded by Pierre Ceresole, a Swiss pacifist in 1920 with the specific intention of working practically for peace through international work camps. The workcamps continue and in 1987 almost one and a half thousand people participated. There were 58 camps in Great Britain and a further 430 throughout the world organised by other SCI branches. Many of the camps include work with children, but there are also manual and work/study camps. An example of the latter being the East-West study camp involving equal numbers of participants from the East and West. IVS's work has expanded. In 1987 70 people were placed as long term volunteers in Southern Africa. Experienced and skilled people are placed according to local demand in agriculture, engineering, teaching etc. In Britain, IVS works through 26 local groups providing voluntary work in the community. IVS is also placing greater emphasis on development education with the SCI Africa-Asia-Europe exchange programme being an integral part of this. A network of local development education groups is being built up.

Journal: *'Service'*, quarterly membership journal.

VOLUNTARY SERVICE OVERSEAS
(VSO)

9 Belgrave Square, London SW1X 8PW (01-253 5191).

Contact: Neil McIntosh, Director.

Citizen Diplomacy

Status: Registered charity.

Patrons: The Duke of Edinburgh; Lord Garmoyle (Hon Chairman); Geoffrey Barnett (Hon Treasurer).

Membership: 7,000.

Staffing: 180 full time; 10 part time.

Income: £7,063,000 for 1986/87.

Sources of income: Overseas Development Administration (85% of total expenditure) and charitable donations from companies and trusts.

Aims and Objectives: VSO aims to assist less developed countries by providing a recruitment agency to select and place volunteers in answer to the Third World's requests.

In 1986/87, 1,150 volunteers were placed in 40 different countries in six broad categories of work: agriculture, forestry and fisheries; education and librarianship; health; business and commerce; technical trades, craft and engineering; community and social development. The volunteers are skilled and experienced people, with an average age of 31 years. VSO also provides volunteers for the United Nations Volunteers Scheme. There are over 70 local groups in Britain and VSO also administers development education awards for returned volunteers wishing to spread their knowledge and interest in the local community.

Affiliations: VSO is a member of the British Volunteer Agencies Liaison Group (BVALG), the Regional Conference on International Voluntary Service (RCIVS), the International Broadcasting Trust (IBT) and the EEC–NGO Network.

Journal:
'*Orbit*' quarterly membership magazine.

7. Reconciliation work: Northern Ireland

Reconciling within Northern Ireland

by Paul Sweeney, Director,
Northern Ireland Voluntary Trust

The 'Troubles', as people locally refer to the current period of civil unrest in Northern Ireland, are now into their twentieth year, and a solution, as such, seems as elusive as ever. A whole generation has become accustomed to the highly charged political atmosphere, and the world's press has exhausted its vocabulary in seeking to describe the latest horrific atrocity. The tribal cleavages perpetuate prejudices, fears and suspicions, and the whole cycle becomes viciously self-fulfilling as whole communities live polarised, sectarianised and mutually exclusive lives. This week has witnessed at least one funeral per day in Belfast, and as I write the whine of the Army helicopter above denotes yet another red alert in North Belfast.

Paradoxically Northern Ireland is inhabited by people renowned for their warmth and friendliness, and the most abnormal aspect of life is the degree of normality that actually pertains as the silent majority get on with the day-to-day business of living. The fact that on several occasions it appeared that the social fabric of life was going to disintegrate into civil war, and didn't, speaks legions; and whilst the potential for an escalation of communal violence remains acute, clearly there are nevertheless many latent 'forces for the good' in operation throughout Northern Ireland, which have made not insignificant contributions to providing hope, space, and positive alternatives. Located within this social phenomena has been the evolution of a wide range of reconciliation initiatives established and nurtured by scores of very committed and energetic individuals with a tremendous sense of social vision and collective drive to encourage positive social change.

As with the causes of the current unrest some reconciliation groups ante-date the current 'troubles', and in this regard the Corrymeela Community has consistently provided an important focus and impetus to fostering mutual understanding and tolerance from the mid-1960s onwards. However, over the past twenty years, coinciding with the violence, there has been a multiplicity of initiatives in the field of reconciliation and community relations. Many have had short life spans; others have evolved and developed. Some have attracted less than a score of followers; others have engendered considerable popular movements. Some groups have been established in response to the general sense of malaise and hopelessness; others have their genesis in a particular horrific incident such as the Peace People movement, which was born out of the deaths of the Maguire children in August 1976. Some groups have sought to focus on the political (with a small 'p') scenario, such as the New Ireland Group; others have focused on specific issues such as integrated education.

Whilst most reconciliation initiatives within Northern Ireland would share a broad general theme, there is nevertheless a wide diversity between the aims and objectives of each organisation and their philosophical bases. The Christian faith has provided a strong inspirational base for a number of groups, many of which have sought to encourage ecumenism

Reconciliation work in Northern Ireland

throughout the Churches; others have a strong secular base. Some groups tend to focus primarily on encouraging cross-community contact and social harmony; others major on issues such as fairness and social justice. All social classes have involved themselves; however, a middle class liberal ethos would tend to predominate in most groups. Those active in the field of reconciliation throughout Northern Ireland would be only too aware of the superficiality of working simply with the 'converted'.

In 1969 the British government's response to the new outbreak of sectarianism in Northern Ireland was to establish a Community Relations Commission for Northern Ireland modelled on the Community Relations Commission operating in Britain at that time. The fact that in Northern Ireland we are still seeking a definition and understanding of the term 'community relations' outlines in a small way the magnitude of the task that the Community Relations Commission in Northern Ireland was faced with. On the premise that people reconcile from positions of strength rather than weakness, over a period of four years the Community Relations Commission, via a community development process, sought to empower local groups and individuals within the ghettos of Northern Ireland; and there can be no doubt that as a direct result of this process, a tremendous amount of networking and dialogue across the sectarian divide was encouraged, without which the rapidly worsening situation could have been greatly exacerbated. Lines of communication within and between some of the most divided communities remained open, and many of the relationships forged in this period have been sustained into the late 1980s. Furthermore, many of those active in the Community Relations Commission have since moved on to make considerable contributions to positive social change in Northern Ireland within other organisations, both statutory and voluntary.

If the early 1970s can be characterised as a period synonymous with grassroots community politics, by the mid-1970s the established political groupings temporarily recovered lost ground and sought to establish a devolved Power Sharing Executive Assembly. The demise of the Power Sharing Executive in 1974 was to be the first of a series of failed political initiatives that have punctuated life within Northern Ireland, right up to the current process initiated by the Anglo-Irish Agreement, the jury on which is still out. During this time hundreds of self-help community groups, the Corrymeela Community, the voluntary sector generally, a host of children's community holiday schemes, and a range of small-scale cross-community initiatives kept the light of reconciliation burning.

August 1976 saw the birth of the Peace People, a phenomenon that within weeks had thousands of ordinary people from some of the hardest hit areas joining side by side in peace marches. It appeared that the silent majority could remain silent no longer. For a short intense period in contemporary Irish history, even the most sceptical thought that perhaps, just perhaps, a social mass movement could engender a dynamic for positive social change within the hearts and minds of Northern Ireland. For a host of human, sociological and political reasons this was not to materialise. Nevertheless, out of this process has emerged a series of important lessons concerning the promotion of peace and tolerance in a divided society.

By the 1980s it became clear that the integrity and complexity of the divisions within Northern Ireland would preclude a 'quick fix' solution. As Martin Luther King explained, 'True peace is not merely the absence of tension, it is the presence of justice'. The processes that have lead to the current situation have taken place over a long period of time. Likewise, peace and the promotion of justice is a slow, gradual, unspectacular, often unglamorous journey. This is all the more difficult when one looks at the limited capacities within those groups committed to promoting real peace and justice. Generally speaking, reconciliation groups operating within Northern Ireland are relatively small-scale, unfocussed, isolated, grossly under-resourced, and very often overdependent on a handful of extremely active, at times charismatic, leaders within each group. This is in no way to demean the tremendous contribution of each group, but to highlight the ad hoc, marginal, low-prestige response that society, and government in particular, has afforded reconciliation groups. This is in stark contrast to the current well-resourced, macho, militaristic solutions to problems requiring sensitive, visionary and multi-faceted approaches.

Reconciliation groups and force of circumstances led government in Autumn 1987 to spell out a new commitment towards the promotion of 'community relations' within Northern Ireland. A central plank to this policy has been, for the first time, a public recognition that there exists within Northern Ireland two very strong, equally valid, traditions, and that diversity, built upon mutual understanding, can be a healthy starting point in seeking to effect positive social change. In addition to a more aggressive push on equality of opportunity within the workforce, a

Community Relations Unit has been established within the Northern Ireland Office under the direct supervision of the Secretary of State and his Ministers. Hopefully these initiatives at government level will provide a more fertile environment for reconciliation groups, who are now uniquely well placed to build upon the experiences of the past twenty years. Sufficient resources will have to be provided, and those active in this field know only too well that there will be setbacks. Nevertheless, there is within Northern Ireland sufficient goodwill, nurtured over the years by scores of reconciliation groups, to work towards a more tolerant, caring and just society. For this potential to be maximised it has to be acknowledged that real progress can only begin when, at another level, political leaders engage in constructive dialogue both within Northern Ireland and the island of Ireland, and within the United Kingdom and Ireland. Like the young boy with his finger in the dyke, reconciliation groups within Northern Ireland, in a way that can never be measured, have made a major contribution to keeping the fabric of society intact, whilst awaiting a much longed for acceptable political settlement.

List of contents

All Children Together (ACT)
Anglo-Irish Encounter
Belfast Charitable Trust for Integrated Education (BELTIE)
British Irish Association
Community Conflict Skills
Community of the Peace People, Fredheim
Co-operation North
Corrymeela Community
Fellowship of Reconciliation, Northern Ireland
Harmony Community Trust
Interchurch Group on Faith and Politics
Northern Ireland Conflict and Mediation Association
Northern Ireland Peace Forum
PACE – Protestant and Catholic Encounter
Peace and Reconciliation Group, Derry
Peace Education Resource Centre, Belfast
Ulster Quaker Peace Committee
Ulster University, Centre for the Study of Conflict (see Section I, Universities).
Women Together

ALL CHILDREN TOGETHER (ACT)

13 Belfast Street, Belfast BT7 1FY (0232-227 335).

Contact: Joanne McKenna, Director.

Status: A company limited by guarantee, recognised as a Northern Ireland charity by the Department of Inland Revenue.

Origins: ACT was formed in the early 1970s by a group of Catholic parents whose children were attending non-Catholic Schools in Northern Ireland.

Directors: Mr I. J. Hamilton; Rt Hon W. B. McIvor; Mrs C. F. Linehan; Mrs Y. A. Gilmour; Mr G. E. Hewitt; Mr G. C. French; Mr W. Brown; Mrs M. Connolly; Sister Anna Hoare.

Membership: 120.

Staffing: 2 full time (one of which is an ACE-sponsored trainee).

Income: £73,130 for 1986/87.

Sources of income: The Nuffield Foundation has provided signficant support towards the development of particular schools. Donations have also been received from the Sir Halley Stewart Trust, CAF, Lever Brothers, Boots Charitable Trust, Joseph Rowntree Charitable Trust, Grent Trust, Dunmarry Protestant and Catholic Encounter, Northern Ireland Voluntary Trust, Puckham Charitable Trust, and Rothmans. Grant-aid is received from the Department of Education for Northern Ireland.

Aims and objectives: ACT is an interdenominational association of parents which believes that the high degree of religious segregation in the Northern Ireland education system is an obstacle to the solution of Northern Ireland's problems. It was formed to advance integration by consent and help counteract the situation whereby Roman Catholic grant-aided schools (though open to all) are almost totally attended by Roman Catholic children, and state controlled schools (though also open to all) are mostly attended by Protestant children, and are looked on as Protestant church related schools. ACT provides technical advice and guidance to parent groups. It meets with government, church representatives and other voluntary groups to promote the potential of integrated schools to improve community relations.

ACT advises parent groups on fund-raising and itself raises funds for new schools and their continued upkeep. In doing this, it works in co-operation with Belfast Charitable Trust for Integrated Education (BELTIE) (see separate entry). A key aim is to help the new schools become grant-aided by the Department of Education.

Reconciliation work in Northern Ireland

ACT was instrumental in founding Lagan College in 1981, the first planned, shared, all-ability college for boys and girls in Northern Ireland. It also supported the development of Forge Integrated Primary School, which opened in 1985; it supported the first planned, shared school outside the Belfast area, the All Children's Integrated Primary School, Newcastle, Co Down, which opened in 1986; it supported the Bridge Primary School, opened in 1987 and started by parents from Banbridge, Co Down.

ACT is setting up a resource centre of legal and technical information and advice for new parent groups. It holds an annual conference and organises seminars.

Journals and recent publications:
'ACT-LETT', biannual newsletter circulated within Westminster, Dail Eireann and Washington as well as to membership. A bibliography on integrated education.

ANGLO-IRISH ENCOUNTER

London Office:
9 St James's Square, London SW1Y 4LE, (01-930 2233). *Contact*: Donald Cape, Administrator.

Dublin Office: Institute of Public Administration, 57–61 Lansdowne Road, Dublin 4, (0001-686 233). *Contact*: Mary Clear, Secretary.

Status: Non-governmental organisation.

Origins: Initiated in 1983 by the British and Irish governments.

Hon Officers: Joint Chairmen: Sir Oliver Wright (London); Dr T. K. Whitaker (Dublin).

Staffing: London: 2 part time. Dublin: 1 part time.

Income: £25,000 for 1986/87 (UK Section).

Sources of income: Foreign and Commonwealth office for the UK section.

Aims and objectives: Encounter aims 'to contribute to the improvement of relations between the Irish and British peoples in the interest of peace, reconciliation and stability'.

It organises conferences and seminars (e.g. 'Irish Studies in Britain' in 1985, 'The Role of the Media in British-Irish Relationships' in 1986, and 'Britain and Ireland within the European Community' in 1987).

Publications: Reports of conferences.

BELFAST CHARITABLE TRUST FOR INTEGRATED EDUCATION
(BELTIE)

74 Whitewell Road, Belfast BT36 7ES (0232-774 258).

Contact: J. Mulvenna, Director.

Status: Registered charity.

Origins: Founded in October 1984.

Trustees: Mrs Murial Pritchard (Chairman); Judge McKee (Vice Chairman); Miss Anne Trundle (Secretary); Anthony Spencer (Treasurer);, John Carson; Trevor Greene; Maura Hendron; Patricia Mallon.

Staffing: 1 full time; 2 part time.

Income: £119,000 for 1986/87.

Sources of income: Donations have been received from: the Wolfson Foundation; Joseph Rowntree Charitable Trust; American Irish Foundation; Bernard Sunley Charitable Foundation; Lankelly Foundation; Drapers Charitable Trust; A. E. Reed Charitable Trust; Garfield Weston Foundation; Hillcote Trust; Women Caring Trust and other trusts; unions and individuals.

Aims and objectives: BELTIE aims to ensure that by the year 2000 there will be places in integrated schools in the City of Belfast for about one-third of the pupils in the city. An integrated school provides a Christian-based education for Protestant and Catholic children on terms of equality. The education is child-centred and stresses parent involvement and respect for the rights and duties of parents.

BELTIE motivates and supports groups who want to open an integrated school, and in doing so is developing the initiative of those parents who founded Lagan College, the first example, in 1981. It has been particularly instrumental in the development of Hazelwood College and Hazelwood Primary School which opened in Autumn 1985 and which received financial support of £138,000 from the Trust in 1986. It also helps schools either to obtain grant-aid from the Northern Ireland Department of Education or to raise funds elsewhere.

In September 1987 a central group for which BELTIE is providing administrative support, was formed to represent the integrated education movement in the Province to charitable bodies and funding agencies. (By 1987 there were 2 comprehensive schools, 5 primary schools, 4 nursery units, and 2 other schools in formation.)

BELTIE plans from 1990 to place its main emphasis on the transformation of existing schools and to offer development assistance, advice, information, financial and material aid to 'open-door' segregated schools, and such other segregated schools as wish to become planned integrated schools.

Journals and recent publications:
'*Integrated Education in Belfast*', quarterly bulletin.
'*Planning Study*', a document to inform, support and motivate parents who want to open an integrated school.

BRITISH IRISH ASSOCIATION

9 Poland Street, London W1V 3DG (01-437 4185).

Contact: Marigold Johnson, Secretary.

Status: Registered charity.

Origins: Founded in 1972.

Patrons: Professor J. C. Beckett; Sir Charles Carter; Lady Ewart Biggs; Robert Kee; Dr Anthony Kenny; The Earl of Longford; Lord Moyne; Sir David Orr; Senator Eoin Ryan; Dr T. K. Whitaker; David Astor (Chairman, Executive Committee).

Staffing: 1 part time.

Income: Some £14,000 for 1986/87.

Sources of income: There is no membership therefore no subscription income. No financial aid is accepted from governments. The Joseph Rowntree Social Service Trust provide the office accommodation. Other supporting trusts have been the Esmée Fairbairn Trust, the FCI Trust, the Allen Lane Trust, the Walter Guinness Trusts and the Ireland Fund. Donations have also been given by banks and companies.

Aims and objectives: The Association exists to promote better relations between the communities of both islands. Its main activity is the organisation of large annual conferences where eminent public figures from Britain, the Republic and Northern Ireland meet by invitation for private discussion of sensitive issues.

COMMUNITY CONFLICT SKILLS

84 Drumaney Road, Cookstown, Co Tyrone, Northern Ireland (06487-37011).

Contact: Mari Fitzduff, Co-ordinator.

Status: Independent group.

Staffing: 1 part time.

Income: £10,000 for 1987/88.

Source of income: Joseph Rowntree Charitable Trust.

Reconciliation work in Northern Ireland

Aims and objectives: This pilot project started formally in November 1987 with funding for one year from JRCT. Its aims are to:

'Explore practical possibilities of effecting attitudinal and behavioural change between groups and individuals in Northern Ireland;

Develop, collect and provide materials and programmes for organisations willing to tackle sectarianism both within their own institution and with their membership;

Organise training and support possibilities for trainers, group workers, tutors, mediators or educators wishing to develop their own confidence and skills in tackling areas of conflict between the two main communities in Northern Ireland. This could be for those who see such work as part of their primary work, or who require additional skills to extend their work in the community, educational, trade union, church, youth sectors, etc;

Co-ordinate and publicise the developing work of different agencies and individuals working in this field, in order to avoid duplication of efforts, training and programme development.'

The Project aims to work with and through existing agencies developing training in such areas as: intergroup skills, prejudice reduction, issues of justice, political assertion and handling conflict, etc.

Journals and recent publications:
Fitzduff, Mari '*Community Conflict Skills Handbook*', 1988 (a training manual for anti-sectarian work in Northern Ireland).

COMMUNITY OF THE PEACE PEOPLE

'Fredheim', 224 Lisburn Road, Belfast BT9 6GE (0232-663 465).

Contact: Ann McCann, Administrator.

Status: The Community is an independent group, but it has also set up a registered charity, the Peace People Charitable Trust, and a company limited by guarantee, Peace Forms Ltd.

Origins: The Community of the Peace People started in 1976 when the driver of an IRA getaway car was shot dead by a pursuing British Army patrol. The car crashed, killing three young children and gravely injuring their mother. The Peace People movement was set-up by Ciarán McKeown, Betty Williams and Mairead Corrigan (the aunt of the dead children) after a series of rallies protesting against this incident and the continuing violence. In 1977 Betty Williams and Mairead Corrigan were awarded the Nobel Peace Prize.

Reconciliation work in Northern Ireland

Membership: 150 adults plus 100 young members of Youth of Peace.

Staffing: 5 full time.

Combined annual income: £80–100,000 for 1986.

Sources of income: The largest amount of financial help is received from the camp support groups particularly in Norway and in the USA (where the support group is established as Peace People Inc). The Northern Ireland Department of Education supplies grant-aid and funds have also been given by the American Ireland Fund, Dublin, the Public Welfare Foundation, USA, the Northern Ireland Voluntary Trust, and the Barrow and Geraldine S. Cadbury Trust.

Aims and objectives: The Peace People work for the creation of a just and peaceful society in Northern Ireland by nonviolent means, seeking to build such a society from the bottom up, through the efforts of ordinary people. They promote dialogue between political groups, inform people about political and social issues, and support people organising locally to solve local problems for themselves.

They campaign for the creation in Northern Ireland of a justice system of the highest standards and with respect for human rights and human dignity. They work through an open democratic structure, with local groups and an annual assembly in which all members can vote.

Advice and support is given particularly to prisoners and their families. Alternative transport is provided for prison visits (which otherwise is via paramilitary groups), social events and holidays are arranged for wives and children.

Summer peace camps have been organised since 1978 in Norway for teenagers, and in Durham for younger children. In 1987 camps were also arranged in Germany (for a wider age range), in France for children and exchange visits set up in Sweden.

The Farm Project at Kilcranny House near Coleraine started in 1985. It is both a small residential community and an educational resource centre where visitors from all backgrounds can work and develop in mutual understanding and friendship.

Affiliations: The Community is affiliated to the International Fellowship of Reconciliation, the Northern Ireland Football Association, and the Northern Ireland Youth Clubs Association.

Journals and recent publications:
'*Peace by Peace*' fortnightly newspaper sold door to door.
'*Know Your Rights*' (Advice on questioning, search and arrest).

CO-OPERATION NORTH (Belfast)

7 Botanic Avenue, Belfast BT7 1JG (0232-321 462)
(*also see entry in Part Two – Funding sources*).

CO-OPERATION NORTH (Dublin)

37 Upper Fitzwilliam Street, Dublin 2
(0001-610 582/3/4/8).

Contacts: Winston McColgan, Chief Executive; Tommy Fegan, Deputy Chief Executive.

Status: Two associated private companies, both registered as charities.

Origins: Founded in 1979.

Boards: A common Board of Directors serves both companies. Its Council and Board are representative of trade, industry, tourism, education, trade unions and national, cultural and sporting organisations, North and South. Chairman: T. P. Brand (1986), Dr Louden Ryan (1987).

Staffing: 30 full time (combined Dublin/Belfast offices). Of these 10 are employed under Government-assisted employment schemes.

Annual budget: IR £965,000/Stg £865,000 in 1987.

Sources of income: Business in Ireland, North and South including staff secondments and rent-free premises from local companies; business corporations in the United States and Great Britain; Irish and British Governments (approximately 10% of total budget); the European Community.

Aims and objectives: Co-operation North is a non-political, non-denominational organisation founded to build understanding and respect between the people of Northern Ireland and the Republic of Ireland. Its aim is, through practical co-operation in the economic, social and cultural spheres, to break down the barriers of misunderstanding and ignorance which have created suspicion and mistrust and have contributed to tension and violence.

In order to achieve these aims Co-operation North:
 commissions research;
 facilitates direct contact between groups and individuals across the social and economic spectrum;
 provides a two-way information flow through its reference centres in Belfast and Dublin;
 acts as a catalyst to motivate joint projects and activities by companies, agencies and voluntary bodies.

Co-operation North is both a fund-raising and a grant making body. Its activities are grouped under three main programmes:
 Business Programme: publication of information guides, operation of cross-border referral service,

organisation and sponsorship of exchange visits, joint seminars and conferences to stimulate cross-border business co-operation and trade;

Youth and Education Programme: North/South exchanges assisted between youth clubs, schools and teachers;

Community Programme: networking and exchange links made between community groups North and South, and the promotion and organisation annually of large scale popular events involving people from both sides of the border.

Journals and publications:
'*Co-operation North News*', quarterly newsletter also distributed in Britain and the USA; '*The Co-operation North Guide*', A Directory.

'*Peace and Reconciliation Projects in Ireland*', Revised Second Edition 1984 (Reprinted 1986 by Irish Council of Churches).

'*A Far Far Better Way*', a booklet by the first Chairman, Brendan O'Regan 1979 (revised 1986) adopted as the Co-operation North Charter.

A series of short publications and research papers have been produced on common problems and opportunities for co-operation.

The following associated organisations have been established with the sole purpose of raising funds for Co-operation North's work:

London:
Co-operation Ireland, c/o TSB England and Wales, 61–63 Kennington Road, London SE1 7PZ (01-928 9234).
Contact: Carley Brown, Executive Secretary.

New York:
Co-operation Ireland Inc., Grace Plaza (5th Floor), 1114 Avenue of the Americas, New York, NY 10036, USA (212-819 5612).
Contact: Connolly Cole, Executive Director.

CORRYMEELA COMMUNITY

8 Upper Crescent, Belfast BT7 1NT (0232-325 008).

Ballycastle Centre: Ballycastle, Co Antrim, N Ireland BT54 4QU (02657-62626).

Contact: Rev John Morrow, Leader.

Status: Registered charity and company limited by guarantee.

Origins: Established in 1965 after initiatives from Ray Davey, the Chaplain of Queens University, Belfast, and a group of his students and other interested people who sought to break the stereotypes of church work in Northern Ireland.

Membership: Some 150 formal 'community' members.

Staffing: 25 full time; 3 part time, plus 10 one-year volunteers and many short-term summer volunteers.

Income: £335,000 for 1986/87.

Sources of income: Letting at Ballycastle Centre (27% of total revenue income); members and friends; donations from trusts and foundations.

In 1981, the Ford Foundation grant-aided a conference, 'Models of Political Co-operation'.

Aims and objectives: The Corrymeela Community is a group of Christians, both Protestant and Catholic, who believe themselves to be called together as 'an instrument of God's peace' in the Church and in the world. It is a dispersed community. The formal members and friends carry on the Community's work by becoming involved wherever they live and work, through their churches, and in social, political and professional concerns.

Corrymeela runs two centres:

Ballycastle, a base where people from different traditions can meet and talk freely. It also serves as a refuge and place of rest for many victims of violence. A conference and education programme on the roots of social conflict is developed with the help of the staff who themselves are directly involved in youth, church, schools and other community work.

Corrymeela House, in Belfast, is the administrative office base for field workers, and a meeting place for Belfast Corrymeela groups and other groups sharing some similar aims.

Corrymeela's work of reconciliation and understanding includes extensive work with school groups and families; a week-long biannual summer festival with some 2,000 participants; Corrymeela International arranges exchange visits; Corrymeela Link has been a support group in Britain active since 1976.

Journals and recent publications:
The Corrymeela Papers: '*Understanding the Signs of the Times*'; '*Declaration of Faith and Commitment for Christians in Northern Ireland*'.

Davey, Ray '*An Unfinished Journey*' an anthology of 21 years of Corrymeela by its founder, and '*Take Away this Hate*' an autobiography.

McCreary, Alf '*Corrymeela*'.

Reconciliation work in Northern Ireland

FELLOWSHIP OF RECONCILIATION, Northern Ireland

67 Woodvale Road, Belfast BT13 3EZ (0232-753 613).

Contacts: Denis Barritt and Jens Wikinger.

Status: Charitable.

Origins: Set up in 1949 by members of the Peace Pledge Union.

Membership: About 100.

Staffing: None paid.

Income and sources: Not disclosed.

Aims and objectives: A Christian pacifist group sharing the objectives and principles of the International Fellowship of Reconciliation, with particular reference to Northern Ireland.

The Fellowship has been active in anti-nuclear weapons campaigns and has also undertaken various activities aimed at reconciliation in Northern Ireland. It runs summer play-schemes and work-camps which bring Catholic and Protestant children and their parents together.

HARMONY COMMUNITY TRUST

122 Great Victoria Street, Belfast BT2 7BG (0232-243 223/234 771).

Contact: D. F. Harrison, Secretary.

Status: Registered charity.

Staffing: 5 full time (including 1 ACE worker); 2 part time.

Income: £68,000 in 1986.

Sources of income: The Department of Education for Northern Ireland contributed 44% in 1986. Other income from trusts, companies and individuals.

Aims and objectives: The Trust formed in 1975 has set up a children's holiday centre with an emphasis on reconciliation. Children from all over the Province, especially from Belfast and Londonderry visit the holiday centre. In 1986 a Rural Education Project was launched for school groups.

Holiday centre address: Glebe House, Kilclief, Nr Strangford, Co Down BT30 7NZ (039686-374).

INTERCHURCH GROUP ON FAITH AND POLITICS

c/o Iona, 211 Churchill Park, Portadown BT62 1EU, Co. Armagh, Northern Ireland (07672-330 366).

Contact: Rev Brian Lennon SJ.

Status: Independent group.

Origins: Started in 1983.

Membership: 16.

Staffing: None paid.

Income: £500 in 1987.

Sources of income: Sales of publications; Churches Emergency Fund; an anonymous trust.

Aims and objectives: The Group explores the conflict in Northern Ireland from a Christian perspective, identifying both the fears of different groups and the common ground between them. It is made up of people from different religions and political traditions. It organises conferences and seminars and produces publications which stimulate further group discussions.

Recent publications: The Group has published several pamphlets, including:
'Breaking Down the Enmity: Faith and Politics in Northern Ireland', 1985; *'Understanding the Signs of the Times'*, 1986 (raises questions for Catholics and Protestants in the light of the Anglo-Irish Agreement); *'A Declaration of Faith & Commitment'*, 1986; *'Towards an Ireland that Works'*.

NORTHERN IRELAND CONFLICT AND MEDIATION ASSOCIATION

c/o 46 University Street, Belfast BT7 1HB (0232-244 003).

Contact: Oliver Johnston.

Status: Independent group seeking charitable status.

Membership: 70.

Staffing: None paid.

Income: about £1,000 for 1987/88.

Aims and objectives: The Association aims to enable people to handle conflict positively by increasing their access to concepts, skills and services in the constructive management of disputes.

In the three years between 1987 and 1990 the Association's priorities are to:

  Establish and maintain a support network for individuals and representatives of organisations;

  Develop a set of principles as a Code of Practice;

Promote the concepts throughout Northern Ireland;

Set up an Information Service;

Provide a Brokerage Service for people requiring training, services and research.

A copy of the strategy is available from the Association.

NORTHERN IRELAND PEACE FORUM

c/o Corrymeela Centre, 8 Upper Crescent, Belfast 7 (0232-647 106).

Contact: Eileen Carragher, Chairperson.

Status: Independent group.

Origins: The Forum started in 1976.

Membership: Some 15 organisations mainly based in or near Belfast.

Staffing: None paid.

Aims and objectives: The Forum is open to any group concerned with peace and reconciliation in Northern Ireland. The Forum now meets on a quarterly basis and is reconsidering the future direction of its role as a co-ordinatory body.

PACE: An Association for Protestant and Catholic Encounter

103 University Street, Belfast BT7 1HP (0232-232 864).

Contact: Barbara Wright, Office Secretary.

Status: Charitable.

Origins: PACE was started in 1968 by a group of Catholics and Protestants who felt the need to meet together to learn as much as they could about each other, and to discuss freely their points of agreement and disagreement.

Patrons: Reverend Dr Cahal Daly, Bishop of Down and Connor, Professor Norman Gibson.

Officers for 1987–88: Denis Murphy and James Shannon (Joint Chairmen); Miss Frances Hickey (Hon Secretary); E. Gourlay (Hon Treasurer).

Membership: Individuals 2,000; Local PACE groups 11.

Staffing: 2 part time.

Annual income: Not disclosed.

Source of income: Community Relations section of the Department of Education.

Aims and objectives: PACE seeks to:

Promote harmony and goodwill between the religious and political communities in Northern Ireland;

Demonstrate that, although people may be separated by difference of conviction, there are many activities in which they can freely unite in order to work together for the common good of all;

Work with all who desire the establishment of a social order based upon justice and charity, and enlivened by mutual respect and understanding, thus leading to the elimination of the factors which produce harmful divisions in our society.

The central group provides support to the local groups which exist in East Belfast, South Belfast, Cavehill/Glengormley, Dunmarry/Finaghy, Holywood, Larne, Newcastle, Omagh and Ormeau, to develop mutual trust through talking and working together.

Journals: '*PACE Journal*', three times a year, circulated widely and in Europe and the USA; '*Newspace*', occasional membership newsletter.

PEACE AND RECONCILIATION GROUP

18a London Street, Londonderry BT48 6RQ (0504-369 206).

Contact: Peter Simpson, Overseer.

Status: Registered charity.

Officers: Margaret O'Donnell; Chair, Alan Faulkner, Vice-Chair.

Staffing: 1 full time; 2 part time. All paid workers are employed under ACE).

Income: £3,800 for 1985/86.

Sources of income: During 1985/86 support was received from the Women Caring Trust, the Esmé Mitchell Trust, the Blackburn Trust, the Derry City Council, and Cork Peace Group.

Aims and objectives: The Group is a small number of people from different political and religious backgrounds who aim to promote peace and reconciliation within the city of Londonderry and its outlying districts. The Group became autonomous in 1980 having originally been affiliated since its beginning in 1976 to the Northern Ireland Peace Movement.

The Group runs and participates in practical projects which contribute towards mutual understanding and co-operation. It operates a mini-bus which it also makes available for many different community groups, and organises many sporting activities as a way of bringing together different groups for friendly and open

Reconciliation work in Northern Ireland

exchanges. The first Action for Community Employment (ACE) worker began in 1986 on a project examining cultural divisions in Northern Ireland.

PEACE EDUCATION RESOURCE CENTRE

Inter-Church Centre, 48 Elmwood Avenue, Belfast BT9 6AZ (0232-663 145).

Contact: Norman L. Richardson, Peace Education Officer (Irish Council of Churches).

Status: Charitable.

Origins: The Centre opened in 1984 and is run as part of the Irish Commission for Justice and Peace/Irish Council of Churches joint peace education programme, a collaborative venture started in 1978.

Staffing: 1 full time.

Income: Not known.

Sources of income: The Joseph Rowntree Charitable Trust, the Ireland Fund, the Esmé Mitchell Trust and the Church of the Brethren (USA), all helped with the costs of start-up resources, library equipment and publicity. Other sources include the Conference of European churches, salary funding by the Department of Education for Northern Ireland for the Peace Education Officer, the Irish Churches and sales.

Aims and objectives: The Irish Commission for Justice and Peace (a Roman Catholic body) and the Irish Council of Churches (which represents eight Protestant denominations) aim through their joint peace education project to provide resources for schools and churches to assist education in peace and cross-community knowledge and understanding. The Centre acts as a sales facility for pupil texts and teachers' background books, as a peace library and as an advice and information service for teachers.

Affiliations and projects with other bodies: The Council and Commission join with the Irish Catholic Aid Agency (Trócaire) and Christian Aid, Ireland, to promote a Peace Projects Scheme for schools. Information is sent to all schools in Northern Ireland and the Republic of Ireland each autumn.

Journals and recent publications:
A resource centre catalogue and a schools' magazine 'Issues' (three editions by Autumn 1987) are both sent free to all schools and colleges, individuals and organisations concerned with education, voluntary or statutory.

ULSTER QUAKER PEACE COMMITTEE

c/o Renmore Avenue, Portadown, Co Armagh (0762-333 219).

Contact: Elsa Peile, Secretary.

Membership: 9 (including convenor and secretary, each representing different Quaker meetings in Northern Ireland).

Staffing: None paid.

Income: £250 for 1986/87.

Sources of income: The Wainwright and Allen Fund supported the revision and reprint of their Peace Testimony leaflet. An appeal for the peace education project (see below) raised £58,000 from individual Quakers, Quaker meetings and from charitable trusts.

Aims and objectives: The Committee aims to represent the views of Quakers in Ulster on issues relating to peace and other concerns. Its work is mainly centred around the organisation of educational meetings, in particular its annual conference (held in 1987 on 'The Links Between Poverty and Violence'). However, in 1986 and 1987 funds were raised for a full-time post for three years based at Magee College under the auspices of Centre for Study of Conflict, to foster peace education and education for mutual understanding, particularly in western areas of Northern Ireland.

Affiliations and projects with other organisations: The Committee works closely with the Dublin Quaker Monthly Meeting Peace Committee and Quaker Peace and Service, London. It has representatives on the Northern Ireland Peace Forum and links with Christian CND and with the World Disarmament Campaign.

Publications:
'The Quaker Peace Testimony' a pamphlet.

WOMEN TOGETHER

Room 6, Bryson House, 28 Bedford Street, Belfast BT2 7FE (0232-326 446).

Contact: Anne Wilson, Secretary (Office hours: Mon-Fri 9.30 am – 1.30 pm).

Status: Charitable.

Origins: Started in 1970 through the initiatives of its founder, Ruth Agnew, who felt 'called' to develop women's involvement in reconciliation.

Officers: Ruth Agnew (Life President); Maeve Mulholland (Chair).

Reconciliation work in Northern Ireland

Membership: 100.

Staffing: 1 part time.

Income: Some £2,250 for 1987.

Sources of income: Women's church groups in Germany have sent support; grants from Women Caring Trust and other funds.

Aims and objectives: Women Together aims to:

Bring together women who believe that violence in all its forms must be opposed in the interest of promoting peace in the community;

give them the corporate strength to resist undesirable pressures and to use their influence for peace in their homes, their streets and neighbourhoods;

foster a sense of pride in their locality and enable them as a group to alert the local authorities to the needs of the neighbourhood and to bring effective pressure on the appropriate bodies to fulfil their obligations;

offer them a wide range of activities in which they can engage as a relief from their home commitments and as a means of working together.

It consists of small groups of women working among women and children who have suffered from violence and unrest. The work is not publicised, to safeguard the people involved.

Groups exist in Finaghy, East Belfast, Greenisland, Lisburn, Whitehead. In addition to its other varied activities, the groups raise funds each year for a particular charity.

Affiliations and joint projects: The Groups are also involved with the Peace Forum; Glebe House (holiday home for children from both sides of the community); Children's Community Holidays; the Visitors' Canteen at the Maze Prison; Meals for the Elderly; Anti-Intimidation Group; Voluntary Service, Lisburn; Battered Wives/Women's Aid; supporting Integrated Education Work with other Reconciliation Groups; attending Ecumenical Services; and the Northern Ireland Hospice.

PART TWO
SOURCES OF FINANCIAL SUPPORT

Charity law - peace in our time

by Adrian Longley, Solicitor and Legal Advisor, National Council for Voluntary Organisations

This year (1988) marks the fiftieth anniversary of Neville Chamberlain's return from Munich, having, as he claimed, helped to secure 'peace for our time'. Chamberlain's hopes were of course shattered by Hitler's invasion of Poland in September 1939; and although there has been no universal conflict since 1945, scarcely a day passes without reports of 'wars and rumours of wars' in some parts of the globe. Bearing in mind the threat to the existence of life from the proliferation of nuclear and chemical weapons, it might not unreasonably be supposed that movements for the promotion of peace would be vigorously – and officially – encouraged. Yet, none of the bodies registered with the Charity Commissioners in 1987 – and since 1981 between 3,500 and 4,000 have been added to the Register every year – will have been established for that specific purpose. To understand why – and to assess the implications for promoters, subscribers and the public at large – it is necessary to look briefly at the origins and development of the legal meaning of charity over the past 400 years.

The Legal Meaning of Charity

To St. Paul in the first century A.D. charity was the greatest of three Christian virtues; and it would have been with the Pauline meaning predominantly in mind that Pope in the eighteenth century was impelled to write:

'In Faith and Hope the world will disagree,
But all Mankind's concern is Charity'.

The Law's concern is more pragmatic – and mundane. Charity means an institution – of a special kind – formed otherwise than for commercial gain. Given that each of the four has been so formed, what is it that links, for example, *War on Want* and *Christian Aid* (each a charity) on the one hand and distinguishes both from the

United Nations Association and the *Campaign for Nuclear Disarmament* (neither a charity) on the other. The answer is that whilst each of the four is a voluntary organisation, only two, War on Want and Christian Aid are established for purposes which the law regards as 'charitable'.

As the report of the Goodman Committee (1976) stated, 'there is no neat encapsulated definition of charity'. The nearest to it (and for that matter the most modern) is a judicial classification of 1891 by Lord MacNaghten which postulated four main heads:

1. The relief of poverty;
2. The advancement of education;
3. The advancement of religion;
4. Some 'other purposes beneficial to the community'.

Underpinning the classification of charity there is a statutory reference point to which the courts still look for guidance: the preamble (introduction) to an Act of Parliament of Elizabeth I passed in 1601 which listed certain activities then regarded as charitable.

> 'The relief of aged, impotent, and poor people; the maintenance of sick and maimed soldiers and mariners, schools of learning, free schools and scholars of universities; the repair of bridges, havens, causeways, churches, sea banks and highways; the education and preferment of orphans, the relief, stock or maintenance of houses of correction; marriages of poor maids; supportation, aid and help of young tradesmen, handicraftsmen and persons decayed; the relief or redemption of prisoners or captives; and the aid or ease of any poor inhabitants concerning payment of fifteens, setting out of soldiers, and other taxes.'

This is not to say the meaning has been fixed since Tudor times. As Lord Hailsham pointed out in the House of Lords eight years ago, 'the legal conception of charity (is) not static but moving and changing'. In effect, the law moves by a process of analogy, so that, for example, the 'aid or ease of any poor inhabitants concerning payment of fifteens, setting out of soldiers and other taxes' in the preamble permits a trust for a regimental mess or for the poor of the regiment to be charitable today.

With one exception (the relief of poverty) an over-riding requirement is benefit to the public or to what the law regards as a sufficient section of the public.

In the context of the **relief of poverty**, poverty is a relative term; it does not mean destitution; it may be paraphrased as 'having to go short', taking into account an individual's 'station in life'. Moreover, relief does not have to be in the form of cash; an organisation providing clothes or other goods following a natural or man-made disaster can be charitable – always assuming the victims to be poor.

Unlike the other heads of legal charity, benefit may be confined to a small number of people, for instance, one's poor relations.

In the context of the **advancement of education**, the subject matter of the education – presented, so far as possible, without bias – must be of discernible merit. The writings of Shakespeare and the musical compositions of Delius unquestionably qualify, but not the collection of Victoriana described as 'junk' in a case decided in 1965. A careful distinction has to be drawn between the imparting of knowledge on the one hand and mere information on the other. Propaganda with its element of indoctrination is not allowed. Whatever the subject matter, there must always be elements of instruction and study. Thus the results of research must be disseminated to the public at large.

The **advancement of religion** is not confined to Christianity. Judaism, Islam, Oriental and Transatlantic faiths are all eligible, but not humanist or ethical systems not founded on a belief in a Supreme Being or Intelligence exercising control over human destiny. There must be a degree of evangelism. As Lord Denning has pointed out, when a man says his prayers in the privacy of his own bedroom, he may truly be said to be concerned with religion, but not with the advancement of religion. On this reasoning a trust for nuns as been rejected as charitable by the House of Lords because the order was enclosed. The efficacy of continuous prayer – and thereby benefit to the public at large – could not be *proved*.

The fourth judicial head, **other purposes beneficial to the Community**, does not comprise each and every purpose which might, in a general sense, be considered 'beneficial to the community'. A trust will only be charitable if it is within 'the spirit of intendment' of the Elizabethan preamble. For example, the reference in the preamble too 'aged, impotent and poor people' has been construed disjunctively so as to allow help to be given to the old or sick who are not, at the same time, in financial need; and it is by virtue of this head that gifts 'unto my country England'; for the preservation of the Seas of the World (particularly those near the United Kingdom) from pollution and of flora and fauna in a particular district have been held charitable.

Not surprisingly, the rationale of particular judgments can strike some people as perverse. Anti-vivisection is not charitable, medical research being of benefit to mankind; but the prevention of cruelty to animals passes the test, not, as might be supposed – and as is the case in Eire – because of any benefit to the animals themselves, but on account of the noble feelings of humanity and morality which are thereby aroused in members of the human race.

Purposes which are overtly designed to bring about fundamental changes in the structure of society, whether at home or overseas, and are therefore essentially political do not qualify – largely on the grounds that the courts have no way of judging whether a proposed change in the law will or will not be for the public benefit. One result of this view is that organisations for the promotion of international friendship or understanding cannot be charitable, though the promotion of good race relations *within the realm* now qualifies. In the words of the Charity Commissioner's Report for 1983 and in the light of the Race Relations legislation, 'the matter is no longer one for the Court to judge. The nation through Parliament has already decided that it is for the public benefit and the matter has ceased to be political.'

Of what practical significance, it may be asked, are these archaic – and arcane – distinctions in the last quarter of the twentieth century?

The answer lies in the unique tax privileges afforded to organisations which are charities at law. 'In this world' wrote Benjamin Franklin in 1789, 'nothing can be said to be certain except death and taxes'. Charities, however, are the exception that proves the rule. Technically, they are not subject to the legal embargo on perpetual trusts and, of far greater practical importance today, they are exempt from most forms of direct taxation. These privileges have been reinforced in the 1986 Finance Act which stimulated giving to charity by individuals and corporations.

How can peace be charitable?

If, then organisations whose primary purpose is the promotion of peace are, as such, ineligible for registration with the Charity Commissioners, is all endeavour in this field to be denied the tangible – and intangible – benefits of charitable status?

The position may not always be as hopeless as at first sight it seems to be. Much will in practice depend upon the main thrust of an organisation's actual activities; and in this connection there is a vital difference between an organisation's *declared objects* (which must be exclusively charitable in the strict legal sense) and *the means* by which those objects are to be achieved. The latter need not – and, by definition, cannot – be exclusively charitable, so that charity trustees may properly undertake all manner of operations – from employing staff and holding property to arranging lectures and exhibitions and raising and investing funds – provided these are wholly directed towards the achievement of their primary charitable objects. Indeed, as we have seen, although charities are precluded from bringing pressure on Government to procure changes in policies or administrative practices, 'where such action is in furtherance of its purposes, a charity may present to a Government Department *a reasoned memorandum* advocating changes in the law' (The Charity Commissioners – September 1986).

The raison d'etre of an organisation concerned with peace issues may in some cases be held to be charitable, even though the specific purpose of promoting peace is not. By examining the opportunities that exist under the different heads of charity and some of the organisations which have been able to obtain charitable status, we can develop some practical ideas for those hoping to get a peace organisation registered as a charity.

'Poverty, sickness and disease' – a combination of the first and fourth heads – 'wherever the same may occur' – and from whatever cause (including war) may be relieved by appropriate charitable trusts. Indeed, one such trust – *Give Peace a Chance* – which declares these objects has been registered with the Charity Commissioners in 1986. Furthermore, as the promoters of *Give Peace a Chance* have also found, there is no bar to the registration of a trust for the advancement of public education (the second judicial head) 'concerning the history and current activities of peace movements through the provision of educational facilities, including publications, films, displays and the creation of a National Peace Museum'.

Impartial instruction about movements for peace is entirely acceptable, whereas the advocacy of a particular peace philosophy is not. This distinction is vividly illustrated by the cases of the *British Atlantic Committee* and the *Disarmament Study Trust*. The former has existed for some 30 years as a kind of NATO public relations outlet (there are equivalent bodies in other NATO member countries) and was recognised as a charity in 1972. But in 1982, at the height of the 'peace' campaign against the Cruise and Pershing missile deployments, its status was challenged by supporters of CND (which had been denied charitable recognition.) They claimed that the BAC was in receipt of government money (which it was) and had responded to government appeals to do more to publicise the aims of NATO's existing defence policy – and that it could not, as a result, be regarded as a non-partisan, charitable body. Faced with the potential loss of its charitable status, the BAC responded by setting up a new separately funded organisation called *Peace Through NATO*, which was designed to handle the campaigning side of its activities (but would be an entirely separate and independent body in its own right). The stated objects of Peace Through NATO are to 'influence specialist groups and associations' – notably the unilateralists – who have 'made inroads, claiming to speak for their professions'. These objects are, of course, non-charitable.

The BAC then reverted to its original role – in accordance with its declared charitable objects: 'to advance the education of the inhabitants of the United Kingdom in the aims of the Atlantic Treaty and the supporting NATO organisations, and in the duties and responsibilities of the government and citizens of the United Kingdom under the Treaty and the need to promote links between member-states of NATO'. Its activities include the staging of lectures, seminars and conferences, research, publishing and 'co-ordinated activities'.

The *Disarmament Study Trust* was established in the early 1980s to foster 'the advancement of education for the public benefit, including, in particular, research into and teaching about the history of the formation and implementation of decisions and obligations throughout the world relating to disarmament and restrictions on the manufacture, supply and accumulation of armaments of all kinds, and the publication of the results of such research'. In March 1983, the Trust was refused registration by the Charity Commissioners on the grounds that 'disarmament is a provocative and intrinsically political subject, and even though the academic activity might be of high scholarship and socially useful, the interests which it serves must by the nature of the subject be those interested in achieving political goals and seeking to influence policy.... The study of disarmament cannot be considered as a neutral subject and must by its nature be a political issue'. The decision was condemned by the Trust's legal adviser as 'a totally political judgement which has no logical basis' (The Guardian, 28 March 1983), but was nevertheless accepted by the trustees, who then proceeded to establish a new organisation, the *London Centre for International Peacebuilding*. This organisation, though not itself entitled to charitable status, was linked in a supportive capacity to a charity, the *Caroline Gourlay Trust*, formed for permitted educational purposes in this field.

These two cases demonstrate not only the highly technical – some would say highly artificial – distinction between objects which are acceptable as legally charitable and those of an ostensibly comparable educational character which are not; they also indicate the practical steps which can be taken to resolve the problem.

In relation to the third judicial head, the advancement of religion, the Founder of Christianity may have announced that he came 'Not to send peace but a sword'. He also commended the peacemakers as being the Children of God; and whilst many followers of religion have over the centuries demonstrated a marked preference for the sword, to the extent that belief in a Deity connotes the essential Brotherhood of Man, most of the advocates of orthodox religious belief at least claim to be promoting peace. In any event, there is a strong presumption that a religious body satisfying the relevant criteria is legally charitable.

It is, however, the fourth head, which includes certain purposes beneficial to the community, which still offers the greatest scope to promoters in this field. Indeed, those who agree with Vegetius in the fourth century A.D. ('Let him who desires peace, prepare for war') or subscribe to the views of the present Chief of the Defence staff (the Armed Services are the 'greatest of all the Social Services' for without them all the rest would be worthless) will not look in vain to this category. Trusts to promote the defence of the realm from the attack of hostile aircraft (and thereby contribute to the efficiency of the Armed Forces), for the purpose of increasing the efficiency of the police or of a particular hospital, to enable boys to become officers in the Royal Navy and the Mercantile Marine have all been accepted as charitable. In short, bodies which promote the idea of a strong defence system can claim with some justification to be promoting peace just as actively as those which describe themselves as peace organisations. Reunions, social functions and similar events for the benefit of members of ex-servicemen's associations are, however, excluded.

In the United States of America a gift to the *World Peace Foundation*, an overtly campaigning body, has been accepted as charitable. Over here, a declared aim to act as 'a catalyst in society working at the grass roots in the cause of peace, justice and freedom' has led to an application by the *United Nations Association* being rejected by the Charity Commissioners. By the same token and in line with the Commissioners' thinking in relation to the *Disarmament Study Trust* referred to above, the operations of the *Campaign for Nuclear Disarmament*, implying a fundamental shift in the defence and foreign policies pursued by all British Governments since the war, are unacceptably political. On the other hand, although *War on Want* and *Christian Aid* (both of which, as we have seen, are charities) have on several occasions been censured by the Charity Commissioners for indulging in activities of a political character, neither has been removed from the Register largely because (unlike CND) their raison d'etre is undeniably charitable in the legal sense. Similarly, *Oxfam*'s charitable status remains undisturbed notwithstanding the alleged partisan character of some of its publications.

Charting a course through the system

That the system is on occasion perverse and without logic cannot be gainsaid. What critics tend to overlook is the flexibility which the existing rules permit. As Lord Glenarthur reminded his fellow peers during a debate on Charity Law on 5 March last year, 'the range of organisations which fall within the definition of Charity is far wider than is commonly believed'. And the range is never closed.

It is significant that none of the three Committees reporting in this area since the war – Nathan in 1952, the House of Commons Expenditure Committee in 1975 and Goodman in 1976 – recommended radical reform. Indeed, examination of the legal meaning of charity was expressly excluded from the terms of reference of the Efficiency Strutiny undertaken last year by Sir Philip Woodfield into the Supervision of Charities.

Even if the legal meaning were examined yet again with a view to modernisation, it is most unlikely that the promotion of peace would eventually be seen as a charitable object in its own right.

Goodman's proposals that the list of charitable activities in the preamble to the Elizabethan Statute should be replaced by statutory guidelines reflecting social, economic and legal changes over the past 400 years is silent in this respect. Ben Whitaker's dissenting view – that the test should be the relief of deprivation – would be of little practical help. The idea put forward by the Charity Law Reform Committee (which met regularly in the early 1970s) that all non profit distributing organisations ought to be accorded charitable status may be totally discounted: if adopted, it would have the effect of conferring fiscal benefits on bodies as diverse as political parties and trade unions on the one hand and social and sporting clubs on the other and would be strenuously resisted by the Inland Revenue.

The promoters of organisations designed to bring about 'peace for our time' have in effect a clear choice. If they wish to secure the fiscal and other benefits available to charities they must recognise and conform to the constraints of charity law as currently interpreted by the courts – and it must be remembered that the Charity Commissioners are an extension of the High Court.

In broad terms this means that they are limited to the impartial advancement of public education in areas acceptable to the Charity Commissioners and the Inland Revenue, for example, peace movements generally (*Give Peace a Chance*), the duties and responsibilities of Government and citizens in a particular international context (the *British Atlantic Committee*) or to those elements of the fourth judicial head which cover the efficiency of the armed forces and the Defence of the Realm.

Whatever the precise nature of the organisation's objects both the Charity Commissioners and the Inland Revenue will require to be satisfied that the promoters' actual activities will faithfully match their declared intentions. It is therefore essential that the proposed governing instrument be cleared in draft with the Commissioners and the Revenue before formal adoption. With a charity being placed on the Commissioners' Register at the rate of one for every half hour of the working week, the current procedure – especially in a somewhat contentious field of this nature – can be lengthy, running into months, if not, in some cases, years.

The alternative is to establish an organisation (whether linked to a charity or not) which, while totally free to promote the cause of peace by any lawful means (including political campaigning without restriction), is ineligible for the benefits, both tangible and intangible, of charitable status. This organisation can exist alongside a charitable body constituted and operated within the confines of charitable law. Such a dual arrangement allows the charitable work to be undertaken with charitable funds and the non-charitable work to be undertaken with non-charitable funds. In this connection, it cannot be too strongly emphasised that whilst a non-charitable body may in appropriate circumstances assist a charity, the promoters and managers of a charity may never directly support, whether financially or otherwise, activities whose purpose is not legally charitable.

In the final analysis the promoters' modus operandi – and hence, their organisation's status – will be largely determined by individual circumstances and personal preference.

In a year which sees not only the fiftieth anniversary of the Munich Agreement but the tercentenary of his birth, Pope (whose comment on Charity has already been noted) may perhaps be allowed the last word.

'For Forms of Government let fools contest;
Whate'er is best administered is best'.

(The views expressed in this article are the personal views of the author, and do not necessarily reflect those of NCVO.)

Check-list for organisations seeking charitable status

1. Think first. Don't rush into applying for charitable status as quickly as you can. Decide why you want to be a charity. What tax and rate benefits will you make use of, and how much will this be worth in financial terms? What grant sources do you intend to approach, and what is the likelihood of your getting grant support?

2. Decide whether you think any or all of your work could qualify as being charitable (having read this article). If some only, then you could consider a 'dual structure'. If all, then you may be able to register the existing or proposed organisation.

3. Take proper professional advice. 'Peace' in the context of charitable status is a difficult and complex area. Proper advice on (a) whether to apply for charitable status and (b) the actual application, will be invaluable if your application is to be successful. The NCVO offers an advisory service for registration and a number of solicitors specialise in or are experienced in charity registration applications.

4. If at the end of the day you decide you don't want to or that you can't obtain registration as a charity, then you may still be able to obtain grant support from charitable sources provided that the projects you are seeking support for are charitable. You may need to discuss this with the grant-maker first, and you may possibly need to find a third party organisation to receive the grant on your behalf. Informal advice on this might be obtained from the Grant Secretaries of the leading trusts in the peace/security field.

5. Remember that in Scotland and Northern Ireland, no charity registration procedure exists, and you will need to get recognition as a charity from the Inland Revenue.

1. UK sources

Introductory note

The following list of some 160 charitable trusts in the UK results largely from a review of the accounts held at the Charity Commission of some 400 to 500 trusts.

They were initially identified from the annual reports and accounts of organisations profiled in the first half of this book, from directories and from the pursuit of likely titles, names and words in the Charity Commission index.

The resulting list shows very few trusts, only about 20 in all, with any specific focus on aspects of peace, security and international relations. These have been separately listed in the index as have those trusts with a particular interest in overseas aid, development education, or Northern Ireland.

These notes on trusts have been compiled solely for this particular guide and need to be read in this context. They do not aim to give a full picture of the trust's grant-making interests. Instead they indicate from the evidence of selected relevant grants that the trust appears to have some potential interest in the field of concern, or in certain of its aspects. For most trusts the listed grants total up to only a small proportion of the trust's annual grant-making. There are very few trusts with clearly stated policies or priorities to support this area of charitable work, which produce an annual report or supply information to the public – the contrast with trusts and foundations in the USA is most striking.

Several trusts did not wish to be listed as they said their funds were committed in advance and they were concerned at the prospect of receiving a flood of applications they would be in no position to assist. We have been careful to note these provisions in their entries.

All trusts were sent a draft entry which they were asked to amend and/or update. Most have been helpful in this respect. All were asked to supply details on how and when applications should be presented and what, if any, further information is available for applicants.

Grant seekers are advised to consult the *'Guide to Major Grant Making Trusts'* and the *'Directory of Grant Making Trusts'* to gather further information about trusts. We have not listed various exclusions such as 'no grants to individuals or to organisations which are not registered charities'. This is common practice. However, from an examination of grant-making records there appear to be many occasions on which stated exclusion policies have been overridden.

List of contents

* Non-charitable funds

Allen Lane Foundation
Mrs M. K. Allen Will Trust
A. S. Charitable Trust
Atlantic Peace Foundation
Avenue Charitable Trust
Baring Foundation
Elizabeth Barker Fund (*see British Academy*)
Philip Baxendale Trust
Beaverbrook Foundation
Benham Charitable Settlement
C. T. Bowring (Charities Fund) Ltd
E. and H. N. Boyd and J. E. Morland Charitable Trust Ltd
Brecher and Co Charitable Trust
British Academy
Britten Pears Foundation
T. B. H. Brunner's Charitable Trust
Harold Buxton Trust
Noel Buxton Trust
Barrow and Geraldine S. Cadbury Trust
* Barrow Cadbury Fund Ltd (*see Barrow and Geraldine S. Cadbury Trust*)
C. L. Cadbury Charitable Trust
Edward Cadbury Charitable Trust
Edward and Dorothy Cadbury Trust (1928)

UK Sources

Henry T. and Lucy B. Cadbury Charitable Trust
J. and L. A. Cadbury Charitable Trust
J. C. Cadbury Charitable Trust
Paul S. Cadbury Charitable Trust
Richard Cadbury Charitable Trust
William Adlington Cadbury Charitable Trust
Vera and Maxwell Caplin Charitable Trust
Catholic Fund for Overseas Development (CAFOD)
Chase Charity
* Cheney Peace Settlement
Christian Aid
Hilda and Alice Clark Charitable Trust
J. Anthony Clark Trust
Roger and Sarah Bancroft Clark Charitable Trust
Cobb Charitable Trust
Commonwealth Foundation
Commonwealth Relations Trust
Commonwealth Youth Exchange Council
Ernest Cook Trust
Co-operation North
John and Edythe Crosfield Charitable Trust
Delves Charitable Trust
Dinam Charity
Dulverton Trust
Edith M. Ellis 1985 Charitable Trust
Enkalon Foundation
Ericson Trust
European Human Rights Foundation
Esmée Fairbairn Charitable Trust
Allan and Nesta Ferguson Charitable Trust
Firbank Charitable Trust
Fitton Trust
Gatsby Charitable Foundation (see Sainsbury Family Charitable Trusts)
J. Paul Getty Jr General Charitable Trust
Simon Gibson Charitable Trust
A. B. and M. C. Gillett Charitable Trust
Gillett Trust
Give Peace A Chance Trust
GNC Trust
Godinton Charitable Trust
T. W. Greeves Trust
GSC Trust, Gwen Catchpool Charity
Walter Guinness Charitable Trust
Harbour Foundation Ltd
Virginia Worsfield Harington Charitable Trust
L. G. Harris and Co Ltd Charitable Trust
Headley Trust (see Sainsbury Family Charitable Trusts)
Hedley Foundation Ltd
Hickinbotham Charitable Trust
Walter Higgs Charitable Trust
Hilden Charitable Trust
Hillcote Trust
Lady Hind Trust
P. H. Holt Charitable Trust
Inchcape Charitable Trust Fund
Inter-Church Emergency Fund for Ireland
Invicta Trust

Irish Ecumenical Church Loan Fund Committee
J. G. Joffe Charitable Trust
Joicey Trust
Sir Cyril Kleinwort Charitable Settlement
Ernest Kleinwort Charitable Trust
Kleinwort Benson Charitable Trust
Lankelly Foundation
Lansbury House Trust Fund
Leigh Trust
Leverhulme Trust
Linbury Trust (see Sainsbury Family Charitable Trusts)
Lloyd's Charities Trust
Lyndhurst Settlement
M. B. Charities Ltd
Manor Charitable Trust
Marsden Charitable Trust
* Maypole Fund
Mercers' Charitable Foundation
* Mercury Provident plc
Victor Mischon Trust
Esmé Mitchell Trust
Samuel Montagu Charitable Trust
John Moores Foundation
Moorgate Trust Fund
Morel Charitable Trust
S. C. and M. E. Morland Charitable Trust
Network Foundation
New Moorgate Trust Fund (see Moorgate Trust Fund)
New Sheffield Trust
Northern Ireland Voluntary Trust
Nuffield Foundation
Oak Foundation
Oakdale Trust
One % Fund
Oppenheimer Charitable Trust
Oxfam
P. F. Charitable Trust
Harry Payne Trust
Headley Pitt Trust
Puckham Charitable Trust
Radley Charitable Trust
Rank Foundation Ltd
Rank Xerox Trust
Miss E. F. Rathbone Charitable Trust
Albert Reckitt Charitable Trust
Eva Reckitt Trust Fund
Rest-Harrow Trust
Mr C. A. Rodewald's Charitable Settlement
Rotary Foundation Scholarships
Rothley Trust
Rowan Charitable Trust
Joseph Rowntree Charitable Trust
* Joseph Rowntree Social Service Trust Ltd
J. B. Rubens Charity Trustees Ltd
* Earl Russell Peace Foundation Trust
Sainsbury Family Charitable Trusts
Schroder Charity Trust
Scott Bader Commonwealth Ltd

UK Sources

Sears Foundation
Sewell Charitable Trust
Simpson Foundation
Harold Smith Charitable Trust
Stephen R. and Phillipa H. Southall Charitable Trust
W. F. Southall Trust
Sir Halley Stewart Trust
C. B. and H. H. Taylor Trust
Tzedakah
Van Neste Foundation
Howard Walker Charitable Trust
Philip Walker Charitable Trust
A. F. Wallace Charity Trust
War on Want
Warbeck Fund Ltd
Wates Foundation
Weinberg Foundation
Westcroft Trust
Garfield Weston Foundation
Westward Trust
Whitaker Charitable Trust
H. D.H. Wills 1965 Charitable Trust
Wolfson Foundation
Women Caring Trust
Zochonis Charitable Trust

UK FUNDS BY SCALE OF GRANT MAKING:

Over £500,000 per annum

Baring Foundation
Barrow and Geraldine S. Cadbury Trust
British Academy
Christian Aid
Commonwealth Foundation
Dulverton Trust
Esmée Fairbairn Charitable Trust
Gatsby Charitable Foundation (see *Sainsbury Family Charitable Trusts*)
J. Paul Getty Jr General Charitable Trust
Headley Trust (see *Sainsbury Family Charitable Trusts*)
Hedley Foundation Ltd
Sir Cyril Kleinwort Charitable Settlement
Ernest Kleinwort Charitable Trust
Leverhulme Trust
Linbury Trust (see *Sainsbury Family Charitable Trusts*)
Mercers' Charitable Foundation
Moorgate Trust Fund
New Moorgate Trust Fund (see *Moorgate Trust Fund*)
Nuffield Foundation
Oak Foundation
Rank Foundation Ltd
Joseph Rowntree Charitable Trust
Joseph Rowntree Social Service Trust Ltd
J. B. Rubens Charity Trustees Ltd
Wates Foundation
Garfield Weston Foundation
Wolfson Foundation

£100,000–£499,999 per annum

Allen Lane Foundation
Barrow Cadbury Fund Ltd
Beaverbrook Foundation
Benham Charitable Settlement
Noel Buxton Trust
Edward Cadbury Charitable Trust
Paul S. Cadbury Charitable Trust
William Adlington Cadbury Charitable Trust
Chase Charity
Commonwealth Relations Trust
Commonwealth Youth Exchange Council
Ernest Cook Trust
Dinam Charity
European Human Rights Foundation
Simon Gibson Charitable Trust
Godinton Charitable Trust
Hilden Charitable Trust
Lady Hind Trust
P. H. Holt Charitable Trust

UK Sources

Inchcape Charitable Trust Fund
Irish Ecumenical Church Loan Fund Committee
J. G. Joffe Charitable Trust
Kleinwort Benson Charitable Trust
Lankelly Foundation
Leigh Trust
Lloyd's Charities Trust
M. B. Charities Ltd
Manor Charitable Trust
John Moores Foundation
Northern Ireland Voluntary Trust
Oxfam
P. F. Charitable Trust
Rank Xerox Trust
Rotary Foundation Scholarships
Rowan Charitable Trust
Sears Foundation
Sir Halley Stewart Trust
Tzedakah
Van Neste Foundation
Warbeck Fund Ltd
Weinberg Foundation
Whitaker Charitable Trust
H. D. H. Wills 1965 Charitable Trust
Zochonis Charitable Trust

£50,000–£99,999 per annum

C. T. Bowring (Charities Fund) Ltd
Brecher and Co Charitable Trust
Catholic Fund for Overseas Development
 (*development education funding only*)
J. Anthony Clark Trust
Delves Charitable Trust
Enkalon Foundation
Joicey Trust
Lyndhurst Settlement
Marsden Charitable Trust
One % Fund
Oppenheimer Charitable Trust
Miss E. F. Rathbone Charitable Trust
Rothley Trust
Schroder Charitable Trust
Harold Smith Charitable Trust
W. F. Southall Trust
Howard Walker Charitable Trust

£20,000–£49,999 per annum

Mrs M. K. Allen Will Trust
Avenue Charitable Trust
C. L. Cadbury Charitable Trust
Edward and Dorothy Cadbury Trust
J. C. Cadbury Charitable Trust
Richard Cadbury Charitable Trust

Roger and Sarah Bancroft Clark Charitable Trust
Edith M. Ellis 1985 Charitable Trust
Fitton Trust
A. B. and M. C. Gillett Charitable Trust
GNC Trust
Walter Guinness Charitable Trust
Harbour Foundation
Walter Higgs Charitable Trust
Inter-Church Emergency Fund for Ireland
Esmé Mitchell Trust
Samuel Montagu Charitable Trust
Oakdale Trust
Harry Payne Trust
Puckham Charitable Trust
Radley Charitable Trust
Albert Reckitt Charitable Trust
Eva Reckitt Trust Fund
Scott Bader Commonwealth Ltd
C. B. and H. H. Taylor Trust
Philip Walker Charitable Trust
A. F. Wallace Charity Trust
Westcroft Trust

£10,000–£19,999 per annum

T. B. H. Brunner's Charitable Trust
Henry T. and Lucy B. Cadbury Charitable Trust
J. and L. A. Cadbury Charitable Trust
Cheney Peace Settlement
John and Edythe Crosfield Charitable Trust
Virginia Worsfield Harington Charitable Trust
Hickinbotham Charitable Trust
Victor Mishcon Trust
Earl Russell Peace Foundation Trust
Simpson Foundation

£5,000–£9,999 per annum

Hilda and Alice Clark Charitable Trust
Cobb Charitable Trust
Allan and Nesta Ferguson Charitable Trust
Morel Charitable Trust
S. C. and M. E. Morland Charitable Trust
Headley Pitt Trust
Rest-Harrow Trust
Mr C. A. Rodewald's Charitable Settlement
Westward Trust

Under £5,000 per annum

Elisabeth Barker Fund
Philip Baxendale Trust
E. and H. N. Boyd and J. E. Morland Charitable Trust Ltd
Harold Buxton Trust

UK Sources

Ericson Trust
Firbank Charitable Trust
Give Peace A Chance Trust
T. W. Greeves Trust
G.S.C. Trust, Gwen Catchpool Charity
L. G. Harris and Co Ltd Charitable Trust
Hillcote Trust
Maypole Fund
New Sheffield Trust
Sewell Charitable Trust
Stephen R. and Phillipa Southall Charitable Trust

No information on grants total

A. S. Charitable Trust
Atlantic Peace Foundation
Britten Pears Foundation
Vera and Maxwell Caplin Charitable Trust
Co-operation North
Gillett Trust
Invicta Trust
Lansbury House Trust Fund
Mercury Provident plc
Network Foundation
War on Want
Women Caring Trust

TRUSTS WITH PARTICULAR INTERESTS:

Peace and defence

A. S. Charitable Trust
Atlantic Peace Foundation
Britten Pears Foundation
Noel Buxton Trust
Barrow and Geraldine S. Cadbury Trust
Elisabeth Barker Fund (see Royal Academy)
Barrow Cadbury Fund Ltd (see Barrow and Geraldine S. Cadbury Trust)
Vera and Maxwell Caplin Charitable Trust
Cheney Peace Settlement
Commonwealth Relations Trust
Dinam Charity
Dulverton Trust
Esmée Fairbairn Charitable Trust
Allan and Nesta Ferguson Charitable Trust
Give Peace A Chance Trust
Hillcote Trust
Lansbury House Trust Fund
Maypole Fund
Network Foundation
New Sheffield Trust
One % Fund
Puckham Charitable Trust
Radley Charitable Trust
Eva Reckitt Trust Fund
Mr C. A. Rodewald's Charitable Settlement
Rotary Foundation Scholarships
Joseph Rowntree Charitable Trust
Joseph Rowntree Social Service Trust Ltd
Earl Russell Foundation Trust
W. F. Southall Trust
Sir Halley Stewart Trust
Westcroft Trust

Overseas aid and/or Development education

Catholic Fund for Overseas Development
Christian Aid
John and Edythe Crosfield Charitable Trust
Walter Higgs Charitable Trust
Samuel Montagu Charitable Trust
Oxfam
Rank Xerox Trust
Rowan Charitable Trust
Harold Smith Charitable Trust
Philip Walker Charitable Trust
War on Want
Warbeck Fund Ltd

UK Sources

Northern Ireland

Allen Lane Foundation
Paul S. Cadbury Charitable Trust
Chase Charity
Co-operation North
Enkalon Foundation
Inter-Church Emergency Fund for Ireland
Irish Ecumenical Church Loan Fund Committee
Lankelly Foundation
Esmé Mitchell Trust
John Moores Foundation
Northern Ireland Voluntary Trust
Women Caring Trust

ALLEN LANE FOUNDATION

32 Chestnut Road, London SE27 9LF.

Correspondent: The Secretary.

Trustees: Mrs Christine Teale, Mrs T. Schmoller, Mrs Clare Morpurgo, B. C. G. Whitaker.

Annual grants total: £286,000 in 1986/87.

Policy and practice: The Foundation has general charitable objects with a strong interest in community relations and work with the disadvantaged. It has a particular interest in Northern Ireland. It does not support academic research or international projects.

A review of the Foundation's accounts for 1985/86 lodged at the Charity Commission has shown support for the following organisations with some relevance to the scope of this book:

United Nations Association Trust	£1,500
Prisoners' Wives and Families	£1,000
Harmony Community Trust, Northern Ireland	£1,000
Fourth World Educational and Research Association Trust	£1,000
Northern Ireland Council for Voluntary Action	£1,000
British Council of Churches	£2,000
Minority Rights Group	£5,000
Protestant and Catholic Encounter	£500

Mrs M. K. ALLEN WILL TRUST

c/o Messrs Dawson and Co (ref A.F.N.), 1 St Peter Street, Bedford ML4 02PN (0234-64245).

Trustee: A. F. Niekirk.

Annual grants total: £27,584 in 1985/86.

Policy and practice: The Trust supports naval or military charities or institutions. In 1985/86 grants included the following:

Army Benevolent Fund	£1,000
Ex Services Mental Welfare Society	£900
Royal United Services Institute for Defence Studies	£1,500
Imperial War Museum Trust	£1,484

A. S. CHARITABLE TRUST

31 Green Street, London W1Y 3FD.

Correspondent: R. St George Calvocoressi.

Trustees: R. St George Calvocoressi, C. W. Brocklebank, Sir Thomas Hare.

Policy and practice: The Trust has general charitable objects and a national and international scope. The Trust is sympathetic to projects for Third World Development; peacemaking and reconciliation; training in Christian Lay Leadership; Christ-centred social action; charismatic Christian groups involved in any of the above. Preference is for charities known to the Trust or in which they have a special interest or knowledge. Appeals by large charities and individuals are not considered.

Over recent years CHIPS, Christian International Peace Service, has been the major beneficiary. Small grants have been made to Traidcraft, Christian Engineers in Development, International Ecumenical Fellowship and Dunamis.

Presentation of applications: Correspondence cannot be answered as funds are fully committed.

ATLANTIC PEACE FOUNDATION

Bertrand Russell House, 45 Gamble Street, Nottingham NG7 4ET (0602-784 504).

Correspondent: Ken Fleet, Trustee.

Trustees: Ken Fleet, Ann Kestenbaum, Michael Barrett Brown.

Annual grants total: Not known. In 1987 the Foundation said it had a total fund of about £20,000 with some £1,500 annual interest as income.

Policy and practice: The Foundation makes occasional grants for research into peace and conflict. The accounts for 1983/84 lodged with the Charity Commission show an unsecured, interest-bearing loan of £10,000 to the Russell Press. Two of the trustees are also Directors of the Bertrand Russell Peace Foundation (which has four Directors).

Support has been given in recent years for:
  A study of middle-eastern conflict, 1982–84 by Tony Simpson;
  Research on chemical weapons, in 1984 by A. Hay;
  Publication of a handbook for peace studies in schools, 1985 by Chris Sewell.

AVENUE CHARITABLE TRUST

c/o Messrs Sayers, Butterworth, 18 Bentinck Street, London W1M 5RL.

Correspondent: S. G. Kemp.

Trustees: Hon F. D. L. Astor, Hon Mrs B. A. Astor, S. G. Kemp.

Annual grants total: £43,000 in 1986.

Policy and practice: The Trust has general charitable objects. A review of the accounts for 1985 lodged at the Charity Commissioners showed the following grants with some relevance to the scope of this book:

Anti-Slavery Society	£1,000
Defence Research Trust	£5,000
Runnymede Trust	£500
Save the Children Fund	£100
South African Council of Churches	£500

Presentation of applications: In writing; there are no application forms.

THE BARING FOUNDATION

8 Bishopsgate, London EC2N 4AE (01-283 8833).

Correspondent: Mrs T. M. Meldau, Secretary.

Members of Council of Management: Sir John Baring, Sir Lindsay Alexander, Sir Mark Baring, Mr N. H. Baring, Mrs T. A. Baring, Mr R. D. Broadley, Lord Howick, Lady Lloyd.
Barry Till (Adviser to the Council).

Annual grants total: £1,800,090 in 1986.

Policy and practice: In 1986 and in previous years the Foundation followed a general policy to make grants only to national charities and to those which are 'local' to London. In 1987 it agreed to extend its range for local appeals to include Merseyside and the North East i.e. Tyne and Wear and Teeside.

The Foundation produces a short public annual report with tabular analyses of the number of donations made by categories and a 5 year summary of donations by categories, from which the following extract has been taken for 1986:

The Arts	£306,000	17.0%
Church and Religion	£17,000	1.0%
Conservation	£178,000	9.9%
Education	£223,000	12.4%
International	£124,000	6.9%
Medicine	£233,000	12.9%
Social Welfare	£650,000	36.1%
Youth	£26,000	1.4%
Miscellaneous	£43,000	2.4%
Total	£1,800,000	100.0%

Detailed reports for 1985 and earlier years listing all separate grants, are lodged at the Charity Commission.

UK Sources

Grants relevant to this book made in previous years have been as follows:

Under **Education**:

In 1985
European Educational Research Trust (corporation subscription)	£500

In 1984
Commonwealth Institute	£5,000

In 1983
Ditchley Foundation	£10,000

Under **International**:

In 1985
Royal Institute of International Affairs (corporation subscription)	£3,519
Minority Rights Group	£1,000
Oxfam	£8,000
British Institute of International and Comparative Law	£1,000
British Executive Service Overseas	£5,000
Save the Children Fund (for a new UK education project re the Third World)	£25,000

In 1984
International Institute for Strategic Studies	£5,000
Save the Children Fund	£10,000
David Davies Memorial Institute for International Studies	£2,500

In 1983
Overseas Development Institute (3rd of 3)	£1,000
Intermediate Technology Development Group	£30,000

In 1982
Council for Arms Control	£5,000

Under **Miscellaneous**

In 1985
British North American Research Association (2nd of 3)	£1,500

PHILIP BAXENDALE CHARITABLE TRUST

134 Chorley New Road, Bolton, Greater Manchester.

Correspondent: G. Whittle.

Trustees: P. S. Baxendale, G. Whittle.

Annual grants total: £2,860 in 1984.

Policy and practice: The Trust has general charitable objects. The funds are apparently fully committed and in 1984 only two grants were made.

A review of the Trust's most recent accounts at the Charity Commission showed that in 1979 (when the total grant allocation was £14,090) the following grants with some relevance to the scope of this book were made:

Intermediate Technology Development Group	£1,000
Foundation for Alternatives	£1,000
Parliamentary Democracy Trust	£1,100

BEAVERBROOK FOUNDATION

11 Old Queen Street, London SW1H 9JA (01-222 7474).

Correspondent: M. A. C. Marshall.

Trustees: Lord Beaverbrook (Chairman), Lady Aitken (Deputy Chairman), Rt Hon Lord Robens, Hon Laura Mallet, Sir Barrie Heath, T. M. Aitken, Lady Beaverbrook, Basil de Ferranti.

Annual grants total: £386,420 for year ending September 1986.

Policy and practice: The Foundation has a policy to support 'such charitable objects of an educational and general nature as the trustees may think fit.' It gives only to charities in UK and Canada, a considerable amount to medical work and no grants to individuals. The Foundation has no stated priorities within its grantmaking but reviews all applications on their merits with a practical requirement that an organisation clearly itemises its request. A review of the accounts for 1985 at the Charity Commission showed the following grants with some bearing on the scope of this book.

RAF Museum	£50,000
Imperial War Museum Redevelopment Appeal	£25,000
Save the Children Fund	£20,000
RAF Ex-POW Association	£1,000

Grants ranged between £170 and £100,000 with the largest grant to the Sir Max Aitken Museum Trust. The majority of grants are in the £1,000 to £5,000 range.

Presentation of applications: The trustees meet three times a year and applicants are advised to present their applications in the New Year or mid year. No guidance is available for applicants on either presentation or policy.

BENHAM CHARITABLE SETTLEMENT

Mullions, Boughton, Northampton NN2 8RQ (0604-842 357).

Correspondent: Mrs H. M. Benham.

Trustees: Mrs H. M. Benham, E. D. D'Alton, P. Schofield.

Annual grants total: £132,030 in 1986.

Policy and practice: The Trust has general charitable objects with a preference for charities in Northamptonshire known to the trustees, and to national charities, or to the branches in Northamptonshire of national charities.

A review of the Trust's accounts lodged at the Charity Commission showed the following grants with some relevance to the scope of this book made in recent years.

In 1985
Action Aid	£200
Africa Now	£950
Oxfam	£250

In 1986
English Speaking Union	£100
Intermediate Technology Development Group Ltd	£100
International Voluntary Service	£150
Minority Rights Group	£200
Northern Ireland Voluntary Trust	£200
Oxfam	£150
Project Trust	£400
Stantonbury Campus	£100

Presentation of applications: With charity registration number.

C. T. BOWRING (CHARITIES FUND) LTD

The Bowring Building, PO Box 145, Tower Gate, London EC3P 3BE (01-283 3100).

Correspondent: P. L. Eckersley, Charities Fund Administrator.

Trustees: The Directors.

Annual grants total: £69,729 in 1986.

Policy and practice: The Fund has general charitable objects and a broad grant-making policy with larger grants in the medical, social welfare and cultural areas e.g. to hospices, Guys Hospital and the Philharmonic Orchestra. Grants are only made to registered charities.

A review of the Fund's accounts lodged at the Charity Commission has shown the following grants with relevance to the scope of this book.

In 1986
English Speaking Union	£350
European Atlantic Group	£100
European Educational Research Trust	£250
Ulster Defence Regiment	£100
Voluntary Service, Belfast	£250

In 1985
Co-operation Ireland	£2,500

Presentation of applications: In writing to the Fund Administrator.

Information available for applicants: Published accounts of the holding company.

E. AND H. N. BOYD AND J. E. MORLAND CHARITABLE TRUST LTD

19 Queenswood Road, Moseley, Birmingham B13 9AU.

Correspondent: H. N. Boyd.

Trustees: H. N. Boyd, Esther Boyd, Janet Morland.

Annual grants total: £1,400 in 1986/87.

Policy and practice: The accounts at the Charity Commission for 1986/87 show the small grants to the following (in the range £150–£20) with some relevance to the scope of this book: Chile Relief Fund, Greenpeace Environment Trust, Oxfam, Survival International, VSO, War on Want, Water Aid, World Government for the Age of Enlightenment (T. M.), Warwicks Monthly Meeting, Staffordshire Monthly Meeting, Warwickshire Peace Education Officer, Ulster Peace Education Officer.

BRECHER AND CO CHARITABLE TRUST

Messrs Brecher & Co, 78 Brook Street, London W1Y 2AD (01-493 5141).

Correspondent: H. A. Brecher.

Trustees: D. J. Brecher, H. A. Brecher, S. Prevezer, A. A. D. Wiseman.

Annual grants total: £62,594 in 1983.

Policy and practice: General charitable objects within a national and international beneficial area.

A review of the Trust's accounts for 1983 on file at the Charity Commission showed the following grants with some relevance to the scope of this book:

Friends of the Earth Trust	£500
Justice	£139

UK Sources

BRITISH ACADEMY

20–21 Cornwall Terrace, London NW1 4QP (01-487 5966).

Correspondent: Jane Woods, Assistant Secretary.

Annual awards total: £2,815,000 in 1984/85.

Policy and practice: Founded in 1901, The British Academy is the premier national learned society devoted to the promotion of advanced scholarship in the humanities and social sciences. The purposes of the Academy's Charter are promoted in the following ways:

Research grants: Since 1926 the Academy has received Government funds for the support of research, and these are complemented by a number of private funds administered by the Academy for special purposes (*see below for Elisabeth Barker Fund*). They take many forms; grants are made both to individual scholars – ordinarily resident in the United Kingdom and of post-doctoral or equivalent status – for their private research and to learned bodies and other groups.

Exchange agreements: There are now some 20 agreements with other academies and academic institutions overseas. These provide for fixed number of exchange visits of the kind that would be difficult for individual scholars to arrange without official help.

Appointments: The Academy administers two competitions: Readerships and Post-doctoral Fellowships.

Research projects: The Academy sponsors 29 collective research undertakings of its own.

Sponsorship of British schools and institutes overseas

Lectures, discussion meetings and the award of Prizes and Medals for outstanding work in various fields of the humanities.

Publication, primarily of fundamental texts and research aids prepared under the direction of Academy committees. There are limited schemes for supporting publications.

Postgraduate studentships: In 1984 the Academy assumed responsibility from the Department of Education and Science for the administration of the Postgraduate Studentships in the Humanities scheme.

Advice to Government and other public bodies.

Information available for applicants: Annual 'Guide to Awards' giving the various closing dates etc.

ELISABETH BARKER FUND

(see address and telephone number above)

Contact: Jane Lyddon.

Awards: Up to six annual awards of £500 each.

Policy and practice: The Fund was established with the object of promoting world peace and understanding, through the study of recent European history and through associated academic and cultural exchange between European countries, and in particular the countries in Eastern Europe.

Awards may be made to support individual, collective, or institutional projects (including conferences). Awards to individuals may take the form of grants for private study and research in other European countries. UK scholars and institutions may also apply for funds to assist scholars from other European countries to visit Great Britain, or to extend a stay following attendance at a conference.

Presentation of applications: On the standard Academy Research Grants application form. The closing date is 31st March.

BRITTEN PEARS FOUNDATION

The Red House, Aldeburgh, Suffolk, IP15 5PZ (072885-2615).

Correspondent: Mary Perry, Secretary.

Trustees: Isador Caplan, Dr Donald Mitchell, Marion Thorpe, Dr Colin Matthews, Noel Periton, Hugh Cobbe.

Annual grants total: Not disclosed.

Policy and practice: The Foundation has general charitable objects and a national scope with a particular interest in Suffolk. The Britten Pears Library Trust was set up as a subsidiary in late 1973.

There are no accounts filed at the Charity Commission so it has not been possible to gauge the Foundation's grantmaking policy and practice from that source. However it is believed there is an interest in activities and interests within the scope of this book although, like several other funding sources, it did not wish to draw attention to its work.

T. B. H. BRUNNER'S CHARITABLE TRUST

24 Bedford Gardens, London W8 (01-727 6277).

Correspondent: T. B. H. Brunner.

Trustees: T. B. H. Brunner, Helen V. Brunner.

Annual grants total: £12,501 in 1983.

Policy and practice: The Trust has general charitable objects with a special interest in arts, particularly music. Recipients of grants have included the Minority Rights Group (£500) in 1983.

HAROLD BUXTON TRUST

c/o S.P.C.K., Holy Trinity Church, Marylebone Road, London NW1 4DU.

Correspondent: The Secretary.

Trustees: P. Gilbert (Chairman), The Very Rev J. Arnold, R. de Bunsen, The Rev P. Davy, Mrs E. Harris, The Rev Canon C. Hill, The Rev Canon M. Moore, H. Whitbread.

Annual grants total: £3,345 in 1985/86.

Policy and practice: The Trust's objects are 'to promote the realisation of God's Will in human society, primarily through the Catholic religion'. It aims a) to further political, economic and social justice for all people b) to make it possible for Christians engaged in human betterment and reconciliation to visit other peoples c) to support the appreciation of the best living art.

Presentation of applications: Applicants should write to the Secretary. The Trustees meet in May and November each year.

NOEL BUXTON TRUST

27–8 Russell Square, London WC1B 5DS (01-580 5876).

Correspondent: Margaret Beard, Secretary.

Trustees: Mrs E. R. Wallace, Chairman; Hon Simon Buxton, Mrs Leah Harvey, Sir Bernard de Bunsen, R. L. de Bunsen, Lord Noel-Buxton, Professor Hugh Tinker.

Annual grants total: £101,338 in 1986.

Policy and practice: The Trustees' present interests are:

- Child and family welfare;
- Race relations in the UK and abroad;
- The rehabilitation of prisoners and the welfare of their families;
- Education and development in Africa;
- The promotion of international peace and disarmament.

The Trustees are interested in research in the above areas as well as in projects for practical action. Its policy statement says it seldom gives grants of more than £2,000, often considerably less. The Trustees are, however, prepared to consider applications for recurrent grants over a period of several years.

Grants are not made to individuals, nor in respect of students undertaking courses of any kind. The Trust does not contribute towards expeditions.

Grants for International Peace and Disarmament in 1986 included:

Centre for International Peacebuilding	£3,000
Institute of Development Studies, Sussex	£5,000
Lansbury House Trust Fund (War Resisters' International)	£300
Norwich Third World Centre (Alpha)	£200
Quaker Peace Studies Trust (Bradford School of Peace Studies)	£1,000
U.N.A. Trust (Nuclear Freeze and Arms Control Project)	£1,000
U.N.A. Trust (Right from the Start)	£2,000

Grants under other categories included:

International Voluntary Service	£2,000
Minority Rights Group	£5,000
Newham Conflict and Change Project	£500
Northern Ireland Projects Trust	£800
Northern Ireland Voluntary Trust	£5,000

It is also known that the Oxford Research Group has received support in previous years.

Presentation of applications: There is no application form and applications may be submitted at any time.

Information available for applicants: A brief policy statement and list of recent grants.

BARROW AND GERALDINE S. CADBURY TRUST (BGSC Trust)
Barrow Cadbury Fund Ltd (BC Fund Ltd)

2 College Walk, Selly Oak, Birmingham B29 6LQ (021-472 0417).

Correspondent: Anthony Wilson, Secretary.

Trustees/Directors: Catherine R. Hickinbotham, (Chairman), Geraldine M. Cadbury, Rachel E. Cadbury, Edward P. Cadbury, Philippa H. Southall, Charles L. Cadbury, Roger P. Hickinbotham, Anna C. Southall, Richard G. Cadbury, Erica R. Cadbury, Ruth M. Cadbury, James E. Cadbury.

Annual grants total: £843,152 in 1986/87 for BGSC Trust. £208,284 in 1986/87 for BC Fund Ltd.

The Barrow Cadbury Fund Ltd is a benevolent company and able to make grants to organisations which are not registered charities.

UK Sources

Policy and practice: The Trust has general charitable objects. In 1986/87 grants were made in the following categories:

	BGSC	BC Fund
Peace and International Relations	£225,507	£56,475
Race Relations	£204,081	£26,815
Housing, Neighbourhood Development and Services	£43,258	£47,512
Employment	£120,035	£41,012
Penal Affairs	£132,951	£9,750
Health Education and Social Services	£50,400	£650
Northern Ireland	£18,000	£7,250
Society of Friends and other Churches	£26,115	–
Minority Arts	£22,805	£1,416
Personal	–	£17,764

It is worth quoting the introduction to the section 'Peace and International Relations' in the 1986/87 Annual Report – 'Trustee/Directors expect this category to remain a high priority, whether the 'peace' issue concerns international relations or topics within the UK and Northern Ireland. At the international level, proposals which deal with arms control will be approached according to whether they make warfare more 'credible', or whether the steps to secure control and reduction in weaponry will thereby bring about improved political relationships. The Trustees also expect applications to be compatible with their own pacifist principles.

The Trustees remain sympathetic to initiatives in the field of peace education, but generally restrict their grants to the West Midlands. They rarely support research in international relations'.

Barrow and Geraldine S. Cadbury Trust grants in 1986/87 included:

International grants:

Budapest Conference – Christans and War	£1,500
Cape Town University, South Africa, for Centre for Intergroup Studies	£5,000
Committee on South African War Resistance, for refugees	£1,500
Conflict Resolution Centre, USA	£1,000
International Group of Researchers on the ABM Treaty	£3,080
Lincoln Trust, for work in South Africa	£2,750
South Atlantic Council for Falklands-Maldives Study Programme	£5,889
UNIPAL, for Middle East Volunteer placements	£2,500
UN Institute for Disarmament Research, for arms in outer space research project	£21,000
Quaker Council for European Affairs, for Brussels Centre	£2,050
Quaker Peace and Service	£19,750

National Grants:

Bradford University School for Peace Studies, for student placement and temporary staffing	£20,000
British Council of Churches Peace Forum	£2,500
Central London Arts Ltd for Critical Mass, 'The Day the Sheep Turned Pink'	£2,000
Defence Information Group	£10,000
Dunamis, for public programme	£1,000
International Physicians for the Prevention of Nuclear War, for conference	£3,000
Lansbury House Trust Fund, for Alternative Defence Commission	£8,750
Minority Rights Group, for administration	£2,500
Overseas Development Institute, for All Party Group on Overseas Development	£12,000
Play for Life – catalogue of 'peace toys'	£500
Quaker Peace Studies Trust, Bradford University for research fellowships	£5,000
Sussex University, for Armament and Disarmament Information Unit	£10,000
Transnational Institute, for UK programme	£5,000
Verification Technology Information Centre, for administration	£5,000
Woodstock Trust, for Oxford Research Group, administration, publication	£31,700

Barrow Cadbury Fund Limited grants in 1986/87 included:

International grants

British American Security Information Centre, for Washington DC Office	£5,000
Committee on South African War Resistance, for expenses	£500
International Peace Poster Exhibition	£1,000
Western Sahara Campaign	£1,250

National grants

At Ease, for administration	£100
Campaign Against Arms Trade, for administration	£500
Freeze, for Parliamentary post	£2,500
Peace Education Network	£12,000

UK Sources

SANA (Scientists against Nuclear Arms), for administration	£7,500
United Nations Association, for staff position	£11,000
Working Party on Chemical and Biological Warfare	£6,750
World Disarmament Campaign Newsletter	£2,000

West Midlands grants

Birmingham Campaign Against Arms Trade	£75
Selly Oak Peace Council	£100

Presentation of applications: An information brochure is available from the Trust. Full Trustees' meetings are held quarterly in March, late June, October, December. All major applications are considered at such meetings. Small grants in the West Midlands can sometimes be considered much more rapidly. Written applications requested.

Information available for applicants: Annual Reports (with particularly full and helpful statistics of grant-giving but individual allocations not shown). The 1986/87 Report has an introduction entitled 'Prophecy and Reconciliation: Justice and Peace' centring on its peace and international relations programmes.

C. L. CADBURY CHARITABLE TRUST

Joe's Farm, Upper End, Great Comberton, Pershore, Hereford and Worcestershire WR10 3DP (038674-487).

Correspondent: C. L. Cadbury.

Trustees: C. L. Cadbury, Mrs J. S. Cadbury, G. White.

Annual grants total: £26,940 in 1984/85.

Policy and practice: The Trust has general charitable objects and a national and international scope. Support is given to organisations known to Mr C. L. Cadbury and unsolicited applications are not welcomed. A review of the Trust's accounts for 1984/85 at the Charity Commission has shown that the following grants were made which fall within the scope of this book:

Young Friends World Gathering	£200
International Voluntary Service	£250
Africa Now	£100
UNA Trust	£500
Oxfam	£3,000
Lagan College	£500
Woodbrooke College	£1,000
Quaker Peace and Service	£3,000

The 61 grants then made ranged between £20 and £3,000; seven of £1,000 or more.

Presentation of applications: In writing at any time. No acknowledgement is sent to unsolicited requests.

EDWARD CADBURY CHARITABLE TRUST

(see also the Edward and Dorothy Cadbury Trust (1928)), Elmfield, College Walk, Birmingham B29 6LE (021-472 1838).

Correspondent: Mrs M. Walton, The Secretary.

Trustees: J. A. Gillett, C. E. Gillett, C. S. Littleboy, Mrs E. S. Bateman.

Annual grants total: £345,730 in 1980/81.

Policy and practice: The Trust has general charitable objects and a national and international scope. It also has a particular preference for applicants from the West Midlands area.

The most recent accounts lodged at the Charity Commission were for 1976/77 when a total of £118,033 was allocated. These showed the following grants with any possible relevance to the scope of this book:

Action Returned Volunteers	£600
Belfast, Voluntary Service Branch	£500
Society of Friends	£15,305
Selly Oak Colleges	£75,361

EDWARD AND DOROTHY CADBURY TRUST (1928)

(see also the Edward Cadbury Charitable Trust), Elmfield, College Walk, Selly Oak, Birmingham B29 6LE (021-472 1838).

Correspondent: Mrs M. Walton, The Secretary.

Trustees: J. A. Gillett, M. W. Gillett, P. A. Gillett, C. M. Elliott.

Annual grants total: £40,000 in 1983/84.

Policy and practice: The Trust has general charitable objects and a preference for applications from the Midlands though it has a national and international scope.

A review of the most recent accounts for 1983/84 on file at the Charity Commission showed the following allocations with some relevance to the scope of this book:

UK Sources

AFS International Programmes	£300
Belfast East Community Council	£200
British Council for Racial Equality	£100
Fellowship of Reconciliation	£150
Society of Friends	£350
IVS	£150
League of Remembrance	£100
Polish Students Appeal Fund	£200
Russian Immigrant Aid Fund	£50
Selly Oak Colleges	£798
Woodbrooke College	£1,500

Grants then ranged between £50 and £50,000.

HENRY T. AND LUCY B. CADBURY CHARITABLE TRUST

Treharrock, 41 Long Grove, Seer Green, Beaconsfield HP9 2YN (049-465 917).

Correspondent: Mrs E. M. Hambly, Trustee (until March 1988 when Trustees will change).

Trustees: Mrs E. M. Hambly, J. A. Cadbury, R. C. Gillett, K. M. Charity, D. B. Gillett, A. T. Hambly, B. S. Cadbury.

Annual grants total: £16–17,000 in 1986/87.

Policy and practice: The Trust has general charitable objects and a national scope but apparently the funds are already allocated and new applications are not encouraged.

A review of the Trust's accounts for 1983 which were the most recent filed at the Charity Commission showed the following grants with some relevance to the scope of this book:

Woodbrooke College	£500
Quaker Peace and Service	£500
Eritrea Relief Agency	£100

Each Trustee had their own 'quota' of £500 to devote to their own special interests.

Included in these allocations were the following grants:

Intermediate Technology Development Group	£100
United Nations Association	£100
Quaker Peace and Service	£100
International Voluntary Service	£170

J. AND L. A. CADBURY CHARITABLE TRUST

2 College Walk, Birmingham B29 6LE (021-472 1464).

Correspondent: Mrs Sylvia Gale, The Secretary.

Trustee: Mrs L. A. Cadbury.

Annual grants total: £16,675 in 1986/87.

Policy and practice: The Trust has general charitable objects and a national scope with a particular interest in the Midlands. The Trust's accounts for 1986/87 showed a considerable interest in conservation. The two largest grants were to the National Trust (£5,000) and Worcestershire Nature Conservation Trust (£1,000). The remaining hundred grants were parcelled out in small amounts between £25 and £500.

The following grants of £50 to £100 to organisations with some bearing on the scope of this guide book were made: Amnesty International, Anti-Slavery Society, Population Concern, Canon Collins Educational Trust, Y Care International.

J. C. CADBURY CHARITABLE TRUST

Pannell Kerr Forster, Lee House, 6a Highfield Road, Edgbaston, Birmingham B15 3ED (021-455 0431).

Correspondent: R. Harriman.

Trustees: J. C. Cadbury, C. J. C. Cadbury, R. V. J. Cadbury, Mrs E. B. Cadbury.

Annual grants total: £29,230 in 1985/86.

Policy and practice: The Trust has general charitable objects and a national and international scope. Apparently the Trust's current commitments absorb its income so that it cannot entertain unsolicited applications.

The most recent Trust accounts filed at the Charity Commission were for 1975/76. These showed that the Trust then had a strong interest in wildlife conservation and that the following organisations with some relevance to the scope of this book were then supported:

Fircroft Trust	£3,073
Minority Rights Group	£50
Intermediate Technology Ltd	£500
Oxfam	£150
International Voluntary Service	£40

UK Sources

PAUL S. CADBURY TRUST

2 College Walk, Selly Oak, Birmingham B29 6LE (021-472 0417).

Correspondent: Eric Adams, Secretary.

Trustees: Catherine R. Hickinbotham (Chair), Rachel E. Cadbury, Charles L. Cadbury, Roger P. Hickinbotham, Richard G. Cadbury, Ruth M. Cadbury, James E. Cadbury, Anna C. Southall. (These 8 trustees are also trustees of the Barrow and Geraldine S. Cadbury Trust, which has 13 trustees in all.)

Annual grants total: £138,754 in 1986/87.

Policy and practice: The Trust was established with general charitable objects and a national scope with a particular interest in the West Midlands.

Grants were made in the following categories in 1986/87:

Housing, neighbourhood development and services	£91,692	66%
Northern Ireland	£31,000	22%
Society of Friends and other Churches	£10,266	7%
Health, education and social services	£5,772	4%
Penal Affairs	£25	–

59% of grants were made in the West Midlands area.

A review of the Trust's accounts for 1986/87 filed at the Charity Commission showed that 90 organisations then received support with the largest grant being for £13,500 and only two others receiving as much as £10,000. The following allocations with some relevance to the scope of this book were made:

Alliance-Ardoyne Playscheme	£2,000
Cornerstone Community	£2,000
Corrymeela Community	£250
Friends of the Earth	£1,400
Northern Ireland Council for Voluntary Action	£10,000
Warwickshire Monthly Meeting, Society of Friends	£4,000
Warwickshire Monthly Meeting, Education Committee	£150
Woodbrooke College	£25

Presentation of applications: Major applications are considered 3 times a year and those under £1,000 monthly. Informal enquiries by letter or telephone are welcomed.

Information available for applicants: Information leaflet; annual report.

RICHARD CADBURY CHARITABLE TRUST

14 Gaveston Road, Leamington Spa, Warwickshire CV32 6EU.

Correspondent: Mrs M. M. Slora.

Trustees: R. B. Cadbury, Mrs M. M. Slora.

Annual grants total: £23,000 in 1986/87.

Policy and practice: The Trust has general charitable objects and a national and international scope with a bias towards charities local to the trustees.

The Trust has supplied the following list of allocations in 1986/87 with relevance to the scope of this book:

Christian Aid	£300
Woodbrooke College	£500
Oxfam	£350
Far East Broadcasting Association	£100
VSO, Birmingham and District Local Committee	£200

Presentation of applications: Applications should be sent by February, June and October each year.

The Trust does not support appeals from individuals unless they are made through a recognised charitable body or organisation.

WILLIAM ADLINGTON CADBURY CHARITABLE TRUST

2 College Walk, Birmingham B29 6LE (021-472 1464).

Correspondent: Mrs S. Gale, Secretary.

Trustees: Mrs Hannah Henderson Taylor, Mrs Constance Tangye, Alan Cadbury, Brandon Cadbury, Mrs Sarah Stafford, W. James Beech Taylor, Rupert A. Cadbury.

Annual grants total: £194,225 in 1986/87.

Policy and practice: The Trust has general charitable objects and gives support nationally, (excluding London) with a particular interest in the West Midlands.

The Trust's schedule of grants for 1986/87 showed the following allocations with some relevance to the scope of this book:

Quaker Peace Studies Trust	£2,000
Northern Ireland Projects Trust	£1,000
Warwickshire Monthly Meetings Peace Education Officer	£1,000
United Nations Association	£500
Northern Ireland Voluntary Trust	£2,000

UK Sources

Canon Collins Education Trust for South Africa	£500
Quaker Peace and Service	£2,500

The grant range was between £50 and £10,000 with only two grants of £10,000 being made. The majority of grants were between £500 and £2,000.

VERA AND MAXWELL CAPLIN CHARITABLE TRUST

6 Post Office Avenue, Southport, Merseyside PR9 0US.

Correspondent: A. M. Caplin.

Trustees: A. M. Caplin, Mrs V. D. Caplin, E. B. Caplin, D. K. Malies.

Policy and practice: The Trust was established in 1976 with an income of £10,000 with the following objects: 'to advance education in the art or science of government and other branches of political and economic science and in particular the study of relationship to one another of the United Kingdom of Great Britain and Ireland and the other countries of the British Commonwealth'.

Since its establishment no accounts have been lodged with the Charity Commission. The Trust has not replied to correspondence. No examples of beneficiaries have been identified in the course of research on this book.

CATHOLIC FUND FOR OVERSEAS DEVELOPMENT (CAFOD)

2 Garden Close, Stockwell Road, London SW9 9TY (01-733 7900).

Correspondent: Brian Davies, Head of Education Department.

Annual grants total: £71,420 in 1986/87 for development education funding within the UK.

Policy and practice: CAFOD's development education programme seeks to promote understanding and solidarity between people in this country and in the Third World.

The general aims of this programme are to:

Increase awareness of poverty and injustice in the world and the structures which cause them;

Reflect on the injustices of our western lifestyle and consider how we can be freed to live more justly;

Encourage Christians in their social, political and economic choices to act in favour of the poor;

Celebrate the Church's vision of integral human development and her mission to build up the kingdom of God on earth.

The Development Education programme makes support in three areas:

Core-funding to those dioceses with full-time justice and peace workers;

Funding of programmes of organisations with related interests e.g. International Broadcasting Trust, One World Week and Third World First;

Small one-off grants for projects such as exhibitions and films, etc.

Programmes and projects proposed for funding should be in line with CAFOD's general aims in Development Education and be directed mainly at members of the Catholic Church of England and Wales.

The purpose of the fund is to promote new initiatives in Development Education among CAFOD's constituency and draw attention to good practice.

Special encouragement is given to programmes and projects which set out to influence those not reached by other efforts.

Preference will be given to programmes and projects which:

Have clearly defined objectives and can be accomplished within a specific time;

Attempt to break new ground or reach a new public;

Involve educators or those who will in turn influence others;

Can be taken up and followed through by others.

Grants made in 1986/87 included funding towards Justice and Peace Workers in Leeds, Southwark, Salford, Nottingham, Northampton, Plymouth. Programme funding included support towards:

Selly Oak RC Lectureship	£1,000
One World Week	£3,750
International Broadcasting Trust	£5,000
Third World First	£4,000
Returned Volunteer Action	£1,500
Campaign Against Arms Trade, DE Project	£1,000
National Association of Development Education Centres – Workshops	£2,000
Trade Union Research and Education Group – TUIREG	£1,500
Bread not Bombs, DE Project	£1,000
Action for World Development Fund	£3,000

Project funding included support for:

Walk for the World	£7,500
Namibia Support Committee Exhibition	£250

Presentation of applications: There is no

application form. Details of formal information required are given in the guidelines. Decisions on applications are made twice a year.

Further information for applicants: Guidelines for the development education fund; a statement of general policy for grant-making; annual reports.

CHASE CHARITY

34 North End Road, London W14 0SH (01-603 1525).

Correspondent: Calton Younger, Secretary.

Trustees: A. Ramsay, G. Halcrow, R. Mills, Mrs R. A. Moore, Mrs C. Flanders.

Annual grants total: £218,175 in 1985/86.

Policy and practice: The Charity has general charitable objects and a national scope. Whilst it has a specific interest in the arts and the English heritage it has also provided support to organisations in Northern Ireland.

Grants in 1985/86 included the following:

Westrock Whiterock Community Youth Group, W. Belfast	£500
The Matt Talbot Centre, Belfast	£2,000
Belfast Voluntary Welfare Society	£2,000
Action Resource Centre, Northern Ireland	£2,000
The Peace People Trust	£2,000
PACE Association (Protestant and Catholic Encounter)	£1,725
Society of St Vincent de Paul	£2,000

Presentation of applications: Applications may be made at any time. The Trustees meet quarterly. There are long waiting lists.

Information available for applicants: The accounts are filed at the Charity Commission.

CHENEY PEACE SETTLEMENT

Aylesmore Farm, Shipton-on-Stour, Warwickshire (060-885 279).

Trustees: Harry Mister, Geoffrey Tattersall.

Contacts: Howard Cheney, Founder of Settlement, 42 Uplands Park Road, Enfield, Middlesex (01-363 4398), or Harry Mister, Trustee, 3 Upperhead Row, Huddersfield, Yorkshire HD1 2JL (0484-23622).

Annual grants total: £10,000 each year.

Policy and practice: The Settlement was started by Howard Cheney in 1976. It is not a registered charity.

UK Sources

Support is given to a broad range of groups in the vanguard of work to improve human relationships and conditions between themselves and their environment. These have included organisations such as the Soil Association, Friends of the Earth, Greenpeace, Amnesty International as well as those immediately concerned with peace (as conventionally defined) e.g. The Alternative Defence Commission, Peace News and At Ease.

Grants range between £20 to £1,000.

Grants were made in 1986/87 to:
Lansbury House Trust Fund,
War on Want,
Family Planning Association,
Woodland Trust,
Conservation Trust,
War Resisters' International.
Campaign Against Arms Trade.
Peace Tax Campaign,
National Peace Council,
Oxfam.

as well as to those organisations mentioned earlier.

Presentation of applications: The applications can be made at any time and are reviewed continuously; there are no set meeting dates.

CHRISTIAN AID

PO Box 100, London SE1 7RT or Interchurch House, 35 Lower Marsh, London SE1 7Rl (01-620 4444 x 2345).

Contact for development education grants: Barbara Vellacott, Head of the Education Sector.

Development Education Grants Committees: A UK/Ireland Committee comprising Board members and other advisers makes decisions on national grants.

Regional Development Education Committees (five in England and one each in Scotland, Wales and Ireland) encourage imaginative local initiatives.

Annual grants total for development education in the UK: Some £500,000 in 1987/88 of which £170,000 to national organisations and the remainder to regional and other organisations.

Policy and practice: Christian Aid supports development education work. It does not make a specific policy statement or publish criteria for support.

UK/Ireland grants for development awarded between September 1986 and March 1987 included the following:

UK Sources

Action for World Development Fund	£17,000
One World Week	£10,800
Trade Union International Research and Education Group	£9,930
International Broadcasting Trust	£35,000
Bread not Bombs Week	£2,000
The Other Economic Summit	£1,000
Centre for Global Education	£3,300
World Studies 8–13 Project	£7,000
Campaign Against Arms Trade	£3,675
Third World First (first of three)	£10,500
National Association of Development Education Centres (NADEC)	£12,000

Presentation of applications: The UK/Ireland Committee meets in March, June/July and November. Applications need to be received 8 weeks in advance. The Regional Committees meet at different times and information on these should be found out as necessary. There is no application form, but detailed guidelines are prepared.

Information available for applicants: Guidance about information required from the applicant is available.

HILDA AND ALICE CLARK CHARITABLE TRUST

c/o Messrs Thomson McLintock, 15 Pembroke Road, Bristol, Avon BS8 3BG.

Correspondent: The Trustees.

Trustees: R. B. Clark, J. A. Clark, P. T. Clothier, S. Clark, M. P. Lovell, A. T. Clothier.

Annual grants total: £8,450 in 1985.

Policy and practice: The Trust's objects are expressed as follows: 'For such charitable purposes or objects as the trustees shall in their uncontrolled discretion think fit.' In effect the Trust gives mainly to the Society of Friends.

Grants made in 1982, the most recent year for which accounts were filed at the Charity Commission, included:

Quaker Peace and Service	£650
Quaker Home Service Council	£150
Quaker Social Responsibility and Education	£500

(These same grants had been made in 1981 and 1980.)

Presentation of applications: The trustees meet in December. Applications should be made in writing.

J. ANTHONY CLARK CHARITABLE FOUNDATION

15 Pembroke Road, Bristol, Avon BS8 3BG.

Correspondent: Avon Executor and Trustee Co.

Trustees: Avon Executor and Trustee Co, D. M. Parkes, L. P. Clark, J. C. Clark.

Annual grants total: £70,910 in 1984.

Policy and practice: The Trust has general charitable objects. It gives in the main to the Society of Friends and educational projects. There are no records filed at the Charity Commission since 1977, but it is known that the Oxford Research Group has received support.

Presentation of applications: Applications can be made at any time but the Trustees do not reply to unsolicited approaches unless they are able to make a grant or wish for further information.

ROGER AND SARAH BANCROFT CLARK CHARITABLE TRUST

40 High Street, Street, Somerset.

Correspondent: Mrs F. Coole.

Trustees: Priscilla Johnston, Eleanor C. Robertson, Mary P. Lovell, S. Clark.

Annual grants total: around £20,000 in 1987.

Policy and practice: The Trust has general charitable objects. It has a time-limit to 1990. There is a particular interest in the Society of Friends, education and local appeals. The most recent accounts at the Charity Commission were for 1973. These showed two small grants of relevance to the scope of this book to Oxfam and the Fellowship of Reconciliation

Presentation of applications: The trustees meet three times a year. Applications will be acknowledged if a reply paid envelope is also enclosed. The Trust finds it gets inundated with inappropriate appeals and did not wish for the further exposure of an entry in this book.

COBB CHARITABLE TRUST

19 High Street, Trumpington, Cambridge, Cambridgeshire (0223-841 222).

Correspondent: A. Cobb.

Trustees: Mrs C. A. Cobb, F. Applebe, A. Applebe.

Annual grants total: £5,200 in 1986/87.

Policy and practice: Little is known about the Trust's policies but a review of its accounts at the Charity Commission has shown that in 1986/87 the Trust made the following grants which are relevant to the scope of this book:

Campaign for Nuclear Disarmament	£400
Green Deserts Sudan	£400
Quaker Peace	£400
Population Services	£200
Intermediate Technology	£200

THE COMMONWEALTH FOUNDATION

Marlborough House, Pall Mall, London SW1Y 5HY (01-930 3783).

Correspondent: 'Inoke F. Faletau, Director.

Annual income: £1.54 million.

Annual grants total for Fellowships and awards: More than £200,000 in 1983/84 (all for exchanges for less than 3 months).

Policy and practice: The Foundation is an autonomous body with a Board of Governors nominated by the 43 Commonwealth Governments which contribute to it. The Foundation works among the unofficial bodies of the Commonwealth. It co-operates in the activities of professional Commonwealth Associations and has supported the establishment of a series of interdisciplinary professional centres and Commonwealth non-governmental organisation liaison units. It is responsible for a range of Commonwealth Foundation Fellowship and Bursary Schemes e.g. the Fellowship Scheme to Promote Commonwealth Understanding whereby twelve Fellowships are awarded annually to professionals of influence to undertake a one month programme on Commonwealth affairs. Fellowships are not available on personal application.

The following Ad Hoc Awards are available on personal application to the Foundation:

Bursaries for short-term study, refresher courses, advisory visits and training attachments;

Grants for attendance at conferences, seminars and workshops.

These awards are available to professional women and men and members of non-governmental organisations throughout the Commonwealth. Bursaries are tenable for periods not exceeding three months in a Commonwealth country other than the applicant's own.

Presentation of applications: In writing, there is no application form. Three months' notice is generally required.

Information available for applicants: A briefing leaflet, and a guide to conference organisers.

COMMONWEALTH RELATIONS TRUST

28 Bedford Square, London WC18 3EG (01-631 0686).

Correspondent: Mrs Barbara Anderson, The Secretary.

Trustees: The trustees of the Nuffield Foundation now are automatically trustees of this Trust i.e. Lord Flowers, (Chairman), Professor B. M. Hoggett, Professor Sir Hans Kornberg, Professor R. C. O. Matthews, Dr D. A. J. Tyrrell, Sir Brian Young.

Annual grants total: £110,000 in 1986/87.

Policy and practice: The Trust, formerly the Imperial Relations Trust, was set up in 1937 by an anonymous gift to the first Earl Baldwin of Bewdley to strengthen ties which bind together the United Kingdom and other independent countries of the Commonwealth. Fellowships, travel bursaries and grants are given. As its name implies the Trust covers all member countries of the Commonwealth (initially it had only covered a selected few). At the present time Fellowships and Travelling Bursaries are awarded as follows:

Fellowships: One each year to Australia and to New Zealand to enable an experienced teacher from each country to spend a year at the University of London Institute of Education, or any other college in the UK; these are 'matched' with additional Fellowships provided by Australia and New Zealand.

Travelling Bursaries: Bursaries are offered annually to eight national broadcasting organisations of Commonwealth countries for three-month visits to the UK by members of staff; three UK broadcasters from the BBC and the independent sector receive awards for visits to Commonwealth countries overseas, with an emphasis on visits to developing countries.

Similar schemes exist for trade unionists, and adult educators from Australia, Canada and New Zealand to visit the UK and from the UK to visit a Commonwealth country overseas.

One bursary is available each year to a librarian and an adult educator from developing countries for a visit to the UK.

UK Sources

Adult Education Bursaries	£16,712
London University	£6,600
Trades Union Travelling Bursaries	£13,576
Bursaries for broadcasters	£51,716

Support is also available for people travelling from the UK to Commonwealth countries and vice versa.

Information available for applicants: A basic information sheet. Awards are advertised by the national organisations concerned and applications should be addressed directly to them. Details may be obtained from the Secretary.

COMMONWEALTH YOUTH EXCHANGE COUNCIL

18 Fleet Street, London EC4Y 1AA (01-353 3901).

Correspondent: Roderick Gray, Executive Secretary.

Annual grants total: around £148,000 in 1986/87.

Policy and practice: The aim of this financial support is to promote reciprocal exchanges which will develop contact and thereby better understanding between the young people of the UK and other Commonwealth countries. Priority is given to funding:

New or particularly innovative exchange programmes;

Exchanges with Commonwealth countries in Africa, Asia and the Caribbean;

British organisations which have not been previously very active in this field;

Exchanges involving young Britons who would not normally have the opportunity to take part.

An exchange may begin with a visit overseas by a British group or with a visit to Britain by another Commonwealth group. In either case there should be the prospect of a reciprocal visit taking place within a reasonable time scale in the future.

Projects must be organised by an established organisation in the UK and in the partner country and led by a responsible person. Exchanges, particularly outside Europe are expected to last at least 21 days. The participants should be aged between 16 and 25 years and groups should be between 5 and 15 in number. In 1986/87, 77 groups were given assistance, 35 of these were from other Commonwealth countries and 44 from the UK.

Presentation of applications: An application form is available and applications should be submitted at least 9 months before the project begins. The grants sub-committee is made up of representatives of central government, local education authorities and voluntary youth organisations. Applicants are advised to ring about the timing of its meetings as applications are needed a month in advance. The majority of applications should be made in Autumn.

Information available for applicants: Guidelines.

ERNEST COOK TRUST

Estate Office, Fairford Park, Fairford, Gloucestershire GL7 4JH (0285-713 273).

Correspondent: J. G. L. Malleson, Secretary.

Trustees: Lord Saye and Sele, Sir Ralph Verney, Sir Jack Boles, C. F. Badcock, W. R. Benyon.

Annual grants total: £451,111 in 1986/87.

Policy and practice: The major part of the Trust's support is for projects concerned with education in the countryside or enabling city dwellers to enjoy countryside facilities and for research into issues affecting rural society or concerned with conservation of the countryside. Support is also given to organisations assisting travel overseas by young people particularly where the aim is to develop understanding between people of different countries. In recent years the Trust has given support in this educational exchange field to:

The Experiment in International Living (1986)	£20,000
Yes, Student Exchange, Bristol University (1985)	£700

Presentation of applications: Applications can be submitted throughout the year and are considered by the trustees twice a year.

Information available for applicants: A leaflet listing recent grants and outlining policy is available.

CO-OPERATION NORTH (Belfast)

7 Botanic Avenue, Belfast BT7 1JG (0232-321 462).

CO-OPERATION NORTH (Dublin)

37 Upper Fitzwilliam Street, Dublin 2 (0001-610 588/2/3/4).

Policy and practice: The aims of Co-operation North (*see also entry in Part One of this book*) are: 'To promote goodwill and understanding between the people of Northern Ireland and the Republic of Ireland by fostering co-operation in the economic, social and cultural spheres.

To engage in investigation and research into common problems and the opportunities for mutually beneficial co-operation.'

Its main funding programmes are:

School Links: To assist two-way, project-based exchanges between primary and secondary schools in Northern Ireland and the Republic of Ireland. The maximum grant for each group is IR£275 (STG £250). Each school/college is expected to be responsible for a considerable part of the cost of each exchange.

Youth Links: A grant of up to IR£300 (STG£275) for young groups in Northern Ireland and the Republic of Ireland for two-way, project-based exchanges.

Network '87: A scheme to assist social, cultural, recreational and health organisations in cross-border exchanges. Maximum grants of IR£300 (STG£275) for each group.

Miscellaneous: Co-operation North from time to time supports particularly worthwhile projects involving cross-border co-operation which do not fall within the above schemes.

Information available for applicants: A range of leaflets is available about each of the schemes. These include entry forms in most cases.

JOHN AND EDYTHE CROSFIELD CHARITABLE TRUST

Grove Lodge, Admiral's Walk, London NW3 6RS.

Correspondent: J. F. Crosfield

Trustees: J. F. Crosfield, Mrs E. M. Crosfield, R. J. Crosfield.

Annual grants total: £13,400 in 1985.

Policy and practice: Its objects are 'To help deprived children and deprived adults who are sick or old. To support medical research and preserve the ecology'.

The Trust has a national and international scope but it is understood that regular support is made to certain charities each year and new applications cannot be considered.

DELVES CHARITABLE TRUST

Pannell Kerr Forster, Lee House, 6a Highfield Road, Edgbaston, Birmingham B15 3ED (021-455 0431).

Correspondent: R. Harriman.

Trustees: Mrs M. Breeze, J. J. Sloan, J. Breeze, G. Breeze, Miss E. Breeze, C. Breeze.

Annual grants total: £82,950 in 1985/86.

Policy and practice: The Trust has general charitable objects and can provide support both to national and international causes.

The most recent accounts lodged at the Charity Commissioners were for 1979/80 and showed subscriptions and donations to:

The Intermediate Technology Develoment Group	£5,000
Minority Rights Group	£500
Oxfam	£3,000
Quaker Peace and Service	£3,000

Presentation of applications: The Trust cannot consider applications as its funds are committed.

DINAM CHARITY

29 Boltro Road, Haywards Heath, West Sussex RH16 1BW (0444-459 316).

Correspondent: The Secretary.

Trustees: The Hon Mrs Mary M. Noble, The Hon Mrs G. R. Jean Cormack, The Hon Edward D. G. Davies, The Hon Jonathan H. Davies.

Annual grants total: £101,325 in 1985.

Policy and practice: The Trust was set up in 1926 by David Davies. It has general charitable objects with a particular interest in the development of international understanding.

The most recent accounts on file at the Charity Commission for 1979 showed that the major part of its grant-making (78%) was then allocated to the David Davies Memorial Institute of International Studies (£16,000). Other grants were made to:

War on Want	£1,350
Atlantic College	£400

THE DULVERTON TRUST

5 St James's Place, London SW1Y 1NP (01-629 9121).

Correspondent: Major General M. J. Tomlinson, Secretary.

Trustees: Lord Dulverton (Chairman), Hon Robert Wills, Sir David Wills, Col S. J. Watson, Maj Gen Sir John Nelson, C. A. H. Wills, Miss Catherine Wills, J. W. Watson, Sir Ashley Ponsonby, Hon Michael Wills, Lord Taylor of Gryfe, the Earl of Gowrie.

Annual grants total: £1,204,000 in 1986/87.

Policy and practice: The Trust has supplied the following account of its policy in this area. 'Grants may be made for all charitable purposes but are generally made only to registered charities because of conditions in their trust deed to this effect. The detailed policy of

UK Sources

the Trust is reviewed annually at the first meeting of the financial year. At the policy review on 2 May 1985 the Trustees confirmed that principal activity would be directed to five main categories; industrial understanding, peace and security, conservation, youth and education and religion. Activity would also be continued to a lesser degree in the fields of preservation (natural resources), general welfare and East Africa.

In the general context, the exclusions of the Trust are listed in full in 'The Guide to the Major Grant Making Trusts. It should be noted that among these exclusions are universities, including research grants. No grant is ever made to an individual. The policy governing exclusions is dictated by the finite limitations of the funds available to the Trust. In these circumstances the Trust just cannot do everything and remain effective.

Although Peace and Security is one of the major categories of the Trust, a fixed sum of the order of 8% of the available revenue is usually made available within any one financial year. The only significant variation of policy since 1984 was made by Trustees in May 1985 when it was decided that 'the emphasis for the support of the Trust in this general category should be directed principally towards the limitation of subversion and terrorism within the United Kingdom'.

The Trust has provided signficant support over recent years to the Council for Arms Control and the British Atlantic Committee. From time to time the Trust will vary their support, within this overall category, from one national charity to another. Thus the scale of specific grants in the past may prove to be misleading.'

In 1985 recipients in the category of 'Peace and Security' were:

British Atlantic Committee	£45,000
Council for Arms Control	£48,000
Institute for the Study of Conflict	£1,000
Royal Institute for International Affairs	£10,000

Grants were also made under its 'Education' category to organisations falling within the ambit of international relations as defined by this book. These were:

English Speaking Union	£780
United World Colleges	£20,000
International Broadcasting Trust	£5,000
David Davies Memorial of International Studies	£15,000
U.N.A. Trust	£6,500

Presentation of applications: To the Secretary in writing with not more than three typed sheets including a summary of funding. Accounts are not required initially. Applications are considered by Trustees at their quarterly meetings.

EDITH M. ELLIS 1985 CHARITABLE TRUST

Messrs Waterhouse & Co, 4 St Paul's Churchyard, London EC4M 8BA.

Correspondent: A. P. P. Honigmann, Trustee.

Trustees: A. P. P. Honigmann, E. H. Milligan.

Annual grants total: £26,000 in 1986.

Policy and practice: Its objects are as follows: 'General charitable purposes including religious and educational projects and projects in the international field specially related to economic, social and humanitarian aid to developing countries. Ecumenical and Quaker interests are favoured.'

Grants are 'Modest contributions towards launching new schemes or tiding over moments of shortfall in experiments within the general purposes outlined above.' The accounts on file at the Charity Commission do not list individual grants and no replies have been made by the Trustees in response to correspondence.

ENKALON FOUNDATION

25 Randalstown Road, Antrim BT41 4LJ (08494-63535 x 601).

Correspondent: J. W. W. Wallace, Secretary.

Trustees: R. L. Schierbeek (Chairman), J. A. Freeman, D. H. Templeton.

Annual grants total: between £90–£100,000 in 1986/87.

Policy and practice: The Foundation is interested in cross community groups, self-help, assistance to the unemployed and groups helping the disadvantaged. The priorities may vary from year to year. Grants are made up to a maximum of £6,000.

Recent grants have been made to:
  The Corrymeela Community,
  Community of the Peace People,
  Lagan College, Belfast,
  Children's Community Holidays,
  Ulster Peoples College,
  Harmony Community Trust,
  Community Technical Aid.

A grant was made to the Northern Ireland Voluntary Trust in 1986/87.

Presentation of applications: Applications should be in writing. Decisions are made at three monthly intervals.

Information available for applicants: Guidelines.

ERICSON TRUST

Flat 2, 53 Carleton Road, London N7 0ET.

Correspondent: Mrs A. M. C. Cotton.

Trustees: C. B. Cotton, Mrs A. M. C. Cotton, A. Weston.

Annual grants total: £3,000 in 1987.

Policy and practice: The Trust has general charitable objects and a national and international scope. It apparently gives to certain charities on a yearly basis and is interested in funding new and innovatory projects but prior commitments give little leeway for this.

During 1987 £1,000 was donated to Oxfam. This was the only grant with any bearing on the scope of this book. In previous years support has been given to organisations in Northern Ireland. Most donations are in the £200 to £300 range.

Presentation of applications: Applications are considered at a meeting in February each year.

EUROPEAN HUMAN RIGHTS FOUNDATION

95a Chancery Lane, London WC2A 1DT.

Correspondent: Peter Ashman, Honorary Administrator.

Trustees: Theo van Boven, Martin Ennals, Martin Kriele, Keba Mbaye, Peter Nobel, Paul Seighart, Nicole Questiaux.

Annual grants total: £158,000 in 1986.

Policy and practice: The Foundation was established in 1980. It is a registered Dutch charity and not confined to giving grants to organisations which are registered charities. Its objectives are the promotion and protection throughout the world of civil, economic, social and cultural rights, as they are at present laid down in the international instruments, as well as the furtherance of endeavours to realise aims of a humanitarian nature in general. The Foundation makes small grants, seldom exceeding about £3,000, to individuals and/or non-governmental organisations for awards, projects, studies and research in these fields, favouring small projects of an innovative nature.

Recent grants have been made to the following projects on the following themes (the Foundation does not list individual organisations):

Human rights as an issue in education;

A study of rights of the child;

A medical charity which rehabilitates the victims of torture;

An examination of the social facts of sectarian division in Northern Ireland.

Presentation of applications: The Foundation provides application forms. These have to be completed by mid April and mid October prior to the Trustees' meetings in May and November each year.

Information available for applicants: An annual report.

ESMÉE FAIRBAIRN TRUST FUND

5 Storey's Gate, London SW1P 3AT (01-222 7041).

Correspondent: Miss R. Sprigg, Organising Secretary.

Trustees: D. L. T. Oppé (Chairman), A. G. Down, J. S. Fairbairn (Treasurer), Sir John Hackett, C. J. M. Hardie, Mrs P. Hughes-Hallett, Sir William Rees-Mogg, Paul Stobart, Andrew Tuckey.

Annual grants total: £1,837,026 in 1986/87.

Policy and practice: The objects of the Trust are:

Economic enlightenment;

The furtherance of knowledge in finance and investment; and

General charitable purposes.

In 1985 the Trust decided to include scientific and technological education as a prime area of concern within its main field, previously confined to economics and finance.

In pursuing the objectives of the Trust as outlined above, the Trustees seek to identify charities whose activities seem particularly enterprising or meritorious but which may not find it easy to attract widespread support.

The Trust makes donations only to UK registered charities. It does not respond to appeals from individuals. Occasionally and exceptionally it may fund a piece of research to be carried out by a named person; in such cases applications should be made through the head of department of a university or similar institute of higher education.

The most recent Trust accounts for 1986/87 show the following categories and totals of grants within each as follows:

Education – Economics and Business Studies	£300,976	16%
Education – Scientific and Technological	£9,000	0.5%
Other Education	277,100	15%
Arts	232,200	13%
Heritage	234,250	13%

UK Sources

Welfare	262,150	14%
Young People	£93,500	5%
Medical	£37,150	2%
Disablement	£70,000	4%
Environment	£87,500	5%
Research	£189,500	10%
Other	£54,500	3%

During that year grants were made to the following:

Other education

Kings College London, Liddel Hart Centre for Military Archives	£7,500

Welfare

Women Caring Trust	£20,000

Environment

Council for Arms Control	£2,000
Intermediate Technology Development	£10,000

Research

Foundation for Defence Studies	£5,000
Institute for European Defence and Strategic Studies	£2,000
International Institute for Strategic Studies	£10,000
IEA – Centre for Research into Communist Economics	£5,000

Other

British Atlantic Committee	£2,000
Ditchley Foundation	£12,000
English Speaking Union	£1,000
Foundation for Defence Studies	£1,000
Oxford University Strategic Studies Group	£2,500

Presentation of applications: The Trustees hold quarterly meetings to consider relevant applications.

Information available for applicants: A brief policy note.

ALLAN AND NESTA FERGUSON CHARITABLE TRUST

102 Oakfield Road, Selly Oak, Birmingham, B29 7ED (021-472 1922).

Correspondent and trustee: Mrs E. Ferguson.

Annual grants total: some £8–10,000 in 1986/87.

Policy and practice: The Trust has general charitable objects and aims to assist in education, overseas development and world peace. There are no records on file at the Charity Commission since 1977 so it is not possible to indicate what allocations have been made which fall within the scope of this book.

FIRBANK CHARITABLE TRUST

c/o Messrs Ambrose Appelbe, 7 New Square, Lincoln's Inn, London WC2A 3RA.

Correspondent: See above.

Trustees: A. Appelbe, Felix Appelbe, V. Thomas.

Annual grants total: £4,105 in 1985/86.

Policy and practice: The Trust has general charitable objects, its largest grant in 1985/86 was to the National Trust (£750). Its other interests are Quaker, educational and social welfare oriented. Grants in 1985/86 included:

Quaker Peace and Service	£500
Religious Society of Friends	£100
Arts for the Earth	£100
Quaker Peace Studies Trust	£50

FITTON TRUST

Messrs Walker Martineau, 10 & 11 Grays Inn Square, London WC1R 5JL (01-242 1545).

Correspondent: See above.

Trustees: Dr R. P. A. Rivers, D. M. Lumsden, D. V. Brand.

Annual grants total: £46,550 in 1984/85.

Policy and practice: The Trust has general charitable objects and grants are made nationally.

The most recent accounts at the Charity Commission were for 1980/81 which showed grants to: Voluntary Services, Belfast; IVS; Corrymeela Community. It is known that a grant was made to the Belfast Integrated Education Charitable Trust (BELTIE) in 1986.

J. PAUL GETTY JR GENERAL CHARITABLE TRUST

149 Harley Street, London W1N 2DH (01-486 1859).

Correspondent: Sir Arthur Drew, Administrator.

Trustees: J. Paul Getty Jr, Rt Hon James Ramsden, C. H. Gibbs, V. E. Treves.

Annual grants total: £1,200,000 in 1986.

Policy and practice: The Trust was established in 1985 for 'all such legally charitable purposes in the UK or outside the UK as the trustees in their absolute discretion from time to time think fit'.

A letter from the Trust at end December 1987 has stated: 'On the whole, unless there is some personal

Trustee involvement, there have been no grants to international or overseas organisations, including exchange and volunteer programmes.

Grants have been made, however, to the following:

Ranfurly Library	£16,000
Medical Foundation for the Care of Victims of Torture (for 3 years)	£10,000
The Butler Trust (for 3 years)	£5,000
NACRO (for 3 years)	£12,000
Scottish and Northern Refugee Councils (for 3 years)	£3,000
Foundation for Defence Studies	£3,000
Interfaith Trust	£5,000
International Family Service, Birmingham	£3,000
Keston College	£5,000
Liverpool 8 Law Centre	£15,000
Hazlewood Integrated School in Northern Ireland	£25,000
Urban Trust	£25,000
Peterhouse School, Zimbabwe	£13,000

all of which might come within the scope of this book. The School in Zimbabwe was given a grant because of family connections. It would normally not have come within the criteria. In other words, there is concern for good relations within the country and care for those arriving here.'

Presentation of applications: The Trustees meet quarterly when equal amounts of the annual income are allocated. Applications should be in writing. It is worth quoting for a new trust of this scale the whole of its *'Guidelines to Applicants'*.

'Please give as simple, but as full a statement as possible to include the following information. Please note that we can only give to those groups with charitable status.

- The objective of the project – how long has it been going, or planned?
- What is new about it? Or what contribution is it making to the community?
- What precisely would the money be used for, and how do you see yourselves arriving at the objectives?
- To what extent are local people involved, e.g. is there contact with local SS, voluntary groups etc?
- Are you members of SCODA (is drug addiction involved)?
- Who would be responsible for seeing the work was carried out, and for spending the grant?
- What resources are required, e.g. capital, people, services with estimated costs?
- Over what period of time would the grant be requested?
- Who else has been approached for funds and with what result?
- Enclose a copy of the annual accounts.
- Name 2 or 3 persons to whom we could refer to hear more about your project.'

Information available for applicants: Guidelines for applicants.

SIMON GIBSON CHARITABLE TRUST

Hill House, 1 Little New Street, London EC4A 3TR.

Correspondent: B. Marsh.

Trustees: B. Marsh, K. R. Pryor, Mrs A. M. Homfray.

Annual grants total: £124,250 in 1986.

Policy and practice: The Trust has general charitable objects. It gives mainly to national (rather than local) UK registered charities. It supports a wide range of organisations. A review of the Trust's accounts at the Charity Commission showed a small recurring grant of £500 made for the 3 years, 1984/86, to the United Nations Association Trust. This was the only organisation, within the range of interest of this guide, to have received support.

Presentation of applications: Applications should be made in writing; they are reviewed between March and April each year.

A. B. AND M. C. GILLETT CHARITABLE TRUST

41 Beauchamp Road, Bishopston, Bristol BS7 8LQ.

Correspondent: M. B. Gillett, Secretary.

Trustees: J. E. Barlow, R. R. Fruchter, H. J. Gillett, J. B. Gillett, J. Gordon.

Annual grants total: £21,750 in 1986/87.

Policy and practice: The Trust has general charitable objects within the UK and abroad with a commitment to human rights, protection of the environment and concerns of the Society of Friends. The resources of the Trust are apparently absorbed by the charities with which it has an association. In 1986/87 the Trust's donations included the following:

Quaker Peace and Service	£6,000
Woodbrooke College	£1,000
Minority Rights Group	£2,000
Prisoners of Conscience Appeal Fund	£3,000

Presentation of applications: The main Trustees' meeting is in May or June and the majority of applications are considered then. There is no application form but applications are made with the prior agreement of the Trustees. Applications from individuals for study or travel are not normally considered.

GILLETT TRUST

5 Furness Road, Eastbourne, East Sussex BN21 4EX (0232-23609).

Correspondent: Dr F. D. Gillett.

Trustees: Dr F. D. Gillett, J. A. Gillett, R. H. Gillett.

Annual grants total: £1,502 in 1973/74.

Policy and practice: The Trust has general charitable objects but apparently the trustees only make grants to charities which are personally known to them. There are no accounts on file at the Charity Commission since 1973/74. These show the following grants:

Social Responsibility Council of the Society of Friends	£155
The Friend	£100
Ethiopia Disaster Emergency Fund	£100
Society of Friends 1% Fund	£30
Fellowship of Reconciliation	£35
United Nations Association	£50

GIVE PEACE A CHANCE TRUST

20 The Drive, Hertford SG14 3DF (0992-586 943).

Correspondent: Gerald Drewett, Secretary.

Trustees: Alex Bryan, Eleanor Barden, Anne Brewer, John Endersby, Allen Jackson.

Annual grants total: £4,000 in 1987.

Policy and practice: The Trust was founded in 1986 by a group of Quakers who were seeking a legal way to divert taxes from military purposes to peace-building purposes. Its aim is to record the history and current activities of the peace movements, and it produces exhibitions and publications which will form the nucleus for locally-inspired and charitably-based Peace Education Centres. Its ultimate aim is a National Peace Museum, or a series of provincial museums. The Provincial Museum cum Peace Education Centre is seen as an integrated concept. It is an active Trust which seeks funds for projects it identifies from applications received.

Presentation of applications: Applications can be for very small personal grants, e.g. for historical research which results in something tangible; or larger projects which are moderate in terms of their financial need.

GNC TRUST

c/o Messrs Price Waterhouse, Livery House, 169 Edmund Street, Birmingham, West Midlands B3 2JB.

Correspondent: See above.

Trustees: R. N. Cadbury, Miss C. J. Chandler, Mrs J. E. B. Yelloly, G. T. E. Cadbury.

Annual grants total: £39,800 in 1984.

Policy and practice: The Trust has general charitable objects, a national scope and a particular interest in the Midlands, Avon, Cornwall and Hampshire. A review of the most recent accounts on file at the Charity Commission (when a total of £11,250 was disbursed) showed the following grants with relevance to the scope of this book.

Quaker Peace and Service	£1,500
Woodbrooke College	£3,500

GODINTON CHARITABLE TRUST

Godinton Park, Ashford, Kent TN23 3BW (0233-20773).

Correspondent: A. W. Green.

Trustees: R. J. Eddis, Moran Caplat, M. F. Jennings.

Annual grants total: £113,450 in 1986.

Policy and practice: The Trust has general charitable objects and a national range. A review of the most recent accounts for 1986 on file at the Charity Commission showed the following allocations with some relevance to the scope of this book:

VOS	£250
Project Trust	£250
Army Benevolent Fund	£500
Russian Immigrant Aid Fund	£250

Donations ranged between £50 and £3,000 with the majority being within £250 and £500.

UK Sources

T. W. GREEVES TRUST

8 Middle Park Close, Selly Oak, Birmingham B29 4BT (021-475 3582).

Correspondent: T. W. Greeves.

Trustees: T. W. Greeves, Mrs I. H. Greeves, E. M. Wood.

Annual grants total: £2,321 in 1985.

Policy and practice: The Trust has general charitable objects but gives particularly to the Society of Friends. Recent grants made by the Trust include:

Oxfam	£250
UNICEF	£250
Ulster Quaker Service	£250
Society of Friends	£900
Woodbrooke College	£100

Most grants were between £20 and £250.

Applications are not solicited and do not usually receive a reply.

GSC TRUST, GWEN CATCHPOOL CHARITY

c/o Ambrose Appelbe, Solicitors, 7 New Square, Lincoln's Inn, London WC2A 3RA (01-242 7000).

Correspondent: Ambrose Appelbe.

Trustees: Ambrose Appelbe, J. Greaves, A. Wallis, O. Wallis.

Annual grants total: £2,975 in 1985/86.

Policy and practice: A review of the Trust's accounts at the Charity Commission showed the following grants with relevance to the scope of this book:

Woodbrooke College	£1,050
Religious Society of Friends	£300
International Voluntary Service	£250
Nippansan Myohoji (Peace Mission)	£150
Oxfam	£150
Voluntary Service Overseas	£150
Medical Foundation for the Care of Victims of Torture	£100
War on Want	£100
UNA Trust	£50

WALTER GUINNESS CHARITABLE TRUST

Biddesden House, Andover, Hampshire (0264-790 237).

Correspondent: Lord Moyne.

Trustees: Lord and Lady Moyne, F. B. Guinness, M. C. Butterworth.

Annual grants total: £25,807 for 1985/86.

Policy and practice: The Trust has general charitable objects and a national and international grant-giving range. A review of the Trust's accounts for 1985/86 lodged at the Charity Commission showed the following grants with some relevance to the scope of this book:

Amnesty International	£20
British Irish Association	£600
British Mexican Society Earthquake Relief Fund	£100
Christian Aid	£100

Lord Moyne has written the following caution for new applicants – 'The Trustees are not able to give individual students grants. They have a long list of causes which they support and are actively seeking to reduce this by concentrating on long-standing commitments. They are not able to reply to appeals to which they are not able to respond'.

HARBOUR FOUNDATION LTD

8–10 Half Moon Court, Bartholomew Close, London EC1A 7HE.

Correspondent: S. A. Simmonds.

Trustees: Council of Management.

Annual grants total: £24,810 in 1982.

Policy and practice: The Foundation's objects are:

The relief of poverty, suffering and distress amongst refugees, homeless and displaced persons throughout the world;

The advancement of education, learning and research of persons and students of all ages and nationalities throughout the world and to disseminate the results of this research;

General charitable purposes.

The Trust which can make grants both nationally and internationally is apparently not in a position to make new commitments because of those already made. The most recent records at the Charity Commission were for 1982 and presented no examples of grant-aid. The Foundation has not replied to correspondence.

UK Sources

VIRGINIA WORSFOLD HARINGTON CHARITABLE TRUST

Sladen Green, Binley, Andover, Hampshire.

Correspondent: Mrs V. W. Harington.

Trustees: V. W. Harington, R. J. V. Harington, G. C. Sagar.

Annual grants total: £14,144 in 1986/87.

Policy and practice: The Trust has general charitable objects and a national scope. A review of its accounts on file at the Charity Commission has shown the following grants in 1986/87 with some relevance to the scope of this book.

Christian Aid	£2,000
Intermediate Technology	£1,500
War on Want	£2,000
Save the Children	£500
Oxfam	£1,500
Corrymeela Community Link	£1,000

1983/84
Defence Research Trust (Foundation for Alternatives)	£500

1979/80
Amnesty International	£500

L. G. HARRIS AND CO LTD CHARITABLE TRUST

Stoke Prior, Bromsgrove, Hereford and Worcester B60 4AE (0527-31441).

Correspondent: The Secretary.

Trustees: L. G. Harris, B. Middleton.

Annual grants total: £2,825 in 1986/87.

Policy and practice: The Trust has general charitable objects and grants are made both nationally and locally.

Apparently no unsolicited approaches can be considered. Thirty two grants ranging between £20 and £500 were made in 1986/87.

Recent grants with some relevance to the scope of this book have included:

In 1986/87
Society of Friends	£500
Society of Friends, Sudan Relief Fund	£250

In 1983/84
National Peace Council	£100

In 1982/83
Parliamentary Group for World Government	£50

HEDLEY FOUNDATION LTD

c/o Messrs MacFarlanes, 10 Norwich Street, London EC4A 1BD (01-236 7411).

Correspondent: See above.

Trustees: The Directors.

Annual grants total: £530,000 in 1986/87.

Policy and practice: The Foundation's beneficial area is national and overseas. It has a particular interest in the disabled and underprivileged.

The most recent Foundation accounts at the Charity Commission were for 1985/86 and showed the following grants with some relevance to the scope of this book:

Fleet Air Arm Museum	£1,000
Imperial War Museum	£1,000
Minority Rights Group	£500
Northern Ireland Voluntary Trust	£1,000
Oxfam	£2,500

Presentation of applications: At any time with latest audited accounts and Charity Commission Registration Number.

HICKINBOTHAM CHARITABLE TRUST

69 Main Street, Bushby, Leicester LE7 9PL (0533-431 152).

Correspondent: Mrs C. R. Hickinbotham.

Trustees: Mrs C. R. Hickinbotham, P. F. J. Hickinbotham, R. P. Hickinbotham.

Annual grants total: £18,976 in 1985.

Policy and practice: The Trust has general charitable objects but particularly supports local charities in Leicestershire and Quaker charities generally. The most recent accounts at the Charity Commission were for 1977 and included:

International Voluntary Service	£1,000
Society of Friends, Leicestershire	£120
Society of Friends	£130
Oxfam	£100
Voluntary Service Overseas	£75

out of a total grant allocation of £17,790.

Presentation of applications: In writing.

Further information for applicants: No grants are made to individuals and replies are not sent to unsuccessful applicants.

WALTER HIGGS CHARITABLE TRUST

12 Heaton Drive, Edgbaston, Birmingham B15 3LW (021-454 0322).

Correspondent: D. C. Y. Higgs.

Trustees: D. C. Y. Higgs, Mrs A. J. Higgs, Lady E. P. Higgs.

Annual grants total: £20,000 in 1986/87.

Policy and practice: The Trust can give for general charitable purposes nationally, but mainly supports charities in the Midlands and West Midlands. The accounts for 1985/86 show a total of 15 grants (most of which (12) were between £8 and £420). Larger grants were given to:

The Arkleton Trust	£15,000
UNA Trust	£1,000

The Trustees stress that their income is committed in advance and they have little leeway to consider new applicants.

HILDEN CHARITABLE FUND

Gort Lodge, Sudbrook Lane, Richmond, Surrey TW10 7AY (01-948 2720).

Correspondent: A. Rampton, Trustee.

Trustees: G. J. S. Rampton, I. Caplan, J. R. A. Rampton, D. S. Rampton, C. H. Rodeck, E. K. Rodeck, D. Chesworth, B. M. H. Rampton, A. Rampton, H. M. C. Rampton.

Annual grants total: £263,000 in 1986/87.

Policy and practice: The Fund has general charitable objects. One third of the income is reserved for work in the Third World and it also has a particular interest in minorities, however defined, in the UK. It no longer gives to well established causes. The '*Guide to Major Grant-Making Trusts, 1986*' says: 'The Fund currently believes that its modest resources should be applied to areas where little or no help is likely to be available from elsewhere'. At present the Fund is confining its funding to its existing commitments to some 30–50 organisations and states that new applications cannot be entertained.

A review of the Fund's accounts lodged at the Charity Commission has shown that the following grants with some relevance to the scope of this book have been made in recent years:

Northern Ireland Voluntary Trust (annually)	£15,000
Britain/Tanzania Society (annually)	£4,000
Intermediate Technology Development Group (annually)	£10,000
Tools for Self Reliance (annually)	£5,000
Save the Children for perinatal work in uplands of Peru (last two years)	£40,000
Minority Rights Group (annually)	£3,000

HILLCOTE TRUST

29 Galton Road, Westcliffe-on-Sea, Essex SS0 8TE (0702-45860).

Correspondent: J. S. Coe, Trustee.

Trustees: J. S. Coe, Mrs D. J. Coe, G. S. Hemingway.

Annual grants total: £2,180 in 1986/87.

Policy and practice: The Trust has general charitable objects and its deed states clearly that it gives not only to registered charities but also to 'such other charitable purposes as recognised as such by law'. It gives small grants to organisations concerned with peace, reconciliation, conservation and social and therapeutic aid.

In 1986/87 the following grants with relevance to the scope of this book were made.

Armament and Disarmament Information Unit	£100
Belfast Charitable Trust for Integrated Education	£500
Canon Collins Education Trust	£500
Lagan College	£500
Peace Education Project	£100

Presentation of applications: Applications are considered in January, each year.

LADY HIND TRUST

Wells and Hind, Solicitors, 14–16 Fletcher Gate, Nottingham NG1 2FX (0602-506 201).

Correspondent: Wells and Hind, Solicitors.

Trustees: W. D. Crane, J. A. L. Barratt, C. W. L. Barratt, W. F. Whysall.

Annual grants total: £134,584 in 1985.

Policy and practice: The Trust has general charitable purposes. Its accounts lodged at the Charity Commission have not listed individual grants since 1982. The accounts for 1981 showed the following grants with some relevance to the scope of this book:

Far East Prisoners of War and Internees Fund	£1,000

UK Sources

International Voluntary Service, Derby Branch	£500
Roosevelt Memorial Travelling Scholarship	£1,000

Presentation of applications: Applications are considered quarterly. They must be accompanied by audited accounts dated within 12 months of the application being made. There is no application form.

P. H. HOLT CHARITABLE TRUST

c/o Ocean Transport and Trading plc, India Buildings, Liverpool, Merseyside L2 0RB (051-236 9292).

Correspondent: P. E. V. Hughes, The Secretary.

Trustees: Not disclosed.

Annual grants total: £227,233 in 1986/87.

Policy and practice: Grants are made for charitable purposes in Great Britain, particularly in the Merseyside area also where 'original work or work of special excellence is being undertaken'.

The Trust made grants under the following headings in 1986/87:

Community	£92,192
Education	£29,956
Visual arts, music, theatre	£32,731
Health	£37,414
Marine	£34,940

The following grants with some likely relevance to the scope of this book were then made:

Recipients of 'Community' grants included:

International Voluntary Service, NW	£200
International Voluntary Service, Tuesday Club	£250
Voluntary Service Overseas – Liverpool	£300
Voluntary Service Overseas	£500

Recipients of 'Education' grants included:

British Atlantic Committee	£200
British Association for the Advancement of Science	£250
Overseas Development Institute	£200
Royal Institute of International Affairs	£495
Runnymede Trust	£400

Over 300 grants are made, many of them between £100 and £500.

Presentation of applications: Applications may be sent at any time.

INCHCAPE CHARITABLE TRUST FUND

40 St Mary Axe, London EC3A 8EU (01-283 4680).

Correspondent: The Secretaries.

Trustees: The Earl of Inchcape; Sir David Orr, S. Rabin, G. H. Turnbull, C. R. Armstrong, R. C. Williams.

Annual grants total: £109,000 in 1986.

Policy and practice: The Trust has general charitable objects and particularly supports the work of national and international charities especially those in the Commonwealth. Over 200 grants a year are made, with the largest amount by value going to benevolent organisations with military connections, to medical research and to educational and youth charities. The most recent accounts, lodged with the Charity Commission were for 1984/85 and showed that the following grants with some relevance to the scope of this book were then made:

Commonwealth Youth Exchange Council	£500
English Speaking Union	£100
European Atlantic Group	£100
Mountbatten Memorial Trust	£2,500
Northern Ireland Voluntary Trust	£250
Overseas Student Trust	£3,000
Oxfam	£100
Royal Commonwealth Society	£2,500
United Kingdom Council for Overseas Student Affairs	£100
United World College	£3,500
Voluntary Service Overseas	£250

Presentation of applications: Applications which are reviewed quarterly should be accompanied by the current annual report and accounts.

INTER-CHURCH EMERGENCY FUND FOR IRELAND

Inter-Church Centre, 48 Elmwood Avenue, Belfast BT9 6AZ (0232-663 145).

Correspondent: Dr R. D. Stevens, Secretary. (Dr Stevens also administers the Irish Ecumenical Church Loan Fund Committee.)

Fund Committee: The Fund Committee of 12 members is jointly appointed by the Roman Catholic Church and the Irish Council of Churches. Its two Co-Chairmen are F. Jeffrey and the Very Rev Canon P. J. Early.

Annual grants total: STG £23,300 in 1987.

Policy and practice: The Fund supports relief and reconciliation work and ecumenical youth and community work. It administers gifts given by the Conference of European Churches Emergency Fund for Ireland and the European Catholic Bishops' Fund for Ireland, as well as contributions from other churches and individuals. All applications for grants are carefully investigated by the Secretary. Grants are not made for running costs, CABx, pre school playgroups, mixed holidays outside Ireland, or uniformed youth organisations.

Grants made in 1987 included:

Ballyduff Playscheme	£250
Holiday Projects West	£2,000
Community Relations in Schools	£1,000
Northern Ireland Peace Forum	£50
Northern Ireland Children's Holiday Scheme	£1,500
Glencree Centre for Reconciliation	£2,000

The highest grants were £2,500.

Presentation of applications: There is an application form. The Fund Committee meets three times, usually in June, October and February/March.

Information available for applicants: Guidance for applicants.

INVICTA TRUST

c/o Messrs E. A. Purcell and Co, 4 Quex Road, London NW6.

Correspondent: E. H. Feingold.

Trustees: A. Hirsch, E. H. Feingold, M. Gelley.

Annual grants total: Not known.

Policy and practice: The Trust was set up in 1986 with the following objects:

To advance education in and the religion of the Orthodox Jewish Faith;

The relief of poverty;

Such other purposes as are recognised by English law as charitable.

It is understood that the Trust has been supportive to Play for Life.

IRISH ECUMENICAL CHURCH LOAN FUND COMMITTEE

Interchurch Centre, 48 Elmwood Avenue, Belfast BT9 6AZ (0232-663 145).

Correspondent: Dr R. D. Stevens, Secretary.

Fund committee: H. R. Roberts (Chairman), Rev Canon R. Richey, Rev Canon W. J. Arlow, R. W. Jess, R. C. Lewis-Crosby, J. Smyth, T. A. Peoples, Rt Hon D. W. Bleakley, Miss H. McMillen, Dr R. D. Stevens.

Current capital: £110,000 in 1987.

Policy and practice: The Fund has been set up to promote the spiritual, physical, moral and social welfare of all the people of Ireland by making low interest loans to Christian communions and other bodies e.g. community and reconciliation organisations and co-operatives.

Loans of up to £10,000 are made, with an interest rate of not less than 3% (normally 5%). They are repayable within a ten year period. Some form of security is required and not more than 60% of total costs of a project are covered. Loans made in 1987 included:

Christian Renewal Centre, Rostrevor (for 3 years)	£10,000
Saltshaker Centre, Antrim Road, North Belfast (for 5 years)	£5,000

and loans were made in earlier years to Belfast Charitable Trust for Integrated Eduacation (BELTIE), Harmony Community Trust, Northern Ireland Children's Holiday Scheme, Cornerstone Community.

Presentation of applications: There is an application form. The Fund Committee meets twice a year in early September and early March.

Information for applicants: Background information sheet.

J. G. JOFFE CHARITABLE TRUST

Allied Dunbar Centre, Station Road, Swindon, Wiltshire SN1 1EL (0793-28291).

Correspondent: J. Joffe.

Trustees: V. L. Joffe, D. J. Palmer.

Annual grants total: £294,714 in 1986/87.

Policy and practice: The Trust has general charitable objects. Funds are apparently fully committed to charities of special interest to the Trustees.

There is a strong policy in favour of projects in or working on behalf of Third World development. A review of the Trust's accounts lodged at the Charity Commission has shown the following grants with some relevance to the scope of this book.

In 1986/87

Mminority Rights Group	£6,000

UK Sources

Anti-Slavery Society	£25,000
Foundation for Alternatives	£5,000
Protestant and Catholic Encounter	£2,500

In 1983/84

The Soweto Black Women's Charitable Trust	£17,500
Educational Trust for Southern Africa	£5,000

Information available for applicants: The Trustees have written 'There is normally no purpose in submitting applications for grants as the Trust's funds are fully committed for some years ahead. Regrettably applications cannot be acknowledged'.

JOICEY TRUST

Messrs Dickinson Dees, Cross House, Westgate Road, Newcastle-upon-Tyne, NE99 1SB (091-261 1911).

Correspondent: N. A. Furness, Appeals Secretary.

Trustees: Lord Joicey, Lady Joicey, Hon J. M. Joicey, R. H. Dickinson.

Annual grants total: £73,825 in 1986/87.

Policy and practice: The Trust has general charitable objects, and makes grants to charities in the North-East particularly North of the River Tyne. Other grants are exceptional. A review of the Trust's accounts for 1986/87 lodged at the Charity Commission showed the following allocations with some relevance to the scope of this book:

Atlantic College	£300
International Voluntary Service	£250

Presentation of applications: Applications need to be submitted by early June and mid November, for meetings in early July and mid January.

KLEINWORT BENSON CHARITABLE TRUST

10 Fenchurch Street, London EC3M 3LB (01-623 8000).

Correspondent: Philip Prain.

Trustees: Kleinwort Benson Trustees Limited, Philip Prain.

Annual grants total: £190,000 in 1986.

Policy and practice: The Trust has general charitable objects and responds only to national applications. A review of the Trust's accounts at the Charity Commission showed that in recent years its grant-making has included the following examples which have relevance to the scope of this book:

In 1986

Airey Neave Refugee Trust	£100
British Executive Service Overseas	£500
Centre for World Development Education	£250
Ditchley Foundation	£500
ESU	£500
Fleet Air Arm Museum	£250
Intermediate Technology	£500
Overseas Development Institute	£250
Royal Air Forces Association	£350
Royal Institute of International Affairs	£1,410
Voluntary Service Overseas	£500

In 1985

United World Colleges (International) Ltd	£1,500
Imperial War Museum Redevelopment Appeal	£500
Books for Development	250

In 1984

Justice Educational Research Trust	£500
Miriam Dean Refugee Trust Fund	£150

Presentation of applications: In writing.

SIR CYRIL KLEINWORT CHARITABLE SETTLEMENT

The Lawn, Speen, Newbury, Berkshire RG13 1QN (0635-43151).

Correspondent: Mrs A. J. Claridge, Trust Officer.

Trustees: Kleinwort Benson Trustees Ltd, D. A. Acland, D. A. Peake, A. C. Heber Percy.

Annual grants total: £649,150 in 1986/87.

Policy and practice: The Trustees are particularly interested in the fields of education, job-creation, conservation, arts, medical research and care, population control and youth development. Specific recipients of grants have not been listed in the accounts lodged with the Charity Commission since 1984/85. These accounts showed the following grants with some relevance to the scope of this book.

Population Concern	£10,000
Ross McWhirter Foundation	£1,000
Trust for Education in International Living	£8,600

In 1982/83

Ditchley Foundation	£5,000
South Atlantic Fund	£15,000

Presentation of applications: Applications should be in writing. The Trustees meet twice a year in May and November.

ERNEST KLEINWORT CHARITABLE TRUST

10 Fenchurch Street, London EC3M 3LB (01-623 8000).

Correspondent: The Secretary.

Trustees: Kleinworth Benson Trustees Ltd, Mrs J. N. Kleinwort, Sir Kenneth Kleinwort, Lady Kleinwort, The Earl of Limerick, F. A. James.

Annual grants total: £977,826 in 1986/87.

Policy and practice: The Trust's objects are for 'general charitable purposes in restricted fields'. It makes grants on a national basis and on a worldwide basis for conservation and planned parenthood. It makes the following types of grant:

Donations towards specific projects;

Annual subscriptions (mostly confined to Sussex);

Temporary loans for short periods to launch specific projects.

In 1986/88 a grant was made to the International Institute for Environment and Development (£30,000). A review of the Trust's accounts lodged at the Charity Commission did not show any further grants with any likely relevance to the scope of this book.

Presentation of applications: Applications should be made in writing. Decisions on grants are made usually within a month of the application being received.

Information available for applicants: Policy Statement, 1987.

LANKELLY FOUNDATION

34 North End Road, London W14 0SH (01-603 1525).

Correspondent: Calton Younger, Secretary.

Trustees: L. H. A. Smith, A. Ramsay Hack, C. Heather, W. J. Mackenzie.

Annual grants total: £257,550 in 1987.

Policy and practice: The Foundation has general charitable objects. *A Guide to the Major Grant-Making Trusts* 1986 states 'The Lankelly Foundation was established in 1968 and the Hambland Foundation, by the same anonymous Settlor in 1977. The two Foundations have the same Trustees, one of whom is also a Trustee of The Chase Charity. Although there are links, the Chase Charity is independent of these two Foundations. Applications cannot be transferred between the Charity and the Foundations, but in some cases applicants to one may be advised that their case better suits the other and be invited to submit a fresh application. In general, the Trustees make grants of up to £10,000, but from time to time on their own initiative and anonymously, they fund a project on the grand scale.'

The most recent accounts lodged at the Charity Commission were for 1986/87 and showed the following grants which have relevance to the scope of this book:

Upper Donegal Road, Social and Recreational Committee	£3,000
Northern Ireland Voluntary Trust	£10,000
St Columba's Church, Whiterock, Belfast	£4,000
Northern Ireland Association of Youth Clubs	£5,000
Derry Film and Video	£5,000
Voluntary Service Belfast	£7,500

Grants in 1987/88 included:

North Coast Charitable Trust for Integrated Education	£20,000
Belfast Charitable Trust for Integrated Education (BELTIE)	£15,000
Holiday Projects West, Londonderry	£5,000
Northern Ireland Council for Voluntary Action	£10,000

Presentation of applications: There are no application forms. Applications should be concise but applicants should not be inhibited. Trustees do not normally see applications but receive papers prepared in the office from correspondence, literature, interviews and visits. The Trustees meet quarterly but plan their programme well ahead.

LANSBURY HOUSE TRUST FUND

6 Endsleigh Street, London WC1H 0DX.

Correspondent: Margaret Melicharova

Trustees: Trevor Davies (Acting Chairman), Godric Bader, April Carter, Alec Davison, Harry Mister, Tony Smythe.

Consultants: Adam Curle, Michael Randle, Margaret Melicharova, Anthony Weaver.

Policy and practice: The Trust supports educational research for the peaceful resolution of conflict. It has no capital fund and provides support in three ways:

It initiates a project and appoints a co-ordinator who is responsible for raising funds from other sources e.g.

UK Sources

the Alternative Defence Commission and its co-ordinator, Michael Randle.

If approached by an existing body with a project which matches the Fund's educational brief it will channel money raised for that project through the Fund e.g. in 1987 the Peace Education Project of the Peace Pledge Union, the Student Peace Project, the Chemical and Biological Weapons Working Party (*see separate entries*).

Where some funds have accrued from investment and commissions small grants of between £50 and £100 are made for educational work.

THE LEIGH TRUST

Marks, Green & Company, 44a New Cavendish Street, London W1M 7LG (01-486 4663).

Correspondent: C. M. Marks.

Trustees: David Bernstein, Lord Bernstein, Dr R. M. E. Stone, H. B. Levin, J. Warton.

Annual grants total: £179,195 in 1985/86.

Policy and practice: The Trust has general charitable objects and makes its support available both nationally and overseas, with the proviso that grants are made only to registered charities. The most recent accounts at the Charity Commission were for 1985/86 and showed an emphasis on social welfare, medicine and health. The following grants were made which have some relevance to the scope of this book:

Fourth World Educational and Research Trust (re Institute for Social Inventions)	£1,500
London School of Economics	£16,000
Prisoners of Conscience Appeal Fund	£500
National Society for the Welfare of Prisoners Abroad	£500

Presentation of applications: '*A Guide to Major Grant-Making Trusts*', 1986 states 'Initial applications should state clearly the use to be made of any donation. Applicants will be expected to provide a detailed budget, and to give details of other donations or grants received for the same purpose. It is likely that one or more Trustees or officers of the Leigh Trust will wish to visit any premises or projects of the applicants. It would be of help to the Trustees if applications could be accompanied by letters of support from individuals or organisations wholly independent of the applicants.

Further information may be obtained from the Secretary at the above address'.

THE LEVERHULME TRUST

15–19 New Fetter Lane, London EC4A 1NR (01-822 6938).

Correspondent: Sir Rex Richards, Director.

Trustees: Sir David Orr, (Chairman), Viscount Leverhulme, Sir Kenneth Durham, C. F. Sedcole, M .R. Angus.

Annual grants total: £5.2 million in 1986.

Policy and practice: The Trust is restricted to purposes of research and education. Within the fields of research and education a grant must be for research and teaching fellowships, studentships and the like. The Trustees are precluded from making capital grants for endowments, sites or buildings, or from giving grants for equipment. They cannot make block grants or grants for such purposes as administration and running costs or to meet deficits. They cannot contribute to appeals.

The terms of the Trust, on the other hand, impose no restrictions as to the fields of study for which grants may be made and set no geographical limits to eligibility. These are matters within the discretion of the Trustees.

Grants made by the Trustees are currently classified under four heads:
  Grants to institutions for research;
  Grants to institutions for academic interchange;
  Grants to institutions for education;
  Grants to individuals under schemes administered by the Research Awards Advisory Committee.

Grants to institutions for research were made under the following headings in 1986: Business Studies, Industrial Relations and Economics; Government, Law and International Relations: Social Policy and Welfare; Medicine and Health; Education; Basic and Applied Sciences; Combined Studies; Humanities; Fine Arts; Libraries, Archives and Museums.

The following are examples identified as being of relevance to this book within the past 3 years.

In 1986

University of Manchester, Defence Research and Development and British Industrial Performance (over 1 year)	£15,000
University of Birmingham, Impact of de-Stalinisation on Soviet industrial relations, 1953–64 (over 3 years)	£54,200

In 1985

Royal Institute of International Affairs. Research fellowship for research on collective management of international issues in Latin America (over 2 years)	£38,800

Foundation for Alternatives.
Research assistance for research on conventional defence of Europe (over 2½ years) £24,900

University of Glasgow.
Research assistance for research on East European attitudes to West Europe and their policy implications (over 3 years) £34,450

University of London, London School of Economics and Political Science.
Research fellowship and assistance for research on Soviet-Third World economic relations since 1950 (over 2 years) £70,950

In 1984

All Souls College, Oxford.
Research fellowship for research on the external policy of the United States, 1945–1980 (over 3 years) £71,000

International Institute for Strategic Studies.
Research fellowship and assistance for research on regional crisis and the central balance (over 3 years) £132,900

Oxfam.
Research fellowship for research on development and indigenous peoples (over 1 year) £10,500

The September 1987 newspaper announcement of the awards to individuals under schemes administered by the Research Awards Advisory Committee showed that one grant was made which falls within the parameters of this book – to C. R. Mitchell, Professor of International Relations, City University 'Conciliatory gestures in international politics'.

In all 30 fellowships, 44 grants, 29 Emeritus fellowships and 14 Study Abroad studentships were announced. Research fellowships and grants may vary in size but do not usually exceed £6,800. Emeritus fellowships do not exceed £4,625 a year. Study Abroad studentships, for people under 30, are £6,300 a year.

Policy and practice: Grants to institutions are decided at the Trustees' meetings which take place four times a year, in February, April, July and November. In order to be considered at these meetings, applications should be in the hands of the Director at the latest by 15th November, 15th April, 1st May and 1st September preferably well before.

Awards to individuals are made by the Research Awards Advisory Committee once a year in Spring. Application forms are available from the previous 1st September from the Secretary.

Information available for applicants: A booklet on policies and application procedures is available. Annual details of grants of more than £10,000 are published. A Quinquennial report is also published.

LLOYD'S CHARITIES TRUST

Lloyd's, Lime Street, London EC3M 7HA (01-623 7100).

Correspondent: M. J. Crick, Secretary.

Trustees: The Council of Lloyds.

Annual grants total: £488,989 in 1985.

Policy and practice: The Trust has general charitable objects and gives to national and international registered charities and not to local causes or local branches of national charities. (The smaller Lloyds Patriotic Fund which is supported by the Trust in addition to having its own income makes grants to ex-servicemen in need (excluding RAF). Total grants in 1983 amounted to £26,000.)

The most recent accounts lodged at the Charity Commission were for 1985 and showed that the Trust's grant making included the following examples with some relevance to the scope of this book:

Commonwealth Youth Exchange Council	£500
English Speaking Union	£1,000
European Cultural Foundation	£250
International Voluntary Service	£750
International Voluntary Service, Northern Ireland	£250
Co-ordinating Committee, Oxfam	£4,000
Save the Children	£6,000
UNICEF	£2,500
Voluntary Services Overseas	£1,250

THE LYNDHURST SETTLEMENT

Bowker Orford & Co, Chartered Accountants, 15–19 Cavendish Place, London W1M 0DD (01-636 6391).

Correspondent: See above.

Trustees: M. Isaacs, A. P. Skyrme, P. D.Schofield.

Annual grants total: £96,000 in 1987.

Policy and practice: the Settlement's objects are as follows: 'To encourage research into social problems with special emphasis on safeguarding civil liberties and extending the rights of minorities.'

Protection of the environment is also seen as an important civil liberty. Preference is given to smaller charities with low administration costs and grants are only made to registered charities.

The Settlement's allocations in 1987 included the following grants of relevance to the scope of this book:

Minority Rights Group	£1,000
Survival International	£1,500
The Civil Liberties Trust	14,500
National Council for the Welfare of Prisoners Abroad	£4,000
Friends of the Earth Trust	£3,000
Medical Council for the Care of the Victims of Torture	£2,000
Prisoners of Conscience Appeal Fund	£2,000

Presentation of applications: A brief description of aims and objectives is needed in the first approach.

M B CHARITIES LTD

Metal Box plc, Queen's House, Forbury Road, Reading RG1 3JH (0734-581 177).

Correspondent: Miss P. Axtell, Secretary, Subscriptions and Donations Committee.

Trustees: G. J. Armstrong (Chairman), E. Cameron, F. Lyttle, G. C. Zanbuni.

Annual grants total: £168,717 in 1985.

Policy and practice: The Trust supports national charities for general charitable purposes. The most recent accounts filed at the Charity Commission were for 1982 and showed the following grants which have relevance to the scope of this book:

European Educational Research Trust	£1,000
Quaker Peace and Service	£1,000

Presentation of applications: The Council of Management meets quarterly.

MANOR CHARITABLE TRUST

36 Old Jewry, London EC2R 8BS (01-382 6000).

Correspondent: The Secretary.

Trustees: Sir Andrew H. Carnwath, M. J. Verey, Sir Ashley Ponsonby, Sir John Baring, P. Baring, A. D. Loehnis.

Annual grants total: £360,080 in 1985/86.

Policy and practice: The Trust has general charitable objects and a national scope. It is believed that the income is largely committed to specific educational projects. Otherwise the Trustees prefer those charities which are known to them.

The most recent accounts on file at the Charity Commission were for 1982/83 when the following grants with some relevance to the scope of this book were made:

Ditchley Foundation	£25,000
Voluntary Service Overseas	£7,500

Presentation of applications: In writing but applicants cannot expect any acknowledgement unless they are successful.

MARSDEN CHARITABLE TRUST

34 Brae Road, Winscombe, Avon BS25 1LJ (093484-2300).

Correspondent: A. H. Marsden.

Trustees: A. H. Marsden, D. J. Ironside.

Annual grants total: £53,585 in 1983.

Policy and practice: The Trust has general charitable objects and gives both within the UK and overseas.

The most recent accounts on file at the Charity Commission were for 1983, and showed that grants then ranged between £500 and £4,250 and included the following with some relevance to the scope of this book:

Afghanistan Support Committee	£500
British Refugee Council	£500
Christian Aid	£500
Earth Resources Research	£1,000
Oxfam	£2,000
Society of Friends	£4,250
Woodbrooke College	£500

Presentation of applications: Grants are made in April and October. The Trustees do not correspond with applicants or deal with Trust matters on the telephone. The charity registration number must always be given.

Further information available for applicants: The Trustees have written that they are embarking on support of a major project outside the area of interest of this book. It will absorb a great deal of the Trust's resources so that the pattern of other giving will be greatly restricted for the next few years and the amounts spent in the area of interest of this book will be small and arise from existing contacts.

MERCERS' CHARITABLE FOUNDATION

Mercers' Hall, Ironmonger Lane, London EC2V 8ME (01-726 4991).

Correspondent: G. M. Wakeford.

Trustees: The Mercers' Company.

Annual grants total: £1.4 million in 1986.

Policy and practice: The Foundation has general charitable objects and a national scope. There are no accounts on file at the Charity Commission since the Trust deed of 1983, so it is not possible to gauge its policies from its schedule of donations or its likely interest in the field of activity covered by this book. The Mercers' Charitable Fund has amalgamated with the Foundation. The Fund made a grant of £5,000 to the South Atlantic Fund in 1982. It is understood that the British Council of Churches Human Rights Advisory Group received support in 1986.

MAYPOLE FUND

Box 25, 136 Kingsland High Street, London E8 2NS.

Correspondent: The Maypole Fund Committee.

Annual grants total: around £4,000 in 1988.

Grant Range: up to £500.

Policy and practice: The Maypole Fund was set up in 1986 by a group of women active in the peace movement. It gives grants to women and women's groups with imaginative ideas and projects designed to further world peace with justice, nuclear disarmament, anti-militarism, and international links between women or these purposes.

In 1987, 23 awards were made. Maypole has written to say that 'Eleven of the awards went to women in Peace Groups or to Women's Peace Groups and some of the applications involved supporting publication of leaflets or reports, production of a songbook, a video and help with mounting two exhibitions. Two awards helped with the costs of conferences. Three helped to pay for the travel of women from or to other countries in connection with peace events. We paid the tax or insurance on two vehicles to be used for peace activities; helped buy some shrubs and trees for a peace grove; provided a creche; a telephone helpline; payment of fines; purchased a word processor.

Three individual women received grants; a young women's group; and an older woman. We decided to give help to two groups concerned with male violence.'

Presentation of applications: Twice a year in mid-March and mid-September.

MERCURY PROVIDENT plc

Orlingbury House, Lewes Road, Forest Row, East Sussex RH18 5AA (034282-3739).

Directors: W. Ashe, P. Castle Stewart, D. Donahaye, E. Gerwin, P. Mackay, C. Nunhofer, M. van Boeschoten.

Company Secretary: C. Nunhofer.

Status: Mercury started in 1974 as a Provident Society and converted to a plc in 1986 to be able to offer shares to the public. It takes its philosophical base from Rudolf Steiner, founder of anthroposophy.

Deposits: over £1.95 million.

Policy and practice: Mercury Provident is a deposit-taking institution which helps finance socially beneficial enterprises; these may be products or services, or projects which are socially creative in their working structures. A central aim is the promotion of fuller consciousness in money matters.

Mercury depositors are asked to make several choices that are normally made for them by conventional banks. Depositors are asked to choose what interest rate they need (not want); they are asked to choose the projects in which their money is to be used; they are asked to choose the term and notice of their deposit. And in all of this they are asked to consider the effect of their choices on the projects they wish to encourage. The rate at which money is lent is chosen by depositors plus a small percentage to cover operational costs. Low-interest deposits can be passed on as low-interest loans. Depositors' money must be secure when lent, but some projects do not have conventional property security to back a loan. In such cases Mercury is innovative in arranging human support-group security in various forms.

In its first ten years Mercury has helped to finance over a hundred enterprises. These were all small-scale. Mercury has lent to organic growing, curative and medical work, housing associations, employment initiatives, education, publishing, toy and instrument making, and wholefood shops. It encourages projects to develop socially creative organisational structures: co-operatives, charities, and other schemes in which ownership, control and rewards are as widely distributed as possible.

Over six hundred people have deposited with Mercury since 1974. The list of projects receiving loans as at December 1987 includes Exchange Resources (*see separate entry*).

Two types of Mercury shares are on offer to enlarge Mercury's capital base;

> Shares without dividends or interest, akin to a gift to Mercury's work, unredeemable, but able to be sold to a

UK Sources

third party. Owners have a vote at company General Meetings.

Ordinary shares with no voting rights but with the probability of dividends. Buyers select the rate of return they need from those offered: three, five or seven percent.

Further information available: A shares prospectus; newsletter for depositors and shareholders; list of projects, December 1987.

VICTOR MISHCON TRUST

Messrs Victor Mishcon and Co, 125 High Holborn, London WC1V 6QP (01-405 3711).

Correspondent: See above.

Trustees: Lord Mishcon, The Lady Mishcon, P. A. Cohen.

Annual grants total: £18,208 in 1985/86 (£46,385 in 1984/85).

Policy and practice: The Trust has general charitable objects, a national and international range and a particular interest in the relief of poverty. A review of the Trust's accounts at the Charity Commission showed the highest grants as £2,000 but no grants falling within the scope of interest of this book since 1982/83.

Then, out of a total allocation of £35,400, the following donations with some relevance to this book were made:

Justice Educational and Research Trust	£100
Writers and Scholars Educational Trust	£25
World Disarmament Campaign	£20

ESMÉ MITCHELL TRUST

PO Box 183, Donegall Square West, Belfast BT1 6JS (0232-245 277).

Correspondent: Northern Bank Executor and Trustee Co Ltd.

Trustees: Lord Dunleath, P. J. Rankin, Commander D. J. Maxwell.

Annual grants total: £48,000 in 1987.

Policy and practice: This Northern Ireland Trust has general charitable objects and gives principally in Northern Ireland. The Trust has given support to a joint project of the Irish Commission for Justice and Peace and the Irish Council of Churches, the Peace Education Resources Centre, Belfast (*see separate entry*).

Presentation of applications: There is no formal application form but applicants are expected to submit a copy of their accounts, most recent annual report, tax and legal or charitable status and information about other sources of finance along with a description of the proposed project and list of officers.

SAMUEL MONTAGU CHARITABLE TRUST

10 Lower Thames Street, London EC3R 6AE.

Correspondent: The Secretary to the Trustees.

Trustees: Sir Michael Palliser, A. T. J. Stanford, A. J. Wadsworth, J. R. Young.

Annual grants total: £34,188 in 1986.

Policy and practice: (The Trust was called the Montagu Drayton Charitable Trust until mid 1986.) The Trust has general charitable objects and has made the following grants with some relevance to the scope of this book:

In 1986
British Executive Service Overseas	£1,000
Imperial War Museum Redevelopment Fund	£250

In 1985
Canterbury Diocesan Board of Education International Youth Year	£500
Centre for World Development Education	£350
Oxfam	£900
Voluntary Services Overseas	£300
Save the Children	£420

Presentation of applications: Applications can be made at any time and are considered about every six weeks.

JOHN MOORES FOUNDATION

South Lodge, Old Southport Road, Formby, Nr Liverpool, Merseyside L37 0AQ (051-653 6364).

Correspondent: Ms Linda Lazenby.

Trustees: Dr M. Cole, G. A. Slater, Mrs J. Moores.

Annual grants total: £198,350 in 1986/87.

Policy and practice: The main objective of the Foundation is to 'promote self esteem and a sense of personal value'. Essentially the aim is to provide grant aid to groups and organisations to whom funds are not readily available. The Foundation concentrates its funding in the more disadvantaged areas of

UK Sources

Merseyside. It has a small budget for Northern Ireland where it aims to support cross community work.

The Foundation does not make grants to national charities, nor for academic research, for buildings, for services to the elderly and handicapped or for the arts.

The Foundation states that the Trust income is not derived from any investments which would help the South African government as the Trustees abominate apartheid.

In 1986/87 grants were divided into the following categories:

Northern Ireland	£11,886
Advice	£43,634
Community	£36,946
Youth	£33,077
Race	24,503
Equality for Women	£19,190
Social Welfare	£12,668
Community Education	£10,694
Unemployed	£5,500
Health	£250

Grants given to projects in Northern Ireland in 1986/87 included:

Waterside Churches Community Advice Centre	£1,000
Antrim Family and Rape Crisis Group	£790
Forum for Community Work Education	£1,200
Well Women Centre, Belfast	£250

Presentation of applications: Applications may be made at any time. Preliminary enquiries are welcome from eligible organisations. Applicants who wish to discuss a potential application informally before making a formal application should telephone the Trust Officer.

The Trust does not have an application form, but requires a letter, on one or two pages, and the most recent audited accounts.

MOORGATE TRUST FUND

1 South Audley Street, London W1Y 6JS (01-491 4606).

Correspondent: D. G. Parry, Secretary.

Trustees: D. F. Martin-Jenkins, P. C. Pratt, D. G. Parry, I. H. Garnett-Orme, Sir D. A. Scott, R. A. Lloyd.

Annual grants total: £1,483,000 in 1986/87.

Policy and practice: The Trust Fund has general charitable objects with a national and international range. It indicates that all applications are considered on their merits. It is run in tandem with the New Moorgate Trust Fund. The most recent accounts on file at the Charity Commission were for 1985/86 and showed that the following grants with some relevance to the scope of this book were made:

IVS	£1,000
Mexican-British Friendship	£10,000
Oxfam	£5,000
Ulster Defence Regiment Benevolent Fund	£5,000
United World Colleges (International) Ltd	£10,000
War on Want	£1,000

Presentation of applications: By letter to the Secretary.

New Moorgate Trust Fund:

Address and correspondent as for *Moorgate Trust Fund*.

Annual grants total: £1,383,500 in 1986/87.

In 1986/87 grants ranged between £1,000 and £50,000 with the largest grant being made to a social welfare charity in South Africa. Other grants with relevance to the scope of this book included:

Airey Neave Memorial Trust	£2,000
Army Benevolent Fund	£3,000

MOREL CHARITABLE TRUST

34 Durand Gardens, London SW9 0PP (01-582 6901).

Correspondent: S. E. Gibbs, Trustee.

Trustees: J. M. Gibbs, W. M. Gibbs, S. E. Gibbs.

Annual grants total: £6,000 in 1984.

Policy and practice: The Trust has general charitable objects. In particular, the Trust's policy is to support the arts, organisations working for improved race relations, inner city projects and Third World projects.

The most recent accounts on file at the Charity Commission were for 1982 and included the following grants with some relevance to the scope of this book:

Corrymeela Link	£200
International Broadcasting Trust	£200
Third World Publications	£300
Quaker Community Relations Committee	£200
Christian Aid	£300
Africa Centre	£500
Voluntary Service Overseas	£500

UK Sources

S. C. AND M. E. MORLAND'S CHARITABLE TRUST

88 Roman Way, Glastonbury, Somerset BA6 8AD (0458-32162).

Correspondent: S. C. Morland.

Trustees: S. C. Morland, Mrs M. E. Morland, J. C. Morland, J. E. Morland, S. Morland, E. Boyd.

Annual grants total: £8,490 in 1986/87.

Policy and practice: The Trust has general charitable purposes and supports Quaker charities and others of which the Trustees have special interest. Its grants can be made both nationally and overseas.

Mr Morland writes 'most grants continue year after year, there is little surplus to support new applicants – so we disappoint most of them'.

Presentation of applications: Applications are only acknowledged if a reply paid envelope is also sent.

NETWORK FOUNDATION

Registered Office, 9 Thorpe Close, Portobello Road, London W10 5XL.

The Network Foundation has a membership of people of wealth who make an annual financial contributon to support and assist its aims. These include a commitment to foster non-exploitative practices and there is believed to be a strong interest in the environment, human rights and peace. Research into the funding of other organisations has shown that financial support has been given to GreenNet, Nuclear Weapons Freeze and Survival International. (The Foundation, a registered charity and company limited by guarantee has a subsidiary non-charitable company, the Network for Social Change Ltd, which is not constrained to supporting charitable purposes.) The Foundation which is in the early stages of its development, and without strong administrative back-up, was not happy to receive the exposure of being included in this book.

Readers should note that **projects are chosen and sponsored by the Network itself. Unsolicited applications cannot therefore expect a reply**.

NEW SHEFFIELD TRUST

National Westminster Bank plc, Trustee and Income Tax Department, 17 York Street, Sheffield S1 1YW.

Correspondent: The Manager.

Trustees: J. E. B. Holtom, Mrs E. P. Holtom, D. R. Brayshaw.

Annual grants total: £4,750 in 1986.

Policy and practice: The Trust has general charitable objects and gives particularly to peace and international community relations, world development, Quaker activities.

There are no accounts at the Charity Commission since 1977. These showed the following allocations (out of a total expenditure of £5,010) with relevance to the scope of this book:

Friends Service Council	£1,000
Ulster Quaker Service Committee	£550
Voluntary Service, Belfast	£200
Fellowship of Reconciliation	£100
Intermediate Technology Development Group Ltd	£100
War on Want	£60

Presentation of applications: In writing – they are not acknowledged.

NORTHERN IRELAND VOLUNTARY TRUST

4th Floor, Murray House, Murray Street, Belfast BT1 6DN (0232-245 927).

Contact: Paul Sweeney, Director.

Trustees: David Cook (Chairman), Denis Barritt, Claire Curry, Eamonn Deane, Mari Fitzduff, Sheelagh Flanagan, Jim Flynn, Felicity McCartney, Sam McCready, Aideen McGinley, Bill McStay, Ben Wilson.

Annual grants total: £340,438 in 1986/87.

Policy and practice: In its annual report for 1986/87 the Trust states that it 'concentrates its resources on helping new organisations to start up or on existing groups developing new projects and on experimental and innovative efforts to tackle social problems in the areas of greatest need. Priority is given to projects which encourage community involvement and self help, which improve understanding and communication within and between communities and which help local people in areas of need to acquire the skills, knowledge and self confidence to tackle serious social problems.

The majority of grants are made to locally based projects but help is also given to voluntary organisations covering a wider geographic area when they are developing a new project that will directly support and benefit the efforts of locally based groups or tackle pressing social need.'

The report for 1986/87 also states that: 'At the present time the trustees are particularly interested to receive applications under the following headings:

Unattached young people
Women's Groups
Unemployment
Community Arts
Welfare Rights
Community Health Initiatives
Community Care
Common Interest/Networking Projects
Neighbouring Communities
Cultural Awareness and Mutual Understanding
Centres for Reconciliation
Community Education and Training
Crime Prevention
Rural Areas

The Community Volunteering Scheme (NIVT provides a management agency for this latter category which is separately funded by the Department of Economic Development.)

Grants by category for 1986/87 were as follows:

Environment/Community Development	£84,430	25%
Unattached Young People and Crime Prevention	£15,736	5%
Community Care and Poverty	£36,950	11%
Unemployment/Community Enterprise	£25,400	7%
Women's Groups	£41,850	12%
Common Interest/Networking/ Mutual Understanding and Cultural Awareness	£23,325	7%
Inter Community Contact Grant Scheme	£24,795	7%
Community Arts, Education and Communication	£54,402	16%
Rural Community Projects	£34,000	10%

The NIVT, in its policies and practice, is concerned with community development. In the context of Northern Ireland, the NIVT believes that the process of good community development work has great potential to contribute to an improvement of relations between local communities.

The relatively new 'Inter-Community Contact Grants Scheme' is described in the 1986/87 annual report:

'The NIVT, since its inception, has provided support for projects which attempt to improve understanding within and between communities and to bridge the traditional divisions in Northern Ireland through a variety of means. In 1986 these areas of work were given an even greater priority and appear in the Trust's guidelines as specific areas of interest. In addition, the Department of Education for Northern Ireland agreed to provide an additional £50,000 per year for each of three years for a specific programme to support cross-community contacts. This fund provides assistance to groups from across the political/religious divisions, to organise meetings, conferences, discussions and residential courses which enables them to look at common concerns and issues or to explore their different heritage. Through this the scheme seeks to offer an opportunity to foster respect, mutual understanding and an increased appreciation of their own and other traditions and an awareness of things that are shared in common.

In the situation of Northern Ireland where people by and large are separated by housing, education, employment, fear and prejudice, opportunities to meet and discuss common issues are unfortunately all too few. This scheme provides support and encouragement for groups seeking to make those contacts. The scheme was announced in September 1986 in Belfast.

It its first seven months, the projects which received grants reflect a range of issues. These include improving individual skills in the area of understanding and dealing with conflict; an emphasis on links between adjacent communities; a growing movement of people concerned with the question of segregated/integrated education in Northern Ireland; and groups concerned about the overt effects of sectarianism and intimidation. The Department of Education agreed to the allocation of the remaining grant aid for 1986/87 to other projects supported by the NIVT with a strong cross-community or reconciliation element to their work'.

In 1986/87 44 grants were made with a grant range of £100 to £4,000 and included the following allocations:

Banbridge Area Parents for Integrated Education	£1,200
Conflict and Mediation Group	£250
Columbanus Community of Reconciliation	£500
Cornerstone Community	£595
FCWE (Pilot Peace Studies Course)	£250
Fellowship of Reconciliation in Ireland	£440
Neve Shalom Follow-up	£145
PACE Conference	£450
Peace People Farm Ltd	£4,000
Peace and Reconciliation Group	£600
Women's Information Group	£1,000

Information available for applicants: Guidelines for grant seekers; annual report for 1986/87; leaflets on special awards schemes.

UK Sources

THE NUFFIELD FOUNDATION

28 Bedford Square, London WC1B 3EG (01-631 0566).

Correspondent: James Cornford, Director.

Trustees: Lord Flowers, (Chairman), Professor B. M. Hoggett, Professor Sir Hans Kornberg, Professor R. C. O. Matthews, Dr D. A. J. Tyrrell, Sir Brian Young.

Annual grants total: £3.4 million in 1987.

Policy and practice: The objects of the Foundation, as laid down in the Trust Deed, are:

a) The advancement of health and the prevention and relief of sickness, particularly by medical research and teaching;

b) The advancement of social well being, particularly by scientific research;

c) The care and comfort of the aged poor;

d) The advancement of education.

Two types of grant are made: major grants and small grants.

Major Grants: These are grants in response to ad hoc proposals. They are called Major Grants to distinguish them from Small Grants which are dealt with by means of self-contained schemes. There are no formal limits, upper or lower, in the size of Major Grants. The Trustees aim to support experimental or developmental projects which may act as a model or example for others and which cannot be supported from public funds. In considering research they prefer new projects and seldom make grants for work already underway. Research projects should generally have a practical application. Applicants should submit an outline proposal to the Foundation and they will be advised whether the project is suitable for consideration.

Small Grants and Fellowships Schemes: These are schemes for the support of self-contained academic research projects in the sciences and the social sciences.

Peace and security research are not among the Trustees' current priorities but applications can be considered under the special schemes in the social sciences, details of which can be obtained from Theresa O'Neill, at the address above. Booklets describing the Foundation's work and listing grants are also obtainable from the Foundation.

Examples of recent grants within the scope of interest of this book (from the Foundation's Triennial Report, 1983–85).

Social Research and Experiment

Tools for Self-Reliance:
Field visits to Zimbabwe and Tanzania
(1983) £7,640

British Pugwash Group, towards the cost of organising a symposium on SDI (1985) £10,000

Dunamis, for a seminar on East/West, North/South relations to be followed by publications and sound tapes to be sold to schools and colleges £3,000

University of Edinburgh, Department of Sociology to Dr Donald MacKenzie for a programme of interviews for a project on the development of strategic missile technology £19,416

Education:

Forge School, Belfast, to help establish an integrated primary school following the successful establishment of Lagan College £45,000

Small grants scheme in Social Sciences

Dr M. Mowlem, Department of Politics, University of Newcastle-upon-Tyne. A study of control and accountability in the civil nuclear power industry (1983) £1,880

Dr David Robertson, Sub Faculty of Politics, University of Oxford. The British nuclear deterrent: the strategic and moral logic of a small nuclear force (1983) £1,135

Mr Paul Byrne, Department of European Studies, Loughborough University. The Campaign for Nuclear Disarmament (1984) £650

Dr Peter Lyon, Institute of Commonwealth Studies, London. The Commonwealth as an international organisation (1985) £850

Working parties and specialist conferences in the Social Sciences:

Dr C. R. Mitchell, Conflict Management Research Group, Department of Systems Science, City University. Future relations between Britain and Argentina (1984) £912

Dr Dilys Hill, Department of Politics, University of Southampton. Human rights and foreign policy (1985) £1,000

Dr Martin McCauley, School of Slavonic and East European Studies, London. The Soviet under Gorbachev (1985) £1,000

Dr E. R. J. Owen, St Antony's College, University of Oxford. An examination of the Suez crisis and its consequences in the light of current research (1985) £1,000

Mr Peter Shearman and Dr Mary McAuley, Department of Government, University of Essex. The superpowers, Central America and the Middle East (1985) £1,000

UK Sources

Exclusions: The Foundation does not entertain applications for the following activities except for particular schemes or when the activity is part of a project which is otherwise acceptable:

  Organisation of conferences;

  Attendance at conferences;

  The publication of books or other writings, and the production of films;

  The purchase of apparatus or other equipment;

  Day-to-day running expenses or accommodation needs;

  Work for degrees or other qualifications;

  Provision for sport or recreation;

  Exhibitions.

The Foundation does not contribute to appeals and cannot respond to requests for financial help made by or on behalf of individuals in personal difficulty or distress.

Presentation of applications: The Trustees meet six times in the course of the year, usually in February, April, June, July, October and December. Closing dates are around six weeks before the meetings. Applicants will be informed of their decisions immediately after the meeting. Grants are formally offered not to applicants but to the institutions to which they are attached. The Foundation requires an assurance that the institution concerned will be willing to administer any grant made. Work on the project can begin as soon as the grant has been offered and accepted.

Further information for applicants: Detailed booklets published annually with full guidance for applicants and triennial reports are available from the Foundation.

OAK FOUNDATION (UK) LTD

35 Belgrave Square, London SW1X 8QB (01-245 1251).

Correspondent: Roger Harrison, Executive Director.

Policy and practice: The Foundation was registered with the Charity Commission in mid 1987 and has general charitable objects and a national and international scope. The Foundation has reported that during the period 1988/90 support will be made available in the following areas:

  Education: Research and development of improved techniques for the recognition and remediation of early learning disability, where children are underperforming in school despite average or above average ability level.

  Human Rights: The rehabilitation of the bodies and minds of the victims of torture.

  Third World: The provision of assistance to enable disadvantaged people in Southern Africa to improve the quality of their lives.

No information is available on the scale of grant-making but the Foundation is believed to have between £1–2 million at its disposal for these purposes.

Presentation of applications: Applications will be considered in any form. A preliminary telephone call is recommended.

OAKDALE TRUST

Low Furrow, Pebworth, Stratford-upon-Avon, Warwickshire CV37 8XW.

Correspondent: B. Cadbury.

Trustees: B. Cadbury, Mrs F. F. Cadbury, R. A. Cadbury, F. B. Cadbury, Mrs O. H. Tatton-Brown, Dr R. C. Cadbury.

Annual grants total: £42,000 in 1986/87.

Policy and practice: The Trust has general charitable objects, a national and international scope with a particular interest in activities in the West Midlands. The Trust has supplied the following list of relevant organisations which it has supported recently:

  Quaker Peace and Service

  Amnesty International

  Quaker Peace Studies Trust

  International Boy's Town

Presentation of applications: Applications may be sent at any time. Only successful approaches are acknowledged.

ONE % FUND

Committee on Sharing World Resources, Quaker Peace and Service, Friends House, Euston Road, London NW1 2BJ (01-387 3601).

Correspondent: Pat Saunders, Secretary.

Trustees: Friends Trust Ltd.

Annual grants total: £54,778 in 1986.

Policy and practice: The Fund was set up in 1968 and is administered by the Committee on Sharing World Resources on behalf of the London Yearly Meeting of Quakers. The Fund comes mainly from contributions by those Friends who tax themselves, and if possible, donate up to 1% of their income.

UK Sources

Projects are supported according to whether they are:
  Collective and self reliant;
  Increase food production;
  Based on low cost, appropriate technology;
  Educate public opinion and/or influence the British Government.

In 1986, the Fund reviewed its policies and reaffirmed its policy to use one third of its income for projects related to development education. Its 1986 report states:

'The more we examine the international structures which keep the poor in poverty, the more we realise that we are the oppressor. Therefore, the multiplier effect of informing and inspiring those working as development educators, campaigners, and activists – both through our own work and through our grants to others – was seen to be a necessary part of our response.'

In 1986, the following grants were given in the UK under this category:

Ara Study Tours	£200
Action for World Development Fund	£1,000
Bread not Bombs	£250
Campaign Against Arms Trade	£1,000
International Broadcasting Trust	£500
Legumes Theatre Co/Skate Aid	£250
National Association of Development Education Centres	£400
One World Week	£1,300
Quaker Council for European Affairs	£3,500
Quaker Peace and Service Development Education Project	£3,000
Quaker Peace and Service Development Education Programme	£3,500
The Other Economic Summit + Brandtland Report Seminar	£750
Tools for Self Reliance	£1,000

Presentation of applications: The Committee meets in April, July and November and applications should be sent at least a month in advance.

Further information available for applicants: An annual report is available on request.

OPPENHEIMER CHARITABLE TRUST

17 Charterhouse Street, London EC1N 6RA (01-404 4444).

Correspondent: J. J. I. Hawkins.

Trustees: E. G. J. Dawe, S. P. Shoesmith, T. W. H. Capon, N. Casselton Elliott, J. J. I. Hawkins.

Annual grants total: £52,315 in 1986.

Policy and practice: The Trust has general charitable objects and a national and international scope. The Trust gives grants only in areas where companies of the De Beers group operate. It has a particular interest in medicine and health, the young and the aged, and general welfare. A review of the Trust's accounts lodged with the Charity Commission has shown that in 1986 grants ranged between £50 and £3,500 except for a large grant of over £25,000 to the Diamond Industry Educational Charity. The following grants made in recent years have some bearing on the scope of interest of this book:

In 1986
Overseas Development Institute Ltd	£100
English Speaking Union of the Commonwealth	£1,100
Voluntary Service Overseas	£250
United World Colleges	£1,000
Project Trust	£100
Operation Raleigh	£1,000

In 1985
Africa Centre	£500

In 1984
Anti-Slavery Society	£500
Voluntary Service, Belfast	£250

Presentation of applications: Applications are considered at meetings in January, April, July and October each year.

OXFAM (Development Education Grants in the UK.)

274 Banbury Road, Oxford OX2 7DZ (0865-56777 x 2408).

Correspondent: Peter Davis, National Education Advisor.

Development Education Committee: Ten members including three Oxfam trustees – the Chair, Vice-Chair and another trustee.

Annual grants total for development education: £200,000 in 1987/88.

Policy and practice: In its support and promotion of development education programmes Oxfam is guided by three principles.

The first is that these programmes are essentially concerned with the ways in which society is changing today: and should lead people to a critical understanding of these changes and towards constructive involvement in them.

The second is that these development education programmes should help to reflect the aspirations of people in the countries of Asia, Africa and Latin America who are working to bring about beneficial changes to their own lives.

The third is that they should at the same time contribute to the education of our own people: in knowledge, in responsibility, and in the skills needed to shape society.

The committee has agreed the following constituent groups, areas of work and regions in development education grant-aid as priorities:

Projects and programmes with primary school age children;
Adult and community projects and programmes;
Work with trade unions;
Programmes in Scotland and Wales;
Programmes associated with Oxfam's Education Department;
Small grants scheme (up to £300 per application);
Programmes in the voluntary and statutory youth sector.

Core budget support is provided for organisations within these priority areas. Applicants are asked to note the following factors:

Project specifications should include information on proposed evaluatory methods;
Notice will be taken of groups and projects developing innovatory work;
Projects will be expected to incorporate procedures for good reporting, publicity and dissemination of their work.

Within the main grants scheme, a discretionary small grant scheme also operates. Its total fund is £3,000 a year for grants between £25 and £300 for local school and community education projects.

Education and Public Opinion Forming Grants in 1986/87 included:

National Association of Development Education Centres	£10,000
Trade Union International Research and Education Group	£8,000
World Studies 8–13 Project	£6,000
Campaign Against Arms Trade	£1,000
Bread not Bombs Week	£2,500
Centre for Global Education, York	£4,000
Centre for International Studies	£3,500

Support also to many local development education centres and groups.

Director's Discretionary (for grants which do not fall readily into Oxfam's other categories of grant making). Examples in 1986/87 included:

UNA London	£10,000
Women's Peace Alliance	£1,500
World Development Movement	£5,000

Presentation of applications: Applications should be made in writing and guidelines for both the development education grants scheme and the small grants fund are available upon request.

The Committee meets three times a year in May, September/October and February. The heavy demands on its resources mean that the majority of funding decisions are made at the May meeting (except for the small grants). The small grants scheme is discretionary, and applications can be made to the secretariat throughout the year.

Further information for applicants: The terms of reference of the committee; list of priorities for grant making; guidelines about how applications should be prepared and detailed notes on the information required for both major and small grants.

P F CHARITABLE TRUST

25 Copthall Avenue, London EC2R 7DR (01-638 5858).

Correspondent: The Secretary.

Trustees: R. Fleming, V. P. Fleming, P. Fleming, G. A. Jamieson.

Annual grants total: £469,000 in 1987.

Policy and practice: The Trust's policy is to make contributions to medical research, hospitals, religious and educational bodies and other legal charities. It has a national scope.

The most recent accounts on file at the Charity Commission were for 1983/84 when the grants were in 15 categories: animals, birds, fish; restoration of buildings; youth clubs and associations; old peoples' welfare organisations; welfare (rehabilitation); welfare (miscellaneous); welfare (settlements); welfare (housing associations); universities and schools; the arts; miscellaneous.

Grants included the following with some relevance to the scope of this book:

Welfare miscellaneous:

IVS	£200
Oxfam	£500

UK Sources

Miscellaneous:
Northern Ireland Voluntary Trust	£1,000
Voluntary Service Overseas	£600
Voluntary Service, Belfast	£300

It is known that a grant has since been made to the Belfast Integrated Education Charitable Trust (BELTIE).

HARRY PAYNE TRUST

25 Bury Green, Wheathampstead, St Albans, Herts AL4 8DB (058-283 2878).

Correspondent: R. King, Secretary.

Trustees: H. S. Burnett, Mrs A. K. Burnett, J. E. Payne, R. King, D. F. Dodd, R. C. King, R. I. Payne, Mrs B. J. Major.

Annual grants total: £21,600 in 1985/86.

Policy and practice: The Trust has general charitable objects and usually restricts its work to Birmingham and the West Midlands.

A review of the accounts for 1985/86 on file at the Charity Commission has shown the following grants of some relevance to the scope of this book – to Woodbrooke College and to International Voluntary Service.

Presentation of applications: Applications should be written to the Secretary and accompanied by up-to-date audited accounts. Trustees meet in June and December each year and applications should reach the Secretary by the beginning of May or the beginning of November.

HEADLEY PITT TRUST

Maybank, Ulley Road, Kennington, Ashford, Kent (0233-23831).

Contact: D. H. Pitt.

Trustees: Mrs M. N. Pitt, D. H. Pitt, H. C. Pitt.

Annual grants total: £7,275 in 1986/87.

Policy and practice: The Trust has general charitable objects and a particular interest in the Society of Friends and charities in Ashford. Although the Trust's main interest is in housing for old people, a review of the Trust's 1985/86 accounts filed at the Charity Commission showed three grants of around £50 with some relevance to the scope of this book to Quaker Peace Studies Trust, Quaker Peace and Service, Quaker Festival Appeal. In 1984/85, a larger grant of £1,026 was made to the Society of Friends.

Presentation of applications: Applications may be made in writing at any time.

PUCKHAM CHARITABLE TRUST

41 Beauchamp Road, Bishopston, Bristol BS7 8LQ.

Correspondent: M. B. Gillett, Secretary.

Trustees: A. N. Gillett, D. B. Gillett, R. C. Gillett.

Annual grants total: £47,615 in 1986/87.

Policy and practice: The Trust supports aspects of international relations and environmental issues. Apparently preference is given to applications where the area of work is unlikely to command support from the public and to small headquarters organisations which promote new ideas. The schedule of donations made in 1986/87 has shown the following grants with relevance to the scope of this book:

Network Foundation	£7,200
Caroline Gourlay Trust	£7,000
United Nations Association Trust	£4,000
Fellowship of Reconciliation	£1,500
Society of Friends Geneva	£1,100
Friends World Committee for Consultation	£1,063
Foundation for Alternatives	£1,000
International Voluntary Service	£1,000
Woodstock Trust	£600
Indian Volunteers for Community Service	£500
Lansbury House Trust Fund	£500
Quaker Peace and Service	£352
Centre for World Development Education	£300
All Children Together (Northern Ireland)	£250
Federal Trust	£200

Presentation of applications: Most applications are considered at the main annual Trust meeting in April or May. They are made with the prior agreement of trustees.

RADLEY CHARITABLE TRUST

53 Sherlock Close, Huntingdon Road, Cambridge CB3 0HP (0223-356 312).

Correspondent: P. Radley.

Trustees: P. Radley, Mrs M. A. Radley, P. F. Radley, K. Allchin.

Annual grants total: £23,926 in 1986/87.

Policy and practice: The Trust supports social and international causes and education in these areas. It makes grants to Quaker bodies, international and peace work, for racial equality, community projects, education and conservation. It is a policy of the trustees to support applicants unlikely to have general public support or appeal. Grants are normally between £250 and £500.

The following grants with relevance to the scope of this book were made in 1986/87:

Friends Peace and Service	£500
Bradford School of Peace Studies	£400

Presentation of applications: By letter, enclosing a reply paid envelope.

RANK FOUNDATION LTD

12 Warwick Square, London SW1V 2AA (01-834 7731).

Correspondent: J. A. Wheeler.

Trustees: R. F. H. Cowen (Chairman), Lord Charteris, W. J. L. Clarke, Mrs S. M. Cowen, Sir John Davis, E. E. L. Giusseppi, J. D. Hutchison, Sir Hector Laing, Mrs R. L. Newton, V. A. L. Powell, Joseph Rank, M. J. de R. Richardson, D. R. W. Silk, M. J. M. Thompson.

Annual grants total: £3,274,000 in 1985.

Policy and practice: The Foundation describes its policy as:

The promotion, by means of the exhibition of religious films, of the Christian religion, Christian principles, Christian religious education and the study of the history of the Christian faith. Also the promotion of the Christian religion by an other lawful means.
The promotion of education.
The promotion of any other objects or purposes which are exclusively charitable according to the laws of England in force from time to time.

The Foundation's report, 1984/86, provides the following breakdown into categories of donations made in the five-year period, 1981/86.

Agriculture and Farming	£174,000	2%
Animal Conservation and Welfare	£143,618	1%
Community Service	£850,383	9%
Cultural	£105,250	1%
Education	£983,724	10%
Elderly	£147,500	2%
Handicapped and Deprived	£433,152	4%
Medicine	£1,462,037	15%
Religious Education and Fabric	£4,455,230	45%
Youth	£1,076,830	11%
Total	£9,831,724	100%

The Foundation's Report for the 3 years 1984/86 shows that the following groups which have some relevance to the scope of this book received support of £5,000 and more:

Belfast Charitable Trust for Integrated Education (BELTIE)
Corrymeela Community
Imperial War Museum
United World Colleges of the Atlantic

It is known that smaller sums have been allocated to (for example):

Oxfam (1985)
Centre for Conflict Studies, Ulster University (1987)

Presentation of applications: Audited accounts should be sent with the application. Preliminary enquiries are welcomed.

Information available for applicants: A brochure; report for 1984–86.

RANK XEROX TRUST

Parkway, Marlowe, Bucks SL7 1YL (0628-890 000).

Correspondent: The Secretary.

Trustees: H. Orr-Ewing, D. P. Hornby, R. E. G. Magnin.

Annual grants total: £142,582 for year ending October 1985.

Policy and practice: The Trust is concerned with the advancement of education, the relief of poverty and the promotion of any other charitable purpose.

A review of recent accounts at the Charity Commission has shown that a grant of £4,000 was made in 1984/85 to 'Africa Now'. This appears to be the only grant with any relevance to the subject area of this book.

Presentation of applications: There is no application form and applications are received continuously.

MISS E. F. RATHBONE CHARITABLE TRUST

Rathbone Bros & Co, Port of Liverpool Building, 4th Floor, Pier Head, Liverpool L3 1NW (051-236 8674).

Correspondent: Rathbone Bros & Co.

Trustees: Dr B. L. Rathbone, J. F. W. Rathbone, W. Rathbone Jnr, J. R. Leigh, Miss J. A. Rathbone.

Annual grants total: £71,000 in 1986.

Policy and practice: The Trust has general charitable objects and whilst having the ability to give support nationally, has a particular interest in work in Merseyside and a preference for charities known to the Trust or in which they take a special interest. Only occasional donations are made for overseas work – it is known that the Trust has given support to the United Nations Association Service (UNAIS).

ALBERT RECKITT CHARITABLE TRUST

Southwark Towers, 32 London Bridge Street, London SE1 9SY.

Correspondent: J. Barrett, Secretary.

Trustees: Sir Michael Colman, B. N. Reckitt, Mrs M. Reckitt, A. M. Bell, H. C. Shaw, Mrs G. M. Atherton, Mrs S. C. Bradley, D. F. Reckitt, J. Hughes-Reckitt.

Annual grants total: £28,220 in 1985/86.

Policy and practice: The Trust has general charitable objects and its policy is to support national organisations by means of donations or yearly subscriptions.

The most recent accounts on file at the Charity Commission were for 1973/74 when a total sum of £8,386 was allocated. A particular interest in the Society of Friends and local organisations was then shown; for example small grants of £15–£75 were made to Friends Service Council, International Voluntary Service, Westminster Meeting of the Society of Friends, Woodbrooke Council, and Hull Friends Meeting.

Presentation of applications: Submissions should be made before the end of March.

EVA RECKITT TRUST FUND

1 Serjeants' Inn, London EC4Y 1JD (01-353 2000).

Correspondent: George Bunney.

Trustees: A. R. H. Birch, G. Bunney, Mrs D. Holliday, C. Whittaker.

Annual grants total: £44,762 in 1987.

Policy and practice: The Trust's objects are the 'relief of hardship caused by civil unrest, political or legal injustice or war; betterment and education of the poor'.

The Trust made available a schedule of its grants for the five years, 1983/87. Grants are made under the following headings:

Overseas	Ireland
Housing Projects	Community Projects
Medical	Victims' Support
Educational	Disabled
Relief of Hardship	Environment
Prisoners/Ex-offenders	General
Arts	

The schedule showed the following grants with particular relevance to the scope of this book:

	1985	1986	1987
Overseas:			
Canon Collins Educational Trust	£7,140	£4,070	£1,000
Quaker Council for European Affairs	£400	£400	£400
Educational:			
Campaign Against Arms Trade	£250	–	–
Human Rights Book Week	£100	–	–
Oxford Research Group	–	£600	–
Society for Cultural Relations with the USSR	£500	£500	£1,000
Ireland:			
Voluntary Service, Belfast	£250	£250	£250
General:			
Central American Peace Walk	£750	–	–
Minority Rights Group	£500	£500	£500
Peacemakers' Relief Society	£250	–	–

Grants ranged between £45 and £7,140 with the majority being between £250 and £1,000.

Presentation of applications: Meetings are held regularly about every two months. Applications should be in writing and should indicate the level of support asked for and, if possible, other sources of income and applications made.

REST-HARROW TRUST

Clark Whitehill, Chartered Accountants, 25 New Street Square, London EC4A 3LN (01-353 1577).

Correspondent: Clark Whitehill.

Trustees: Miss E. R. Wix, first CB Trustee Ltd.

Annual grants total: £6,504 in 1986/87.

UK Sources

Policy and practice: The Trust has general charitable objects with a national and international scope and a particular interest in innovatory projects to assist disadvantaged groups.

The accounts for 1986/87 lodged at the Charity Commission included the following small grants with some relevance to the scope of this book, all in the range £25–£100: Belfast Charitable Trust for Integrated Education (BELTIE), Intermediate Technology Development Group, IVS, UNICEF, VSO, and Wateraid.

The majority of grants are between £25 and £100. Four grants were some £1,000. The Trust has pointed out that only a tiny proportion of its modest funds is given to projects relevant to this book.

Presentation of applications: Decisions on grants are made periodically during the year.

MR C. A. RODEWALD'S CHARITABLE SETTLEMENT

Kleinwort Benson Trustees Limited, The Lawn, Speen, Newbury, Berkshire RG13 1QN (0635-43151).

Trustees: Kleinwort Benson Trustees Limited.

Correspondent: The Secretary.

Annual grants total: £6,150 in 1986/87.

Policy and practice: The Trust has general charitable objects with a national and international scope. The policy of the Trustees is 'not limited but their main aims are to enhance; (i) the protection of Humane Freedom, (ii) the promotion of the study of Greek Civilisation, (iii) support for arts, civic amenities and social welfare in the Manchester area'.

A review of the Trust's accounts filed at the Charity Commission showed that 46 grants, ranged between £50 and £600, were made in 1986/87 and included the following allocations with some relevance to the scope of this book:

In 1986/87
Cobden Trust	£200
Minority Rights Group	£600
NIACRO	£50
The Prisoners of Conscience Fund	£400
War on Want	£50

In 1985/86
British Council of Churches – Human Rights Forum	£50
Cobden Trust	£200
Minority Rights Group	£600
Prisoners of Conscience Appeal Fund	£400

Unipal	£100
United World Trust	£50

In 1984/85
Chile Relief Fund	£100
Cobden Trust	£200
Educational Trust for South Africa	£100
Minority Rights Group	£600
Prisoners of Conscience Appeal Fund	£500

Presentation of applications: Applications should be made in writing and are considered quarterly.

ROTARY INTERNATIONAL IN GREAT BRITAIN AND IRELAND

Kinwarton Road, Alcester, Warwickshire B49 6AV (0789-765 411).

Contact: Mrs D. Honey.

Rotary Foundation Scholarships: 30 grants annually (worldwide 400–500 awards). Total awarded for scholarships from UK: £300,000 for 1986/87.

The purpose of the scholarships is to further international understanding and friendly relations among peoples of different countries, rather than to enable beneficiaries to achieve any particular qualification. Both women and men are eligible. The six types of Rotary Foundation Scholarship are:

Vocational Scholarships, for those who are secondary school graduates and who have been employed or engaged full-time in a vocation for at least 2 years at the application deadline. Applicants must not be eligible for a Graduate or Undergraduate scholarship.

Teacher of the Handicapped Scholarships, for those who have been employed or engaged full-time as teachers of the physically, mentally or educationally handicapped for at least two years at the application deadline.

Journalism Scholarships, for those who have been employed in a full-time position in print or broadcast journalism for at least 2 years at the application deadline.

Graduate Scholarships, for those who will have received a bachelor's degree or its equivalent before commencement of scholarship duties.

Undergraduate Scholarships, for those who are studying at the university level but who will not have completed a bachelor's degree before the commencement of scholarship duties.

Grants for University Teachers, for qualified teachers in higher education to enable them to teach for one scholarship year at a suitable educational institution in another country.

UK Sources

Starting in 1987 are special scholarships awarded each year through international competition. These awards are made in the fields of peace studies, agriculture (developing country applicants only) and Japanese studies. In the UK, the peace studies scholarship may be held at the universities of Hull, Keele, Lancaster and Leeds.

A Scholarship may be undertaken in almost any field of study in a country or territory with Rotary clubs. Each scholarship is assigned both a sponsor and a host Rotarian counsellor who provides orientation, advice, and assistance in preparing for and completing a successful study period in another country. Selection is made at least once a year in advance and the scholarships are awarded for one year only.

Presentation of applications: Through the Rotary Club in the district where the applicant lives, studies or works.

Information available for applicants: Published information on scholarships available from HQ office.

ROTHLEY TRUST

Mea House, Ellison Place, Newcastle upon Tyne NE1 8XS (0632-327 783).

Correspondent: P. L. Tennant, Secretary.

Trustees: I. H. Clegg, Dr H. A. Armstrong, R. R. V. Nicholson, J. R. Barrett, R. P. Gordon.

Annual grants total: £65,020 in 1985/86.

Policy and practice: The Trust has general charitable objects with a national scope and a particular interest in the North Eastern region of England.

A review of most recent accounts for 1985/86 lodged at the Charity Commission showed the following grants with some relevance to the scope of this book:

Children's International Summer Villages, N. E. Branch	£455
IVS regional office, Edinburgh	£100
Newry and District, Community Service Council	£420
Northern Ireland Voluntary Trust	£1,030
Project Trust	£100
Quaker Peace and Service	£250

Grants ranged between £50 and £3,870 with the majority under £500.

Presentation of applications: In writing.

ROWAN CHARITABLE TRUST

c/o Coopers and Lybrand, Bridewell House, 6 Greyfriars Road, Reading, Berks RG1 1JG (0734-597 111).

Correspondent: The Trustees.

Trustees: D. D. Mason, J. M. McKenzie.

Annual grants total: £100,000 in 1985.

Policy and practice: The Trust aims to further humanitarian causes. It particularly considers agencies working for development and human rights overseas as well as those working in deprived areas in Britain.

The most recent accounts at the Charity Commission were for 1985 and showed the following grants with some relevance to the scope of this book:

Action for World Development Fund	£850
Christian Aid	£30,000
Intermediate Technology Development Group	£30,000
UNICEF	£10,000

It is also known that the Trust in 1986 gave some support to the British Council of Churches Peace Forum (*see separate entry*).

JOSEPH ROWNTREE CHARITABLE TRUST

Beverley House, Shipton Road, York, N. Yorks YO3 6RB (0904-629 241).

Trustees: Ruth Bailey, Andrew D. Gunn, Christopher J. Holdsworth, Gillian E. Hopkins, Geoffrey Hubbard, W. Grigor McClelland, Roger Morton, Joyce Pickard, Rosemary A. Pyle, Michael H. Rowntree, Carol Saker, David Shutt, Hilary Southall.

Correspondent: Steven Burkeman, Secretary.

Annual grants total: approximately £1.01 million in 1987.

Policy and practice: The Trust's basic information sheet for 1988/89 states: 'Trustees' decisions are informed by the fact that they are members of the Society of Friends (Quakers). The Trust prefers to support *practical* work which, to quote Joseph Rowntree, will assist in 'searching out ... underlying causes of problems', rather than narrow academic research or the provision of direct relief. This leads to Trustees to support innovatory projects in order to help them get established rather than supporting work which is well-proven and should be the responsibility of others'. It also states that at the time of writing, Trustees wish to support charitable activities which:

UK Sources

Help to demonstrate how international peace may be pursued through the development of policies for defence and/or disarmament aimed at reducing both the risk of nuclear war, and the amount of the world's resources devoted to preparation for war;

Reinforce the democratic process, and the rights of citizens, in Britain, and encourage socially responsible behaviour by large public and private organisations:

Work towards a more peaceful and just society in a) Northern Ireland and b) South Africa and Namibia;

Explore ways in which disputes at various levels may be resolved through the use of non-violence, or through mediation;

Aim at teaching young people about the pursuit of peace and justice in a world context;

Seem likely to contribute to a Society that is economically more equitable;

Tackle the causes and effects of racial discrimination in Britain;

Are closely associated with the Society of Friends (Quakers).

The following information has been made available from the Trust's Triennial Report, 1985/87.

Defence and Disarmament: 'The Trust has a longstanding concern in this area rooted in its Quaker witness. In recent years, this has been translated into support for a number of studies aimed at exploring policy alternatives to the nuclear arms race; and at generating a more balanced and informed debate amongst opinion formers and decision shapers in this field. Projects which promote world peace will remain a basic element in Trust grant-making, though the emphasis in specific projects supported may change in response to changing circumstances.' Some grants of £5,000 and over:

University of Sussex, Armament and Disarmament Information Unit (1985/86/87)	£85,810
Oxford Research Group (1985/86/87)	£50,491
Verification Technology Information Centre (1986/87)	£34,115
Defence Information Groups (1985/86/87)	£30,815
Alternative Defence Commission (1985/86/87)	£30,770
London Centre for International Peacebuilding (1985/86/87)	£26,500
Council on Christian Approaches to Defence and Disarmament (1985/86/87)	£17,225
International Group of Researchers on the ABM Treaty (1987)	14,750
Working Party on Chemical and Biological Weapons (1985/86/87)	£13,925
Transnational Institute (1986/87)	£12,833
British Seismic Verification Research Project (1987)	£10,600
University of Bradford School of Peace Studies (for research on defence conversion and SDI)	£28,064
University of Reading Politics Dept (1987)	£10,000
United World Trust (1987)	£7,375
Royal Institute of British Architects (1986/87)	£5,000
Karen Payne for pre-production costs for film 'Turning the Tide' (1987)	£5,000
SCOPE (ENUWAR) University of Essex (1987)	£5,000

Education for Peace and Development: 'The Trust has supported initiatives aimed at introducing a global and peace dimension into classrooms and community education, including work on third world/first world issues, the peaceful resolution of conflict, and defence and disarmament. As a rule, the Trust does not fund educational work recognised as the responsibility of others, or direct development work, though one or two exceptions are reported here.' Some grants of £5,000 and over:

Centre for Global Education, University of York (1985/86/87)	£42,189
Mildred Masheder, for her book – 'Let's Co-operate' (1985/86/87)	£25,917
University of Lancaster, Richardson Institute for Conflict and Peace Research (1985/86/87)	£21,474
University of Bradford, School of Peace Studies (1985/86)	£15,575
United Nations Association (1985/86/87)	£13,000
Carmarthen Centre for Development Education (1986/87)	£12,000
Tools for Self-Reliance (1986/87)	£11,000
Sheffield Post-16 Peace and Conflict Studies Working Party (1986/87)	£10,986
Centre for World Development Education (1987)	£8,363
Centre for Peace Studies, St Martin's College, Lancaster (1985/86)	£6,500
Returned Volunteer Action (1985/86)	£7,500
World Young Women's Christian Association (1985 and 1987)	£5,500
World Education Berkshire (1985/86/87)	£5,500
World Studies in Bradford (1985/86)	£5,000

Non-violence and Mediation: The Trust has supported a series of initiatives in this area and intends to retain this interest. Some of the projects focus on international disputes, others on disputes in the community or between neighbours. Examples include:

UK Sources

Newham Conflict and Change Project (1985–87)	£30,000
South Atlantic Council (1985–87)	£15,704
Reading Mediation Centre (1986–87)	£6,500

Presentation of applications: Applications in writing should follow the Trust's guidance rules. The Trust meets in March, June, September and December and applications need to be made some two months in advance. Often applicants meet representatives of the Trust prior to formal consideration by Trustees.

Information available for applicants: Guidance notes for applicants, 1988/89; Triennial Reports – 1982/84 and 1985/87 (published spring/summer 1988).

JOSEPH ROWNTREE SOCIAL SERVICE TRUST LTD

Beverley House, Shipton Road, York YO3 6RB (0904-625 744).

Correspondent: Lois Jefferson, Secretary.

Trustees: Professor Trevor A. Smith (Chairman), Michael H. Rowntree, Pratap Chitnis (Chief Executive), Elinor M. Goodman, Christopher J. Greenfield, Archy Kirkwood, MP, Richard S. Rowntree, David T. Shutt.

Annual grants total: about £500,000 each year.

Policy and practice: It is worth reproducing the policy of the Trust as set out in their leaflet dated October, 1984.

'The Joseph Rowntree Social Service Trust Ltd is not a charitable trust but is structured as a limited company. It therefore pays tax on its income and was deliberately set up by the Founder in this way to avoid restrictions incurred by grant-making charitable trusts in return for their tax exemption. Put at its simplest this enables it to give grants for political, propagandist and pressure group work which cannot be made by those bodies registered under charitable law.

The Trust has two subsidiary bodies, the JRSST Charitable Trust, which can incur expenditure on those rare occasions when, in close connection with their non-charitable work, Trustees wish to fund some activity which can legally be paid for with tax-exempt money: and JRSST (Investments) Ltd which is the holding company for the Trust's assets.

Political grants: The Trustees collectively do not support the policy and programme of any one political party but over the years have attempted to live up to the Founder's reputation as a radical and reformer. Individuals or groups from nearly all the parties represented in the House of Commons – and all the major ones – have received grants at some time for particular purposes. Grants are not usually made for the normal administrative and campaigning costs of official Party organisations but fringe groups (such as the Bow Group, the Labour Co-ordinating Committee or the Liberal Summer School) and individual politicians with ideas or projects of importance to research or publicise have been successful with applications, and on occasions when it has seemed desirable to Trustees that particular political developments should be fostered, then more central grants to parties have been made (such as those to the Labour Party for research assistance to the then Shadow Cabinet before public money was available for that purpose and to the alliance of the Liberal and Social Democratic Parties when it was formed).

The Trust has made grants to political movements from abroad but these have been rare and normally only in a part of the world in which the Trust has had an interest since its earliest days, for example Southern Africa.

Propagandist and pressure groups: The form and practice of charitable law is notably confused. Some registered charities seem to be able to undertake quasi-political activity without any complaint by the Charity Commissioners, where others find themselves censured. Some charities have obtained permission to use small amounts of their charitable income for political activities closely related to their main purpose. The Trust will not normally fund such groups but will reserve help for the large number of pressure groups which provenly cannot obtain charitable status but which need assistance either for a particular purpose or for a limited period of time. Amnesty International, Friends of the Earth and the National Council for Civil Liberties in their early years are examples of such organisations.

Other Trust activities: The Trust maintains a building in Poland Street, London W1, where free accommodation is given for periods not exceeding ten years to small organisations which qualify for Trust help. But the space available is not large, the number of applicants great, and vacancies are rare. Similar facilities are available in the Birchcliffe Centre, Hebden Bridge, where there is also a Conference Centre and Hostel managed by Pennine Heritage Ltd.

There are a number of projects, such as the establishment of a producer-cooperative or the starting of a small newspaper or magazine, which cannot be supported by charities but which, if they are of more than usual interest, may qualify for Trust help. Sometimes individuals with a personal crusade of importance will be given an award to enable them to develop their interest.

Trustees are anxious not to define their interests so narrowly as to discourage applicants who may have something valuable to do or say. Anyone who needs help for a useful and important idea which clearly cannot be funded by the more conventional charitable trusts should feel free to apply for a grant – recognising, though, that many more applications are received than the Trust can find.'

Grants: Their report for the three years 1982 to 1985 lists 165 organisations which have received support from the Joseph Rowntree Social Service Trust and its subsidiary, the JRSST Charitable Trust. The following 26 organisations whose work falls within the scope of this book were amongst those grant-aided.

- Bradford University – School of Peace Studies
- British Friends of Peace Now
- British Irish Association
- British Nuclear Test Veterans Association
- British Pugwash Group
- Campaign Against Arms Trade
- Center for International Policy – Washington
- Committee on the Administration of Justice in Northern Ireland
- Committee on South African War Resistance
- Cumbrians Opposed to a Radioactive Environment
- European Nuclear Disarmament
- European Proliferation Information Centre
- Independent Commission on Disarmament and Security Issues
- Medical Campaign Against Nuclear Weapons
- Namibia, Visit of Parliamentarians
- Orlov Defence Fund
- Pax Christi
- South Atlantic Study Group
- Trade Union CND
- UK Coalition for a Nuclear Weapons Freeze
- UK-USSR Medical Exchange Programme
- United Nations Association
- United Nations Parliamentary Group
- World Disarmament Campaign
- York Peace Centre
- York University: Northern Ireland Research

During 1982–85 personal grants were made to 55 individuals. They are not named in the triennial report.

Presentation of applications: By letter at any time. Trust staff give applications a preliminary assessment. If applications 'pass' this phase, discussions may take place between applicants and the secretariat before a final submission is made to the Trustees.

The Trustees normally meet in the middle of the third month of each quarter. Applications must arrive at least a month prior to a quarterly meeting.

Requests for sums under £1,500 can be dealt with after the initial vetting by postal decision of any three Trustees including the Chairman.

Further information for applicants: A basic information leaflet (quoted extensively in this entry).

J. B. RUBENS CHARITY TRUSTEES LTD

Rolls House, 7 Rolls Buildings, Fetter Lane, London EC4A 1NH.

Correspondent: J. R. Rubens, Charity Trustees Ltd.

Trustees: M. L. Phillips, M. D. Paisner, Mrs R. Phillips, P. R. Smith.

Annual grants total: £669,800 in 1985/86.

Policy and practice: The Trust has general charitable objects with a national and international scope. Support is mainly to Jewish charities with the largest grant to the Jewish Philanthropic Association for Israel and the Middle East (£384,500). Little is known about the specific policies of the Trust. A review of the Trust's accounts lodged at the Charity Commission showed the following grants with some relevance to the scope of this book:

In 1985/86
Council of Christians and Jews £1,000

In earlier years
Victims of Persecution	£40,000
European Educational Research Trust	£7,000
Airey Neave Memorial Trust	£2,000
South Atlantic Fund	£5,000

EARL RUSSELL PEACE FOUNDATION TRUST

Beverley House, St Stephen's Square, Hull SU1 3XG (0482-24532).

Correspondent: A. O. Cullen, Secretary.

Trustees: Mrs Valerie Gribbin, Mrs Gilda Susan Haskins.

Annual grants total: £13,450 in 1986/87. (Income of the Trust is between £10,000 to £11,000 p.a.).

Policy and practice: The income of the Trust shall be paid out or used at the absolute discretion of the trustees to the furtherance of the cause of world peace and for no other purpose.

UK Sources

Presentation of applications: Applications at any time with no prescribed format but the Earl Russell Peace Foundation Trust is fully committed with regular recipients.

THE SAINSBURY FAMILY CHARITABLE TRUSTS

13 New Row, St Martin's Lane, London WC2N 4LF (01-836 6477).

Correspondent: Hugh L. de Quetteville.

The nine Sainsbury Family Charitable Trusts include: the Elizabeth Clark Charitable Trust, the Gatsby Charitable Foundation, the Headley Trust, the Jerusalem Trust, the Kay Kendall Leukaemia Fund, the Linbury Trust, the Lisa Sainsbury Foundation, the Monument Trust, the Monument Historic Buildings Trust.

One letter to the above office will ensure that an appeal is considered by whichever of the Trusts is the most appropriate. The Gatsby, Headley and Linsbury Trusts are those which have supported work within the scope of interest of this guide.

Applications may be made in writing at any time. No policy statements or guidelines for applicants are supplied.

The Gatsby Charitable Foundation

Trustees; H. O. N. & V. Trustee Ltd and CTS Stone.

Annual grants total: £4,481,000 in 1986.

Policy and practice: The Gatsby Charitable Foundation was set up in 1967 and in its earlier years showed a more marked emphasis on alternative approaches to economic development and social welfare than is now apparent. Its main grant areas are technical education, mental health and social services. A review of the Foundation's accounts filed at the Charity Commission has shown the following allocations with some relevance to the scope of this book:

In 1985/86
Centre for European Policy Studies	£120,699
Organisation for Economic Co-operation and Development	£8,566
Royal Institute for International Affairs	£50,000

In 1984/85
Intermediate Technology Development Group	£38,000
Oxfam	£16,500

In earlier years
Institute for Development Studies	£76,362
Anti-Slavery Society	£3,250

Headley Trust

Trustees: The Hon T. A. D. Sainsbury, H. O. N. & V. Trustee Ltd, Mrs S. M. Sainsbury, J. W. R. Lindsey.

Annual grants total: £735,000 in 1986.

Policy and practice: The Trust has general charitable objects and a national scope. In 1986 grants ranged between £40,000 and £30 with 17 grants of £1,000 and over.

A review of accounts filed at the Charity Commission has shown that the following grants, with some relevance to the scope of this book, have been made in recent years:

In 1986
Anglo-Israel Association	£1,000
Imperial War Museum	£10,000
Sandy Gall's Afghanistan Appeal	£1,000
Schools' Third World Project	£2,187

In 1984
Lagan College, Belfast	£20,000

Linbury Trust

Trustees: W. M. Pybus, Miss J. S. Portrait

Annual grants total: £814,322 in 1985/86.

Policy and practice: The Trust has general charitable objects and a national scope. A review of its accounts at the Charity Commission showed that in recent years it has made the following grants which have some relevance to the scope of this book:

In 1985/86
Anglo-Polish Medical Foundation	£100
Band Aid Trust	£500
European Cultural Foundation	£1,000
School's Third World Project	£3,750

In 1984/85
Bilderberg Association	£8,400
Justice Educational and Research Trust	£3,000

In 1983/84
European Educational Research Trust	£5,000

SCHRODER CHARITABLE TRUST

120 Cheapside, London EC2V 6DS (01-382 6000).

Correspondent: The Secretary.

Trustees: None, the Trust is an unlimited company.

Annual grants total: £99,576 in 1985/86.

Policy and practice: The stated preference is for national, registered charities. The range of giving is broad with beneficiaries in the fields of health, social welfare, refugees, education and the arts.

A review of the most recent accounts for 1985/86 filed at the Charity Commission showed that the Trust gave money to over 300 recipients with grants ranging between £50 and £5,000, the majority being for £1,000 and less. They included the following with some relevance to the scope of this book:

Arab-British Chamber Charitable Foundation	£100
Army Benevolent Fund	£700
British Atlantic Committee	£100
British Commonwealth Ex-Services League	£300
British Council for Aid to Refugees	£150
British Mexican Society	£500
Co-operation Ireland	£100
Ditchley Foundation	£200
English Speaking Union Educational Trust	£795
European Educational Research Trust	£100
Foundation for Defence Studies	£250
Overseas Development Institute	£100
RAF Benevolent Fund	£100
Save the Children Fund	£525
UK Committee for the United Nations Children Fund	£150
Ulster Defence Regiment Benevolent Fund	£500
Voluntary Service Overseas	£400

Presentation of applications: Applications are considered on a monthly basis.

SCOTT BADER COMMONWEALTH LTD

Wollaston, Wellingborough, Northants (0933-663 100).

Contact/Correspondent: Michael Jones, Secretary.

Trustees: The Board of Management.

Annual grants total: £24,850 in 1985/86.

Policy and practice: Its objects are 'To assist distressed and needy persons of all nationalities – To provide recreational facilities within the United Kingdom – To establish and support charitable institutions whose objects include the advancement of education. Preference is given to purposes in which the Trust and its members have special knowledge, interest or involvement'.

The Trust, from an examination of its accounts for 1985/86 lodged at the Charity Commission gives almost equal total amounts to local, national and international concerns.

In 1985/86 its grant-making included the following allocations with relevance to the scope of this book:

National grants:

Gandhi Foundation	£200
The Other Economic Summit	£1,000

International grants:

Voluntary Service Overseas	£250
Intermediate Technology	£4,000
Quaker Peace and Service 1% Fund	£400
Green-peace Foundation	£1,000
The International Institute for Peaceful Change	£1,000
Pugwash	£250
Change	£250
Fourth World Review	£100

A sum of £5,000 was set aside for a 'South African project (not yet identified)'.

Presentation of applications: There is no application form. Annual allocations are made between October and November but small grants are considered at any time.

SEARS FOUNDATION

40 Duke Street, London W1A 2HP (01-408 1180).

Correspondent: D. J. R. Ward.

Trustees: L. Sainer, G. Maitland Smith, D. J. R. Ward.

Annual grants total: £183,122 in 1986/87.

Policy and practice: The Foundation has general charitable objects and a national scope. A review of the Foundation's accounts with the Charity Commission showed it makes grants under the following headings: Health; Facilities for aged; Sick and disabled; Arts; National charities; Miscellaneous. The 'miscellaneous' category totalled £21,850 in 1986/87 and included the following grants with some relevance to the scope of this book:

In 1986/87

Save the Children Fund	£500

UK Sources

| Research Foundation for Study of Terrorism | £500 |
| Mountbatten Training Limited | £500 |

In 1984/85
Save the Children Fund	£34,719
Voluntary Service, Belfast	£500
Cruse, Northern Ireland	£250

Presentation of applications: In writing.

SEWELL CHARITABLE TRUST

37 Hogback Wood Road, Beaconsfield, Bucks HP9 1JT (04946-2947).

Correspondent: J. B. Sewell.

Trustees: J. B. Sewell, Mrs J. M. Fishpool, C. B. Sewell, Mrs J. P. Hilken, Mrs J. Sewell.

Annual grants total: £3,500 in 1987.

Policy and practice: The Trust has general charitable objects. Grants are only made to charities of the Society of Friends, or closely connected to the Society. The Correspondent has written that whilst the Trust is involved in funding work within the ambit of this guide it applies the connection with the Society of Friends very strictly.

SIMPSON FOUNDATION

Messrs Witham, Weld & Co, 70 St George's Square, London SW1V 3RD.

Correspondent: C. E. T. Bellord.

Trustees: G. B. Shaw, C. E. T. Bellord, M. H. Kelleher.

Annual grants total: £16,050 in 1984/85.

Policy and practice: The Foundation has general charitable objects with a national scope, and 'charities favoured by the Founder in his lifetime and others with similar objects – in the main Catholic.'

The most recent accounts filed at the Charity Commission were for 1974/75 when out of a total of £3,275, £500 was granted to the Catholic Institute for International Relations, an allocation within the scope of interest of this book.

Presentation of applications: Applications may be presented in writing at any time but telephone approaches will not be accepted.

HAROLD SMITH CHARITABLE TRUST

28 Wilton Road, Bexhill-On-Sea, East Sussex TN40 1EZ.

Correspondent: A. P. Silk.

Trustees: W. D. G. Wallace, B. V. Norgan, Mrs S. E. Norgan.

Annual grants total: £96,000 in 1986/87.

Policy and practice: The Trust has general charitable objects. Its accounts for 1986/87 at the Charity Commission showed that all grants were £1,000 and over. However the only grant falling within the scope of this book was £2,000 to Voluntary Service Overseas.

Presentation of applications: Applications may be made continuously but must be accompanied by a reply paid envelope.

THE STEPHEN R. AND PHILLIPA H. SOUTHALL CHARITABLE TRUST

Porking Barn, Clifford, Hereford HR3 5HE.

Correspondent: Mrs P. H. Southall.

Trustees: S. R. Southall, Mrs P. H. Southall.

Annual grants total: £4,070 in 1979.

Policy and practice: The Trust's objects cover general charitable purposes. The most recent accounts filed at the Charity Commission were for 1976/77. The grants made in that year totalled £3,252. Most were very small; 69 grants were made and the highest sums given were in the range £250 and £100 and made to only 11 organisations. Grants included the following (all £100 or under): Oxfam, Brothers to All Men, International Voluntary Service, Friends of Peace and International Relations, Society of Friends: Yearly Meeting Fund, and Friends Service Council.

W. F. SOUTHALL TRUST

Rutters Solicitors, 2 Bimport, Shaftesbury, Dorset SP7 8AY.

Correspondent: Stephen T. Rutter.

Trustees: A family trust with seven trustees.

Annual grants total: £63,000 in 1986.

Policy and practice: The Trust makes grants mainly within the UK though it can give internationally. Its objects cover the Society of Friends, peace education, alcohol and drug addiction and related charities.

UK Sources

In 1986 the following grants were made:

Quaker Peace and Service	£9,500
Friends World Committee for Consultation	£3,000
Woodbrooke College	£1,500
Quaker Social Responsibility and Education	£6,500
Quaker Home Service	£6,500

Grants between £100 and £500 included: Christian Aid, Fellowship of Reconciliation, International Fellowship of Reconciliation, International Voluntary Service for Peace, Oxfam, Voluntary Service Overseas, Peace Education Project, and a number of smaller charities.

Presentation of applications: Trustees meet twice a year but most of the grants are made in the Autumn. These applications should be sent by September. All should include a reply paid envelope. The Trust is not in a position to correspond with all applicants.

Information available for applicants: Applicants are asked to remember that this is principally a Quaker Trust.

SIR HALLEY STEWART TRUST

88 Long Lane, Willingham, Cambridge CB4 5LD (0954-60707).

Correspondent: Mrs Polly Fawcitt, Secretary.

Trustees: Sir Charles Carter (Chairman), Professor Harold C. Stewart, Sir Ronald C. Stewart, Dr Joan Haram, William P. Kirkman, Ian Halley Stewart, Professor John Lennard-Jones, Professor Phyllida Parsloe, Michael S. R. Collins, George Russell, Barbara Clapham (Associate Trustee), Professor W. Jacobson (Associate Trustee).

Annual grants total: approx £400,000 in 1986/87.

Policy and practice: The accounts filed at the Charity Commission are prefaced with the following outline of the Trust's objects: 'Its purpose is primarily to provide grants for the research into the prevention of human suffering, with the view to making such pioneer research work self-supporting at the earliest possible moment. The trust deed gives three principles to which the trustees should have regard in administering trust income:

To furthering for every individual such favourable opportunities of education, service and leisure as shall enable him or her most perfectly to develop the body, mind and spirit.

In all social life whether domestic, industrial or national, to securing a just environment, and

In international relationships to fostering goodwill between all races, tribes, peoples and nations so as to secure the fulfilment of hope of "Peace on Earth" '.

A large proportion of the Trust's funding goes to pioneer medical research but a list of the Trust's grants showed the following allocations for 1985 onwards with some relevance to the scope of this guide:

Education grants:

Forge Integrated Primary School, Belfast (1985/87)	£26,232
Mill Strand Integrated Primary School Coleraine, N. Ireland (1987/89)	£30,000

Social and economic grants:

Advisory Board of the Churches on Human Rights and Responsibilities in the UK and Irish Republic (1985/87)	£1,000
Standing Advisory Commission on Human Rights, Belfast, for research programme on discrimination amongst the Catholic Community (1986/87)	£10,000
United Nations Association International Service (1986/87)	£12,479
Farset Youth Project, Belfast (1986)	£500
Farset Youth and Community Development Ltd (1987/88)	£20,000
Anglo-Nordic Productions Trust (1986)	£4,000

Presentation of applications: A preliminary telephone call to the Secretary is recommended before a written application is presented. Applications are considered three to four times a year.

Information available for applicants: A booklet about the Trust's grant-making between 1974 and 1984.

C. B. AND H. H. TAYLOR TRUST

16 Stocks Wood, Birmingham B30 2AP.

Correspondent: Mrs H. H. Taylor.

Trustees: Mrs H. H. Taylor, Mrs C. H. Norton, Mrs E. J. Birmingham, J. A. B. Taylor, W. J. B. Taylor, Mrs C. M. Penny.

Annual grants total: £20,785 in 1984/85.

Policy and practice: The Trust has general charitable objects. Apparently this family trust limits its grants to charities in which family members have a personal interest. It is able to give both nationally and overseas. It has a strong Quaker commitment.

The most recent accounts at the Charity Commission were for 1983/84 when a higher sum of £29,875 was allocated. Grants included:

Woodbrooke College	£3,250
Quaker Peace and Service	£2,500
Friends World Committee	£1,800

UK Sources

Selly Oak Colleges	£1,000
The Friend	£750
Centre for Black and White Christian Partnership (Selly Oak Colleges)	£500
Voluntary Service, Belfast	£250
United Nations Association Trust	£250

Presentation of applications: New applications can be submitted for Trust meetings in April and November. It appears that many recipients are regular commitments. These organisations need to make their applications when they are due accompanied by a copy of the accounts of the previous year.

TZEDAKAH

Messrs Leonard Finn & Co, 8 Brentmead Place, London NW11 9LH (01-458 1141).

Correspondent: L. I. Finn.

Trustees: Tzedakah Limited.

Annual grants total: £207,870 in 1985/86.

Policy and practice: The Trust is concerned with 'Relief of poverty – Advancement of education and religion – General charitable purposes'.

A review of the Trust's accounts at the Charity Commission showed the following grants with some relevance to the scope of this book in 1985/86.

Band Aid	£675
Friends of Refugees of Eastern Europe	£125
Russian Immigrant Aid Fund	£777
Society of Friends	£2,128

The Trust's major grant of £30,000 went to the Bresslov Foundation. The Trust's funds are apparently fully committed.

VAN NESTE FOUNDATION

15 Alexandra Road, Clifton, Bristol BS8 2DD.

Correspondent: F. J. F. Lyons, Secretary.

Trustees: M. T. M. Appleby (Chairman), F. J. F. Lyons, Mrs B. Stevens, G. J. Walker.

Annual grants total: £122,380 in 1986/87.

Policy and practice: The Foundation has general charitable objects. A review of the Foundation's accounts at the Charity Commission showed that the following grants with some possible relevance to the scope of this book were made in 1986/87:

Responsible Society	£10,000
Northern Ireland Community Educational Association	£10,000

Presentation of applications: In writing. Not all applications are acknowledged.

HOWARD WALKER CHARITABLE TRUST

Messrs Bury & Walkers, Solicitors, Permanent Building, Regent Street, Barnsley, South Yorkshire S70 2EQ (0226-89131 x 232).

Correspondent: See above.

Trustees: P. O. Walker, Mrs C. Walker, D. M. Grunwell.

Annual grants total: £63,680 for 1986/87.

Policy and practice: The Trust has general charitable objects and a national and international grant-making scope. Apparently grants are only made to charities known to the Trust.

In 1986/87 accounts lodged at the Charity Commission showed the following grants with relevance to the scope of this book:

Prayer for Peace	£100
International Broadcasting Trust	£150
South Yorkshire World Development Education	£250
War on Want	£300
Christian Aid	£500
Oxfam	£500
Action Aid	£500
Tear Fund	£1,250

Presentation of applications: There is no application form and applications are considered periodically. Only successful grantees are acknowledged.

PHILIP WALKER CHARITABLE TRUST

Messrs Bury & Walker, Solicitors, Permanent Building, Regent Street, Barnsley, South Yorkshire S70 2EQ (0226 89131 x 232).

Correspondent: See above.

Trustees: M. J. M. Walker, Mrs J. R. Lees, Mrs H. E. Porteous.

Annual grants total: £23,243 in 1986/87.

Policy and practice: The Trust has general charitable objects. Its accounts for 1986/87 at the

Charity Commission showed grants between £25 and £1,250 and support to medical, youth and local Barnsley activities. The following grants with some relevance to the scope of this book were also made:

IVS	£500
Howard Walker Charitable Trust	£1,250
Friends of the Earth Trust	£100
War on Want	£500

Presentation of applications: Grant applications are reviewed at intervals. Only successful applicants are acknowledged.

A. F. WALLACE CHARITY TRUST

Warne Investment & Financial Services Ltd, 2 London Wall Buildings, London EC2M 5PP (01-628 0881).

Trustees: F. A. Wallace, A. J. W. F. Wallace.

Annual grants total: £31,460 in 1984/85.

Policy and practice: The Trust has general charitable objects and a national and international scope. It is apparently the policy of the Trustees to consider all appeals. There were no accounts on file at the Charity Commission since 1973/74 when the following grants were made with some relevance to the scope of this book (out of a total of £25,044).

British Atlantic Committee	£100
Royal Institute of International Affairs	£105

WAR ON WANT (UK-based funding)

Central Office, 36–39 Great Guildford Street, London SE1 0ES (01-620 1111).

Contact: John Denham, National Campaigns Officer.

Policy and practice: War on Want has to date made no rigid distinction between its campaigning work and its work in fostering development education. As a result it has no specific ear-marked budget for grant-aid to groups working in the UK. So far the major part of its funding has been devoted to international groups based in the UK with which it has strong working relationships and some activities in development education centres. It has not encouraged applications but rather encouraged co-operative work on specific projects. The following projects based in Britain were funded in 1985/86:

Education/Information Programme (CARILA)
Central America Human Rights Co-ordination
Central America Information Service
Film El Salvador
Latin American Debt Campaign
Nicaragua Solidarity Campaign
Development Under Fire (Film on Nicaragua)

Presentation of applications: There are no set procedures or times by which applications should be prepared for consideration by a committee.

Information available for applicants: Annual reports.

WARBECK FUND LTD

4 Chiswell Street, London EC1Y 4UP (01-638 9476).

Correspondent: L. C. Lowrence, Secretary.

Trustees: The Directors, J. A. Barnett, M. B. David, N. Sinclair.

Annual grants total: £206,170 in 1985/86.

Policy and practice: The Fund has general charitable objects and a national and international scope. Payments, however, have to be made to a UK charity. It gives predominantly to Jewish causes. The most recent accounts on file at the Charity Commission were 1985/86 when 176 grants were made ranging between £8 and £117,300 (the largest grant being to the Jewish Philanthropic Association).

The following donations were the only ones with any relevance to the scope of this book: African Educational Trust, which received £2,000, and smaller grants (all under £100) to International Voluntary Service, Save the Children Fund, and UNICEF.

Presentation of applications: In writing.

WATES FOUNDATION

1260 London Road, Norbury, London SW16 4EG (01-764 5000).

Correspondent: Sir Alan Goodison, Director.

Trustees: Mrs M. Jean Edwards (Chairman), Anne Ritchie, David Wates, Julia Brodie, Jane Wates, Michael Wates, Paul Wates.

Annual grants total: £1,066,356 in 1986/87.

Policy and practice: The Foundation has general charitable objects, and a UK and international scope. Its information leaflet states its present policy as: 'the alleviation of distress and the improvement of the quality of life, especially in the urban community. Within these broad aims, which are reflected in a wide pattern of grants, the Trustees currently have a special

UK Sources

interest in the well-being of young people in all its aspects, both spiritual and physical.'

No grants are made to individuals nor, as a rule, to 'large well-established charities, to national associations or in response to national appeals. The majority of grants are made to projects in the South-East, but there are exceptions.

Practical projects involving people are preferred to research. *'The Guide to Major Grant-Making Trusts'*, 1986, says that the Trustees have approved the following percentage allocations to heads of expenditure:

Education and science	10%
Health	15%
Community projects and the disadvantaged	35%
Church and religious projects	5%
Arts	5%
Overseas	5%
Heritage, conversation and the environment	10%
Miscellaneous and reserve	10%
Administration	5%

Grants in the year 1986/87 included the following:

Council on Christian Approaches to Defence and Disarmament	£1,000
Commonwealth Institute	£5,000
Imperial War Museum Development Appeal	£5,000
United World College of the Atlantic	£5,000
Voluntary Services Overseas	£5,350
Council for Science and Society	£10,000
British Executive Service Overseas	£10,000
Voluntary Service, Belfast	£16,100

Presentation of applications: The Trust has written that the subjects of peace, security and international relations do not fall within the Trustees' current focus of active interest.

Applications can be made at any time by letter including lastest accounts, to the Director. Grant allocation meetings are held quarterly. Recipients must have charitable status.

Further information for applicants: An information sheet and a report from 1978–1983; the report of recent years is in preparation.

WEINBERG FOUNDATION

9–15 Sackville Street, Piccadilly, London W1X 1DE.

Correspondent: M. A. Weinberg.

Trustees: F. Mauwer, N. Ablitt.

Annual grants total: £388,301 in 1985/86.

Policy and practice: The Foundation has general charitable objects. A review of the most recent Foundation accounts for 1982/83 lodged with the Charity Commission showed the following allocations (out of a total of £210,583) with some relevance to the scope of this book:

Minority Rights Group	£1,000
Greepeace	£500
Parliamentary Democracy Trust	£750

WESTCROFT TRUST

32 Hampton Road, Oswestry, Shropshire SY11 1SJ.

Correspondent: Dr Edward P. Cadbury.

Trustees: Edward P. Cadbury, Mary C. Cadbury and 3 others.

Annual grants total: £44,000 in 1985/86.

Policy and practice: The Trust has general charitable objects and a national scope. (Charities in developing countries can be helped via a UK agency.) All appeals are considered: where they involve the Trustees' own fields of interest, knowledge or association preference will be given. Well funded and patronised national appeals are usually rejected as are appeals to build up capital funds. Education for peace and for the practice of medicine are favoured and so are projects in Shropshire. Otherwise in education and in the fields of the arts and religion grants are generally restricted to Quaker causes.

The Trust support in 1985/86 included grants to the following organisations:

Advisory Board of the Churches on Human Rights and Responsibilities in the UK and the Irish Republic
Bradford University, School of Peace Studies
Canon Collins Trust
Coleraine Women's Aid
Derry Women's Aid
Harmony Community Trust
International Voluntary Service
Lansbury House Trust Fund
Lifeline International
Lionel Penrose Trust
Miriam Dean Refugee Trust

Oxfam
Oxford Project for Peace Studies
Play for Life
Northern Friends Peace Board
Quaker Council for European Affairs
Quaker Peace Studies Trust
Quaker Peace and Service
Quaker Social Responsibility and Education
UNA North West Region Appeal
United World Education and Research Trust
University of Lancaster, Richardson Institute
Voluntary Service Overseas
Women Caring Trust.

Presentation of applications: There are no application forms or acknowledgements except with a reply paid envelope. Applications are dealt with at about 2 month intervals.

GARFIELD WESTON FOUNDATION

c/o Bowater House, 68 Knightsbridge, London SW1X 7LR (01-589 6363).

Correspondent: H. W. Bailey.

Trustees: William Garfield Weston, Garfield Howard Weston, W. G. Galen Weston, G. Grainger Weston, Miriam L. Burnett, Barbara E. Mitchell, Nancy R. Barron, Gretchen A. Bauta, Wendy C. Rebanks, Camilla H. W. Dalglish.

Annual grants total: £5,098,800 in 1986/87.

Policy and practice: The Foundation has general charitable objects (with a particular interest in education, medicine and religion) and a national scope. The largest grants were given in 1986/87 to the Great Ormond Street Children's Hospital (£3 million) and the Weston Provident Fund (£1 million); but in all about 180 grants were made, the majority between £250 and £10,000.

In 1986/87 grants of relevance to the scope of this book included:

Schools Partnership Worldwide	£5,000
Co-operation Ireland	£2,000
Women Caring Trust	£250
Commonwealth Countries League	£200

In 1984/85, £25,000 was given to the Commonwealth Youth Exchange Council.

WESTWARD TRUST

4 The Chestnuts, Winscombe, Avon BS25 1LD.

Correspondent: D. J. Ironside.

Trustees: D. J. Ironside, Mrs J. Ironside, Mrs E. M. Axford, J. M. Ironside, Mrs R. M. Dodd.

Annual grants total: £6,800 in 1983.

Policy and practice: The Trust has general charitable objects and a national scope. The trustees do not encourage unsolicited applications because of the breadth of their current charitable contacts.

The most recent accounts at the Charity Commission were for 1982 and included the following grants:

Society of Friends	£3,814
The Friend Publications Ltd	£100
Fellowship of Reconciliation	£150

Mr Ironside has written that their 'problem is that our own contacts and interests are such that (a) we are never short of things to give to and (b) we very rarely give to unsolicited applications'. He felt that the inclusion of the Trust in the book would 'result in a lot of worthy people wasting time and expense in sending us applications.'

WHITAKER CHARITABLE TRUST

Currey & Co, Solicitors, 21 Buckingham Gate, London SW1E 6LS

Correspondent: See above.

Trustees: P. E. D. Dunning, D. W. J. Price.

Annual grants total: £123,645 in 1986/87.

Policy and practice: The Trust has general charitable objects and a national and international scope. Its major interest is educational, in particular in the United World College of the Atlantic, which receives the major part of its grant allocation. Grants made in 1986/87 included:

United World College of the Atlantic	£102,500
Minority Rights Group	£1,000
Northern Ireland Council Society	£1,500
Voluntary Service, Belfast	£500

H. D. H. WILLS 1965 CHARITABLE TRUST

12 Tokenhouse Yard, London EC2R 7AN (01-588 2828).

Correspondent: W. W. Sutherland.

UK Sources

Trustees: J. Kemp-Welch, Hon V. M. G. A. Lampson, J. B. S. Carson, M. D. H. Wills.

Annual grants total: £135,212 in 1985/86.

Policy and practice: The Trust has general charitable objects and its scope is the UK, the Channel Islands and the Irish Republic. A review of its accounts filed at the Charity Commission has shown that in 1985/86 grants included the following allocations relevant to the scope of this book:

United World Colleges (International Ltd)	£55,000
United World College of the Atlantic	£5,400
British Atlantic Committee	£1,000
The European Atlantic Movement (TEAM)	£500
Imperial War Museum Trust	£250
Belfast Charitable Trust for Integrated Education	£100
Co-operation Ireland	£100

Although one further grant was for over £50,000, most of the remaining 100 or so grants were in the range £50–£5,500. The Ditchley Foundation received support in previous years.

Presentation of applications: There are no application forms and no specific dates for making applications; apparently few new applications can be considered.

WOLFSON FOUNDATION

18/22 Haymarket, London SW1Y 4DQ (01-580 6441).

Correspondent: Dr Alun Jones, Director and Secretary.

Trustees: Sir Isaac Wolfson (President), Lord Wolfson (Chairman), Lord Dainton, Lady Wolfson, Sir Raymond Hoffenberg, Professor Barrie Jay, Sir Randolph Quirk.

Annual grants total: £9 million in 1987.

Policy and practice: The Trustees make grants to further the development of the following areas:

Medicine and Health Care, including research and the prevention of disease; the care and treatment of the sick, disadvantaged and disabled.

Science and Technology in Higher Education, particularly where benefits may accrue to the development of industry and commerce in the United Kingdom.

Arts and the Humanities in Higher Education and the support of institutions such as libraries and museums, galleries and theatres, and academies and colleges as well as the conservation and restoration of historic buildings.

Grants are made only to registered charities or to exempt charities such as universities.

The Foundation makes several types of grants which are not necessarily independent of each other – for capital projects, for research projects, for specific projects, for schemes designated by the trustees.

Further information is available in the Foundation's 'Guidelines for Applicants'. The Foundation does not, as a rule, make grants for research or other projects which are considered to be the proper responsibility of another funding body such as a Research Council.

The most recent accounts at the Charity Commission were for 1985 and showed the following grants touching upon the scope of interest of this book:

Royal Institute for International Affairs (for 2 years for its library)	£40,000
University of East Anglia (to establish a chair of environmental risk and assessment)	£250,000

The Foundation's Report, 1955–1985, lists grants made between 1981 and 1985 and shows support to the following:

Minority Rights Foundation	£5,850
The Justice Trust	£1,000

Presentation of applications: Applications are advised to approach the Director informally before making a formal application; there is no application form. The trustees normally meet twice a year and closing dates for applications are mid-March and mid-September.

Further information for applicants: Guidelines for Applicants; Report of the Wolfson Foundation, 1955–1985.

WOMEN CARING TRUST

5 Storey's Gate, London SW1P 3AT (01-799 1002).

Correspondent: Mrs M. Callander, General Secretary.

Trustees: Lady Fisher and The Lady Hunt of Tanworth (Co-Chairmen), Mrs Christopher Bland, Mrs Anne Dickson (NI), Mrs Michael Garland, Mrs Betty Lushington, Mrs Iona McFerran, (NI), Mrs Robin Phillips, Mrs Joyce Rose, Sir Leonard Smith, Lady Quinlan.

Annual grants total: Not known.

Policy and practice: The Trust is a non-political, non-sectarian fund-raising charity formed in 1972 to help women and children in Northern Ireland.

It provides the opportunity for people in Britain to express their sympathy for the suffering of their fellow citizens in Northern Ireland by giving practical help and enabling the Trust to continue its work among families who, through no fault of their own, are caught up in the Troubles.

The Trust supports community organisations all over the Province. It has helped to supply and maintain a fleet of playbuses for 3–5 year olds, enabling them to play in comparative safety off the streets for a few hours every day. Playschemes, Youth Clubs, Community Centres and holidays by the sea and in the countryside for groups of 'mixed' children have all been helped. Integrated schools have received support. Groups and organisations which received grants during 1987 included:

Cornerstone Community, Belfast

Fellowship of Reconciliation in Ireland, Belfast

Forge Integrated Nursery and Primary Schools, Belfast

Glebe House, Co Down (annual grant)

Peace and Reconciliation Centre, Co Derry (annual grant)

Resource Centre, Co Derry (annual grant)

Voluntary Service, Belfast (annual grant)

Women Together, Belfast

In 1987 the Trust gave 72 grants.

Presentation of applications: There is no application form; the Trustees meet 6 times a year. All profits are carefully reviewed with advisers in Northern Ireland, specifically the Voluntary Service Belfast and the Irish Council of Churches.

Information available for applicants: Annual report; basic information sheet about the kinds of projects supported.

ZOCHONIS CHARITABLE TRUST

PO Box 498, 12 Booth Street, Manchester M60 2ED (061-236 9721).

Correspondent: Spicer & Oppenheim, Chartered Accountants.

Annual grants total: £361,000 in 1986/87.

Policy and practice: The Trust has general charitable objects. A review of the Trust's recent accounts at the Charity Commission has shown the following grants with some relevance to the scope of interest of this guide (it appears that the Trust has some preference for activities in the Manchester area and has given support for activities for young people, people with disabilities and to the arts).

In 1986/87
Books for Development	£30,000
Minority Rights Group	£5,000
British Executive Service Overseas	£5,000
Overseas Students Trusts	£10,000

In 1985/86
Overseas Development Institute	£10,000
United World College of the Atlantic	£5,000

UK SOURCES:
Awards and Prizes

List of contents
Frank Cousins TGWU Award
Right Livelihood Award
UNA Media Peace Prize
UNESCO Prize for Peace Education

FRANK COUSINS TGWU PEACE AWARD

Transport and General Workers' Union, Transport House, Smith Square, London SW1P 3JB (01-828 7788 x 347).

Correspondent: Regan Scott, Secretary to the Award Panel.

Award panel: Neil Kinnock, Brian Nicholson (Chairman of the TGWU Executive), Joan Ruddock, Ron Todd, Norman Willis, plus another TGWU Executive Committee member.

Award: £4,000 each year.

Aim: The award is to assist the cost of research, travel and other activities related to projects which promote peace, disarmament and/or arms conversion. The award is made to a person or a project. The awards which started in 1984 have been made to Joan Ruddock, Scientists Against Nuclear Arms and Olive Gibbs.

Applications/nominations: The award is announced during September in the relevant journals and newsheets of the Labour movement calling for applications, from individuals or organisations, detailing the exact way in which the award would be used. There is no application form. The closing date for applications is the end of October.

RIGHT LIVELIHOOD AWARD FOUNDATION

Registered office: Ragnall House, 18 Peel Road, Douglas, Isle of Man (registered as a charity on the Isle of Man).

Correspondent: The above is the address for the receipt of donations. For information on the awards, contact the School of Peace Studies, University of Bradford, West Yorks BD7 1DP. (0274-737143)

Contact: Paul Ekins, Research Director.

Trustees: Jakob von Uexkull, Founder/Chairman; Birgitta Hambraeus, Monika Griefahn.

Annual cash awards: Some US $100,000 (plus honorary, non-monetary awards).

Policy and practice: The Right Livelihood Awards are popularly known as the 'Alternative Nobel Prize'. They are presented in the Swedish Parliament in Stockholm on the day before the Nobel Prizes in the same spirit as Alfred Nobel, who wanted to honour those who 'during the past year have conferred the greatest benefit on mankind.'

'A crucial feature of the Right Livelihood Award is its holistic approach to the challenges of today. It brings together those who are working for peace and disarmament, human rights and social justice, sustainable economic development and environmental conservation, and for human development, whether through the improvement of health and education, through cultural and spiritual renewal, or through the addition to the stock of human knowledge and benign technologies. The complexities and interdependencies of our world demand such an integrated approach.' Recipients are chosen by an international jury which includes Trustees of the Foundation. The Award is funded in part from endowment income and by donations from individuals all over the world.

The cash award is never given for personal use but for work in progress. Nominations need to be made by May 31st. Anyone may nominate a person other than themselves or a project not their own.

During the first eight years 1980–1987 the Awards have been presented to:

Dr Hassan Fathy (Egypt)
Plenty International relief organisation (USA, Guatemala, Lesotho)
Dr Mike Cooley (Britain)
Bill Mollison (Australia)
Patrick van Rensburg (Botswana, Zimbabwe)
Petra Kelly (West Germany)
Anwar Fazal/Consumer Interpol (Malaysia)
Sir George Trevelyan/The Wrekin Trust (Britain)
The Participatory Institute for Development Alternatives (Sri Lanka)
Erik Dammann/The Future in Our Hands (Norway) (Honorary Award)
Amory and Hunter Lovins/The Rocky Mountain Institute (USA)
High Chief Ibedul Gibbons (Palau, Pacific)
Dr Manfred Max-Neef/CEPAUR (Chile)
Dr Leopold Kohr (Austria)
Self-Employed Women's Association (India)
Winefreda Geonzon/FREE LAVA (Philippines)
Dr Wangari Maathai/GREEN BELT MOVEMENT (Kenya)
Iman Khalifeh (Lebanon) (Honorary Award)
Janos Vargha/DUNAR KÖR (Hungary)
Pat Mooney (Canada) and Cary Fowler (USA)
Lokayan (India) 'Dialogue with the People'
Theo van Boven (Holland) (Honorary Award)
Dr Alice Stewart (Britain) and Dr Rosalie Bertell (Canada)
Evaristo Nugkuag/AIDESEP (Peru)
The Ladakh Ecological Development Group (India)
Dr Robert Jungk (Austria) (Honorary Award)
The Chipko Movement (India)
Professor Hans-Peter Durr (West Germany)
Frances Moore-Lappé (USA)
Mordechai Vanunu (Israel)
Professor Johan Galtung (Norway) (Honorary Award)

In late 1987 a conference 'Peace through Disarmament, Development and a Healthy Productive Environment' was held with 1987 award recipients as speakers.

A 'UK Right Livelihood Society' is in the process of being established.

UNA MEDIA PEACE PRIZE

United Nations Associations UK, 3 Whitehall Court, London SW1A 2EL (01-930 2931/2).

Award: £1,000.

The prize is open to a person, team or organisation for an item or range of work in the UK media that has been properly nominated and is judged to have contributed best to international understanding and peace in the previous year.

The previous year's winner is invited to judge the succeeding year's award and is assisted by a panel of professional and interested assessors.

Material can range from a single 'letter to the editor', cartoon, advertisement, news report, article or programme to extended series or features, and be from the UK press or broadcasting media at local, regional or national levels. Recipients can be professional or amateur.

The prize includes a trophy with a symbol designed by Ruth Brock. The money may in exceptional circumstances be divided between more than one winner. Certificates of Merit are awarded for other nominated work.

Nominations of work, whether their own or others, can be made by an individual using a form obtainable from the Director of the UNA.

UK Sources

Nominations: must be received by the 31st of January each year.

Awards: are announced in April each year.

UNESCO PRIZE FOR PEACE EDUCATION

UNESCO, Division of Human Rights and Peace, 7 place de Fontenoy, 75700 Paris, France (010-331 456 83817).

Award: Approximately US $60,000 each year.

Aims: The Unesco Prize for Peace Education promotes action designed to 'construct the defences of peace in the minds of men' by rewarding a particularly outstanding example of activity designed to alert public opinion and mobilise the conscience of mankind in the cause of peace.

The Prize is awarded annually to an individual, group of individuals or an organisation, and financed from the interest of a large donation to UNESCO by the Japan Shipbuilding Industry Foundation.

A jury of nine persons, appointed for 3 years by the Director General, serves as the International Commission for Peace in the Minds of Men.

Laureates of the Unesco Prize:

- 1981 Mrs Helena Kekkonen (Finland) and the World Organisation of the Scout Movement;
- 1982 Stockholm International Peace Research Institute (SIPRI);
- 1983 Pax Christi International;
- 1984 International Physicians for the Prevention of Nuclear War (IPPNW);
- 1985 General Indar Jit Rikhye (India) and the Georg-Eckert Institute for International Textbook Research (Federal Republic of Germany);
- 1986 Professor Paulo Friere (Brazil);
- 1987 Ms Laurence Deonna (Switzerland) and the 'Servicio Paz et Justitia en America Latina'.

Nominations: The closing date for nominations is fixed each year but is generally 31st March. Nominations may be made by member States of Unesco, intergovernmental organisations, non-governmental organisations granted consultative status with Unesco and persons whom the Director-General deems qualified in the field of peace.

UK SOURCES:
UK Governmental Sources

List of contents

Commission of the European Communities (EEC)
Economic and Social Research Council
Foreign and Commonwealth Office
Fulbright Awards
Joint Twinning Committee of Local Authority Associations (*see entry in Part I*)
Ministry of Defence
NATO Research Awards
NATO International Scientific Exchange Programmes
Youth Exchange Centre

COMMISSION OF THE EUROPEAN COMMUNITIES

Directorate-General for Development, Co-operation with Non-governmental Organisations (VIII/D/3), rue de la Loi, 1049 Brussels 200, Belgium (010-322 235 6883).

Contact: Karen Birchall, DG VIII.

Total annual allocation for development education: Throughout EEC about 5 million Ecus in 1986/87. Total spent within the UK about 1 million Ecus in 1986/87.

Policy and practice: The European Community operates a scheme to co-finance projects run by non-governmental organisations in the member states. The scheme to assist development education started in 1979. Now, some 10% of the overall co-financing budget has been earmarked to educate the public in the EEC countries on development issues, on North/South interdependence and its impact on our daily lives and on those of peoples in developing countries. The EEC pays up to half the cost of a project. The upper limit from January 1988 is 80,000 Ecus each year (this unit of European currency runs at some £0.7). This contribution may cover e.g. salaries and allowances, materials production, equipment purchase, etc. Projects must have a European dimension e.g. dealing with E.C. policies or relations with developing countries, or involving collaboration with NGOs from other Member States, or reaching a European target group.

Projects funded in the past have included courses for schools, churches and workers, co-ordination of work at EEC level, production of audiovisual materials, and organisation of campaigns. Organisations must be non-profit making. Those which have received support in the UK to date include:

  Action for World Development Fund (WDM)
  Catholic Fund for Overseas Development
  Catholic Institute for International Relations
  Centre for International Studies

UK Sources

Centre for World Development Education
Change
Christian Aid
International Broadcasting Trust
Minority Rights Group
National Association of Development Education Centres
Oxfam
Quaker Peace and Service
Returned Volunteer Action
Scottish Education and Action for Development
Selly Oak Development Education Centre
Third World First
Trade Union International Research and Education Group
Voluntary Service Overseas
War on Want
Welsh Centre for International Affairs

Presentation of applications and information available: Criteria of eligibility of NGOs and projects can be found in *"General Conditions for the Co-financing of Projects to raise Public Awareness of Development Issues . . ."* (doc. VIII/271/87/EN) Most up-to-date version from Karen Birchall, DG VIII, (*see above*).

Decisions on co-financing are made throughout the year. Applicants can also receive useful information/exchange services from the NGO-EEC Liaison Committee (which has a sub-committee on education for development) at: 76 Rue de Laeken, 1000 Brussels, Belgium (010-322 218 3167).

ECONOMIC AND SOCIAL RESEARCH COUNCIL (ESRC)

160 Great Portland Street, London W1N 6BA (01-637 1499).

Contact: C. J. Caswill, Director of Information Division.

Council members: Professor Peter Hall (Chairman), B. Allison, Professor G. Bain, Dr W. Birch, Professor J. Blondel, Professor G. Brown, I. C. R. Byatt, A. M. G. Christopher, Sir Hugh Cortazzi, G. Davies, Professor J. Griffith Edwards, Sir Christopher Foster, Professor H. Hanham, Professor P. Levy, Dr G. McCrone, Professor A. Maynard, Dr J. Metters, Professor H. Newby, Dr A. S. Noble, K. V. Thomas, Dr G. Winfield. Secretary: David Stafford.

Boards and Groups:
Research Grants Board: Professor G. Brown (Chairman), J. P. Moore (Secretary).

Training Board: Dr G. Winfield (Chairman), Dr P. B. Long (Secretary).

Research Development Groups:
Industry, Economy and Environment: G. Davies (Chairman), Mrs C. Hadjimatheou (Secretary).
Human Behaviour and Development: Professor P. Levy (Chairman), Dr D. A. Statt (Secretary).
Society and Politics: Professor J. Blondel (Chairman), Dr A. P. Bruce (Secretary).
Research Resources Advisory Group: Professor H. Newby (Chairman), Dr A. W. Williams (Secretary).

Budget: £27.7 million for 1988/89, of which £15.84 million was for research (grants, centres etc.) and £7.47 million for Postgraduate Training Awards.

Policy and practice: ESRC was incorporated by Royal Charter in 1965 as the Social Science Research Council and changed its name in 1984. Its functions as laid down in its charter are: 'to encourage and support by any means research in the social sciences by any other person or body; to make grants to students for postgraduate instruction in the social sciences; to provide and operate services for common use for carrying on such research; to provide advice and to disseminate knowledge concerning the social sciences'.

Research Funding: ESRC has two principal modes of research funding: Research Initiatives (where specific areas are identified and research proposals invited) Research Centres, and the Research Grants Scheme (where applicants in recognised institutions submit research proposals on any topic within the Council's remit). Full details are given in the *Research Funding* booklet which is available from Registrars of academic institutions. In September 1987 ESRC set up a new independent Board to administer its responsive Research Grants Scheme thus separating this area from its own research activities.

Applications for funding are selected according to research excellence, contribution to social science understanding, and timeliness. Each year between £4 and £5 million is reserved for research grants, available for proposals between £5,000 and £250,000.

Postgraduate Training: ESRC offers studentships for full-time postgraduate students undertaking advanced courses or research training. Bursaries for vocational diploma or certificate courses in business and managment studies are also available. Full details are given in the *Studentship Handbook* and the *Bursary Handbook* which are available from academic institutions or ERSC.

Presentation of applications: Applications are

invited from UK academic institutions regardless of discipline. The closing dates are 15th April, 15th August and 15th January for which decisions are made by mid August, mid January and mid May. Further details are in the *'ESRC Research Funding'* booklet and proposal form available from academic registrars.

Information available for applicants: Annual Report; Corporate Plan; Newsletter; Annual Register of funded research. Information on current grants can be obtained from the Information Department.

FOREIGN AND COMMONWEALTH OFFICE

London SW1A 2AH.

The Department grant-aids certain organisations. There is no formalised procedure for making applications and recipients develop appropriate working contacts within the Foreign and Commonwealth Office.

The following list of non-governmental, and statutory organisations supplied by the Finance Department shows a total of £4,875 million provision for grant-aid in 1987/88 and that well over half this sum (55%) was provided to the Commonwealth Institute.

In addition the Department funds policy studies by the Royal Institute of International Affairs at the rate of about £50,000 a year. The Arms Control and Disarmament Department gives some support to the Council for Arms Control for activities, such as seminars or papers. In 1986/87 this amounted to about £5,500.

Grants: General expenses and grants to non-governmental and statutory organisations (1987/88 Provision):

Commonwealth Institute	£2,665,000
Marshall Aid Commemoration Commission	£775,000
The Great Britain/East Europe Centre	£126,000
Great Britain/USSR Association	£140,000
Great Britain/China Centre	£120,000
North Atlantic Assembly	£256,000

Other grants in aid to UK based organisations:

Franco-British Council (British Section) Ltd	£106,000
British Atlantic Committee	£60,000
British Youth Council	£44,000
United Nations Association	£24,000
British Yugoslav Society	£12,000
European Movement (British Council) Ltd	£10,000
Anglo-Irish Encounter	£26,000
Afghanistan Support Committee	£25,000
Peace through NATO	£110,000
Fund for International Student Co-operation	£76,000
West India Committee	£10,000

Grants in aid to non-governmental organisations engaged in the explanation of arms control and defence issues	£20,000

Other grants in aid (to organisations based abroad):

International Committee of the Red Cross	£240,000
International Commission of Jurists	£10,000
College of Europe, Bruges	£3,000
UK Immigrants Advisory Service	£10,000
Trilateral Commission	£2,000

FULBRIGHT AWARDS

The Fulbright Commission, (United States – United Kingdom Educational Commission), 6 Porter Street, London W1M 2HR (01-486 7697).

Contact: Peter Calladine, British Programme Administrator.

The Origins of the Commission: Inspired by his early experience as a Rhodes Scholar at Oxford, Senator William Fulbright sponsored legislation in the United States after the Second World War to use funds from the sale of surplus war property for programmes of education and cultural exchange.

The purpose of the Fulbright programme is to further mutual understanding between the United States and other nations. The programme operates in more than 100 countries, and in 43 of them binational commissions have been established to administer it.

The British binational commission was set up in 1948. Since 1965 the United Kingdom Government has contributed to its funding, and at present provides one third of the Commission's annual budget.

Under the provisions of the Fulbright-Hays programme, a number of grants are available to citizens of the United Kingdom and dependent territories for academic study or assistance for the travel costs of lecturing or research, in the United States of America. The awards are competitive and are made by the Commission in London in co-operation with the Board of Foreign Scholarships in Washington.

Applicants must be citizens of, and ordinarily resident in the United Kingdom or its dependent territories. Some basic criteria are listed below; full details should be obtained from the Commission.

UK Sources

Awards for Postgraduate Students: These cover round-trip travel and full maintenance for one academic year, and may include some assistance with tuition costs. There are no strictures regarding the disciplines favoured and no age limits. Applicants must have at least an upper second class honours degree, or its equivalent. Some 25 awards are made each year. No list of awards is available from the Commission.

Travel Grants for Visiting Lecturers and Research Scholars: Applicants must hold an appointment to undertake lecturing or research at an approved American institution of higher learning.

Grants to *Visiting Lecturers* are confined to those who have been invited to lecture at a University or College or at some other approved institution of higher learning in the United States.

Senior Research Scholars normally should have achieved professional standing in their chosen field and should be planning advanced work of a post-doctoral nature at an approved institution of higher learning in the United States.

Junior Research Scholars normally should not be older than 30 years on the closing date for the competition, and should have a PhD or its equivalent, or be expecting to complete requirements for a PhD before departing for the United States. All scholars should have good reasons for pursuing their work in the United States.

Applicants must be planning a minimum stay of about four months at one academic institution in the United States. The Commission stresses that it is the objective of this programme that a maximum amount of time be spent in the United States. Preference is therefore given to those applicants who intend to spend a full academic year there. Of this time about two-thirds should be spent at one university or recognised research institution. Applications for the summer months only will not be considered. About 35 awards are made each year.

Presentation of applications: Application forms are available from July each year and no requests for them can be made after 30th October 1987. Applications have to be made by the first week in November and shortlisted candidates are interviewed in January.

Information available for applicants: Detailed guidelines of criteria and benefits are available. No information is available on the types of awards made to date.

MINISTRY OF DEFENCE

Whitehall, London SW1A 2HB

Ministry of Defence Lectureship Scheme: The MOD Defence Lectureship Scheme, which currently funds six Defence Lectureships at British universities, began in 1968 with the aim 'to improve the scope and level of discussion of defence subjects among informed public opinion'. The MOD finances each Lectureship for an initial five years, renewable for a further five years if the performance of the Lecturer is considered by the MOD and university to be satisfactory. At the end of the ten year period it is hoped that the University can absorb the post on its own payroll. Lecturers are employed by the university. The Lecturers teach courses such as Strategic Studies and undertake defence-related research, and enable a department to devote more attention to the defence aspects of its discipline.

As at 1 January 1988, Defence Lectureships were held at:

The Centre for Defence Studies, University of Aberdeen;

The Department of International Politics, University College of Wales, Aberystwyth;

The Centre for Russian and Eastern European Studies, University of Birmingham;

The Centre of International Studies, University of Cambridge (two Lectureships);

The Department of War Studies, King's College, University of London.

Research and Development Contracts in Universities and Colleges: The MOD continues to place agreements and contracts with universities and other institutions of higher education for academic/scientific research and development. This work is a necessary part of the defence programme. The MOD does not publish details of these arrangements. In a written Parliamentary answer by T. Sainsbury in Hansard on 21 January 1988, it is stated that the defence research establishments then had 753 research agreements and 76 contacts with British universities, polytechnics and other institutes of education. The cost of this research and development in the academic sector was £14 million in financial year 1986/87. The forecast for 1987/88 was some £18 million.

Joint Research Council/MOD research grants: This scheme is aimed at supporting research in the universities and similar institutions of higher education, which is not only of high academic quality but also likely to be of relevance to defence, thereby contributing to the strengthening of both the UK science base and the defence research programme. The Government's intention to make such arrangements was announced in the Statement of Defence Estimates 1985 (paragraph 537).

The scheme operates alongside the Research Councils' research grant award procedures, with the MOD participating. The MOD will fund up to 50% of a joint research grant, the decision being based mainly on the level of defence relevance. There are currently over 100 joint grants in operation under this developing scheme and the objective is to achieve £5 million of MOD funding per annum.

NATO RESEARCH AWARDS

(Cultural Relations and Liaison with Universities)

NATO Fellowship Programme

Aim: The Fellowship Programme promotes study and research leading to publication on aspects relevant to the North Atlantic Alliance.

Conditions: Candidates are selected on the basis of their special aptitude and experience for carrying through a major project of research. They must be nationals of a member state i.e. Belgium, Canada, Denmark, France, Federal Republic of Germany, Greece, Iceland, Italy, Luxembourg, Netherlands, Norway, Portugal, Spain, Turkey, United Kingdom and United States.

The following research subjects areas were defined as appropriate for Fellowships in 1988/89:

International and external problems arising for Western security;

Public perceptions of the Atlantic Alliance and of Soviet threat;

In the context of Article 2 of the Washington Treaty, analysis of the Alliance's role in the development of more stable, peaceful, and friendly international relations;

The European contribution to NATO;

NATO strategy and emerging technologies.

Awards; 180,000 Belgium francs (or the equivalent currency for each member state) to each Fellow. Additional travel costs within the NATO areas are granted. (Awards therefore are within the £2,000–£3,000 range.) Some 20–25 fellowships are awarded annually.

Applications: Forms are obtainable from designated national authorites. For the UK this is the British Council, 65 Davies Street, London W1Y 2AA (01-499 8011).

Regardless of present residence, applicants should submit their applications to the appropriate authority of the country of which they are a national no later than mid December. Awards are published the following April.

Information available for applicants: An information brochure.

For further information contact: Dr Fernand Welter, NATO Information Service, Cultural Relations and Liaison with Universities, 1110 Brussels, Belgium (010 322-241 00 40/44 00/44 90); or the British Council at the above address.

NATO Institutional Research Fellowships

Aims: The NATO Institutional Research Fellowships stimulate collaboration between relevant university departments or recognised Centres of Strategic and International Studies by supporting research projects on current topics of interest to the Atlantic Alliance involving such departments or Centres.

Applicants must be qualified academic institutions of a member state of NATO i.e. competent university departments, strategic study centres or research teams headed by experts of international standing.

Awards: 200,000 Belgian francs plus transport costs.

Applications: Forms are obtainable from the British Council (*see address above*) and should be returned no later than mid December.

Further information for applicants: Information brochure.

NATO INTERNATIONAL SCIENTIFIC EXCHANGE PROGRAMMES

Aims: The Science Programme, established in 1958, aims to enhance the scientific and technological capabilities of the Alliance through a variety of activities aimed at promoting international scientific co-operation in a wide range of disciplines.

Unlike most international scientific programmes, which are institution or project oriented, the NATO International Scientific Exchange Programmes are focused on individual scientists; they promote collaboration through the international mobility of scientists.

Although support is most often provided to the university sector, projects with an industrial interest are also encouraged in an effort to further co-operation across both national boundaries and research sectors.

Contact: NATO Scientific Affairs Division, B-1110 Brussels, Belgium. (010 322-241 00 40)

UK Sources

Advanced Study Institutes (ASIs)

Aims: To disseminate advanced knowledge not yet in university curricula and foster international scientific contacts through high-level teaching course. Each course is for two weeks, and the level is post-doctoral; lecturer-student ratio is about 1:6 with a participation of 70–100 scientists of different nationalities.

Awards: Travel and living costs of lecturers; part of travel and living costs of students; part of organisational expenses. About 60 awards are made each year.

Applications: Forms are available from NATO Scientific Affairs Division. Deadlines mid January, April and September for meetings to be held the following year.

Advanced Research Workshops (ARWs)

Aims: To assess the state-of-the-art in a given scientific area and to formulate recommendations for future research. Working meetings are held for three to five days for 30–50 prominent experts in their subjects, from NATO and other countries. Participation is usually by invitation only.

Awards: Travel and living costs of main speakers; part of travel and living costs of other participants; part of organisational expenses. About 50 awards are made each year.

Applications: Forms from NATO Scientific Affairs Division. Deadlines – mid January, April and September for meetings to be held at least nine months after the deadline.

Collaborative Research Grants (CRGs)

Aims: To stimulate collaboration between laboratories in different countries and thus enhance the effectiveness of research. Assistance is provided for international travel and living expenses of members of research teams collaborating on a joint research project. Funding is for reciprocal visits abroad of one to four weeks. Awards are for one year extending to two, with the possibility of up to two renewals.

Awards: International travel and living expenses abroad for members of research teams. About 400 awards are made each year plus some 150 renewals.

Applications: from NATO Scientific Affairs Division. Deadlines – 31st March, 15th August, 30th November; decisions about three months later.

Special Programmes

Aims: To concentrate effort and support for a limited period of five years on a few emerging areas of science or those undergoing rapid change. Examples of activities sponsored: Advanced Research Workshops, Advance Study Institutes, Collaborative Research Grants, research and lecture visits, short duration fellowships, special initiatives.

Applications: On special forms to NATO Scientific Affairs Division.

NATO Science Fellowship Programme

Aims: The intention is to stimulate the international exchange at postgraduate and postdoctoral level between NATO countries. NATO fellowships cover not only science and technology but also medical, agricultural and environmental sciences, industrial psychology and sociology.

Applications: An information brochure is available. Application forms for NATO Science Fellowships are available from and should be returned by the 31st December to: Science and Engineering Research Council (SERC), Fellowship Section, Polaris House, PO Box 18, North Star Avenue, Swindon SN2 1ET (0793-26222 x 2253).

YOUTH EXCHANGE CENTRE (see also Part I – Citizen Diplomacy, Central Bureau for Educational Visits and Exchanges)

Seymour Mews House, Seymour Mews, London W1H 9PE (01-486 5101).

Correspondents: Gordon Blakely and David Evans, Co-Directors.

Annual grants total: about £800,000.

Annual number of grants: about 750 (excluding the Commonwealth Youth Exchange Council).

Policy and practice: The Centre gives grants to support continuing and constructive links between British youth groups and young people in another country. The aim is to foster better understanding and establish firm contact with a partner community. Young people without the opportunity for international experience are the main target group.

Grants are considered for two way, reciprocally arranged projects with Western and Eastern Europe, the USA and Pakistan. (Programmes for other Commonwealth countries are arranged by the Commonwealth Youth Exchange Council which has a separate entry. The CYEC is, however, supported financially by the Youth Exchange Centre.) The YEC is interested to learn of exchanges taking place elsewhere. In very exceptional circumstances it may help and support an innovative exchange as a pilot project. The Centre cannot underwrite the full cost of an exchange. Support is given to the round-trip travel costs and the hosting costs in Britain. Typical travel grants cover about one third of the costs. There is increasing competition for the limited funds available and priority is given to the development of new exchanges or to innovatory projects.

Presentation of applications: Application forms are available and must be submitted at least 12 weeks before a visit is scheduled. They are considered by Regional Grants Committees which meet between October and June.

Information available for applicants: Information leaflet (also listing the kind of exchanges that are not considered).

2. North American sources

Introductory note

There are a large number of US foundations, and one based in Canada, which give to 'peace' or which have peace and international relations as part of their policy or programme. The amount of money available from these foundations is colossal in relation to the much more limited support for this sector by UK foundations.

The reasons for this are various. Firstly, most UK foundations are older than their US counterparts, and their objects and policies reflect an earlier age when peace issues were less to the fore. Secondly, many US foundations see the promotion of peace as an important issue for them to be involved in. This is not the case in the UK, where the number of large trusts with a commitment to peace and security as part of their work can be counted on one hand. Thirdly, charity law in the UK has frightened people away from supporting peace initiatives, both because of what the Charity Commission recognises as being charitable and because many of the trusts see peace as a political minefield, rather than a genuinely charitable activity.

But just because there are large funds available in North America and a scarcity in the UK, it does not follow that UK-based organisations should be targeting their fund-raising across the Atlantic. There are a number of hurdles to be overcome, if any money is to be obtained:

1. The US interest in peace is markedly different from the UK's. There is a stong interest in Western Hemispheral issues, such as the situation in Central America. There is a more emphatic anti-Communist strand in the America viewpoint; a US book on ethical investment even lists trade with the Eastern Bloc as one of the ethical issues on which to rule out investing in a company, whereas in the UK such enterprise would be widely applauded. Geographically, Western Europe abuts Eastern Europe, and this proximity makes the issues of short and intermediate range nuclear weapons a more direct concern in Europe.
2. Whereas US foundations wanting to grant-aid overseas might be prepared to devote some of their funds to third world causes, they are less likely to want to 'invest' in the UK.
3. The US tax laws normally inhibit many US charities from making grants to external organisations which do not have tax-exempt status with the Internal Revenue Service. This means that an intermediary agency with US-exempt status might have to be used as a channel for the grants.

But this does not make it impossible to fund-raise in the US. It simply means that some thought has to be given to the sorts of activity or project in which US foundations might be interested and the particular foundation be approached.

Generally speaking any of the following criteria could make a grant more likely.

1. The organisation or project is of world-standing.
2. The work being funded is of special interest in the US (e.g. strategic issues which particularly concern the US).
3. The work for which funding is sought is to take place in the US (e.g. US-Europe research, attendance at conferences).
4. The work for which funding is sought will involve US agencies (e.g. an international conference or seminar).
5. The project is a joint project being undertaken

with a US agency, and the US agency becomes responsible for securing the funding from US sources.

Many UK organisations have been successful in obtaining grants from US foundations, including some quite small agencies and initiatives. So it is possible.

In the following listings we give information on those US foundations which give substantially in the area of peace and international relations, and we note any UK grants made by the foundation in the latest year for which accounts were available. This information has been gleaned from the directories of charities at the Foundation Centre, the *'Grant Seekers Guide'* produced by the National Network of Grantmakers, *'Search for Security'*, a specialist guide to peace funding produced by the now-defunct Forum Institute, and other sources. These were then followed up by a search of the Internal Revenue Service returns made by the foundations, in which it is mandatory to list grant beneficiaries and which, unlike in the UK where such information is confidential, must be publicly filed.

We have used our own judgement in deciding whether to include or omit a particular foundation, the main criteria being the amounts of the grants budget devoted to peace or international relations and whether the prime concern of the foundation is this area of work. Within the foundations listed, all political standpoints are supported from left-radical community initiatives through to hawkish think-tanks attempting to affect US policy formation.

List of contents

Arca Foundation
Ark Foundation
Bydale Foundation
Carnegie Corporation of New York
Carthage Foundation
Compton Foundation
C S Fund
Donner Canadian Foundation
Ford Foundation
General Service Foundation
German Marshall Fund of the United States
Joyce Mertz-Gilmore Foundation
Glickenhaus Foundation
Harry Frank Guggenheim Foundation
John Simon Guggenheim Memorial Foundation
George Gund Foundation
William and Flora Hewlett Foundation
HKH Foundation
W. Alton Jones Foundation, Inc
Henry P. Kendall Foundation
Max and Anna Levinson Foundation
Henry Luce Foundation
John D. and Catherine T. MacArthur Foundation
Andrew W. Mellon Foundation
Ruth Mott Fund
Stewart R. Mott and Associates/Stewart R. Mott Charitable Trust
A. J. Muste Memorial Institute
New Land Foundation, Inc
New World Foundation
North Shore Unitarian Univeralist Veatch Program
John M. Olin Foundation
Albert Parvin Foundation
Pew Charitable Trusts
Ploughshares Fund
Public Welfare Foundation
Smith Richardson Foundation
Rockefeller Brothers Fund
Rockefeller Family Fund
Rockefeller Foundation
Samuel Rubin Foundation
Sarah Scaife Foundation
Scherman Foundation
Florence and John Schumann Foundation
Sequoia Foundation
Alfred P. Sloan Foundation
Starr Foundation
Sunflower Foundation
Threshold Foundation
Tides Foundation
Topsfield Foundation
United States Institute of Peace
Weyerhauser Foundation, Inc
Winston Foundation For World Peace
Youth Project

North American Sources

ARCA FOUNDATION

1425 21st Street, NW, Washington, DC 20036, USA (202-822 9193).

Correspondent: Margery Tabankin, Executive Director.

Annual grants total: $698,500 in 1985.

Grant range: $5,000–$30,000.

Policy and practice: The Arca Foundation was established in 1952 'to help promote the well being of mankind throughout the world'. It now gives grants primarily to organisations concerned with US foreign policy applications in Central America. The Foundation also gives to organisations concerned with public information, issues in South Africa, and civil liberties and justice. Support is given for operating budgets, seed money, technical assistance, publications, conferences and seminars.

There are no geographical limitations but grants are not made to individuals.

Grants made in 1985 included the following:

Central America:
Foreign Policy Education Fund, Washington, DC, to support Americans for Peace in the Americas — $20,000

Indian Law Resource Center, Washington, DC, to assist Nicaraguan Indian efforts to negotiate a peace settlement — $7,500

South Africa:
Center for Development Policy, Washington, DC, to support educational work with US opinion leaders regarding apartheid — $25,000

Public interest/other:
Pro Peace, Inc, Los Angeles — $10,000

Parliamentarians for World Order Conference Fund, New York — $10,000

Five Continent Peace Initiative

Presentation of applications: Grant applications should be made by letter and include a two or three page project summary with a budget. More detailed proposals are requested if the application passes the screening process. These should be returned by mid-March or mid-September.

Information available for applicants: Annual report.

ARK FOUNDATION

250 Lafayette Circle, Suite 301, Lafayette, CA 94549, USA (415-283 7920).

Correspondent: Linda Lazare, Senior Associate.

Annual grants total: $400,000 in 1986.

Grant range: $100–$10,000.

Policy and practice: The Ark Foundation primarily 'supports projects that will have a positive impact on US relations with the Soviet Union and other countries with which we currently have conflicts'.

Through its operating organisation, Ark Communications Institute (ACI), a variety of such programmes are being developed. These projects focus on the use of creative initiative by individuals to make a difference in global issues.

The expanding agenda of ACI has necessitated a reduction in the number of grants made to outside organisations.

'Within the framework of global communications and relations, ACI look for projects that demonstrate creativity and originality, significance, leverage, identifiable applications and sound management.'

Grants made in 1986 included the following examples:

Pepperdine University, American/Russian Writers' Conference — $20,000

Parliamentarians Global Action — $5,000

Nuclear Weapons Freeze Campaign — $1,000

Foundation for the Arts of Peace — $5,000

Earth Trust, US/Soviet Film Initiative — $5,000

Presentation of applications: Monthly board meetings review grants.

Information available for applicants: Guidelines for project selection.

BYDALE FOUNDATION

500 Fifth Avenue, New York, NY 10110, USA (212-719 9393).

Correspondent: Milton D. Solomon, Vice President.

Annual grants total: $605,750 in 1986.

Grant range: $5,000–$15,000.

Policy and practice: The Foundation supports a wide range of programmes and projects with the intention of increasing international understanding, improving higher education, and enhancing public policy research.

Grants made in 1986 included the following examples:

Parliamentarians for World Order	$15,000
American Committee on US/Soviet Relations	$15,000
World Policy Institute	$10,000
Federation of American Scientists	$10,000

Presentation of applications: Deadlines May 1st and November 1st. Scholarships, fellowships and grants to individuals are not awarded.

CARNEGIE CORPORATION OF NEW YORK

437 Madison Avenue, New York, NY 10022, USA (212-371 3200).

Correspondent: Frederic A. Mosher, Program Chair, Avoiding Nuclear War.

Annual grants total: $37.6 million in 1986/87.

Grant range: $4,800–$1.5 million.

Policy and practice: The programme concerned with the avoidance of nuclear war began in 1983 and emphasises: support of independent scholarship to develop new ideas for decreasing the chances of nuclear war; relating these ideas to the concerns of policymakers; serious educational efforts using the results of this work to build broad non-partisan understanding of these ideas, and efforts to improve the US/Soviet relationship or manage it less dangerously.

The first phrase of the Corporation's programme has involved the negotiation of a small number of substantial grants to universities or institutions with very strong, multi-disciplinary programmes concerned with the study of international security, arms control, the Soviet Union, and US/Soviet relations. The Corporation does not anticipate making many more such general support grants, if any. It will continue to support research and analysis of the avoidance of nuclear war and which because of their complexity or technical difficulty require attention by the most competent and credible independent experts and institutions. It will support particular mechanisms designed to link scholarly work to the concerns of policymakers. In its second phase, the programme hopes to find ways to support more effective public education on these issues. It does not, however, at this point expect to support work on elementary, secondary, or undergraduate instruction.

As a matter of charter policy, in this programme the Corporation is not likely to provide direct support for institutions in the United Kingdom. In a few instances it has supported the US end of a collaboration with overseas institutions.

Grants in 1986/87 included the following examples:

Nuclear Control Institute	$105,000
Parliamentarians for World Order Conference Fund, towards public education in the United States about the worldwide implications of the Arms Race	$125,000
Pugwash Conference on Science and World Affairs, towards an international workshop on the prevention of accidental nuclear war	$25,000

Presentation of applications: Applications are accepted throughout the year.

CARTHAGE FOUNDATION

PO Box 268, 25 William Penn Place, Pittsburgh, PA 15230, USA (412-392 2900).

Correspondent: Richard M. Larry, Treasurer.

Annual grants total: $2.5 million in 1986.

Grant range: $5,000–$125,000.

Policy and practice: The Carthage Foundation confines most of its grant awards to programmes that will address public policy questions concerned with national and international issues. It provides either general operating support or specific project grants for a range of activities from seminars to publications.

The Foundations does not support individuals, construction or endowment funds. There are no geographical restrictions.

Grants made in 1986 included the following examples:

Committee on the Present Danger	$75,000
European American Institute for Security Research	$15,000
Institute for Foreign Policy Analysis	$25,000
United States Global Strategy Council	$50,000

Presentation of applications: Requests may be submitted at any time and will be acted on as quickly as possible. Initial enquiries should be in letter form and have the approval of the organisation's Board of Directors. They are normally considered at meetings in the first and fourth quarters of each year.

COMPTON FOUNDATION

10 Hanover Square, New York, NY 10005, USA (212-510 5040).

Correspondent: James R. Compton, President.

Annual grants total: $1.6 million in 1985.

North American Sources

Grant range: $25–$125,000.

Policy and practice: The Foundation's priorities include global-human survival, education, social welfare and social justice, culture and the arts, and religion. Proposals related to global survival receive the greatest portion of funding. It supports research and education to promote greater knowledge and understanding of global problems that threaten human survival and of long-term trends. These problems include nuclear armaments and other aspects of national security; extreme contrasts in wealth in rich and poor countries; and assaults on human rights everywhere in the world. The Foundation makes no grants to individuals.

Preference is given to research by highly qualified individuals within university programmes. The objective is to provide a reliable factual and analytical base and help guide private and public decision making on issues. The Foundation supports selected voluntary organisations working in these fields.

Grants in 1984 included the following examples:

Greenpeace, USA	$3,000
Foundation for the Arts of Peace	$11,000
Institute for East/West Security Studies	$1,000
Physicians for Social Responsibility	$2,700
Union of Concerned Scientists	$10,000
Scientists Institute for Public Information Nuclear Winter Project	$10,000
Institute for the Study of World Politics for Fellowships and Special Projects	$125,000

Presentation of applications: Applications are accepted throughout the year.

C S FUND

469 Bohemian Highway, Freestone, CA 95472, USA (707-829 5444).

Correspondent: Marty Teitel, Executive Director.

Annual grants total: $1.2 million in 1986.

Grant range: $1,000–$50,000.

Policy and practice: The aim of C S Fund is 'to challenge and change the practices and beliefs which justify and shape the peril we collectively face'. The Fund addresses weapons escalation, political repression, contamination of the planet, alteration of the Earth's genetic pool, efforts to reduce the free exchange of ideas and open debate, and limitations on institutional responsibility. The Fund challenges the beliefs that: security is rooted in military strength; nuclear war could be limited and won; the future should be the servant of the present; and that the security of one group can be legitimately subordinated to another.

The Fund supports organisations that further these aims, and utilise public education, research and legal action, as well as other approaches. Projects should demonstrate a national and international impact. The C S Fund does not support individuals, endowments, capital ventures, emergency requests or film or video projects.

Grants in 1986 included the following examples:

SANE Education Fund	$25,000
Institute for Space and Security Studies	$10,000
Institute for Defence and Disarmament Studies	$25,000
International Centre for Development Policy	$25,000

Presentation of applications: The deadlines are January 15th, May 15th or September 15th. A brief proposal of 500 words or less should be submitted. Applicants are notified of the Board's decision.

Information available for applicants: Brochure describing application goals and guidelines.

DONNER CANADIAN FOUNDATION

PO Box 122, Toronto Dominion Centre, Toronto, Ontario M5K 1H1, Canada (416-869 1091).

Correspondent: D. S. Rickerd, President.

Annual grants total: C$2.44 million in 1986.

Grant range: C$95,000–C$325,000.

Policy and practice: The Foundation operates nationally through grants to institutions in the fields of law reform and correction in Canada, international affairs, Canada's North, and oceans and inland waters.

Conflict resolution is one of the four target areas of funding in the field of international affairs. Recent grants have included:

'Meeting the Challenge of International Terrorism' Centre for Conflict Studies, University of New Brunswick	c$95,000
'South Asia: Ontario' Centre for South Asian Studies, University of Toronto	c$325,000
'International Peacekeeping' Centre for International and Strategic Studies and the International Peace Academy, York University, Toronto	c$25,000

Presentation of applications: A preliminary letter with basic details is advised. The Board meets three times a year for which complete information is needed at least eight weeks in advance.

Further information for applicants: Annual Report.

FORD FOUNDATION

320 East 43rd Street, New York, NY 10017, USA (212-573 5000).

Correspondent: Enid Schoettle, Director.

Annual grants total: $199.05 million in 1987; $20.9 million (11%) for international affairs.

Grant range: $5,000–$1.7 million.

Policy and practice: The Ford Foundation seeks to identify and contribute to the solution of problems of national or international importance. It works primarily through grants for experimental/ demonstration and developmental efforts that promise to produce significant advances in various fields.

The Foundation operates six programme areas: urban poverty; rural poverty and resources; human rights; governance and public policy; education and culture; and international affairs. Within the area of international affairs, the Foundation encourages informal analysis and public debate on major global issues. Grants are made for research, training, policy analysis, and dissemination of information in seven major topic areas: the international refugee and migrant issue; international peace and security; international economics and development; US foreign policy; international relations; international law and organisations; neglected fields of foreign area studies.

The Foundation's aim in the international peace and security category is to stimulate (in the US and abroad) consideration of issues critical to the maintenance of international security and the peaceful resolution of disputes. Traditionally, Ford has provided support to major universities and research institutions for research and training on a broad range of security and arms control issues such as: the ethical and moral dimensions of nuclear weapons policies and military competition; US defence policies; Soviet security policies and East-West relations; arms control; the security of developing countries; and conventional military forces and doctrines, etc. Support also is given for studies and workshops on specific policy issues such as US defence manpower policies, the proliferation of nuclear weapons and various aspects of European security, and the development of high school curricula materials on national security in the nuclear age. The international economics and development category supports research on three major themes: how nations cope with international economic forces; the political dimensions of economic relations; and the uncertain future of the international economic system.

The central aim of the Foundation's work in US foreign policy is to increase understanding of the policy-making process and recommend ways of improving it. It includes a post-doctoral fellowship programme for scholars from both the US and abroad.

The Foundation's work in the fields of international relations and international studies focuses on the foreign policies of developing countries and neglected fields of foreign area studies in the United States and the Third World.

Grants to individuals are awarded for graduate fellowship usually either through publicly announced competitions or on the basis of nominations from universities and other institutions.

Grants in 1986 included the following examples:

Rural poverty and resources
Oxfam, England $20,000

Access and equity
World University Service, London $20,000

Peace and Security
Brookings Institution, Washington $130,000
Chulalongkorn University, Thailand $33,000
French Institute of International Relations $137,000
International Peace Research Association, Brazil $22,700
Natural Resources Defence Council $200,000
Research Institute for Peace and Security, Japan $20,000
Government of Thailand, Ministry of Foreign Affairs $17,000
University of Uppsala, Sweden $5,500

US Foreign Policy
Council on Foreign Relations, New York $21,870
Fund for Peace, New York $50,000

International Relations
Arab Thought Forum, Jordan $47,000
Chulalongkorn University, Thailand $3,000
Japan Center for International Exchange $20,000
University of Maryland $5,000

International Studies
Lingnan College, Hong Kong $13,000
University of Zimbabwe $32,000

In 1984 grants in international relations included the following:

University of Aberdeen, Centre for Defence Studies $12,500

North American Sources

University of Edinburgh, Defence Studies	$124,700
University of Lancaster	$113,958
University of Southampton	$225,600

Presentation of applications: Applications are considered throughout the year. There are no forms. Applicants are advised to send a brief proposal first. Notice is usually sent within one month as to whether it falls within the Foundation's programme interests and budgetary limitations.

Information available for applicants: Annual Report; 'Current Interests'; 'The Letter', bi-monthly.

GENERAL SERVICE FOUNDATION

1445 Pearl Street, PO Box 4659, Boulder, Colorado 80306, USA (303-447 9541).

Correspondent: R. W. Musser, President.

Annual grants total: $1.2 million in 1986.

Policy and practice: The Foundation's major areas of interest are population, resources, and non-military aspects of international peace. In the field of international peace it makes contributions only in the following areas:

  Research and education on US International Relations that would contribute to international peace;
  International working groups concerned with increasing understanding and co-operation;
  Policy and programme analysis leading to development of alternatives to war;
  Research and education on the relationships between economic, environmental and political development and international peace.

Contributions are made to organisations tax-exempt under US laws. The Foundation prefers projects and/or programmes which are new, innovative, demonstrational, and/or research in nature.

In general, contributions are not made to operating budgets, nor to annual campaigns of established organisations. Nor does the Foundation ordinarily contribute to capital (physical plant, equipment, endowment), to individuals, nor to relief.

Grants in 1986 included the following examples:

International Peace Research Association	$20,000
Institute for East/West Security Studies, 1987 Alumni Conference in Talloires, France	$25,000
Open Space Institute, Centre on the Consequences of Nuclear War	$21,500
Parliamentarians Global Action, The Five Continent Peace Initiative	$40,000

Presentation of applications: Proposals should be submitted at least two months before the Board meetings in April and November. A brief statement regarding the purpose for which funds will be used and a one or two page summary of the project or programme focusing on the solution to the problem, should be included.

Further information for applicants: Annual Report; application guidelines.

GERMAN MARSHALL FUND OF THE UNITED STATES

11 Dupont Circle, NW, Suite 900, Washington, DC 20036, USA (202-745 3950).

Correspondent: Frank E. Loy, President.

European Address: Ahrstrasse 58, 5300 Bonn 2, West Germany (0228-37 66 71).

Correspondent: David Kramer, Representative for Europe.

Annual grants total: $2.6 million in 1985/86.

Grant range: $450–$910,000.

Policy and practice: The Fund was founded in 1972 by a gift from the Federal Republic of Germany in appreciation of American post-war recovery assistance, to assist in the understanding and resolution of certain contemporary and emerging problems common to industrial societies. The German gift amounted to DM 147 million and was to be transferred in 15 annual instalments (extended in 1986 for a further 10 years). The American Board of Trustees has full discretion in the administration of the Fund.

The Fund operates both nationally and internationally in the fields of economics, social welfare, international relations and environmental conservation, through research, grants to institutions and individuals and fellowships. Major areas of study are:

  International and European-American Programme (Economic interdependence, Euopean-American relations);
  Comparative Domestic Programme (Employment, Environment, Immigration);
  Scholarly Support Programme (Fellowship programme, Scholarly networks);
  Media Programme;
  Special German Programme.

Programmes must have US and European components, preferably Western European. No support is available for work relating to arms control or disarmament, or for graduate or undergraduate studies.

Support is awarded in the form of continuing support, seed money, employee matching gifts, fellowships, internships, special projects, publications, conferences and seminars, exchange programmes and grants to individuals. Grants to individuals include short-term awards for US-European travel for conferences in the Fund's field of interest.

Grants in 1986 included the following examples:

George Mason University, Centre for Conflict Resolution	$12,500
United Nation Association of USA	$15,000
Chicago Council on Foreign Relations for European Representation at Atlantic Conference	$10,000

Also grants to individuals

Presentation of applications: The final proposal should be made on a fund application form. The deadline for fellowships is November 15th with their notification in March. Other deadlines vary. Board meetings are held in February, May and October.

Further information for applicants: Programme policy statement, application guidelines, multi-year report newsletter, information brochure.

JOYCE MERTZ-GILMORE FOUNDATION

218 East 18th Street, New York, NY 10003, USA (212-475 1137).

Correspondent: Robert Crane, Vice President, Program.

Annual grants total: $3.074 million in 1987.

Grant range: $2,500–$35,000.

Policy and practice: The Foundation is interested in programmes which increase participation in and expand the scope of the national security dialogue, and alter the context of the confrontation between the United States and the Soviet Union.

Specifically, the Foundation is interested in programmes which '1) offer alternative ways to conceptualize defense and security issues so as to improve the possibility for nuclear disarmament and generally lessen the possibility of war 2) explore bilateral and multilateral interactions that might increase the prospects for security between and among nations and 3) broaden public participation in the defense and security dialogue in the United States in order to move it beyond its military focus.'

North American Sources

Grants in 1987 included the following examples:

Institute for Defense and Disarmament Studies	$35,000
Search for Common Ground	$10,000
Center for Defense Information	$10,000
Committee for National Security	$10,000
Nuclear Times	$10,000

Presentation of applications: Applicants must submit an application form which is available upon request. Usually proposals received from August through January will be considered by the Board of Directors at their spring meetings; proposals received from February through July will be considered at the fall meetings.

GLICKENHAUS FOUNDATION

Six East – 43rd Street, NY 10017, USA.

Correspondent: Nancy G. Pier, President.

Annual grants total: $154,755 in 1985.

Grant range: $50–$25,000.

Policy and practice: Grants are made primarily for social welfare, health services and international peace organisations.

HARRY FRANK GUGGENHEIM FOUNDATION

527 Madison Avenue, New York, NY 10022, USA.

Correspondent: Karen Colvard, Programme Officer.

Annual grants total: £1.1 million in 1985/86.

Grant range: $15,000–$35,000.

Policy and practice: The Foundation administers an international, interdisciplinary programme of scientific research and study concerning human social problems related to dominance, aggression, violence. 'It has supported research into the neurobiological correlates of aggressive events, models of aggression and violence as social tactics, cross-cultural ethnological studies of aggression and social heirarchy, and other investigations which bear relation to warfare and conflict. The Foundation considers projects from any discipline designed to reveal basic physiological mechanisms to: elucidate fundamental psychological processes; to analyse critical social interrelations; and formulate and test unifying theories of those mechanisms, processes and interrelations.'

North American Sources

Grants are made to individuals for individual projects but not to institutions for institutional programmes. Grants are available for salaries, support staff, equipment, field work, or any other items necessary for the successful completion of a project. The Foundation does not supply funds for general support, institutional overheads, or meetings and conferences. All awards are for one-year terms initially.

Grants made in 1985/86 included the following examples:

Clayton Robarchek, Wichata State University, 'A comparative study of the psychological, sociocultural and ecological contexts of primitive warfare'	$22,543
J. L. P. Thompson, Columbia University, 'Origins of the western concept of legitimate trickery in warfare and international law'	$22,600
Robert Axelrod, University of Michigan, 'Theories of co-operative behaviour', computer models of competition and co-operation	$28,116
Joseba Zulaika, Universidad del Pais Vasco, 'The cultural roots of political terrorism: ritual models of causation'	$22,285

Presentation of applications: Applicants must submit six copies of the application on the Foundation's form. Deadlines are August 1st and February 1st for decisions in December and June respectively.

JOHN SIMON GUGGENHEIM MEMORIAL FOUNDATION

90 Park Avenue, New York, NY 10016, USA
(212-687 4470).

Correspondent: G. Thomas Tanselle, Vice President.

Annual grants total: $7 million in 1987.

Policy and practice: The Foundation aims to improve the quality of education and the practice of the arts and professions; to foster research; and to provide for the cause of better international understanding. It operates nationally and internationally in all fields of science, the humanities and the creative arts. Fellowships are open to citizens and permanent residents, ordinarily between 30 and 45 years of age, of the United States and Canada, of all the other American States, the Caribbean, the Philippines and the French, Dutch and British possessions in the Western hemisphere.

In 1987, the Foundation awarded 273 United States and Canadian Fellowships, two of which were in the field of peace/international relations:

Professor of Political Science and the Film Studies, University of Rochester: Deterrence, stability, and the potential obsolescence of major war.

Professor of International Relations and Political Science and Director, Institute and Transnational Studies, University of Southern California; Turbulence in world politics.

Presentation of applications: Application forms are available from the Foundation on request.

Further information for applicants: Annual Report.

GEORGE GUND FOUNDATION

One Erieview Plaza, Cleveland, Ohio 44114-1773
(216-241 3114).

Correspondent: Henry C. Doll, Acting Executive Director.

Annual grants total: $7.2 million in 1986.

Grant range: $800–$250,000.

Policy and practice: In 1981 the Gund Foundation created a special category within its education programme area for organisations dedicated to the 'pursuit of peace'. Within this category consideration is given to proposals for public education, multi-disciplinary efforts which can lead to a better understanding of the issues, and for policy alternatives which encourage peaceful international relationships and reduce the possibility of armed conflict and nuclear war. Special emphasis is placed on arms control, US-Soviet relations, and the growing importance of global interdependence in advancing world order. Grants for special programmes and new initiatives are given highest priority. The Foundation gives primarily in north eastern Ohio.

Grants made in recent years included the following:

In 1986	
Worldwatch Institute	$60,000
Conflict Analysis Centre	$3,000
In 1985	
International Physicians for the Prevention of Nuclear War	£10,000
Nuclear Control Institute	$10,000

Presentation of applications: Deadlines are 15th of January, April, August and October. There are no application forms.

North American Sources

WILLIAM AND FLORA HEWLETT FOUNDATION

525 Middlefield Road, Suite 200, Menlo Park, CA 94025-3495, USA (415-329 1070).

Correspondent: Roger W. Heyns, President.

Annual grants total: $26.3 million in 1986.

Grant range: $15,000–£2 million.

Policy and practice: The Hewlett Foundation has concentrated its resources on activities in the performing arts; education, particularly at the university and college levels; population issues; environmental concerns; and, more recently, conflict resolution. It also makes grants to a few especially interesting and important projects that are consistent with the broad purpose of the Foundation but fall outside its establishment programme. Grants to projects dealing with arms control/national security have been awarded in this category. There is no particular budget amount set aside for these grants, as they are all special projects, and in 1986 only one new grant was made in this area.

Further grants in the field of peace/international relations were awarded under the conflict resolution and education programmes. The conflict resolution programme includes grants in three categories: i) theory development; ii) mediators and other practitioners of third-party intervention techniques; and iii) organisations that train, educate or promote conflict resolution techniques.

Grants made in 1986 included the following examples:

Special Projects: Arms Control/National Security
Cornell University, Crisis Stability and Nuclear War Project — $20,000
International Institute for Strategic Studies, London — $84,000
Stanford University, Arms Control and Disarmament Project — $150,000

Conflict Resolution
International Peace Academy — $50,000
University of Georgia, 3rd National Conference on Peacemaking and Conflict Resolution — $25,000

International Education
Stanford University, Center for Research in International Studies — $125,000
World Affairs Council of Northern California — $67,000

Presentation of applications: Grants are reviewed continuously for quarterly meetings. There is no fixed limit on grants but applicants should take into account other possible sources of funding. The Foundation will consider multi-year funding. Grants that directly or indirectly support political candidates or influence legislation are not eligible for support. A letter of inquiry addressed to the President should contain a brief statement of the applicant's need for funds and enough information to enable the staff to determine if the application warrants a full and formal proposal. Applicants who receive a favourable response to their inquiry will be invited to submit a formal proposal.

Information available for applicants: Basic policy brochure; annual report.

HKH FOUNDATION

33 Irving Place, 10th Floor, New York, NY 10003, USA.

Correspondent: Harriet Barlow, Advisor.

Annual grants total: $1.2 million in 1986.

Grant range: $5,000–$25,000.

Policy and practice: The Foundation funds in the following areas: reversing the arms race, civil liberties and environmental protection. The Foundation does not give grants to individuals.

Grants in 1985 included the following examples:

Nuclear Weapons Education Fund — $25,000
Americans for Peace in the Americas — $20,000
Fund for Peace — $20,000
Institution for Policy Studies — $25,000

Presentation of applications: The HKH Foundation does not review proposals on a competitive basis instead it consults with activists and researchers to formulate strategic plans for promoting work in these areas. It states, however, that it is interested in discussing 'its thinking and choices with anyone who cares to help us improve the effectiveness of HKH's part in our collective effort to achieve peace, environmental health and freedom of expression'.

W. ALTON JONES FOUNDATION, INC

433 Park Street, Charlottesville, Virginia 22901, USA. (804-295 2134).

Correspondent: R. Jeffrey Kelleher, Director.

Annual grants total: $7.97 million in 1986.

Grant range: $5,000–$212,000.

North American Sources

Policy and practice: The Foundation accepts applications for grants in two programmes according to the following guidelines:

The Sustainable Society Program, which seeks to keep the earth suitable for long-range habitation by preserving the earth's natural resource base; and

The Secure Society Program, The goal of the Foundation's Secure Society Program is to encourage the development of a world that is secure from the peril of nuclear war, without jeopardy to freedom and democracy. Only projects that bear directly on the risk of nuclear war are considered.

In recent years, the Foundation has funded projects falling into the following categories:

Public education through election debates, high school curriculum development, television programmes, lectures, books, films, and museum displays.

Journalist education through roundtables, seminars, expert referral services, journalism schools, newsletters, and bulletins.

Policy development to help government with practical proposals on such matters as long-term strategic policy, technological change, strategic defence, crisis communications, and nuclear proliferation and terrorism.

Expanding the information base through research on the composition of the world's nuclear forces; the biological effects of a nuclear exchange; the factors affecting human behaviour and decision making in a nuclear crisis; the risks and costs of the Strategic Defense Initiative; means of inhibiting nuclear proliferation; and the state of command, control, and communication facilities.

Educating decision makers through such measures as roundtables and seminars for congressmen.

Improving relations between the US and USSR through private exchanges and collaborative projects.

The Foundation does not make grants for building construction or renovation, scholarships, endowments, or directly to individuals or to conduit organisations that pass funds on to others. It usually gives for a specific project rather than for general support.

Grants in 1986 included the following examples:

International Institute for Strategic Studies	$150,000
American Committee on US-Soviet Relations	$75,000
International Council of Scientific Unions	$25,000
Peace Links	$25,000
Esalen Institute, Soviet-American Exchange Program	$25,000

Presentation of applications: There is no standard application form. A full proposal rather than an initial enquiry is preferred.

Information available for applicants: Annual Report; information sheet.

HENRY P. KENDALL FOUNDATION

One Boston Place, Boston, MA 02108, USA (617-723 8727).

Correspondent: Robert L. Allen, Vice-President.

Annual grants total: $2.2 million in 1985.

Grant range: $1,000–$115,000.

Policy and practice: The Kendall Foundation's primary concern is the overall welfare and vigour of the movements it serves: arms control and peace; defence of the natural environment and conservation of energy and resources.

The Foundation prefers grants to organisations that can create legislative, and/or regulative action. Towards this goal, the Foundation encourages research and publicity to influence public policy; grassroots efforts to improve local and national voter registration and voter education; and the education of elected and appointed officials.

Grants in 1985 included the following examples:

World Policy Institute Security Project	$20,000
Search for Common Ground	$6,500
Institute for Soviet American Relations	$5,000
Arms Control Association	$50,000
International Physicians for Prevention of Nuclear War	$45,000
Nuclear Weapons Education Fund	$20,000
Nuclear Psychology Program	$12,500
Lawyers' Alliance for Nuclear Arms Control	$15,000
Institute for Defence and Disarmament (Arms Control Register)	$5,000
Performing Artists for Nuclear Disarmament	$5,000

Presentation of applications: Applications should be one month before quarterly board meetings held in March, June, September and December.

MAX AND ANNA LEVINSON FOUNDATION

1318 Beacon St, Room 6, Brookline, Massachusetts 02146, USA (617-731 1602).

Correspondent: Sidney Shapiro, Executive Director.

Annual grants total: $327,838 in 1986.

Grant range: $1,000–$25,000.

Policy and practice: The Levinson Foundation aims to develop a more humane and rewarding society in which people have greater ability and opportunity to determine directions for the present and future. One of its major interests is the field of international security and nuclear issues. In this, as in its other fields of interest, the Foundation funds activities which promote social change and social justice either by developing the testing alternatives or by responsibly modifying existing systems, institutions, conditions, and attitudes that block promising innovation.

The Foundation does not generally consider proposals for support to individuals or travel or study or projects of primary local significance. It favours projects that cannot obtain traditional funding and that will benefit from small, short-term, start-up and matching grants.

Grants made in 1984 included the following examples:

Center for Education on Nuclear War, Inc	$10,000
Forum Institute	$7,000
Lawyers Alliance for Nuclear Arms Control	$10,000
Nuclear Times Inc	$1,500
Student/Teacher Organisation to Prevent Nuclear War	$10,000

Presentation of applications: Applications are considered in April and September each year but are welcome any time. A brief written proposal of no more than 5 pages is preferred.

Information available for applicants: General policy statement.

HENRY LUCE FOUNDATION INC,

111 West 50th Street, New York, NY 10020, USA (212-489 7700).

Correspondent: Robert E. Armstrong, Vice-President/Executive Director.

Annual grants total: $11.5 million in 1986.

Grant range: $500–$500,000.

Policy and practice: The Foundation was established in 1936 by Henry Robinson Luce in order to make grants to philanthropic organisations for projects in the broad areas of public affairs, higher education, the far East (with a particular emphasis on China) and theology.

It operates throughout the United States and the Far East in the fields of education, public affairs, religion, international relations and American art.

In 1985 the International Institute for Strategic Studies, London received a grant of $200,000 from the Foundation.

Presentation of applications: Applications may be submitted at any time by letter.

Information available for applicants: Annual report.

JOHN D. AND CATHERINE T. MACARTHUR FOUNDATION

140 South Dearborn, Suite 700, Chicago, IL 60603, USA (312-726 8000).

Correspondent: James M. Furman, Executive Vice-President.

Annual grants total: $120.93 million in 1986.

Grant range: $3,500–$750,000.

Policy and practice: The MacArthur Foundation's programme in International Peace and Security aims to strengthen, broaden and integrate research and training in the United States and elsewhere. The programme is intended to draw new people and new disciplines into analysis of security issues. In addition, it hopes to increase public understanding so that citizens can participate more intelligently in decisions about world affairs.

In support of these goals, the Foundation made grants in four major areas in 1986: exchanges and fellowships, grants to individuals for research and writing, international initiatives and collaborations, and public information initiatives.

In 1986, 103 new grants were authorised to institutions, organisations and individuals in the United States and twelve other nations, including Great Britain.

Examples of 1986 grants:

International Initiatives and Collaborations
$3.75 million were committed to fourteen institutions. These funds support programmes that train security experts and Third World leaders, examine the interaction between regional security issues in Europe and the Pacific and suggest alternative models for security and arms control.

North American Sources

Australian National University, Canberra, for Strategic and Defense Studies Centre (over 3 years)	$300,000
Canadian Centre for Arms Control and Disarmament, Ottawa, (over 3 years)	$150,000
Freie Universitat, Berlin, West Germany for the Institute for International Politics (over 3 years)	$300,000
International Institute for Strategic Studies, London, in support of a programme to train analysts from developing countries, to investigate changing security problems in the Third World institutions (over 3 years)	$360,000
Japan Center for International Exchange, Tokyo, in support of exchanges among Asian security analysts and for Center studies (over 3 years)	$150,000
King's College, Cambridge, in support of the interdisciplinary study group on security and scientific issues and the programme on social and political history of peace and conflict (over 3 years)	$150,000
King's College, London, for student support in the Department of War Studies, for a study of European-Japanese strategic relations since 1952, and for a history of the First World War as a formative influence on British policy (over 3 years)	$375,000
Peace Research Institute, Frankfurt (over three years)	$525,000
Royal Institute of International Affairs, London, in support of a project on alternative models for the future of European security and related activities (over 3 years)	$300,000
Stockholm International Peace Research Institute in support of a study to clarify the political, military and economic consequences for Europe and the United States of America forces in Europe (over 3 years)	$375,000
Tampere Peace Research Institute, Finland, in support of multilateral and interdisciplinary seminars to encourage networking among researchers from Europe and the US (over 3 years)	$150,000
World Commission on Environment and Development, Oslo	$250,000

Exchanges and Fellowships

Harvard University, Cambridge, Massachusetts, in support of two fellowships for journalists from Latin America, under the direction of the Nieman Foundation (over 3 years)	$150,000
Institute for East-West Security Studies, New York	$450,000
Institute of International Education, New York	$450,000
International Research and Exchange Board, New York, for Soviet and East European exchanges and the bi-national commissions (over 3 years)	$750,000
Overseas Development Council, Washington, DC, in support for the Council's Center for International Economic and Security Studies, and for support of two visiting fellows (over 2 years)	$200,000
World Peace Foundation, Boston, Massachusetts, in support of a study of inter-American collective security, in collaboration with specialists from Latin America (over 1 year)	$50,000

Public Information Initiatives

The Foundation supports projects in several broad categories which stimulate the growth of publications that address security issues; create public forums for discussion of the issues; enhance networking among public interest organisations; and support the study of peace and security issues in the context of public information and the development of public opinion. Seventeen new grants were given in 1986, totalling over $3.75 million including:

American Committee on US-Soviet Relations, Washington, DC	$350,000
Center for Communication, Inc, New York, in support of a 'space bridge' on the role of the media and public information campaigns in Soviet-American relations	$218,777
National Public Radio, Inc, Washington, DC, in support of radio coverage of defence and security policy issues (over 2 years)	$572,910
Nuclear Times, Washington, DC	$225,000
Public Agenda Foundation, New York (over 2 years)	$700,000
Student Pugwash, Washington, DC, in support of the development of regional chapters, networking, and the new careers project (over 3 years)	$300,000

Grants to individuals for research and writing

These grants are designed to encourage scholars, journalists, and other serious writers to explore the security implications of social, cultural, technical, and economic issues that have not previously been viewed as central to international security – and to take innovative approaches to traditional security concerns. Twenty two grants were awarded in 1986 including three to recipients outside the United States.

An-Na'Im, Abdullah Ahmed, University of California, 'Human Rights and International Relations in Islamic Law'	$40,000
Brigagao, Clovis, University of Estado, Rio de Janeiro, 'Brazil's Regional and International Project – A Security Assessment.'	$22,300
Bunn, George, Stanford University Law School 'US Insider's Account of the Negotiation of the Nuclear Non-Proliferation Treaty'	$50,000
Luckham, Robin, Australian National University, Canberra, 'Weapons and Mass Culture'	$50,000
Tetlock, Philip, University of California, 'Preventing Nuclear War: A Psychological Perspective'	$56,714
Zinser, Adolfo Aguilar, Centro De Investigacion Y Docencia Economica, Mexico City, 'Mexican Concept of National Security – A Crucial Dilemma.'	$54,000

Other grants: Grants totalling $813,000 were made to projects, institutions and organisations outside the main four programme areas.

Cornell University, New York	$37,500
Institute Soviet – American Relations, Washington	$25,000
Lawyers Alliance for Nuclear Arms Control	$25,000
University of Minnesota Foundation for the 'Prospects for Peacemaking: Rethinking National Security and Arms Control'	$40,000
World Affairs Council of Northern California	$40,000

Presentation of applications: There are no deadlines. Applicants should send a letter of no more than two pages.

Information available for applicants: Annual Report.

ANDREW W. MELLON FOUNDATION

140 East 62nd Street, New York, NY 10021, USA (212-838 8400).

Correspondent: J. Kellum Smith Jr, Vice-President and Secretary.

Annual grants total: $66.8 million in 1986.

Grant range: $15,000–$2.5 million.

Policy and practice: The Foundation operates nationally in selected areas of the humanities, cultural activities, higher education, medical and public health education and research, population, conservation and the environment, and public affairs. It makes few grants to non US organisations and no grants to individuals.

Recent grants include the following examples:

In 1985

International Institute for Strategic Studies, London	$450,000

In 1986

Brookings Institution	$375,000
National Academy of Sciences, Committee on International Security and Arms Control	$240,000

Information available for applicants: Annual Report.

RUTH MOTT FUND

1726 Genesee Towers, Flint, Michigan 48502, USA (313-232 3180).

Correspondent: Deborah E. Tuck, Executive Director.

Annual grants total: $1.3 million in 1986.

Grant range: $5,000–$10,000.

Policy and practice: The Fund makes grants in four programme areas: arts; environment; health promotion; and prevention of nuclear war. On the issue of nuclear war, the Fund has supported public education programmes which increase understanding of the problem's scientific complexity and bring together those who are already involved in this work to compound their effectiveness. The Fund does not rule out any area of activity legally acceptable for a private foundation. However, because it believes existing materials are sufficient, it does not encourage requests to fund film or video projects about the probable documented effects of nuclear war. The Fund does not support capital projects or endowments. Donations are limited to charitable organisations in the United States.

Grants in 1984 included the following examples:

International Physicians for the Prevention of Nuclear War	$10,000
Institute for Soviet-American Relations	$2,500
Institute for Space and Security Studies	$10,000

North American Sources

Nuclear-Times	$10,000
Peace Links	$5,000

Presentation of applications: Proposals are accepted throughout the year.

Information available for applicants: Multi-Year Report; application guidelines.

STEWART R. MOTT AND ASSOCIATES
STEWART R. MOTT CHARITABLE TRUST
SPECTEMUR AGENDO

122 Maryland Avenue, NE, Washington, DC 20002, USA (202-546 3732).

Correspondents: Ann Zill, Conrad Martin.

1133 Fifth Avenue, New York, New York 10028, USA (212-289 0006).

Correspondent: Debbie Landau.

Annual grants total: $529,800 in 1984.

Grant range: $1,000–$5,000.

Policy and practice: Together, the Stewart R. Mott Charitable Trust and the Stewart R Mott and Associates carry out the administrative responsibilities for Mr Mott's personal philanthropy. Grants are also made under the name of Spectemur Agendo. Mr Mott's primary interests are: peace, arms control, and foreign policy; family planning and population issues; and government reform and political education. His preference is to support activist projects rather than research-oriented activities, and projects that are national in scope, not local or regional.

Mr Mott supports about five new projects each year. Generally, he donates small amounts, often in the form of benefit tickets, gives 25 to 30 gifts exceeding $1,000 to organisations in which he has a little more interest, makes perhaps a dozen grants of between $5,000 and $125,000 and makes a few very large contributions to organisations with which he is extremely involved. Almost all grants are for general support.

Grants in recent years have included the following:

In 1984:

Amnesty International	$5,000
Conference on the Fate of the Earth	$3,000
Friends of the Earth Foundation	$3,000
International Association of Atomic Veterans	$1,000
Nuclear Times	$3,000
Oxford Research Group	$1,000
Parliamentarians for World Order	$3,000
Ploughshares Fund	$1,000

In 1985

Arms Control Association	$1,000
Albert Einstein Peace Prize Fund	$1,000
Nuclear Free America	$3,000
Oxford Research Group	$1,000
Peace Development Fund	$1,000

Presentation of applications: Throughout the year.

A. J. MUSTE MEMORIAL INSTITUTE

339 Lafayette Street, New York, New York 10012, USA (212-533 4335).

Correspondent: Murray Rosenblithe, Executive Director.

Annual grants and sponsorship total: $148,000 in 1987.

Grant range: $500–$2,500.

Sponsorship range: $142–$42,907.

Policy and practice: 'The A. J. Muste Memorial Institute has, as one of its programs, the funding and fiscal sponsorship of innovative and experimental projects which promote the principles and practice of non-violent social change. They must also be concerned with one or more of the issues to which A. J. Muste dedicated his life: peace and disarmament, social and economic justice, racial and sexual equality, and the labour movement.

The Institute makes a limited number of grants to international, national and local projects, giving priority to those with little chance of funding from more traditional sources and with small budgets. About 25 grants are made annually, ranging up to $2,500. The number of fiscal sponsorship varies, but there is no limit on either the number of sponsorees or the amount of directed funds accepted. Preference is given to new projects and groups over those already in operation for some time. The Institute does not make grants or sponsorships to academic projects or individuals. It does not generally accept proposals from organisations with annual budgets larger than $500,000 or for projects with budgets over $50,000. The Institute also will not accept a new request from a previously funded group for two years after a grant.'

Grants in 1987 included:

Campaign Against US Military Bases in the Philippines, New York	$1,000

International Alliance of Atomic Veterans, Arizona	$1,000
International Fellowship of Reconciliation, Holland	$1,500
Nicaragua Construction Brigades, New York	$1,000
Pax Christi/Canada	$8,000
Peace Museum, Chicago	$5,000
War Resisters International	$2,000
War Resisters League, New York	$1,000
War Resisters League, Connecticut	$2,500

Sponsorships in 1987 included:

Committee for International Nonviolence, Pennsylvania	$4,465
Greenham Women Against Cruise Missiles, New York	$995
War Resisters International	$2,014

Presentation of applications: Applicants should write or telephone the Institute before submitting a proposal and request information on application procedures. Proposals should be less than five pages. Deadlines for submitting grant requests vary from year to year. The board of directors meets approximately eight times a year and grant requests are considered at about five of these meetings.

Information available for applicants: Annual Report.

THE NEW-LAND FOUNDATION INC

200 Park Avenue, Suite 3014, New York, NY 10166, USA (212-867 5500).

Correspondent: Robert Wolf, President.

Annual grants total: $660,000 in 1987.

Grant range: $1,000–$50,000.

Policy and practice: The Foundation 'supports organisations and projects that have a national or international focus in the areas of: environmental protection, mental health, civil liberties, refugee issues, minority education, energy conservation, and arms control and peace. Within peace programmes, the Foundation sponsors a wide range of research projects, activist organisations, and efforts aimed at international co-operation. New-Land takes special interest in alternative security strategies.'

Grants in 1984 included the following examples:

Arms Control Computer Network	$15,000
Campaign for Peace and Democracy/East and West	$2,500

North American Sources

Institute for East-West Security Studies	$10,000
International Student Pugwash	$10,000
Peace Links: Women Against Nuclear War	$5,000
Princeton University Center for Energy and Environment Studies for the 'Finite Deterrance' project	$25,000

Presentation of applications: Applications must be by letter. Proposals are accepted throughout the year for board meetings in the spring and autumn.'

Information available for applicants: Guidelines.

NEW WORLD FOUNDATION

100 East 85th Street, New York, NY 10028, USA (212-249 1023).

Correspondent: Colin Greer, Acting President.

Annual grants total: $1.6 million in 1986.

Grant range: $250–$30,000.

Policy and practice: The Foundation attempts to be responsive to the needs and aspirations of neglected segments of society and to support programmes which have creative and innovative individuals working for them. One programme area is 'the relationship between peoples and nations and the avoidance of war'. This encourages broad-based efforts in the 'avoidance of war', particularly the linkage between domestic issues and traditional reliance on military spending to ensure national security. New World has broadened the base of peace activism to include minority and low-income people. It also seeks to expand public understanding of how genuine world security will be accomplished on the basis of equity and justice. To date, grants have been awarded to organisations for: public education about the consequences of nuclear war and excessive military spending; independent research and analysis; projection of policy alternatives; media information efforts; and initiatives to broaden grassroots participation.

Grants in 1986 included the following examples:

Nuclear Weapons Education Fund, Inc	$100,000
National Sane Education Fund, Ben Spock Center for Peace	$15,000
Centre for Education on Nuclear War	$10,000
Nuclear Times, Inc.	$10,000

Presentation of applications: There are no deadlines. The Board meets three times a year.

Information available for applicants: Biennial Report; programme policy statement.

NORTH SHORE UNITARIAN UNIVERSALIST VEATCH PROGRAM

Plandome Road, Plandome, New York 11030, USA.

Correspondent: Eleanor Vendig, Program Administrator.

Annual grants total: $6 million in 1986.

Grant range: $5,000–$200,000.

Policy and practice: The Veatch Program funds projects in two major categories: denominational and non-denominational.

Its denominational programme supports Unitarian Universalists and other liberal religious projects on a regional, continental and world wide scale. There are few grants in the peace/international relations field.

Support for non-denominational projects are given to projects addressing (i) the rights of individuals, (ii) rights of dissent against national policy and (iii) community service/social welfare.

In category (ii), right of dissent against national policy, one of the issues concentrated on is US military and foreign policy.

The Veatch Program does not give grants to individuals nor for academic research, seminars or publications.

Grants in 1986 included:

Unitarian Universalist Peace Network	$45,000
Coalition for a New Foreign and Military Policy, Washington, DC	$75,000
Business Executives for National Security	$20,000
Institute for Space and Security Studies, Washington, DC	$10,000
Children of War Tour	$36,000

Information available for applicants: Annual Report.

JOHN M. OLIN FOUNDATION

460 Park Avenue, New York, NY 10022, USA (212-486 7220).

Correspondent: Michael S. Joyce, Executive Director.

Annual grants total: $7.7 million in 1984.

Grant range: $1,000–$300,000 (plus larger capital grants).

Policy and practice: The Foundation provides support for projects that reflect or are intended to strengthen the economic, political and cultural institutions upon which the American system of democratic capitalism is based. It also seeks to promote a general understanding of these institutions by encouraging research on the connections between economic and political freedoms, and on the cultural heritage that sustains them.

The Board of Trustees authorises grants in four areas: public policy and research; American institutions; law and the legal system; and strategic and international studies, where grants are awarded for the purpose of examining the relationship between American institutions and international context in which they operate. The Foundation attempts to advance its objectives through support for a myriad of activities including: research; institutional support; fellowships; professorships; lectures; lecture series, and books; scholarly journals; journals of opinion; conferences and seminars; and, on occasion, television and radio programmes.

Grants in 1984 included the following examples:

American Council on Germany	$50,000
The Atlantic Council	$15,000
Harvard University, Center for International Affairs (over 3 years)	$296,922
1985 London Conference on Communism and Liberal Democracy	$12,000
National Strategy Information Center	$100,000
United States Space Foundation	$25,000
James Madison Foundation on educational programmes which link peace/human rights/democracy	$50,000

Presentation of applications: The Board of Trustees meets five times a year and acts on grant requests after the Foundation staff has thoroughly reviewed the proposal. Normally a decision is made within 90 days of receipt. There are no deadlines or application forms.

Information available for applicants: Annual report.

ALBERT PARVIN FOUNDATION

9220 Sunset Boulevard, Suite 230, Los Angeles, CA, USA (213-478 0342).

Correspondent: Albert B. Parvin, Vice-President.

Approximate annual grants total: $287,550 in 1984.

Grant range: $25–$21,000.

Policy and practice: The Foundation was established in 1960 'to promote peace, understanding and goodwill among the nations of the world through education, enlightenment and recognition of achievements toward this objective'.

It operates both nationally and internationally in the fields of social welfare and education through grants for construction projects, for higher education and child welfare, and through fellowships tenable at Princeton University and the University of California by students from new and underdeveloped nations.

Presentation of applications: There are no deadlines.

THE PEW CHARITABLE TRUSTS

Three Parkway, Suite 501, Philadelphia, Pennsylvania, 19102-1305, USA (215-568 3330).

Correspondent: James G. McGann, Program Officer, Public Policy.

Annual grants total: $138.2 million in 1986.

Grant range: $25,000–$2.7 million.

Policy and practice: The Pew Charitable Trusts, represent seven individual charitable trusts funded between 1948 and 1982 by the sons and daughters of Joseph N. Pew, founder of the Sun Oil Company. The Trusts support non-profit organisations dedicated to improving the quality of life for individuals and communities and encouraging personal growth and self-sufficiency. Grants are awarded in the areas of conservation, culture, education, health, human services, public policy, and religion.

The public policy programme at the Pew Charitable Trusts supports research, education, and training programmes in the areas of strategic and international studies and economic and social policy. In 1986, the Trusts committed over $7 million to this programme.

Examples of recent grants include:

Boston University	$25,000
Eisenhower Exchange Fellowship, Inc	$60,000
Foreign Policy Association, Inc	$30,000
Center for Strategic and International Studies Georgetown University (2 grants over 2 years)	$600,000
Greater Washington Educational Telecommunications Association, Inc	$113,000
Hoover Institution, Stanford University	$200,000
School of International Studies, University of Denver (over 2 years)	$100,000

Program for Integrating Economics and National Security, 1986-1989. To improve the linkage between the fields of economics and national security through an interdisciplinary programme of training and research. Programme grants to be awarded in 1987 (over 3 years) $2.7 million

Presentation of applications: Applications can be made throughout the year, but only one request can be submitted within any twelve-month period. Initial contact should be by letter. The Board meets five times a year in February, April, June, September, and December.

PLOUGHSHARES FUND

Fort Mason, San Francisco, CA 94123, USA (415-775 2244).

Correspondent: Sally Lilienthal, President; Wayne T. Jacquith, Executive Director.

Annual grants total: $1.04 million in 1986.

Grant range: $150–$106,800.

Policy and practice: The Ploughshares Fund was established in 1981 to build a constituency of donors concerned with world security and the avoidance of a nuclear holocaust. Ploughshares is a public charitable foundation created to fund organisations and individuals whose work is focused on arms control leading to arms reduction and nuclear disarmament. Encouraging a foreign policy founded on global collaboration, Ploughshares emphasises US-USSR co-operation as the cornerstone of world security.

As a public and charitable foundation, Ploughshares takes advantage of its ability to fund individuals directly and to spend a portion of its resources on lobbying and to make grants outside the United States. Sharing information with others and encouraging and exchanging ideas are part of the process which enables this foundation to carry out its purpose. The Fund has no geographical limitations on its grants, but does not, for the present, fund the production of films.

Grants in 1986 included the following:

Centro Interconfessionale Per La Pace, Rome	$2,250
Council for a Livable World Education Fund	$25,000
Federation of American Scientists Fund	$15,000
Nuclear War Prevention Fund (of Illinois)	$5,000
Women's Action for Nuclear Disarmament	$25,000
World Policy Institute	$20,000

Presentation of applications: The initial request can be in the form of a letter or proposal. It should give the qualifications of the personnel involved with the project as well as a concise description of the methods by which they will carry out their plan. It should identify other current sources of support as well as those with which applications are pending.

Ploughshares sets no deadlines for submitting proposals because decisions on applications are made frequently.

Information available for applicants: Annual Report.

PUBLIC WELFARE FOUNDATION

2600 Virginia Avenue NW, Suite 505, Washington DC 20037, USA (202-965 1800).

Correspondent: C. Glenn Ihrig, President.

Annual grants total: $7.42 million in 1986.

Grant range: $8,000–$250,000.

Policy and practice: The Foundation's scope is worldwide. It aims to promote human welfare through giving with a minimum of overhead and red tape to people whose needs are genuine and urgent, to help them keep themselves within the limits of their resources in a manner which destroys neither the dignity nor the initiative of the receiver. The Foundation strives to improve education, health, living conditions, and human happiness anywhere in the world where circumstances beyond their control have deprived people of development in keeping with their natural abilities.

General purpose grants are made to arms control, peace and disarmament organisations. Funds have been made available for:

Research and educational activities to explore peaceful alternatives to military and nuclear policies;

Efforts to alert the public to the long-term worldwide biological consequences of nuclear war;

Study and analysis of the impact of proposed space weapons defence systems.

Grants in 1986 included the following:

American Committee on US/Soviet Relations	$40,000
Arms Control Association	$250,000
Council on Economic Priorities	$25,400
Herbert Scoville Jr, Peace Fellowship	$40,000
The National Sane Education Fund Options	$30,000
Peace Development Fund	$8,000
Ploughshares Fund	$20,000

Presentation of applications: Applications may be submitted at any time. All requests will be reviewed by the Foundation's screening committee on a daily basis.

Applicants are notified as quickly as possible about the status of their proposals.

Proposals should be concise and informative; no longer than ten pages. The Foundation's funds are a temporary source of support and requests should specify a limited period of need.

SMITH RICHARDSON FOUNDATION

210 East 86th Street, New York, NY 10028, USA (212-861 8181).

Correspondent: Dorothy W. Hurley, Administrative Vice-President.

Annual grants total: $10.45 million in 1986.

Grant range: $5,000–$250,000.

Policy and practice: The Foundation's Public Affairs Program seeks to improve public understanding of, and support for, those elements essential to a strong economy and a free society through: support of specific projects which study public policies that affect business and the economy; sponsorship of educational programmes that enhance public understanding of the requirements for a sound economy and free society; assistance for projects that illuminate the degree of consensus necessary for a free society; and support of scholarship and educational projects that examine foreign policy and national security issues and work towards developing a peaceful, free, and prosperous world.

Grants are given under the following programme titles: domestic public policy; American foreign policies and national security; Central America; unconventional warfare; human rights and global development. The Foundation initiates most of the projects it funds. Within the limits of available resources, the Foundation will look for ways of assisting television and film series dealing with public affairs. No grants are made to individuals.

Grants in 1986 included:

Afghanistan Relief Committee	$35,000
American Foundation for Resistance International	$173,000
Center for Strategic and International Studies	$60,000
European American Institute for Security Research	$10,000
Families for Defence	$49,700
The Heritage Foundation	$48,887
Institute for European Defence and Strategic Studies	$51,000

Stanford University, International Strategic Institute	$110,000
Vietnam Veterans Leadership Program, Inc	$7,500

Presentation of applications: Applications are accepted and reviewed throughout the year. Grants are approved quarterly. There are no application forms.

Information available for applicants: Annual Report.

ROCKEFELLER BROTHERS FUND

1290 Avenue of the Americas, New York, NY 10104, USA (212-373 4200).

Correspondent: Mrs Hilary K. Palmer, Program Associate.

Annual grants total: $6.82 million in 1986.

Grant range: $15,000–$300,000.

Policy and practice: The Fund makes grants in four general areas: 'One World', New York City, non-profit sector, and special concerns. 'One World', its major grant-making focus, has two components: 'Sustainable Resource use' and 'World Security'. Under 'World Security', the Fund seeks to strengthen arms control, improve international relations, and encourage development, trade and finance.

Grants, directly relating to arms issues, are made for the following purposes:

Halting the spread of nuclear weapons capability to other countries and groups;

Determining the effects of nuclear weapons on the world's life support system and the implications of the scientific findings for arms control and security; and

Developing new paths to arms control through interdisciplinary work on specific nuclear and conventional arms issues that includes collaborative efforts between US and Soviet groups.

Grant-making objectives relating to international relations are threefold:

Improving East-West understanding through public information and education, exchanges, internships and joint work with the Soviet Union and, particularly, Eastern Europe on substantive fields of mutual interest;

Strengthening international relations and strategic studies institutes in East Asia and their capacity to relate to one another as well as to their counterparts in the United States; and increasing general American understanding of East Asia as a region of political, strategic, and economic importance to the United States; and

Increasing understanding of common interests among the industrialised nations and helping them deal more effectively with the pressing concerns of less developed countries.

In connection with the implementation of its 'One World' theme, the Fund also supports projects related to the not well understood or explored connections between global resource management and global security. The Fund does not make grants for graduate study, research writing of books, theses, or other individual endeavours.

Grants for 1987 included:

Carnegie Endowment for International Peace	$100,000
Nuclear Control Institute	$75,000
Peace Research Institute, Frankfurt	$23,000
University of Southampton, Programme for Promoting Nuclear Non-Proliferation	$200,000
United Nations Association of United States of America	$150,000

Presentation of applications: Applications are accepted throughout the year. A preliminary letter of enquiry is recommended for an initial approach to the Fund, although submission of detailed proposals is also appropriate.

Information available for applicants: Annual Report.

ROCKEFELLER FAMILY FUND

1290 Avenue of the Americas, New York, NY 10104, USA (212-373 4252).

Correspondent: Donald K. Ross, Director.

Annual grants total: $1.7 million in 1986.

Grant range: $10,000–$50,000.

Policy and practice: Conservation, equal opportunity for women, institutional responsiveness and arms control are the four main grant areas of the Rockefeller Family Fund. The arms control programme of the Family Fund supports efforts to reduce the risk of nuclear war and the economic and social consequences of the arms race. Examples of past grants which fit these guidelines include projects designed to analyse the impact of military spending on various segments of the population; action-oriented research on the environmental hazards associated with the military's nuclear programme; projects to enable citizens to control the weapons programme; and a collaborative effort by Soviet and American physicians to slow the arms race.

North American Sources

Recent grants have included:

Peace Development Fund (1986)	$10,000
Peace Links (1986)	$15,000
Institute for Space and Security Studies, Inc (1986)	$20,000
Institute for Defense and Disarmament Studies (1984)	$20,000
International Physicians for the Prevention of War (1984)	$25,000

Presentation of applications: Applications are accepted throughout the year. Each grant request is referred to a staff programme officer. The Executive Committee reviews proposals every two months. Annual budgetry allocations for specific programme areas are usually made at the Board's December meeting.

Further information for applicants: Annual Report.

ROCKEFELLER FOUNDATION

1133 Avenue of the Americas, New York, NY 10036, USA (212-869 8500).

Correspondent: Lynda Mullen, Secretary.

Policy and practice: The Foundation has in the past made significant contributions in the field of international relations. Lest readers think there is an omission if this Foundation is not quoted, the following extract from a letter on July 1987 by Ms Mullen is reproduced.

'As part of the restructuring associated with the Foundation's new thrust, which centers on the contribution science and technology can make to improving the lives of the poor in the developing world, the Foundation's Board of Trustees terminated the International Relations Division, effective December 31, 1986.'

SAMUEL RUBIN FOUNDATION

777 United Nations Plaza, New York, NY 10017, USA (212-697 8945).

Correspondent: Cora Weiss, President.

Annual grants total: $559,222 in 1986.

Grant range: $1,000–$100,000.

Policy and practice: The Foundation makes grants to national and international organisations for programmes concerned with the pursuit of peace and justice, the search for an equitable reallocation of the world's resources, and the fullest implementation of social, economic, political, civil and cultural rights for all the world's people; some emphasis on organisations located in New York City and Washington, DC.

Grants have been made to:

Fund for Peace	$7,000
Musicians Against Nuclear War	$1,000
Peace Development Fund (fellowship programme)	$7,000
Jobs with Peace Campaign	$5,000

Presentation of applications: There are no formal deadlines. The Board meets in February, June, September and December. A final notification can be expected two weeks after the relevant board meeting.

Information available for applicants: Programme policy statement.

SARAH SCAIFE FOUNDATION

PO Box 268, 3 Mellon Bank Center, Pittsburgh, PA 15230, USA (412-392 2900).

Correspondent: Richard M. Larry, President.

Annual grants total: $8.57 million in 1986.

Grant range: $5,000–$1.08 million.

Policy and practice: The Foundation directs most of its resources to support organisations addressing major domestic and international public policy issues through research, publications and education.

Among the programme areas assisted by grants in 1986 were those concerned with national defence initiatives, the impact of arts and culture on society, the interaction of economic and political thought on policy decisions, the workings of the US legal system, and privatisation of government services.

Grants in 1986 included:

American Bar Association Fund for Public Education, Standing Committee on Law and National Security	$175,000
George C. Marshall Institute	$100,000
Heritage Foundation	$1,075,000
Institute for Foreign Policy Analysis, Inc	$400,000
Hoover Institution on War, Revolution and Peace, Stanford University	$500,000

Presentation of applications: Applications may be submitted at any time. The Directors meet in February, May, September and November. Initial enquiries should be in letter form.

Information available for applicants: Annual Report.

SCHERMAN FOUNDATION

315 West 57th Street, Suite 2D, New York, NY 10019, USA (212-489 7143).

Correspondent: David F. Freedom, Executive Director.

Annual grants total: $2.5 million in 1986.

Grant range: $5,000–$15,000.

Policy and practice: The main areas of interest are disarmament and peace, conservation, family planning, human rights and liberties, the arts and social welfare. Grants are not given for scholarships and fellowships, or to colleges, universities, higher education institutions or to individuals.

Grants in 1984 included:

American Committee on East-West Accord	$5,000
Communicators for Nuclear Disarmament	$7,500
Fund for Peace	$50,000
Parliamentarians for World Order Conference Fund	$10,000

Presentation of applications: There are no deadlines or application forms.

Information available for applicants: 1984 Annual Report and additional information.

FLORENCE AND JOHN SCHUMANN FOUNDATION

33 Park Street, Montclair, New Jersey 07042, USA (201-783 6660).

Correspondent: William B. Mullins, President.

Annual grants total: $3.46 million in 1986.

Grant range: $1,000–$300,000.

Policy and practice: Grants are made for health, higher and secondary education, and community development programmes. Approximately 30% of the grants go to New Jersey institutions and 54% to institutions working on problems that affect all Americans. Current priorities are international relations, population and environment, early childhood development and effective governance.

Grants in 1986 included:

Arms Control Association, Washington, DC	$40,000
Brookings Institution, Washington, DC	$50,000
Council on Foreign Relations, New York	$50,000
John Hopkins Foreign Policy Institute, Washington, DC	$98,670
US Committee of the International Institute for Strategic Studies, Washington, DC	$100,000

Presentation of applications: Proposals should be in writing. Deadlines are mid January, April and October. Board meetings are held in March, June, October and December.

Information available for applicants: Annual Report; application guidelines.

SEQUOIA FOUNDATION

820 A St, Suite 545, Tacoma, Washington 98402, USA (206-627 1634).

Correspondent: Frank D. Underwood, Executive Director.

Annual grants total: $1.98 million in 1985.

Grant range: $1,000–$50,000.

Policy and practice: The Foundation aims to serve the cultural and social needs of the world community. Grants are focused on the stimulation, encouragement, and support of established, voluntary, non-profit organisations set up to meet national and international need in areas of cultural programmes, education, environment, hunger, international peace and world crisis relief. No grants are made to individuals, lobbying, political propaganda nor for conferences or travel.

Presentation of applications: There are no deadlines, the initial approach should be by letter. The Board meets six times a year.

Information available for applicants: Programme policy statement, application guidelines.

ALFRED P. SLOAN FOUNDATION

630 Fifth Avenue, New York, NY 10111, USA (212-582 0452).

Correspondent: Arthur L. Singer Jr, Vice President.

Annual grants total: $20.91 million in 1986.

Grant range: $10,000–$395,000.

Policy and practice: The Foundation's main interests are in higher education, with an emphasis on science, technology, economics, management and public service. It describes its role in arms control and defence policy as 'carefully delimited. It includes only support for various programs designed in one way or another to help teachers deal effectively with the growing interest of undergraduates in systematic instruction on issues of the nuclear age. Courses and seminars on arms control and defense policy are now commonplace at colleges and universities. Yet many of these relatively new instructional programs are led by faculty members who had had little opportunity to master this difficult and complex subject, and who are anxious to deepen their understanding of the technology of nuclear weapons and the history of arms control.'

Grants have been made for summer workshops on issues of the nuclear age.

Grants in 1986 included:
  Committee for National Security
  Arms Control Association
  Institute on Global Conflict, University of California

Presentation of applications: Applications are accepted throughout the year and should be presented as short letters of enquiry rather than fully developed proposals.

STARR FOUNDATION

70 Pine Street, New York, NY 10270, USA (212-770 6882).

Correspondent: Ta Chun Hsu, President.

Annual grants total: $15.7 million in 1986.

Grant range: $150–$2 million.

Policy and practice: The Foundation makes grants largely for education with emphasis on higher education, including scholarships under specific programmes; also limited contributions to hospitals and medical research, cultural programmes, international affairs organisations, and social services.

There seems to be some emphasis on South Africa and Asia.

Grants have been made to:

Trilateral Commission	$10,000
Georgetown University, Center for Strategic and International Studies	$1,000,000
Appeal of Conscience Foundation	$5,000

Presentation of applications: There are no deadlines. The initial approach should be made by letter. Board meetings are held in February and September.

The Foundation does not issue guidelines or a statement of policy.

SUNFLOWER FOUNDATION

305 Madison Avenue, Suite 1166, New York, NY 10165 (212-682 0889).

Correspondent: Katherine Tremaine, President.

Annual grants total: $746,600 in 1985.

Grant range: $2,500–$12,500.

Policy and practice: The Sunflower Foundation supports a wide variety of organisations addressing the root causes of problems in society. Its preference is to support programmes designed to alter public policy or raise public consciousness around progressive issues. There are four major areas of interest:

  Protecting and strengthening the rights of people, including activists believed to be targeted by the government for their political activities;

  Mobilising workers and improve working conditions;

  Influencing and altering US foreign and military policy in the interests of peace and non-intervention; and

  Preserving environmental and natural resources.

It also supports educational efforts, investigative journalism, community education on economic and military issues, and the exchange of ideas among activists working for progressive social change.

Grants have been made to:

Peace Education Project	$2,500
European Nuclear Disarmament, 1983	$5,000

Presentation of applications: A brief description of the proposal should be submitted. It is suggested that requests should not exceed $10,000. The Board meets three times a year and proposals should be made by mid May, September and January in order to be considered by the Board.

Information available for applicants: Application guidelines.

THRESHOLD FOUNDATION

873a Sutter Street, San Francisco, California 94109, USA (415-771 4308).

Correspondent: Drummond Pike, Foundation Manager.

Annual grants total: $358,800 in 1983.

Grant range: $1,000–$50,000.

Policy and practice: Threshold's interests fall into three general categories: '(1) Person, including holistic education, spiritual awakening, issues of male/female awareness, co-operative and intentional communities, traditional indigenous cultures and peoples and nonviolent solutions to discrimination; (2) Planet, including land stewardship, regenerative agriculture, pure air and water, reforestation, appropriate technology, bioregionalism, and all that helps humanity to live more lightly on the planet; and (3) Peace, including conflict resolution, unofficial Tract II diplomacy, and individual and institutional initiatives designed to foster in cultural communication and dialogue'.

Presentation of applications: The Foundation, since Autumn 1984, has not accepted unsolicited proposals.

Information available for applicants: Annual Report.

TIDES FOUNDATION

873 Sutter Street, San Francisco, CA 94109, USA (415-771 4308).

Correspondents: Drummond Pike, President; Dave Moffat, Program Associate/Grants Manager.

Annual grants total: $1.17 million in 1986.

Grant range: $100–$30,000.

Policy and practice: The Tides Foundation works locally, nationally and internationally in five areas of interest: peace education and international affairs; land use, preservation and stewardship; enterprise development and economic public policy; environment and natural resources; and community affairs. The Foundation has grown increasingly concerned with international affairs and the arms race. Therefore, it places high priority on efforts to educate the public about the hazards of a continued weapons race, and those which re-examine ways to limit the possibilities of nuclear accidents. The Foundation's Board believes that bilateral and international efforts to promote better understanding among people as a step toward a non-nuclear future are of vital current importance. The Tides Foundation also supports public education on aspects of military spending through its grants for enterprise development and economic public policy

The Foundation works in three ways: it initiates projects; it awards funds; it administers donor-advised funds.

Grants in 1986 included:

Amnesty International	$2,000
Educators for Social Responsibility	$10,000
Foundation for the Arts of Peace	$11,200
New Israel Fund	$6,000
Peace Brigades International	$500
Women's Action for Nuclear Disarmament Education Fund	$2,000
Youth Project	$2,500

Presentation of applications: Applications are accepted throughout the year and should initially be on one page and itemise the issue(s), the organisation's approach, their target(s), budget and funding to date.

Information available for applicants: Annual Report.

TOPSFIELD FOUNDATION

Route 169, Box 203, Pomfret, Connecticut 06258, USA (203-928 2616).

Correspondent: Susan Graseck, Executive Director.

Annual grants total: $337,693 in 1986 (much of this is committed to Topsfield projects, Grassroots Peace Directory, Access and Options. Only about $50,000 to other projects).

Grant range: $1,000–$10,000.

Policy and practice: The Foundation was established in 1983 'to support efforts concerned with world hunger, population, and peace. Because it feels a particular urgency about the nuclear arms race, grant-making is concentrated among grassroots groups working toward nuclear disarmament. While the Foundation understands that short-term political change is one step, it believes human security results from real change in the hearts and minds of people everywhere. Therefore, the Foundation seeks to enlarge the circle of people involved in disarmament efforts and to translate national concern into debate over public policy. Particular emphasis is given to projects and organisations which build new constituencies and provide avenues of involvement to newcomers. To this end, the Foundation has initiated and funded projects, such as Options, a University Outreach Programme on Nuclear Policy, and Access, a Security Information Service.' These have now become well established and in 1987 largely independent of the Foundation. The Foundation also produces the Grassroots Peace Directory and the International Security News Clipping Service. They do, however, look for ways to give grants to reduce the risk of nuclear war and these grants could increase now that Access and Options have been established.

Grants in 1986 included:

Carnegie Endowment for International Peace	$10,000
Council for a Liveable World, Scoville Fellowship	$12,000

North American Sources

Nuclear Times	$10,000
Jobs with Peace Education Fund	$2,500

Presentation of applications: Applications are accepted throughout the year, and application forms are available from the Foundation.

Information available for applicants: Annual Report.

UNITED STATES INSTITUTE OF PEACE

1550 M Street, NW, Suite 700, Washington, DC, 20005-1708 (202-457 1700).

Correspondent: Dr Kenneth M. Jenson, Director, Grants Program.

Annual grants total: about $1.3 million in 1986/87.

Policy and practice: The Institute was established by an act of Congress as an independent, nonprofit corporation to 'serve the people and the Government through the widest possible range of education and training, basic and applied research opportunities, and peace information services on the means to promote international peace and the resolution of conflicts among the nations and peoples of the world without recourse to violence'.

The Institute runs its own internal programmes, which includes:
  An annual school essay contest;
  A periodic report on the state of world peace;
  A newsletter;
  An intellectual map of the peace field;
  An educational TV series on the history of US-Soviet relations.

Its grants programme is directed primarily at academics, professionals and educators. Applications are welcomed for any work falling within the Institute's mandate and can also be made to foreign nationals though the programme has been publicised little outside the States to date. Its first grants were made in 1986.

The subjects of special interest to the Institute at the present time are
  Research on the relationship between adherence to international human rights standards and international peace;
  research on perceptions of peace across political systems and ideologies, including the comparative status of peace movements and their impact under different political systems, and a comparative assessment and survey of the teaching of peace;
  research on negotiations, including lessons from negotiations between the United States and the Soviet Union, lessons from negotiations between democratic and non-democratic systems, and general lessons in the art of negotiation;
  research on the relationship between domestic political systems and the aggressive use of force;
  research on strengthening the non-use-of-force provisions of the United Nations Charter, including the effectiveness of the United Nations and other international institutions in dealing with low intensity and covert forms of aggression;
  research on the mediation of political change;
  developing curricula and materials for the study of international peace and conflict resolution from high school through post-graduate programs;
  developing curricula and materials for negotiation, mediation, and conciliation theory, teaching, and training;
  assisting media programming, including research and the development of materials particularly for television and radio, that will bring information about issues for international peace and conflict resolution to the broader public.

The Institute also awards three types of fellowships (started in December 1987).

Presentation of applications: Specific application forms must be completed. The first deadline for the fellowship programmes was March 1st, 1988.

Information available for applicants: Procedures for Grant Applications; Biennial Report; Schedule of Grant awards etc.

WEYERHAEUSER FAMILY FOUNDATION, INC

2100 First National Bank Building, Saint Paul, Minnesota 55101, USA (612-228 0935).

Correspondent: Nancy Weyerhaeuser, President.

Annual grants total: $287,850 in 1985.

Grant range: $400–$30,000.

Policy and practice: Since the 1960s the Foundation has placed emphasis on the support of programmes of national and international significance that attempt to identify and correct the causes of maladjustment in our society. It supports international projects that enable people to help themselves via population planning, agricultural improvements, self-government, and peace education.

The Foundation does not normally make grants for projects with limited geographical emphasis, operating budgets, annual campaigns, building and equipment, elementary and secondary education, lobbying or propoganda. Nor does it make grants to individuals, or for scholarships, fellowships and travel. The Foundation stresses that its does not make grants to organisations that are not located in or operating in the United States, although they will make grants to organisations in the United States for international work.

Grants have been made in recent years to:
International Peace Academy, New York, NY
Hubert Humphrey Institute, New York, NY
Oxfam America, Boston, MA

Presentation of applications: Applications to be submitted between January and June: deadline 1st June. The Programme Committee meets annually in late summer to review proposals; the Board meets usually in November.

Information available for applicants: Annual Report; application guidelines; programme policy statement.

WINSTON FOUNDATION FOR WORLD PEACE

401 Commonwealth Avenue, Boston, Massachusetts 02215, USA (617-226 1014).

Correspondents: John Tirman, Executive Director; Nancy Stockford, Program Manager.

Annual grants total: $455,636 in 1986/87.

Grant range: $2,000–$45,000.

Policy and practice: The Foundation was established in 1985 'to contribute to world peace, primarily through the permanent prevention of nuclear war'. It has initially chosen to direct its funding towards public policy. In practice, two general categories of projects have gained support. The first supports the conceptually inventive project that reaches beyond work already underway in the arms control field but still maintains a reasonable prospect of affecting public policy. The second category is concerned with building the infrastructure of the peace movement by improving skills, expertise, means of public education, etc.

Grants in 1986/87 included:

ACCESS, A Security Information Service	$30,000
Center for War, Peace and the News Media	$45,000
Institute for Defense and Disarmament Studies	$12,000
Nashvillians for the Nuclear Arms Freeze	$5,000
United Campuses to Prevent Nuclear War	$16,886
World Policy Institute	$20,600

Presentation of applications: Proposals should be submitted in writing, including a concise statement of the organisation's goals, resources and proposed project. Applications are reviewed at quarterly meetings and the deadlines for these are mid-February, May, August and November.

Information available for applicants: Annual Report.

YOUTH PROJECT

1555 Connecticut Avenue NW, Room 501, Washington, DC 20036, USA (202-483 0030).

Correspondent: Andrea Kydd, Executive Director.

Annual grants total: $3.6 million for 1985/86.

Grant range: $1,000–$80,000 (but most under $30,000).

Policy and practice: The Youth Project supports organisations working to resolve significant social or economic problems. It looks for action-oriented strategies and a commitment to structures that are accountable to local citizens and involve them in the formulation of public policy. It seeks projects that generate citizen participation and have the greatest potential for positive social change. While it does not specify funding categories, four major areas of emphasis have been identified: citizen participation; the economy; the environment; and war and peace.

The Youth Project seldom initiates projects. Rather, it supports the development of effective local, state, regional, and national citizen participation organisation through: seed grants for new and high risk efforts; assistance to organisations that need access to funding sources to establish financial independence; management, fiscal, and legal services; and networking which links similar projects together for mutual support, and connects projects with national and local research, media, and advocacy groups.

The Youth Project has a national office plus seven field offices, each responsible for a distinct geographical area. In addition, the Youth Project administers fifteen donor-advised funds.

Grants in 1985/86 included:

American Friends of END	$20,000
Peace Organisation Assistance Project	$5,000
Washington State Central America Peace Campaign	$21,853

North American Sources

Most of the donor-advised funds also give to projects concerned with Peace/International Relations, for example the Circle Fund:

Campaign Against Nuclear War	$15,000
Centre for Education on Nuclear War	$5,000
PRO-Peace	$5,000
Women's Action for Nuclear Disarmament	$5,000

Presentation of applications: Applications are accepted throughout the year. A cover letter and proposal of not more than ten pages should be submitted.

Information available for applicants: Annual Report.

3. European sources

List of contents

Belgium
Foundation Roi Baudouin/Konig Boudewijnstighting (Prize)
Foundation Paul-Henri Spaak

Denmark
Foundation for International Understanding

Ireland
The Ireland Funds of the United States, Canada and Australia

Italy
Fondazione Rui

Netherlands
Carnegie-Stichting, Watelerfonds (Prize)
European Cultural Foundation

Sweden
Nobelstiftesen (Prize)
NORDSAM, Nordic Co-operation Committee for International Politics

Switzerland
Fondation Charles Veillon
Fonds National Suisse de la Recherche Scientifique

West Germany
Deutscher Akademischer Austauschdienst (DAAD)
Alfried Krupp Von Bohlen Und Halbach-Stiftung
Heinz-Schwarzkopf-Stiftung Junges Europa
Fritz Thyssen Stiftung
Stiftung Volkswagenwerk

Belgium

FOUNDATION ROI BAUDOUIN/ KONING BOUDEWIJNSTIGHTING

Rue Brederode 21, Brederodestraat 21, B-1000 Brussels, Belgium (02-511 18 40).

Correspondent: D. Allard, Advisor.

Annual grants total: US $7.1 million in 1986.

Grant range: No rule except for the King Baudouin Prize which is US $100,000.

Policy and practice: The Foundation aims to support all initiatives likely to improve the living conditions of the Belgian people, taking account of the economic, social, scientific and cultural factors, both at national and international level, which will have an impact on the country's evolution in the years to come. The Foundation conducts its own projects and seldom makes grants to institutions or individuals. It awards the King Baudouin International Development Prize (in 1986 to the International Foundation for Science (Stockholm).

Information available for applicants: Report of operations and financial statement. Relevant literature about the King Baudouin International Development Prize.

FOUNDATION PAUL-HENRI SPAAK

11 Rue d'Egmont, 1050 Brussels, Belgium (010-322 511 8100).

Correspondent: François Danis, Secretaire Général.

Annual grants total: No information made available.

Policy and practice: The Foundation was set up as a centre of thought and action to prolong the European work of Paul-Henri Spaak, particularly in the field of

European Sources

the external relations of the European Communities; to promote any activity contributing to a better understanding of the European ideal and associating new generations with the construction of Europe.

The Foundation was set up to operate nationally, internationally and on a European level in the field of international relations. It proposes to encourage education and scientific research related to its aims through creating specialised professorships in EEC external affairs to be occupied by distinguished foreigners, international fellowships and scholarships, the sponsoring of publications and diffusion of documentation and information on a high level. Lectures and seminars as well as regional, national and international congresses will be organised.

Denmark

FOUNDATION FOR INTERNATIONAL UNDERSTANDING

Kultorvet 2, PO Box 85, 1003 Copenhagen K, Denmark (45-139 418).

Correspondent: Folmer Wisti, Chairman of the Board of the Foundation.

Annual grants total: DKr 200,000 in 1987.

Grant range: Between DKr 25,000 and DKr 100,000.

Policy and practice: The Foundation was set up, in 1973, by Folmer Wisti to contribute to international co-operation on issues of importance in daily life at local and regional level, by the encouragement of local communities, the support of decentralisation and regionalism and the exchange of experience and ideas primarily in the fields of education, social welfare and local government.

It operates internationally in the field of community endeavour. Support is given for seminars and study tours on local community issues, for intensive triennial language courses in English, French, German and Spanish for non-academic young people and for study of developments, problems and achievements in one or more countries. The Foundation supports Det Danske Selskab (the Danish Institute) in its programme of international understanding, particularly the Institute's representatives abroad in their work to organise an exchange of information and contacts. 'Europe of Regions', a conference on decentralisation and regional autonomy, is held annually in Copenhagen. Institutions eligible for support must be independent of party politics, non-profit making and non-governmental. No support is given to individuals.

Recent grants: Grants made in the field of peace and international relations in 1987 included:

The conference *Europe of Regions*

The periodical *Regional Contact*

The book *Industrial Life in Denmark, The Faroe Islands and Greenland Cultural Exchange between Denmark and France* (annual grant over three years).

Presentation of applications: No specific requirements.

Ireland

THE IRELAND FUNDS OF THE UNITED STATES, CANADA AND AUSTRALIA

Kinnear Court, 16–20 Cumberland Street South, Dublin 2, Ireland (0001-714 677 x 114/115).

Correspondent: Judy Hays.

Advisory Committee in Ireland: Colm Cavanagh, Stacia Crickley, Niall Crowley, Michael J. Dargan, Gerald Dempsey, Hugh Frazer, Sir Peter Froggatt, Lady Valerie Goulding, Judy Hayes, Justice Anthony Hederman, Hon Margaret Heckler, Desmond Kenny, James King, Matt Kingston, Maryon Davies Lewis, T. J. Maher, T. Kevin Mallen, James McCarthy, Mairtin McCullough, Larry McGovern, Mrs Patrick McGrath, Jim Milton, Karl Mullen, Justice T. F. O'Higgins, Cormac K. H. O'Malley, Sean O'Siochain, Vincent Poklewski-Koziell, James Sherwin, Mrs Michael Smurfit, Dennis Whelan, Derick Wilson. (This committee makes recommendations on grant-aid to the Boards of Directors in the United States, Canada and Australia.)

Annual grants total of American Ireland Fund: US $2.5 million in 1986/87.

Annual grants total of Ireland Fund of Canada: C $100,000 in 1986/87.

Background: The Ireland Fund is a non-political organisation established in 1976, to raise money in the United States for the promotion of peace, culture and charity in Ireland, North and South. Since that time Funds have been set up in other countries; Canada in 1978, Australia in 1987 and there are plans to set up a fund in Britain.

Policy and practice: The Fund's main areas of interest are peace programmes, cultural programmes and charitable programmes. Priority is given to projects that are innovative, emphasise self help, have a high degree of community involvement and have the possibility of being reproduced elsewhere. Grants are not normally give for more than one year. There are some exceptions to this, however. Grants do not normally exceed £10,000.

Grants made in 1986/87 from the American Ireland Fund included support to the following organisations:
  Community of the Peace People
  Corrymeela/Joint Redemptorist/Irish School of Ecumenics
  Irish Peace Council
  North Belfast Community Resource Centre
  University of Nottingham
  British Irish Association
  Forge Integrated Primary School
  Hazelwood College
  Hazelwood Primary School
  The Housing Association for Integrated Living Ltd
  Irish and British Councils of Churches on Human Rights and Responsibilies.
  Relief of Derry Project
  Tipperary Peace Convention and Song of Peace Contest
  Ulster Quaker Peace Committee

Presentation of applications: The Advisory Committee makes recommendations to each of the Boards of Directors. These meet twice a year to make final decisions on grants. Closing dates for applications are mid January and mid June.

Information available for applicants: Booklets for the two funds in the USA and Canada with names of their Boards of Directors and examples of grant-aid; funding guidelines.

Italy

FONDAZIONE RUI

Viale Ventuno Aprile, 36, 00162 Roma, Italy (06-832 1281/2/3).

Correspondent: Dott Ing Lorenzo Revojera, Secretary General.

Annual grants total: Lit 600 Million in 1987.

Policy and practice: The Foundation was established to promote the further training of university students and intellectuals; to promote cultural activities for youth; to award scholarships to Italian and foreign students and acclimatise the latter to the Italian way of life; to collaborate with national and international organisations to these ends.

It operates nationally in the field of the arts and humanities, and both nationally and internationally in the fields of education, social welfare and studies. It operates also in the fields of international relations and aid to less-developed countries. Programmes are carried out internationally through self-conducted projects and both nationally and internationally through research, fellowships and scholarships, conferences, courses, publications and lectures.

Presentation of applications: No information available.

Information available for applicants: Report of operations and finance.

The Netherlands

CARNEGIE-STICHTING, WATELERFONDS

Vredespaleis, Carnegieplein 2, The Hague, Netherlands (010-3170 469 680).

Correspondent: The Director.

Policy and practice: The Foundation awards the Wateler Peace Prize each year to the person or institution having rendered the most valuable service in the cause of peace or having contributed to finding means of combating war.

This is the only grant the Carnegie Foundation awards.

Recent awards have been made to.
  Alva Myrdal
  Henry Kissinger
  International Commission for Jurists, Geneva
  UNIFIL contingent

European Sources

EUROPEAN CULTURAL FOUNDATION

Jan Van Goyenkade 5, 1075 HN, Amsterdam, Netherlands (010-31200 76 02 22).

Correspondents: Dr R. Georis, Secretary-General; A. N. Van der Wiel, Director.

European Cultural Foundation (UK Committee): temporary address from 1.1.86: c/o English-Speaking Union (Current Afairs Unit), Dartmouth House, 37 Charles Street, London W1X 8AB (01-629 5920). *Correspondent:* Michael F. Cullis, Director.

Annual grants total: Dfl 1.9 million in 1986.

Grant range: Dfl 2,000–Dfl 200,000.

Policy and practice: The Foundation, set up in 1954, is a private, non-profitmaking organisation devoted to the promotion of activities of a multi-national character and European inspiration, in the fields of education, environment, social affairs, the arts and humanities, international relations and the media. The Foundation operates a twofold programme involving grants, and, since 1975, a network of institutes and centres established independently or in co-operation with other organisations throughout Europe. National Committees also operate on its behalf in 15 European countries. The address of the UK Committee is given above.

The Foundation's grantmaking programme gives support to projects involving at least three European countries and of European inspiration. Requests by individuals are not usually considered.

The Foundation makes grants under the following headings:

  Architecture and Archaeology;

  Fine Arts, History, Literature, Music and Cultural Cooperation;

  Employment and Social Problems;

  Education, Language and Youth;

  International Relations, Human Rights and European Cooperation;

  Environment;

  Media.

Every year the Board makes a policy statement. Recent grants have included:

  European Centre for Political Studies (London) (1986)

  London School of Economics and Political Science (1987)

  Plural Societies Foundation, East-West Relations (1987)

  The States General of European Students, Dutch branch (1987)

Presentation of applications: Applications should be in writing. Deadlines for grant applications are mid-February and mid-October each year.

Information available for applicants: Newsletter; guidelines for grants.

Sweden

NOBELSTIFTESEN

Sturegaten 14, POB 5232, S102 45 Stockholm, Sweden (08-663-09-20).

Correspondent: Stig Ramel, Executive Director.

For submission of proposals for the peace prize: The Norwegian Nobel Committee, Drammensveien 19, N-0255 Oslo, 2, Norway.

Peace Prize: 2,175,000 Sw Kroner in 1987 (the same amount for each prize).

Policy and practice: The Foundation was set up in 1900, based on the will of Alfred Nobel, to award annual prizes to those whom, during the preceding year, are judged to have conferred the greatest benefit on mankind in each of the following fields: physics; chemistry; physiology or medicine; literature and peace.

It operates internationally in the fields of science and medicine, literature and peace promotion through the prizes. The Peace Prize is awarded to the individual or organisation who has 'done the most or the best work for fraternity between nations, for the abolition or reduction of standing armies and for the holding and promotion of peace congresses.'

Prize-winners are chosen by the Royal Academy of Sciences, Stockholm (Physics and Chemistry), the Karolinska Institutet, Stockholm (Physiology and Medicine), the Swedish Academy, Stockholm (Literature) and the Norwegian Nobel Committee (Peace). In 1968 the Central Bank of Sweden instituted an Alfred Nobel Memorial Prize in Economic Sciences of the same value as the Nobel Prize.

Presentation of applications: Written proposals regarding prize candidates by qualified persons should reach the Nobel Committee concerned and the Prize Committee Secretary before February 1st. Persons qualified to submit proposals for the Peace Prize are:

  Active and former members of the Norwegian Nobel Committee and the advisers appointed by the Norwegian Nobel Institute;

Members of the national assemblies and governments of the different states and members of the Interparliamentary Union;

Members of the International Court of Arbitration at The Hague;

Members of the Commission of the Permanent International Peace Bureau;

Members and associate members of the Institut de Droit International;

University professors of political science and jurisprudence, history and philosophy, and

Nobel Laureates for Peace.

Recent Peace Awards:

Adolfo Perez Esquivel, Argentine human rights leader, 1980

Office of the United Nations High Commission for Refugees, 1981

Joint award to Alva Myrdal and Alfonso Garcia Robles, 1982

Lech Walesa, 1983

Desmond Tutu, 1984

Elie Wiesel, 1985

International Physicians for the Prevention of Nuclear War, 1986

President Arias of Costa Rica, 1987

Information available: Publications: Annual Report; Les Prix Nobel; Nobel Lectures; Nobel Foundation Directory; Alfred Nobel and the Peace Prize.

NORDSAM

Nordic Co-operation Committee for International Politics, (including Conflict and Peace Research), PO Box 1253 S-11182, Stockholm, Sweden (468 23 4060).

Correspondents: Erland Jansson, Research Secretary; Anne-Marie Bratt, Information Secretary.

Annual grants total: SEK 400,000 in 1986/87.

Policy and practice: NORDSAM is a joint Nordic body responsible for promoting Nordic research in the field of international politics, including conflict and peace research. The members of NORDSAM represent a broad variety of academic disciplines, such as political science, contemporary history, sociology, international relations, international law, and peace and conflict research. They are appointed by the Ministries of Education of their respective countries.

Scholarships and grants are awarded to researchers and advanced students from the Nordic countries. Occasionally support may be given to foreign research within NORDSAM's field of interest. Travel grants are also given for participation in seminars and conferences.

Presentation of applications: Application on forms available from the secretariat must be submitted by 1st October or 1st March.

Information available for applicants: Basic guidelines; bi-annual newsletter *International Studies in Nordic Countries*, free.

Switzerland

FONDATION CHARLES VEILLON

Route de Crissier, 1030 Bussigny-près-Lausanne, Switzerland (021-89-29-11).

Correspondent: Dr Andris Barblan, Secretary.

Policy and practice: Little is known about the Foundation. It did not wish to have its activities publicised. It has said that it is flooded with applications and has to turn down 90% of requests. It has confirmed – 'our objectives cover topics of international interest – support of minorities, regional development of cultural identity, federalism.' It has given support for reconcilation work carried out by the Centre for Conflict Studies at the University of Ulster (*see separate entry*).

FONDS NATIONAL SUISSE DE LA RECHERCHE SCIENTIFIQUE

Wildhainweg 20, 3001 Bern, Switzerland (031-245 424).

Correspondent: P. E. Fricker, Secretary General; Dr R. Bolzern, Social Sciences and Humanities Division.

Annual grants total: 189 million Swiss francs in 1986.

Grant range: 250 Swiss francs to 1.6 million Swiss francs (most grants are under 300,000 Swiss francs).

Policy and practice: Founded in 1952 to grant financial support to basic research when sufficient financial subsidies cannot be made available from other sources, and when research is not undertaken for commercial purposes.

It operates both nationally and internationally in the fields of education, science and medicine, the arts and

European Sources

humanities, law and other professions, and international relations, through grants to individuals and institutions, fellowships, scholarships, conferences, courses, publications and lectures. To be eligible for a research grant, candidates must be resident in Switzerland (regardless of citizenship); candidates for fellowships must be resident in Switzerland or graduates of a Swiss university or Federal Technical Institute. In a determined field of research, the Foundation may empower an external specialised institute to allocate funds. The Foundation also operates an exchange programme with the Royal Society in England.

Grants in 1986 included:

The nuclear issue and politics, L. Mysrowicz, Geneva	Sw fr 9,380
Negotiations about the elaboration of a new international economic order, Prof D. Sidjanski, Geneva	Sw fr 33,391
The impact of the rules of procedure on the disarmament negotiations at the United Nations, Prof A. Berenstein, Geneva (over 2 years)	Sw fr 228,663
Ten exchanges with the Royal Society	Sw fr 18,525

Presentation of applications: The applicants determine their research topics and submit their applications (research plan, required staff and material) to the SNSF. Applications should be submitted twice a year, by the 1st of March and 1st of October.

Information available for applicants: Annual Report, a brief summary in English. Also contact Dr Bolzern.

West Germany

DEUTSCHER AKADEMISCHER AUSTAUSCHDIENST (DAAD)
(German Academic Exchange Service)

Head Office, Kennedyallee 50, D.5300 Bonn 2, Germany (02-28 88 21).

Correspondent: Professor Dr Theodor Berchem, President; Dr Karl Roeloffs, Secretary General.

London Office: 17 Bloomsbury Square, London WC1A 2LP (01-404 4065).

DAAD also maintains branch offices in Cairo, Nairobi, New Delhi, New York, Paris, Rio de Janeiro, San José and Tokyo.

Budget: DM 180 million in 1987.

Policy and practice: Founded in 1925, DAAD promotes international university relations between the Federal Republic and foreign countries. Scholars, professors and students from all disciplines participate in the scheme.

DAAD is funded mainly by the Foreign Office, the Ministry of Education and Science, the Ministry for Economic Co-operation and the states of the Federal Republic of Germany.

In 1987 DAAD supported about 16,000 foreign scholarships and about 9,000 German university students, graduates and academic staff in a variety of short-term or long-term exchange programmes.

ALFRIED KRUPP VON BOHLEN UND HALBACH-STIFTUNG

4300 Essen-Bredeney, Hügel 15, Germany (0201-1881).

Contact: Jürgen Rossberg.

Annual grants total: No information given.

Policy and practice: The Foundation operates nationally and internationally through support of projects in the fields of scientific research and teaching, education, public health, literature, sports, music and the plastic arts. Peace research and international relations are only funded in certain exceptional cases as they are not specified as areas of support laid down in the articles of the Foundation.

It is known that the International Institute for Strategic Studies, London, received a grant of £31,730, in 1985 (Source, the Institute's Annual Report).

HEINZ-SCHWARZKOPF-STIFTUNG JUNGES EUROPA

2000 Hamburg 56, Rissener Landstrasse 195, Germany (0411-816 381).

Correspondent: Kitty Koster, Manager.

Annual grants total: Not made available.

Grant scale: Dm 1,000 usually.

Policy and practice: The Foundation aims to teach young people between the ages of 16 and 35 the fundamentals of free social and economic systems and to promote contact and understanding between young people in Europe. It operates in the European countries, including those of Eastern Europe, in the fields of international relations, culture, political and economic affairs, science and education through seminars, international youth conferences and travel scholarships.

Presentation of applications: A brief written outline of project.

Further information for applicants: Report of operations.

FRITZ THYSSEN STIFTUNG

Am Römerturm 3, Postfach 180346, 5000 Köln 1, Germany (0221-234 471).

Contact: Dr Rudolf Kerscher, Executive Director.

Annual grants total: 6.9 million DM in 1985/86.

Policy and practice: The Foundation aims to promote research and learning in universities and research institutes, particularly in the Federal Republic. Special consideration is given to the rising generation of scientists and scholars. It supports particular research projects of limited duration, mainly in basic research in the humanities; international relations; state, economy and society; medicine and the natural sciences. Within its international relations programme, the Foundation undertakes research projects, notably its 'Environment and International Politics' programme; trains scholars; publishes reports and gives financial support to organisations e.g. International Institute for Strategic Studies, Atlantic Institute for International Affairs and the Institut Universitaire de Hautes Études Internationales. Other areas included and funded within the 'International Relations' category are Law and Economics.

Information available for applicants: Annual Report (in German).

STIFTUNG VOLKSWAGENWERK

3000 Hannover 81, Kastanienallee 35, PO Box 81 05 09, Germany (0511-83810).

Correspondent: Rolf Möller, General Secretary.

Annual grants total: DM 156.6 million in 1986.

Grant range: From about 10,000 DM (for symposia) to some 100,000 DM.

Policy and practice: The Foundation was set up in 1961 by the Federal Republic of Germany and the State of Lower Saxony for the promotion of science, technology and the humanities in research and university teaching. It operates nationally and internationally through grants for specific purposes to academic and technological institutions engaged in research and teaching. The Foundation is free to support any area of science, as well as the humanities, but has limited its funding programme to a range of specific areas. In the case of applications from abroad, co-operation with German research institutions and scholars is usually essential. The Foundation does not provide funds for peace research in the proper sense of the word. Funding under the terms of the programme area 'Research and Training in International Security' is restricted to sub-programmes. For the time being these are: *'Research Competition in Arms Control'* (for German post graduates; last competition deadline until 31 March 1988); *'On-the-job Training Programme in International Security'* (for German junior scholars at extra university research institutes under the direction of Stiftung Wissenschaft und Politik, Ebenhausen); *'Nuclear History Programme'* (organised by Stiftung Wissenschaft und Politik, Ebenhausen, and the University of Maryland. In 1987, 1.8 million DM was given for 'Nuclear History Programme' (see above) to Stiftung Wissenschaft und Politik (Ebenhausen) and University of Maryland, (USA) for a multitude of individual projects.

Applications from foreign research teams are welcomed, but the proposed projects must be related to the Foundation's own work in this field and must contain a substantial element of German involvement and participation.

Grants and training under the category 'Security' ('Sicherheitspolitik') totalled DM 2.7 million in the period 1983–86. Recent grants in the UK have included:

Dr C. M. Davis, Centre for Russian and East European Studies, University of Birmingham, 'Economic Analysis of Defence and Arms Control Issues'.

Professor R. O. Neill, International Institute for Strategic Studies, 'The Implications of Strategic Defences for Western Security Policies'.

Presentation of applications: It is suggested that initial enquiries and discussions of feasibility be directed to the Foundation's advisor in this area: Dr Alfred Schmidt, at Abteilung II: Geistes-und Gesellschaftswissenschaften (address as above). Applications should be presented in German or English. A summary in German will be appreciated. Applications are considered in accordance with their pertinence to programme areas. They must contain sufficient information (including detailed cost schedule) for an objective evaluation by the Foundation and its expert consultants.

Information available for applicants: Annual report (including financial statement); Outlines (information in English, 1983).

4. Japanese sources

List of contents

Foundation of International Education
Honda Foundation
Japan Shipbuilding Industry Foundation
Mitsubishi Ginko Kokusai Zaidan
Niwano Heiwa Zaidan (Niwano Peace Foundation)
Sasakawa Peace Foundation

FOUNDATION OF INTERNATIONAL EDUCATION

2nd Floor, No 32 Kowa Building, 5-2-32 Minami Azabu, Minato-Ku, Tokyo 106, Japan.

Policy: The Foundation aims to assist educational trusts which establish universities and colleges whose principal object is the training of 'internationalists', to promote research and teaching exchange with other countries, and to deepen mutual understanding in international society.

HONDA FOUNDATION

2-6-20 Yaesu, Chuo-Ku, Tokyo 104, Japan.

Policy: The Foundation aims to contribute to the true welfare and peace of mankind by carrying out an international scholarly re-evaluation of modern civilisation; to tackle the problems of environmental destruction, depletion of natural resources, etc.

JAPAN SHIPBUILDING INDUSTRY FOUNDATION

Senpaku Shinko Building, 1-15-16 Toranomon, Minato-ku, Tokyo 105, Japan
(03-502 2371/03-508 2377).

Correspondent: Ryoichi Sasakawa, Chairman.

Annual grants total: US $252 million in 1986, of which US $28 million (11%) was for overseas assistance.

There are seven categories for grants given for overseas assistance including:
  Education: US $3 million
  Culture, Research and Studies: US $10 million
  United Nations: US $6.5 million

Grant range: US $1,000–US $1,000,000.

Policy and practice: The Japan Shipbuilding Foundation was set up by Ryoichi Sasakawa the tycoon/philanthropist determined to 'rid the earth forever of the horror of war', and build 'a heaven on earth where all people can live in harmony as brothers and sisters'. The Foundation attempts to fulfil this aim by generous donations to the World Health Organisation, and to the United Nations. The Foundation gives grants within Japan and to applicants from over 60 other countries in the field of health, education, social welfare, culture, research and international studies.

Recent grants have included:

UNESCO Prize for Peace Education endowment (1979)	US$1,000,000
United Nations University for Peace, establishment of the Sasakawa Endowment for Peace (1983)	US$1,000,000
United Nations University for Peace, Conference on Peace (1983)	US$200,000
The Friendship Force (1986)	US$400,000
Carter Center of Emory University, Chair in International Peace (1986)	US$500,000
Centre for Applied Studies in International Negotiations, Switzerland (1986)	US$430,652

Presentation of applications: No information made available.

Information available for applicants: A report on overseas support and assistance and a short biography of Ryoichi Sasakawa.

MITSUBISHI GINKO KOKUSAI ZAIDAN

2-7-1 Marunouchi, Chiyoda-Ku, Tokyo 100, Japan (03-240 3317).

Correspondent: Seiichi Mitani, Executive Director.

Annual grants total: 67 million yen in 1986.

Grant range: 1 million yen–9 million yen.

Policy and practice: The Foundation was set up in 1981 by the Mitsubishi Bank, Tokyo, to deepen mutual understanding and promote cultural exchanges between Japan and the rest of the World. It provides grants for research in economics, development studies, international affairs and human rights and for exchanges of groups of people (usually aged between 18 and 39 years) for joint research and other activities. The Foundation also organises international conferences. Preference is give to programmes connected with Asia and the Pacific.

No information has been made available about their recent grants.

Presentation of applications: Applications should be submitted in Japanese on or before April 10, or October 10, of each year.

NIWANO HEIWA ZAIDAN (NIWANO PEACE FOUNDATION)

Shamvilla Catherina, 5F, 1-16-9 Shinjuku, Shinjuku-ku, Tokyo 160, Japan (03-226 4371).

Correspondent: Katsunori Yamanoi, General Secretary.

Annual grants total: US $149,425 in 1986.

Grant range: US $2,500–US $15,000.

Policy and practice: The Foundation was established in 1979 'to promote research and activities of peace under the religious spirit in order to contribute to world peace.'

It awards the Niwano Peace Prize (worth 20 million yen) annually to an individual or organisation that is making a significant contribution to world peace through promoting inter-religious co-operation.

Its grants are divided into two categories; research and activity.

Research grants are awarded in the following fields: inter-religious understanding and co-operation, the role of religion today, religious approaches to overcoming impediments to peace, and relationships of science to religion and ethics.

Activity grants are awarded to activities that promote mutual understanding and co-operation internationally or within a country through exchange at a regional level among differing cultures and different religions.

Grants are also awarded to social service, development co-operation, human rights and other activities striving for peace that are being conducted on the basis of religious co-operation and tolerance and transcending religious boundaries.

The Foundation positively welcomes applications from overseas. It will not, however, fund research activity for the benefit of a specific group or political ideology. Grants run for one year and are paid quarterly.

The Foundation also conducts or commissions its own research on similar topics, and operates a Peace Research Institute. It sponsors lectures and symposia throughout Japan, and international exchanges for groups of young people.

Japanese Sources

Research grants in 1986 included:

Kyushu University, 'Naoe Kinoshita's Philosophy of Peace'	US$3,000
University of Tokyo, 'A Study of PVA-PCN (Peace Value-Added Personal Computer Network) as a medium for co-operation among religious non-governmental orgnaisations'	US$4,700
International Christian University, 'Mahatma Gandhi's Peace Movement, Then and Now'	US$4,700

Activity grants in 1986 included:

Cambridge Forum, educational materials for a network of peace and religious organisations in the United States	US$5,000
World Conference on Religion and Peace, 1986	

Presentation of applications: An application form can be obtained from the Foundation. Research and activity grant applications are accepted from April 1st to May 15th; activity grant applications only are also accepted from October 1st to November 15th.

Information available for applicants: Niwano Peace Prize, pamphlet, in English; Research and Activity Grant Guidelines, in English; *Echoes of Peace*, quarterly, in English; *Peace and Religion*, annually, in Japanese; Niwano Peace Foundation Report, quarterly in Japanese.

SASAKAWA PEACE FOUNDATION

Sasakawa Hall, 3-12-12 Mita Minato-ku, Tokyo 108, Japan (03-769 2081).

Correspondent: Setsuya Tabuchi, Chairman.

Finance: An endowment of 50 billion yen is planned; 6 billion yen had been reached by Spring 1987.

Policy and practice: The Foundation was established in September 1986 by Ryoichi Sasakawa, Chairman of the Japan Shipbuilding Industry Foundation, 'to work for world peace through continual and concrete efforts to promote international understanding, exchange, and co-operation'.

Its policies are still at an exploratory stage. In its literature it says the following areas will be given top priority:

Activities aimed at identifying and resolving international, political, economic and social problems, and the creation of new channels for international understanding;

Contributing to the establishment of national stability in developing nations;

Research in Japan on other nations;

Assisting Japanese studies abroad;

Promoting the internationalisation of Japan on a local and regional level.

Presentation of applications: New proposals are encouraged and can be submitted in Japanese or English, an outline of three to four pages is preferred. There are no deadlines for submissions.

Information available for applicants: Information brochure.

Bibliography

Organisations

'*Housmans Peace Diary*', which incorporates the '*World Peace Directory*' listing UK local groups in regions, national groups by country and international organisations.

Day, Alan J. (ed) '*Peace Movements of the World. An International Directory*' Longman, 1987.

'*Armament and Disarmament: An Introductory Guide to Sources*' Armament and Disarmament Information Unit, University of Sussex, 1986.

'*Disarmament Campaigns, International Peace Movement Guide*' Interchurch Peace Council, Amsterdam.

McHugh, Declan (ed) '*Peace Information Resources*', a guide to 31 British collections, National Peace Council, 1987.

Reychler, L. and Rudney, R. '*Directory Guide of European Security & Defense Research*' Leuven University Press and Pergamon – Brassey's, 1985.

'*World Directory of Peace Research Institutions*', 5th edition, UNESCO, 1985.

United Nations Institute for Disarmament Research '*Repertory of Disarmament Research*' UNIDIR, Geneva, 1982. A country by country guide to main academic departments and independent or government statistics.

'*Peace Resource Book*', a Comprehensive Guide to Issues, Groups and Literature. Institute for Defense and Disarmament Studies, Ballinger, 1986.

Miller, Scott and Yuill (eds) '*Many Visions, Many Hands, Women's Peace Directory*' Solid Women Ltd, 1986.

Ellis, Ian M. '*Peace and Reconciliation Projects in Ireland*', Irish Council of Churches, 1986 (3rd edition).

Ryle, Claire and Garrison, Jim '*Citizens' Diplomacy: A Handbook of Anglo-Soviet Initiatives*', Merlin Press, 1986.

'*Volunteer Work*', a guide to medium and long-term voluntary work and service, with information on over 100 organisations recruiting volunteers for projects in the UK and in 153 countries worldwide; published in co-operation with the National Council for Voluntary organisations by the Central Bureau for Educational Visits and Exchanges, 1987.

Funding

UK Sources

FitzHerbert, Luke (ed) '*A Guide to Major Grant Making Trusts*' Directory of Social Change, 1988 (published every 2 years).

'*Directory of Grant-Making Trusts*' Charities Aid Foundation, 1987 (published every 2 years).

'*Independent Funding for Voluntary Action*' Northern Ireland Voluntary Trust, 1987 (funding sources for Northern Ireland).

USA Sources

'*The Foundation Directory*' Foundation Center, NY, 1987 (11th edition).

'*The Foundations Grants Index*' Foundation Center, a cummulative listing of foundation grants (annual).

'*Source Book Profiles*' Foundation Center, a quarterly information service on the 1,000 largest US foundations.

'*Taft Foundation Reporter*', comprehensive profiles and giving analyses of America's major private foundations. Taft Foundation Information Service, 1987 (18th edition).

'*Search for Security: A Guide to Grantmaking in International Security and the Prevention of Nuclear War*' The Forum Institute, 1985, available from Access Security Inc, 1730 M Street NW, Suite 605, Washington DC 20036, $35.

Bibliography

Japanese Sources

The Foundation Library Center of Japan publishes a directory (in Japanese) of Japanese grant making trusts and foundations. Contact: Masaki Kusumi, Information Officer. The Foundation Library Center of Japan, Elements Shinjuku Building 3F, 2-1-14 Shinjuku, Shinjuku-ku, Tokyo, Japan. Tel: (03-350 1857) Fax: (03-350 1858).

Canadian Sources

'*Canadian Directory to Foundations*' 1987 (7th edition), Canadian Center for Philanthropy, Toronto.

'*Canadian Index to Foundation Grants*', 1986 (1st edition) Canadian Center for Philanthropy.

International Sources

Hodson, H. V. (ed) '*The International Foundation Directory*', Europa, 1986 (4th edition).'

Index of organisations

Aberdeen University, Dept of Politics and International Relations	11
Aberdeen University, Centre for Defence Studies	12
All Children Together (ACT)	135
Anglican Pacifist Fellowship	76
Anglo-Irish Encounter	136
Architects for Peace	58
Armament and Disarmament Information Unit (see Sussex University)	23
At Ease	88
Atlantic College (see United World College)	117
Atlantic Institute for International Affairs	39
Baptist Peace Fellowship	76
Belfast Charitable Trust for Integrated Education (BELTIE)	136
Bertrand Russell Peace Foundation (see Russell, Bertrand)	70
Birmingham University, Centre for Russian and East European Studies	12
Book Action for Nuclear Disarmament	58
Bradford University, School of Peace Studies	13
Bradford University, Commonweal Collection	14
British American Security Information Centre (BASIC)	26
British Atlantic Committee	49
British Council of Churches, Division of International Affairs	76
British Council of Churches: Peace Forum	77
British Irish Association	137
British Peace Assembly	72
British Pugwash (see Pugwash Conferences)	33
Buddhist Peace Fellowship	77
Bull Point Peace Bus/Peace Camp	85
Cambridge University, Centre of International Studies	14
Campaign Against Arms Trade	66
Campaign Against Military Research on Campus (CAMROC)	67
Campaign for Defence and Multilateral Disarmament	67
Campaign for Nuclear Disarmament (CND)	50
Christian CND	50
Green CND	51
Labour CND	52
Liberal CND	52
Trade Union CND	51
Youth CND	51
Northern Ireland CND	52
Scottish CND	52
Welsh CND	52
Campaign for the Demilitarisation of the Indian Ocean	49
Catholic Bishops' Conference of England and Wales – Department of International Affairs	77
Catholic Fund for Overseas Development (CAFOD)	105
Catholic Institute for International Relations	105
Catholic Peace Action	78
Central Bureau for Educational Visits and Exchanges	123
Centre for Global Education, University of York	106
Centre for International Studies, Rolle College, Exmouth	107
Centre for Peace Studies, St Martins College of Higher Education, Lancaster	107
Centre for World Development Education	108
Christian Aid	108
Christian CND (see CND)	50
Christian Fellowship Trust	124
Christian Movement for Peace	124
Clergy Against Nuclear Arms	78
Coalition for Peace through Security	67
Commonweal Collection (see Bradford University)	14
Commonwealth Youth Exchange Council	124
Community Conflict Skills	137
Community of the Peace People, (Freidheim)	137
Concord Film and Video Council	88
Conflict Research Society	44
Co-operation North	138
Corrymeela Community	139
Council for Arms Control	26
Council for Education in World Citizenship	109
Council on Christian Approaches to Defence and Disarmament (British Group)	78
Cruise Resistance Network	84
Cruisewatch	84
David Davies Memorial Institute of International Studies	27
Development Education Centres: List of those with paid staffing	120
Diocesan Boards or Councils of Social Responsibility	79
Ditchley Foundation	95
Dunamis	67
East-West Reach	125

Index of Organisations

Ecoropa Ltd	52
Edinburgh University, Defence Studies	14
Electronics and Computing for Peace	59
END Churches Lateral Committee	79
Engineers for Nuclear Disarmament	59
English Speaking Union of the Commonwealth	125
European Atlantic Group	96
European Movement	96
European Nuclear Disarmament (END)	72
European Proliferation Information Centre (EPIC)	27
Exchange Resources, EfP Ltd	88
Ex-Services CND	60
Experiment in International Living	126
Families for Defence	53
Farmers for a Nuclear Free Future	60
Faslane Peace Camp	85
Federal Trust for Education and Research	28
Fellowship of Reconciliation	80
Fellowship of Reconciliation, Northern Ireland	140
Fellowship Party	53
Fircroft College	109
Foundation for Defence Studies	28
Foundation for International Security	29
Freeze Resources Ltd	68
Gandhi Foundation	110
Generals for Peace and Disarmament	60
Glasgow University, Department of Sociology, Media Group	15
Great Britain-China Centre	126
Great Britain-USSR Association	127
Green CND (see CND)	51
GreenNet	88
Harmony Community Trust	140
Institute for European Defence and Strategic Studies	29
Institute for the Study of Conflict	30
Institute for the Study of Terrorism	30
Interchurch Group on Faith and Politics	140
International Council of Scientific Unions (see Scientific Committee...)	36
International Group of Researchers on the Anti-Ballistic Missile Treaty (IGRAT)	31
International Institute for Peaceful Change	68
International Institute for Strategic Studies	31
International Nuclear Non-Proliferation Network (see Southampton University)	21
International Peace Academy	39
International Peace Bureau	73
International Peace Research Association	44
International Physicians for the Prevention of Nuclear War	61
International Society for Research into Aggression	45
International Voluntary Service	131
Inter-Parliamentary Union	96
Joint Twinning Committee of the Local Authority Associations	127
Just Defence	53
Keele University, Department of Politics and International Relations	15
Kent University, Board of Studies of Politics and International Relations	16
Kent University, Centre for the Analysis of Conflict	16
King's College, London	17
Labour Action for Peace	54
Labour CND (see CND)	52
Lancaster University, Centre for the Study of Arms Control and International Security	17
Lancaster University, Richardson Institute for Peace Studies	18
Lawyers for Nuclear Disarmament	61
Legal Support Group	89
Liberal CND (see CND)	52
Local Authorities: Education for Peace	103
Local Authorities: Nuclear Free Zones	93
London Centre for International Peace Building	69
London Mennonite Centre	80
London Nuclear Information Unit	91
London University, Kings College, War Studies Department	17
London School of Economics, Department of International Relations	19
London School of Economics, Centre for International Studies	19
Manchester University, Department of Science and Technology Policy	19
Medical Association for Prevention of War (MAPW)	62
Medical Campaign Against Nuclear Weapons (MCANW)	62
Members of Equity for Nuclear Disarmament	63
Menwith Hill Peace Camp	85
Methodist Peace Fellowship	81
Molesworth Peace Camp	85
Mothers for Peace	128
Musicians Against Nuclear Arms	63
National Association of Development Education Centres	110
National Peace Action Foundation	110
National Peace Council	73
National Steering Committee of Nuclear Free Zone Authorities	92
National Trade Union Defence Conversion Committee	74
North Atlantic Network	74
Northern Friends Peace Board	81
Northern Ireland CND (see CND)	52
Northern Ireland Conflict and Mediation Association	141
Northern Ireland Peace Forum	141
Nuclear Free Zones – Forums and Lists of Local Authorities	93
Nukewatch	84
One World Trust	111
One World Week	111
Open University, Conflict and Security in the Nuclear Age Course	111
Oxfam, Youth and Education Department	112
Oxford Project for Peace Studies	113
Oxford Research Group	32
PACE, An Association for Protestant and Catholic Encounter	141

Index of Organisations

Parents for Survival	63
Pax Christi (British Section)	81
Peace Advertising Campaign	89
Peace and Reconciliation Group, Derry	141
Peace Councils/Peace Centres, Local	86
Peace Education Commission	113
Peace Education Network	113
Peace Education Project: Staffordshire and Warwickshire Monthly Meetings	114
Peace Education Resource Centre, Belfast	142
Peacemakers' Relief Society	89
Peace Pledge Union	54
Peace Tax Campaign	55
Peace Through NATO	69
Peace Through Parliament	70
Pensioners for Peace International	64
Play for Life	114
Polariswatch (see Nukewatch)	84
Prayer for Peace	82
Professions for World Disarmament and Development	74
Psychologists for Peace	64
Pugwash Conferences on Science and World Affairs	33
Quaker Peace and Service	82
Research Foundation for the Study of Terrorism	34
Royal Commonwealth Society	128
Royal Institute of International Affairs	34
Royal United Services Institute for Defence Studies	35
Russell (Bertrand) Peace Foundation	70
Schools' Partnership Worldwide	129
Scientific Committee on Problems of the Environment (SCOPE-ENUWAR)	36
Scientists Against Nuclear Arms (SANA)	64
Scottish Campaign to Resist the Atomic Menace (SCRAM)	55
Scottish CND (see CND)	52
Servas	129
Sheffield Post 16: Peace and Conflict Studies Working Party	115
Snowball	84
South Atlantic Council	37
Southampton University, Department of Politics	20
Southampton University, Centre of International Policy Studies	21
Southampton University, International Nuclear Non-Proliferation Network	21
Stockholm International Peace Research Institute	40
Student Peace Project	115
Sussex University, Institute of Development Studies	22
Sussex University, Science Policy Research Unit	22
Sussex University, Armament and Disarmament Information Unit	23
Teachers for Peace	115
The European Atlantic Movement (TEAM)	55
Third World First	116
Trade Union CND (see CND)	51
Trade Union International Research & Education Group (TUIREG)	116
UK One World Linking Assocation	129
UK-USSR Medical Exchange Programme	130
Ulster Quaker Peace Committee	142
Ulster University, Peace Studies Programme	23
Ulster University, Centre for Conflict Studies	24
United Nations Association	56
United Nations Information Centre	90
United Nations Institute for Disarmament Research	42
United Nations University	41
United Nations University for Peace	41
United Towns Organisation	130
United World College of the Atlantic	117
Upper Heyford Peace Camp	85
Verification Technology Information Centre (VERTIC)	37
Victoria League for Commonwealth Friendship	131
Voluntary Service Overseas	131
Wales University, Department of International Politics	25
War on Want	117
War Resisters International	75
Week of Prayer for World Peace	83
Welsh CND (see CND)	52
Welsh Centre for International Affairs	118
Western European Defence Association	38
Women's International League for Peace and Freedom	57
Women Together	142
Women Working for a Nuclear Free and Independent Pacific	71
Woodbrooke Quaker Study Centre	118
Working Party on Chemical and Biological Weapons	38
World Development Movement	119
World Disarmament Campaign	57
Youth CND (see CND)	51

Index of funding sources

Mrs M. K. Allen Will Trust	160
Allen Lane Foundation	160
Arca Foundation	230
A S Charitable Trust	160
Ark Foundation	230
Atlantic Peace Foundation	161
Avenue Charitable Trust	161
Baring Foundation	161
Elizabeth Barker Fund (see British Academy)	164
Philip Baxendale Trust	162
Beaverbrook Foundation	162
Benham Charitable Settlement	162
C. T. Bowring (Charities Fund) Ltd	163
E. and H. N. Boyd and J. E. Morland Charitable Trust Ltd	163
Brecher and Co Charitable Trust	163
British Academy	164
Britten Pears Foundation	164
T. B. H. Brunner's Charitable Trust	164
Harold Buxton Trust	165
Noel Buxton Trust	165
Bydale Foundation	230
Barrow and Geraldine S. Cadbury Trust	165
Barrow Cadbury Fund Ltd (see Barrow and Geraldine S. Cadbury Trust)	165
C. L. Cadbury Charitable Trust	167
Edward Cadbury Charitable Trust	167
Edward and Dorothy Cadbury Trust (1928)	167
Henry T. and Lucy B. Cadbury Charitable Trust	168
J. and L. A. Cadbury Charitable Trust	168
J. C. Cadbury Charitable Trust	168
Paul S. Cadbury Charitable Trust	169
Richard Cadbury Charitable Trust	169
William Adlington Cadbury Charitable Trust	169
Vera and Maxwell Caplin Charitable Trust	170
Carnegie Corporation of New York	231
Carnegie-Stichting, Watelerfonds (Prize)	257
Carthage Foundation	231
Catholic Fund for Overseas Development (CAFOD)	170
Chase Charity	171
Cheney Peace Settlement	171
Christian Aid	171
Hilda and Alice Clark Charitable Trust	172
J. Anthony Clark Trust	172
Roger and Sarah Bancroft Clark Charitable Trust	172
Cobb Charitable Trust	172
Commission of the European Communities (EEC)	221
Commonwealth Foundation	173
Commonwealth Relations Trust	173
Commonwealth Youth Exchange Council	174
Compton Foundation	231
Ernest Cook Trust	174
Co-operation North	174
Frank Cousins TGWU Award	218
John and Edythe Crosfield Charitable Trust	175
C. S. Fund	232
Delves Charitable Trust	175
Deutscher Akademischer Austauschdienst (DAAD)	260
Dinam Charity	175
Donner Canadian Foundation	232
Dulverton Trust	175
Economic and Social Research Council	222
Edith M. Ellis 1985 Charitable Trust	176
Enkalon Foundation	176
Ericson Trust	177
European Cultural Foundation	258
European Human Rights Foundation	177
Esmée Fairbairn Charitable Trust	177
Allan and Nesta Ferguson Charitable Trust	178
Firbank Charitable Trust	178
Fitton Trust	178
Fondation Charles Veillon	259
Fondazione Rui	257
Fonds National Suisse de la Recherche Scientifique	259
Ford Foundation	233
Foreign and Commonwealth Office	223
Foundation for International Education (Japan)	262
Foundation for International Understanding	256
Foundation Roi Baudouin/Konig Boudewijnstighting	255
Foundation Paul-Henri Spaak	255
Fulbright Awards	223
Gatsby Charitable Foundation (see Sainsbury Family Charitable Trusts)	208
General Service Foundation	234
German Marshall Fund of the United States	234
J. Paul Getty Jr General Charitable Trust	178
Simon Gibson Charitable Trust	179

Index of Funding Sources

A. B. and M. C. Gillett Charitable Trust	179
Gillett Trust	180
Joyce Mertz-Gilmore Foundation	235
Give Peace A Chance Trust	180
Glickenhaus Foundation	235
GNC Trust	180
Godinton Charitable Trust	180
T. W. Greeves Trust	181
GSC Trust, Gwen Catchpool Charity	181
Harry Frank Guggenheim Foundation	235
John Simon Guggenheim Memorial Foundation	236
Walter Guinness Charitable Trust	181
George Gund Foundation	236
Harbour Foundation Ltd	181
Virginia Worsfield Harington Charitable Trust	182
L. G. Harris and Co Ltd Charitable Trust	182
Headley Trust (see Sainsbury Family Charitable Trusts)	208
Hedley Foundation Ltd	182
William and Flora Hewlett Foundation	237
Heinz-Schwarzkopf-Stiftung Junges Europa	260
Hickinbotham Charitable Trust	182
Walter Higgs Charitable Trust	183
Hilden Charitable Trust	183
Hillcote Trust	183
Lady Hind Trust	183
HKH Foundation	237
P. H. Holt Charitable Trust	184
Honda Foundation	262
Inchcape Charitable Trust Fund	184
Inter-Church Emergency Fund for Ireland	184
Invicta Trust	185
Ireland Funds of the United States, Canada and Australia	256
Irish Ecumenical Church Loan Fund Committee	185
Japan Shipbuilding Industry Foundation	262
J. G. Joffe Charitable Trust	185
Joicey Trust	186
Joint Twinning Committee of Local Authority Associations (see entry under organisations)	127
W. Alton Jones Foundation, Inc	237
Henry P. Kendall Foundation	238
Kleinwort Benson Charitable Trust	186
Sir Cyril Kleinwort Charitable Settlement	186
Ernest Kleinwort Charitable Trust	187
Alfried Krupp Von Bohlen Und Halbach-Stiftung	260
Lankelly Foundation	187
Lansbury House Trust Fund	187
Leigh Trust	188
Leverhulme Trust	188
Max and Anna Levinson Foundation	239
Linbury Trust (see Sainsbury Family Charitable Trusts)	208
Lloyd's Charities Trust	189
Henry Luce Foundation	239
Lyndhurst Settlement	189
John D. and Catherine T. MacArthur Foundation	239
Manor Charitable Trust	190
Marsden Charitable Trust	190
Maypole Fund	191
M. B. Charities Ltd	190
Andrew W. Mellon Foundation	241
Mercers' Charitable Foundation	190
Mercury Provident plc	191
Ministry of Defence	224
Victor Mischon Trust	192
Esmé Mitchell Trust	192
Mitsubishi Ginko Kokusai Zaidan	263
Samuel Montagu Charitable Trust	192
John Moores Foundation	192
Moorgate Trust Fund	193
Morel Charitable Trust	193
S. C. and M. E. Morland Charitable Trust	194
Ruth Mott Fund	241
Stewart R. Mott and Associates/Stewart R. Mott Charitable Trust	242
A. J. Muste Memorial Institute	242
NATO International Scientific Exchange Programmes	225
NATO Research Awards	225
Network Foundation	194
New Land Foundation, Inc	243
New Moorgate Trust Fund (see Moorgate Trust Fund)	193
New Sheffield Trust	194
New World Foundation	243
Niwano Heiwa Zaidan (Niwano Peace Foundation)	263
Nobelstiftesen	258
NORDSAM, Nordic Co-operation Committee for International Politics	259
Northern Ireland Voluntary Trust	194
North Shore Unitarian Universalist Veatch Program	244
Nuffield Foundation	196
Oak Foundation	197
Oakdale Trust	197
John M. Olin Foundation	244
One % Fund	197
Oppenheimer Charitable Trust	198
Oxfam	198
Albert Parvin Foundation	244
Harry Payne Trust	200
Pew Charitable Trusts	245
P. F. Charitable Trust	199
Headley Pitt Trust	200
Ploughshares Fund	245
Public Welfare Foundation	246
Puckham Charitable Trust	200
Radley Charitable Trust	200
Rank Foundation Ltd	201
Rank Xerox Trust	201
Miss E. F. Rathbone Charitable Trust	201
Albert Reckitt Charitable Trust	202
Eva Reckitt Trust Fund	202
Rest-Harrow Trust	202

Index of Funding Sources

Right Livelihood Award	218
Mr C. A. Rodewald's Charitable Settlement	203
Rotary Foundation Scholarship	203
Rothley Trust	204
Rowan Charitable Trust	204
Joseph Rowntree Charitable Trust	204
Joseph Rowntree Social Service Trust Ltd	206
J. B. Rubens Charity Trustees Ltd	207
Earl Russell Peace Foundation Trust	207
Smith Richardson Foundation	246
Rockefeller Brothers Fund	247
Rockefeller Family Fund	247
Rockefeller Foundation	248
Samuel Rubin Foundation	248
Sainsbury Family Charitable Trusts	208
Sarah Scaife Foundation	248
Sasakawa Peace Foundation	264
Scherman Foundation	249
Schroder Charitable Trust	209
Florence and John Schumann Foundation	249
Scott Bader Commonwealth Ltd	209
Sears Foundation	209
Sequoia Foundation	249
Sewell Charitable Trust	210
Simpson Foundation	210
Alfred P. Sloan Foundation	249
Harold Smith Charitable Trust	210
Stephen R. and Phillipa H. Southall Charitable Trust	210
W. F. Southall Trust	210
Sir Halley Stewart Trust	211
Starr Foundation	250
Sunflower Foundation	250
C. B. and H. H. Taylor Trust	211
Fritz Thyssen Stiftung	261
Threshold Foundation	250
Tides Foundation	251
Topsfield Foundation	251
Tzedakah	212
UNA Media Peace Prize	219
UNESCO Prize for Peace Education	220
United States Institute of Peace	252
Van Neste Foundation	212
Volkswagenwerk (Stiftung)	261
Howard Walker Charitable Trust	212
Philip Walker Charitable Trust	212
A. F. Wallace Charity Trust	213
War on Want	213
Warbeck Fund Ltd	213
Wates Foundation	213
Weinberg Foundation	214
Westcroft Trust	214
Garfield Weston Foundation	215
Westward Trust	215
Weyerhauser Foundation, Inc	252
Whitaker Charitable Trust	215
H. D. H. Wills 1965 Charitable Trust	215
Winston Foundation For World Peace	253
Wolfson Foundation	216
Women Caring Trust	216
Youth Exchange Centre	226
Youth Project	253
Zochonis Charitable Trust	217

Other Fund Raising Publications

Researching Local Charities	£3.95	......
Arts Funding Handbook	£7.95	......
Raising Money for Women	£5.95	......
Raising Money from Government	£4.50	......
Money/influence in Europe	£3.95	......
Raising Money from Trusts	£2.95	......
Corporate Donor's Handbook	£12.50	......
Industrial Sponsorship & Joint Promotions	£3.95	......
Legacies	£3.95	......
Charity Trading Handbook	£4.95	......
Charity Christmas Cards	£3.95	......

Fund Raising Notes

Complete set of twelve, £5 post free

Finance & Charity Status

Covenants	£5.95	......
Guide to Benefits of Charitable Status	£5.95	......
Accounting and Financial Management	£5.95	......
Investment of Charity Funds	£3.95	......
Socially Responsible Investment	£5.95	......
Directory of Charities	£15.00	......

Promotion and PR

Charity Annual Reports	£4.95	......
Sell Space	£2.95	......
Marketing: A guide for charities	£4.95	......
Advertising by Charities	£5.95	......
Basic PR Guide	£4.50	......

Other Guides

Charities and Broadcasting - A guide to Radio and Television Appeals and Grants
edited by Nicola Parker

A book for voluntary organisations interested in raising money and in better public relations. It includes the first-ever survey of the charitable activities of all BBC and IBA radio stations and television companies, as well as cable operators. Funds for charity worth nearly £35 million in 1987, (an estimated £60 million in 1988) were uncovered. Each entry is illustrated with examples of past appeals and information about 'social action broadcasts'.

£5.95 (ISBN 0-907164-34-X)

Grants for Individuals in Need
edited by Luke FitzHerbert and Helene Bellofatto

Covers over 1,400 charities which make grants for the relief of individual distress, including national and local charities, occupational charities and trade union benevolent funds, ex-services, charities for special needs, and local and parochial charities. Over £70 million is available from these sources. Charities dealing with clients in need will find this as useful, as will social and welfare workers and advice agencies.

£12.50 (ISBN 0-907164-28-5)

Educational Grants Directory
edited by Luke FitzHerbert and Michael Eastwood

The first ever compilation of trusts which make grants for educational purposes either nationally or locally in England and Wales. Over 1,000 grant sources are listed, including funds that support educational visits and exchanges, help handicapped or disabled students, mature students and students from overseas.

£12.50 (ISBN 0-907164-29-3)

Major Companies and their Charitable Support 1989 edition

edited by Michael Norton

This guide contains much more detailed information than has been available up until now on how the top 300 companies operate their community and charitable donations programmes. It is an essential aid for anyone hoping to get support from a major company and its subsidiaries, by showing in detail what they do and do not support. It should repay its cost many times over in showing who, and also who not to approach.

Published December 1988

Paperback, £12.50
(ISBN 0-907164-41-2)

Hardback, £25
(ISBN 0-907164-43-9)

A Guide to Company Giving 1989 edition

edited by Michael Norton

This companion guide gives the facts and figures on company giving for over 1,300 leading companies with brief details of their donations policies. These companies together make donations totalling over £100 million a year.

Published November 1988

Paperback,, £12.50
(ISBN 0-907164-37-4)

Hardback, £25
(ISBN 0-907164-44-7)

A Guide to the Major Trusts 1988-89 edition

edited by Luke FitzHerbert and Michael Eastwood.

This guide provides more detail than has ever been published before on the grant-making policies and practices of major charitable trusts. Besides providing general information on each trust's background, interests and priorities, their grant-making is illustrated with details of actual grants made in the latest year, for which information is available.

It covers over 400 grant-making trusts and foundations which together make grants of about £250 million to charity each year, plus 40 further charities which make grants for medical research.

1988-89 edition available from October 1988

Paperback, £12.50	**Hardback £25**
(ISBN 0-907164-36-6)	(ISBN 0-907164-45-5)

The Directory of Social Change

The Directory of Social Change is an educational charity set up in 1975. Its main activity is as a publisher of books and reference guides for the voluntary sector concentrating on aspects of their fundraising and financial management. It also runs programmes of training courses covering the same field of interest. From time to time the Directory itself undertakes innovatory projects within the voluntary sector.

For further information and to order books, which are mainly sold by mail (prices quoted are post-free), contact:

The Directory of Social Change,
Radius Works,
Back Lane,
London
NW3 1HL

01-435 8171
01-431 1817